FMG PUBLICATIONS® BEST OF

SMITH & WESSON

2010 – 2019

From the publishers of:

BEST OF SMITH & WESSON

2010 – 2019

A collection of content originally published in *American Handgunner* and *GUNS Magazine*.

FORWARD

The very definition of an icon, the Smith & Wesson brand has infused our culture with innovation, amazing products, wartime frenzy to fill orders for our troops and so much more. Since the the 1800s, the public has looked to S&W for personal protection, to help feed their families, to hone their target and competition skills, to protect this country in war time — and to offer tens of thousands of jobs over the decades. Anywhere you go in the world, if you mention Smith & Wesson, people know what you're talking about.

One of the greatest delights of my life so far as been to be the editor of *American Handgunner* magazine and publisher of FMG's other historic firearm magazines. *GUNS Magazine* — the original consumer newsstand gun magazine — celebrates almost 70 years of life this year and remains at the forefront of the genre. *American Handgunner* — celebrating 47 years showcasing everything handguns — is also still robust.

I once had the opportunity to sit at D.B. Wesson's original, personal desk. The chair creaked as I sat and pondered the well-worn roll top before me. I looked at company checks with D.B.'s signature and handled his personal S&W No. 1 revolver — the first cartridge revolver design in the world. To hold — and behold — that kind of living history was a profound experience for a "gun-guy" like me. Today, when I handle a S&W I can't help but remember the history behind the designs. I'm sure you do too.

Both magazines have showcased S&W products on their covers and in their pages literally thousands of times over the decades. This book is just a sound-bite of the total content covered between 2010 and 2019. While many pine for "the old days" of gun making, I think much of that energy is mis-directed. Today's S&W builds the finest firearms ever to come out of their factories. Never hesitating to reach back to embrace their historical designs from the past, today's S&W continues to build on the company's legacy of innovation, design, service — and tradition.

I'm proud to have helped assemble this remarkable line-up of articles, features and stories during my tenure at the magazines and confess, seeing them all together like this is satisfying and heart warming. I think you'll enjoy this romp down memory lane as you read — and re-read — some of your favorite writers as they tell the stories behind these historical guns of Smith & Wesson.

Roy Huntington
Publisher Emeritus • FMG Publications

THE .40 AT 20

GUNS MAGAZINE'S 55TH ANNIVERSARY YEAR COINCIDES WITH THE 20TH FOR THE .40 SMITH & WESSON CARTRIDGE.

Massad Ayoob

It was early 1990, and the venue was the premier firearms industry convention. SHOT, the Shooting and Hunting Outdoor Trade Show —held in Las Vegas that year—saw the introduction of the .40 Smith & Wesson cartridge by Olin/Winchester, which had created the cartridge, and by S&W, which had built the Model 4006 pistol first to be chambered for it.

The new round was a hit of unprecedented proportions. Within a matter of only a few years, it would come to dominate the police handgun market in the United States, and would achieve huge popularity among the armed citizenry as well. It was a classic example of the right thing introduced at the right time.

The '80s had seen the first big wave of the coming tsunami in which the semi-automatic pistol would at long last swamp and drown the traditional police service revolver in North America. Throughout the decade, as the changeover gained momentum, there emerged two strong camps in terms of just what autoloader should replace the old six-shooter. This was seen classically in the rank and file of the Federal Bureau of Investigation, and would play itself out elsewhere, in police departments all over the country.

One camp held firepower was the raison d'etre of a magazine-fed duty sidearm, and they wanted a large reservoir of firepower in their magazines. This side pushed for the paradigm of the period, a 9mm pistol typically taking a 15-round magazine with a 16th in its firing chamber. The S&W Models 459 and 659 fit that profile, as did the Beretta 92 series and the SIG SAUER P226.

The other camp felt "stopping power" was more important than round count, auto pistol that side wanted was tomatic Colt Pistol. There was

little question that a .45 slug hit harder than a 9mm. After all, at 230 grains the .45 bullet was literally twice as heavy as the long-standard 115-grain 9mm. The 1911 of the period carried seven rounds in the magazine and an 8th in the chamber, as did the SIG P220, while the Smith & Wesson Model 645 carried 8+1 and magazines were now available that would let a standard configuration 1911 do the same thing.

Different competent, charismatic instructors and role models pushed in different directions. The FBI saw Bill Vanderpool emerge as the champion of the "high capacity" 9mm, and Urey Patrick as the standard bearer for the .45. When rival teams form on important issues within an organization, it's important the leadership find a way to cut the Gordian knot and resolve the matter with a compromise that satisfies both sides and allows all to move on. In the Bureau, that role fell to John Hall, then head of the Firearms Training Unit at Quantico.

Hall took a novel route: the 10mm

The new .40 S&W chambered M&P40 from Smith & Wesson has been adopted by many law enforcement agencies nationwide. It features a lightweight polymer frame with interchangeable backstraps.

Auto cartridge. He determined through intensive testing that with a 180-grain bullet at a bit under a 1,000 feet per second, this load would meet the penetration and expansion standards the FBI had painstakingly determined through extensive research were necessary to their mission. It was a milder version of the full-power 10mm, which had emerged earlier, championed by Col. Jeff Cooper and based largely on his early work with Whit Collins in creating a wildcat round called the .40 G&A. With the subsonic 10mm load determined, the Bureau chose the Smith & Wesson Model 1076, literally made to the organization's specs, as its next standard issue service pistol.

Smith&Wesson then still employed the legendary Tom Campbell, who had not yet made the jump to Safariland, and master gunsmith and shooter Paul

Liebenberg was on board, too. They were joined on the new cartridge project by an outside consultant, Ed Hobbe. Working from a wildcat Liebenberg had created years earlier called The Centimeter, a short 40-caliber round intended to make Major power factor in IPSC shooting with a narrower cartridge that would allow more rounds in the magazine.

The group determined it could easily duplicate the ballistics of the FBI load for the 10mm, and do so in a cartridge the same overall length as a 9mm Parabellum. This allowed the use of smaller frames with shorter trigger reach, and the double-stack magazines would not make the gun too fat in the frame for he average user to comfortably grasp. While some were predicting all of law enforcement would follow FBI into the big 10mm, S&W had already seen the

early warning signs from departments that would not adopt a pistol requiring a large .45 frame, as the 10mm did, because of universal hand-fit issues.

As a result, the .40 S&W cartridge was born, with Campbell, Liebenberg, and Hobbe the parents who should have been listed on its birth certificate.

At a time when the typical "wondernine" held 16 rounds and the

CHP Chooses Smith's New .40!

By Massad Ayoob • Photos by Roger Andrews

The nation's largest state police agency, the California Highway Patrol, becomes the first major force to adopt the Smith & Wesson 4006. Along the way, Glock gets clocked, and the Double Eagle lands on its nose.

The .40 S&W has proven a versatile cartridge chambered in every size platform from the full-size Colt Combat Elite to pocket-sized guns like the Kahr K40.

Most .40s are suitable for concealment. Mas draws a Glock 27 during an IDPA match in Illinois. The new Glock 22 RTF .40, with light unit attached, rides in this deputy's Safariland security holster.

typical .45 held eight, the S&W Model 4006 exactly split the difference with 12 rounds of .40 caliber. The new load had a "4" in its designation, and in its original load spat a 180-grain bullet at roughly the velocity of a 185-grain standard pressure .45 ACP. This was enough to satisfy the "big caliber" faction. With half again more rounds on board than a GI .45, it had sufficient cartridge capacity to satisfy the "firepower" advocates. It seemed like a perfect compromise, and police began to adopt it in droves, especially after the 4006's quick acceptance by the trend-setting California Highway Patrol and the Alaska State Troopers. Iowa State Patrol and others would go with a double action only version, S&W's 4046.

The Rise Of The Other .40s

S&W's dominion over its proprietary new cartridge did not last long. At that 1990 SHOT Show Gaston Glock spotted the round, and instantly took the concept to his engineering team. The first, rushed prototype of the .40 caliber Glock was little more than a rechambered Glock 17, and it didn't stand up to the snappy recoil and particularly the viciously high slide velocity the .40 S&W round engendered. The prototype Glock's failure to pass the CHP endurance test stung Glock, and prompted a re-engineering that included another frame pin and resulted in a heavier duty pistol all the way across the Glock board.

Meanwhile, Beretta chambered its Model 92 in .40 and dubbed it the Beretta 96. It would eventually be adopted

by state police in Florida, Maryland, Pennsylvania, and North Carolina. SIG took its time, reinforcing its P226 and coming out with its rugged, compact P229. SIG .40s would be adopted by troopers in Massachusetts and Michigan (in both cases replacing the same pistol in 9mm), Ohio, and Arizona, where troopers had previously had the choice of 9mm or .45 SIGs. BATF currently issues the SIG .40, too. Heckler and Koch's USP proved quite popular in .40, becoming the official pistol of the Washington State Patrol, the US Border Patrol, and the Federal Flight Deck Officer program.

However, the Glock 22 was destined to become the most popular of its kind. The design geometry of its grip-frame and magazine accommodated 15 of the .40 S&W cartridges, making the gun a 16-shooter. If a 12-shot .40 had split the difference between a 16-shot 9mm and an 8-round .45 to become an ideal compromise, a 16-shot .40 seemed to go beyond compromise and become the best of both worlds.

Time marched on. The full-size Glock 22 and the 14-shot compact Glock 23 swept law enforcement. Boston, Detroit, Miami, Milwaukee, New Orleans, and countless cities and counties around the nation standardized on the Glock .40. South Carolina became the first state to outfit its troopers with the Glock .40 as soon as the G22 came out, and was followed by Missouri, Oregon, and even Illinois, whose trademark duty pistol had been the S&W 9mm since 1967. In the first decade of the 21st Century, Chief Bill Bratton would make the G22

The power of the .40 S&W is identical with the old .38 WCF albeit in a much smaller package.

Law enforcement had carried the .38 Special (left) for nigh on to 80 years, though some preferred the more powerful .357 Magnum (middle). The switch from the 6-shot revolver to the high capacity self-loading pistol culminated in the wide acceptance of the fledging .40 S&W (right).

Back in the late 1980s, the debate over firepower vs. stopping raged between the fans of the 9mm Luger (above, left) and fans of the .45 ACP (right). The emergence of the .40 S&W (middle) ended the debate for the most part. Improved performance of the 9mm (below, left, as exemplified by Hornady's new Critical Defense ammo) has narrowed the gap in popularity with the .40 S&W, especially in small lightweight pistols, but the .40 S&W is still quite popular in law enforcement, personal defense (with ammo such as Winchester Personal Protection) and competition.

standard issue for new LAPD officers and optional for the rest, and Superintendent Phil Cline would also approve the Glock .40 as optional for Chicago PD. The Feds would go to it in a big way, too. After the S&W 10mm project went south on the FBI, the Bureau adopted the Glock .40 as standard issue a decade ago. It is also in use with US Marshal's Service and the DEA.

Armed citizens had more choice, but the compromise factor was at work there, too. The .40 S&W round has become hugely popular in the "civilian" sector. The compact Glock 23 and subcompact Glock 27, for example, are consistent best-sellers.

Most who have gone with the ".40 compromise" have been happy with it. Many still use the first generation load, a 180-grain JHP at around 980 fps. It basically duplicates the ballistics of the 19th Century .38-40 WCF. Departments such as Nashville PD (G22, Winchester Ranger) and Tulsa PD (G22C, Remington Golden Saber) have had excellent results with 2nd generation transonic ammo, 165-grain JHP at 1,140 fps. Border Patrol reports splendid results with a similar transonic 155-grain at 1,200 fps. These rounds roughly approximate the ballistics of the .357 Magnum with a 158-grain bullet at 1,200 fps. (A subsonic 165-grain, developed for the FBI, is more of a hot .38 Special by comparison.)

A 3rd gen load, the 135-grain JHP at 1,300 fps, equals or exceeds the devastating wound ballistics of the 125-grain .357 Magnum, and is produced by smaller ammo companies such as CorBon and Double-Tap. The South Bend, Indiana Police Department has had tremendous success with its SIG .40s and the CorBon 135. Finally, 200-grain handloads have made inroads in USPSA competition with the .40, but that bullet is not yet seriously in play on the defensive side. Clearly, the .40 S&W is a versatile cartridge giving its user a wide range of load options.

Of late, S&W is back at speed with its very own cartridge, because its polymer Military & Police pistol is making significant inroads. It has been adopted by numerous city, county, and state police departments, with .40 by far the

Though not the most accurate pistol cartridge out there, the .40 S&W has more than enough accuracy for its purpose. Pistol is a Glock 22.

The SIG P226 in .40 was very popular with US law enforcement, although the P229 in .40 has replaced it as SIG's best-selling police pistol in the US today.

The Glock 27 subcompact .40 has proven hugely popular among armed citizens and off-duty cops alike. This one wears Trijicon night sights.

most popular of its four offered calibers. The state troopers of Colorado and Iowa, for example, now carry the M&P40, and the same gun has recently been adopted by the city police of Detroit and Milwaukee.

Not all found the .40 the ideal compromise. The State Police agencies of Georgia, Pennsylvania, and South Carolina eventually traded their .40s for .45 GAP pistols from Glock. North Carolina cashiered the .40 for the .357 SIG. In each case, a perceived need for more power was the reason offered.

The bottom line, however, is the .40 Smith & Wesson cartridge is here to stay. It is the standard issue of more American law enforcement agencies than any other. No caliber since the .38 Special has become so popular so quickly after its introduction. Simply put, the .40 S&W was a brilliant concept, in the right place at the right time. **GUNS**

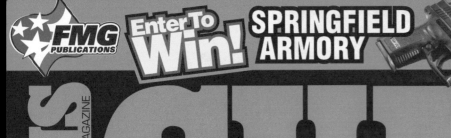

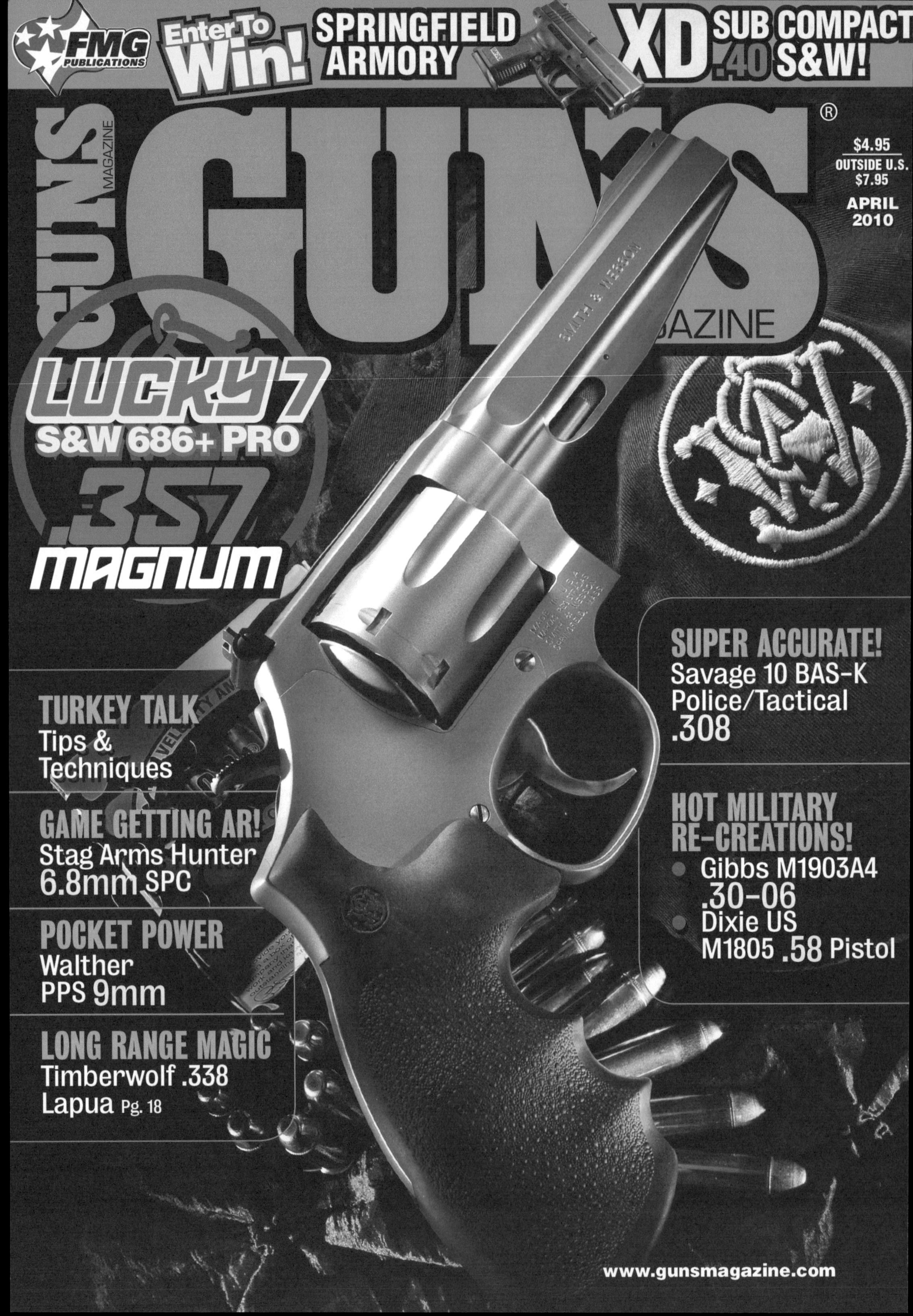

FMG PUBLICATIONS
Enter To Win!
SPRINGFIELD ARMORY
XD SUB COMPACT .40 S&W!
GUNS MAGAZINE
GUNS MAGAZINE ®
$4.95
OUTSIDE U.S. $7.95
APRIL 2010
LUCKY 7
S&W 686+ PRO
.357 MAGNUM
TURKEY TALK
Tips & Techniques
GAME GETTING AR!
Stag Arms Hunter 6.8mm SPC
POCKET POWER
Walther PPS 9mm
LONG RANGE MAGIC
Timberwolf .338 Lapua Pg. 18
SUPER ACCURATE!
Savage 10 BAS-K Police/Tactical .308
HOT MILITARY RE-CREATIONS!
Gibbs M1903A4 .30-06
Dixie US M1805 .58 Pistol
www.gunsmagazine.com

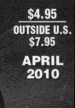

LUCKY 7

Massad Ayoob
Photos: Joseph R. Novelozo

There are three grades of shootability in the shootin' irons available from Smith & Wesson. The standard production grade has set a standard of excellence in the handgun industry worldwide since 1856. At the other end of the scale are the guns from S&W's Performance Center; very much like similarly named sections in the auto industry. The Center turns out special purpose racing iron, some of which gets raced at the national and world championship level, and some of which goes to connoisseurs of those particular machines who can afford to pay for the absolute best.

In this economy more than ever, there are folks who appreciate performance, but just aren't budgeted for top dollar right now. *GUNS Magazine* knows that… and so does Smith & Wesson. That's why, a few years ago, S&W introduced its Pro Series. These are handguns conceptualized and tested in the Performance Center then turned over to the regular Production side of the house, allowing more affordable pricing.

At the time the cover gun was sent to us, it was so new the company hadn't assigned it a stock number, and it came in a box marked "Model 686" and "4" barrel."

Well, it wasn't. This specimen, serial number CML1430, is stamped "686-6" (the "-6" denoting the presence of the internal locking system). It is actually a Model 686-Plus, meaning an L-frame .357 Magnum with 7-shot cylinder. The barrel is 5" long, and shaped in the manner of the company's popular 686 SSR, another revolver in the Pro Series.

Jim Unger, head of revolver production at S&W, calls this configuration the "wedge barrel." Tony Miele, head of the Performance Center, describes it as the "tapered barrel." I can't argue with either one of them. It is wedge-shaped, and it is tapered. Seen from above, the flat-sided barrel narrows a bit, a little more than 1/2" in front of the frame, and then continues in slim, straight lines to the muzzle. Seen from the side, the ejector rod shield is open on both sides, in the SSR style, and what might be called a "half underlug" sweeps up toward the muzzle, growing narrower along the way. This shape may help to reduce friction drag as the gun is being drawn from the holster. It definitely allows smoother, easier re-holstering, which admittedly is more of a tactical concern than a competition concern, and this sweet 7-shooter seems to have "competition" written all over it.

The SSR is named for the Stock Service Revolver division in IDPA, the International Defensive Pistol Association. Because IDPA limits shooters to 6 rounds in their revolvers, the 686 SSR has the conventional 6-chambered cylinder. Says Tony Miele, "We had experienced very good success with the 686 SSR within the IDPA community. The 5" gun is a natural follow-on for ICORE shooters, who can have longer barrels and who can take advantage of the 7th shot."

ICORE is the International Congress Of Revolver Enthusiasts. Their formats seem a bit like the Steel Challenge, where a lighter-barreled revolver is an advantage because it swings faster between the multiple targets. Miele knows the ICORE game, and it sounds as if the new gun will be a fine candidate for it.

A couple of other Performance Center touches adorn this Pro Series gun. The cylinder face is cut for full moon clips,

A key feature of this new model is the sculpted 5" barrel, a work of art in its own right. The front sight, a Patridge style, is pinned to the frame and can be changed to suit the individual's requirements.

A 686+ .357 MAGI FROM S&W'S "PRO

UM
SERIES."

15

LUCKY 7

A 686+ .357 MAGNUM FROM S&W'S "PRO SERIES."

GUNS
MAGAZINE

Mas is happy with the tight 25-yard groups this new Pro Series revolver produces.

Best accuracy was with these SJHP handloads by Chris Christian: 5 shots in .85", the best three tighter than 1/2" center to center, at 25 yards.

the fastest possible reloading system for a wheelgun. The chambers also appear to have been chamfered at the factory, to further enhance reloading speed. The action is not hand-honed like a true Performance Center gun, but this one does have the lighter mainspring the Performance Center uses on its custom L-frames.

The .357 is of course one of our most versatile chamberings, which adds to this gun's desirability. I took the 686-6 to the 25-yard bench with an MTM pistol rest and five loads ranging from mouse-fart to Magnum. They're presented in alphabetical order. Each 5-shot group was measured once overall as an indicator of what it and the gun could do from a solid position in experienced but fallible human hands, and once again for the best 3-shot cluster. Experience and testing have taught me this latter mechanism will give a very close prediction of what the same gun/ammo combination is likely to do for all five shots from a machine rest. All measurements were taken to the nearest .05".

American Eagle, Federal's economy line, has a version of the popular 130-grain full metal jacket .38 Special "Air Force bullet," popular because it's cheap, and may be the best of its kind in speed-driven competitions when allowed because it's a roundnose instead of flat at the tip. This allows it to speedload a little quicker. This is normally an accurate load. The week before the test, my girlfriend won a match with it out of her Bill

A *The Performance Center's new 7-shot M686 .357 Magnum features chamfered chambers for reloading with moon clips. Loose ammunition and conventional speedloaders can still be used.* **B** *The M686 has a narrow, smooth trigger for shooting double action.* **C** *The fully adjustable rear sight is neatly set into the topstrap. The firing pin is fitted to the frame and the hammer has a well-shaped, checkered thumbpiece.* **D** *The Model 686's stainless steel is given a smooth, satin finish. The sights are blued and the hammer and trigger are case hardened.*

With all the ability of a .357 Magnum revolver to fire such a wide range of loads, the new S&W was easy to control in two-handed firing.

You don't need the moon clips. For convenience, Mas used loose rounds for first gunload on each run, seen here ejecting.

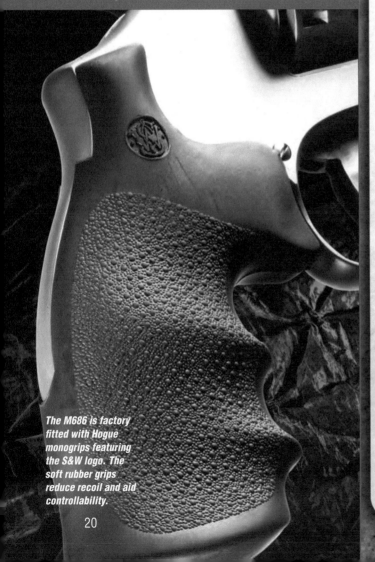

The M686 is factory fitted with Hogue monogrips featuring the S&W logo. The soft rubber grips reduce recoil and aid controllability.

Pfeil-customized S&W Model 67 4". This new S&W didn't like it at all. Although it was OK at 7 yards, at 25 it patterned more than grouped. I can't imagine why, but guns are like us: they seem to have their own, sometimes picky, preferences.

Black Hills manufactured two of our test loads, both light .38 Specials. Their 148-grain mid-range wadcutter cut five easy-to-see holes measuring 1.65" apart. The best three were under an inch, to wit, .95". The other Black Hills product we used was their cowboy load, which uses a truncated cone shaped 158-grain bullet, all lead like the wadcutter, at a moderate velocity. This actually shot tighter than the wadcutter, with a 1.35" overall group and the best three only .90" apart.

Top Load Is A Handload

A handload was next, put together by outdoor writer and pistol champ Chris Christian. Comprising a semi-jacketed Speer 140-grain hollowpoint in a .38 Special case over 6.1 grains of Hodgdon Longshot and a Federal small pistol primer, it was running fast enough to make IDPA's requisite 125,000 power factor (determined by velocity in feet per second multiplied by bullet weight in grains), this fine example of the handloader's art gave the best accuracy of the test. All five shots were well under an inch, measuring .85" center to center. The best three measured .45": a single .45 caliber hole would have bisected them all! You just can't ask for better accuracy than that from a production revolver.

Moving up the power scale, we used a .357 Magnum round at the end. It was Winchester's street-proven 145-grain Silvertip. This opened up slightly, delivering a 2.45", but the best three were still under an inch: 0.95".

Now, let's look at that for a moment. There was one load out of five the test gun just didn't group with. Setting it aside, the other four were all under 2-1/2" for the 5-shot, hand-held group, and three of those four were under 2", and one well under 1". The "best three" measurements, indicative of inherent mechanical accuracy potential, were all under 1" and one was under 1/2". That, my friends, is accuracy with which you can win most any kind of handgun match.

When an outdoor writer tests a new deer rifle, he hunts deer with it and does his darndest to shoot one. It would seem the best way to test a handgun born for competition, would be to shoot a match with it. I therefore set out looking for one. I had already put together an eclectic black basketweave rig for it: Bianchi dress gunbelt, Safariland synthetic 021 competition holster, and a poor man's moon clip carrier: a Don Hume cartridge slide. I was, b'gawd, ready to shoot.

Matchless

Tony Miele had designed this model with ICORE in mind, and I called a club an hour and a half away known to put those on. I discovered they had dropped ICORE a year before. There wasn't another in striking distance. Dang!

Bowling pin shooting is another venue where a 7th shot is a benefit. I checked the calendar. The next one within reasonable driving distance would be after deadline. Double dang!

NRA Action Pistol, as typified by the Bianchi Cup, is fired in 6-shot sequences but the wheelgunner there can certainly benefit from a 7th round in reserve. But there was no NRA Action Pistol match anywhere near me, either. IDPA? The 5" barrel was 1" too long for the rules to allow. PPC? There was only one PPC event on the schedule, and that was a Service Revolver match in Tallahassee, run in accordance with NRA rules, which mandate a 4" maximum barrel length. I had to be there to teach that week anyway.

I was "all gunned up with nowhere to go." So that was that, skunked for any chance to shoot the thing in a match, I took the test gun to my own range and set up a couple of match courses with it, two days before deadline for this article. First, I set up a B-27 NRA police silhouette target. The Service Revolver course is comprised of 48 rounds. Six shots 1-handed in 8

MODEL 686+ PRO SERIES	
MAKER: S&W	
2100 ROOSEVELT AVENUE	
SPRINGFIELD, MA 01104	
(800) 331-0852	
WWW.SMITH-WESSON.COM	
ACTION TYPE:	Double action revolver
CALIBER:	.357 Magnum
CAPACITY:	7
BARREL LENGTH:	5"
OVERALL LENGTH:	10"
WEIGHT:	37.5 ounces
FINISH:	Stainless steel
SIGHTS:	Patridge front, fully adjustable rear
GRIPS:	Hogue monogrip
PRICE:	$1,059

seconds at 3 yards proved the revolver handled well in a single paw, but I hadn't quite sighted it in perfectly yet and the group was in the upper right of the X-ring.

The second stage is draw, fire six, reload, and fire six more, all in 20 seconds from 7 yards. Two handed and holding at 7 o'clock in the X-ring, the smooth Smith made it easy to "clear" this stage, also. The third stage is the same as the second but at 15 yards, and here I got careless and held the sights too far left, and dropped my first point, a 9-ring hit. The match finishes with a draw and six shots each kneeling, standing left hand barricade, and standing right hand barricade, in 90 seconds including reloads. The gun did well in the left hand for an out of the box double action with the non-dominant hand controlling, the way this match must be shot. I finished with the same point score I'd won the Service Revolver match with a week before in Tallahassee.

For a first time over the course, that spoke well for the test gun. Yes, it had adjustable sights, but I had failed to adjust them correctly. Yes, it had a good action for out of the box, but not as good as the well-worn-in Model 64 I'd shot before, whose sights were dead on. Getting the same score under these circumstances tells me this gun is capable of better scores with familiarization and perfect sighting in, and is clearly capable of perfect scores, even national record scores, in this type of shooting.

With none of the tombstone-shaped Bianchi Cup targets on hand, there was only one NRA Action Pistol event I could duplicate on short notice, the Bianchi Plates. A rack of 8" diameter falling plates, six of 'em, is shot twice each from 10, 15, 20, and 25 yards. Back when I shot the Cup, '79 through '88, the times were six, seven, eight, and nine seconds respectively per string, so that's what I set the timer for.

The 5" 686 came up smoothly out of the Safariland holster, even though it was made for a 6" gun, and allowed me to easily clean two-dozen plates at 10 and 15 yards. On the 20-yard line, I got froggy on the trigger and missed a plate. (I dropped it anyway with the 7th shot, "just because," but it still counted as a miss because NRA rules say you can only take one shot at each plate. In NRA Action Pistol, the big advantage of this gun's 7th chamber is you can fire it to make up for a misfire or a skipped chamber.) At 25 yards I missed another, and finished the course with a 460 out of 480 possible. Well, I don't remember ever getting a perfect score on the plate stage at Bianchi Cup, either.

I wasn't testing me, though, I was testing the gun—and this 7-shot 5" passed with flying colors. For those who prefer a revolver, it should also make a neat home defense gun. Recoil wasn't bad at all with the factory-provided Hogue grips even with .357 Magnum rounds, and one more bullet never hurts. Besides, there are lots of folks who, like the late, great Skeeter Skelton, believe a 5" barrel is just the right compromise length for a heavy-duty service revolver.

There was only one misfire during the almost 300 rounds I managed to put through this revolver in the midst of the Great Post-Obama Ammo Drought, and that was from an ancient box of 158-grain .38 Special. (How long ago did they stop making S&W brand ammo, anyway?) If nothing else, it was the perfect reminder of what that 7th chamber is for. Kinda like the gun itself: "better to have it and not need it, than need it and not have it." I'm glad to see Tony, Jim, and the whole team at Smith & Wesson are still working to give us more options that reflect sound engineering, quality manufacturing and, in this case, creative thinking. **GUNS**

Taffin shooting his long-barreled Smith & Wesson 8-3/8" .357 Magnum.

75 YEARS YOUNG

Happy Diamond Jubilee .357 Magnum

John Taffin

To come up with a better revolver for city, county and state police officers, Smith & Wesson took their 3rd Model Hand Ejector .44 Special and chambered it for .38 Special in 1930. This was no ordinary .38. It was loaded heavier and renamed the .38/44 with a muzzle velocity of around 300 fps more than the standard .38 Special. Smith & Wesson offered two basic models of the .38/44, the fix-sighted Heavy Duty for law enforcement use and the adjustable-sighted Outdoorsman for hunters and target shooters.

It wasn't long before experimenters came up with even heavier loads for the .38/44. In 1932, Ed McGivern had high praise for both the revolvers and the new cartridge. He spoke of shooting the Outdoorsman out to 500 yards and called it the finest gun ever turned out by anybody at any time. The .38/44 Heavy Duty was considered "… the finest, strongest, all around general-purpose gun, coming from all angles, that has ever been given to the shooting public." Experimenters like Elmer Keith and Phil Sharpe came up with much heavier loads and Keith's .38/44 load is still a standard today among sixgunners.

The Beginning

The S&W .38/44 Outdoorsman made the .357 Magnum possible and the latter really started in the hunting fields. Sharpe, in his monumental work, *Complete Guide To Handloading*, published in 1937, said, "The .357 Magnum cartridge was born in the mind of the author several years ago. On a hunting trip with Col. D.B. Wesson, Vice-President of Smith & Wesson, a pair of heavy framed Outdoorsman revolvers was used with a large assortment of handloads developed and previously tested by the author. In the field they proved entirely practical, but Col. Wesson was not content to attempt the development of a Magnum .38 Special cartridge for ordinary revolvers, and set to work on a new gun planned in the field."

In 1935 their work with the .38/44, as well as, by ammunition companies, resulted in a new cartridge. The .38 Special case was lengthened and a new name was needed. Wesson, of Smith & Wesson, used the diameter of the bullet, .357" and the French word for a large bottle of champagne, Magnum, and the .357 Magnum arrived. The original load was 15.4 grains of Hercules 2400 under a 158-grain lead bullet and ignited by a large—not small—primer.

The first Magnum sixgun, known appropriately as "The .357 Magnum" was born. The .357 Magnum sixguns were more than simply production guns. Each of the new .357s were specially fitted and finished, and given a registration number in addition to a serial number. In 1935, in the midst of the Great Depression, the new sixgun and cartridge were so popular Smith & Wesson soon dropped the special registration, as they could not keep up with the demand. Back then, $60 was a lot of money, but many shooters were more than willing to pay it to get the finest revolver ever made up to that point.

Remember, 1935 was long before the age of instant communication or even gun magazines, except the *American Rifleman*. Elmer Keith wrote up the .357 for the latter, but opined the barrel was too long and he still preferred the .44 Special. Wesson promoted the new gun and cartridge using both a 6-1/2" and 8-3/4" .357 Magnum-taking elk, antelope and black bear. He even went to Alaska with the hopes of taking a brown bear, but was unable to find one. After contemplation, he felt it was a good thing he had not done so. In later years both of

these early .357 Magnum, revolvers were owned by Col. Rex Applegate, and it was my privilege to be able to handle them. After his death they were sold, so they now belong to a Smith & Wesson collector somewhere.

Keith's .38/44 load used his 173-grain 358429 hardcast bullet, which proved too long for use in the .357 Magnum cartridge due to the length of the Smith & Wesson cylinder. Sharpe designed a 158-grain bullet with a shorter nose and less bearing surface for use in the new cartridge, and published extensive reloading data while warning reloaders not to take this cartridge for granted. In the early 1950s it was left to Ray Thompson to come up with the ideal bullet for the .357 Magnum with his gas-checked 358156. Leading was always a problem with both factory and reloads for the .357 Magnum until Thompson solved the issue. I have never been able to get really good accuracy using plain-based bullets in full-house .357 Magnum loads, but the Thompson gas-checked bullet works perfectly. I consider it the number one bullet for standard weight loads in the .357 Magnum.

The FBI Gun

Smith & Wesson advertised the .357 Magnum as the most powerful revolver ever made, far above any .44 or .45 available. It was not only promoted by Col. Wesson, but Smith & Wesson was also wise enough to present one of the first production 8-3/4" .357 Magnums to the then head of the FBI, J. Edgar Hoover. That barrel length was, of course, too long for law enforcement use, however, 4" and 3-1/2" .357 Magnums soon became very popular with FBI agents.

Soon-to-be General George Patton purchased a 3-1/2" .357 Magnum in Hawaii in 1935 and carried it in tandem with his Colt Single Action .45 during World War I. He called the Smith & Wesson .357 his "killing gun." Even though both his Colt and Smith & Wesson wore ivory grips, contrary to popular belief, they were not finished the same. The Colt was engraved and nickel-plated, while the Smith & Wesson was plain high-polish blue.

Those early .357 Magnums may very well be the finest revolvers to ever come from the Smith & Wesson factory. From 1935 to 1939 approximately 5,200 "Registered Magnums" were manufactured. These guns were basically handfitted, beautifully polished and, in addition to a serial number, had a second number, a registration number, placed on the yoke cuts. Patton's .357 Magnum carried registration No. 506. Registration No. 1 went to Hoover and No. 2 to Sharpe.

GUNS
DEC. '86
HANDLOADING THE .41 MAGNUM
DECEMBER 1986
$2.00 IN CANADA $3.00

COVER STORY
GENERAL PATTON
"Old Blood and Guts"
and HIS GUNS

Win a
SAVAGE
110 K RIFLE

SHOOTING
S&W's NEW
645 AUTO

Speed Shooting
at the
STEEL CHALLENGE

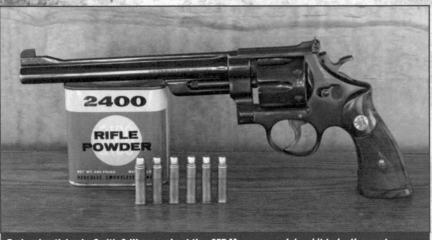

Early advertising by Smith & Wesson about the .357 Magnum proclaimed it to be the most powerful revolver ever offered. The first factory .357 loads were assembled with Hercules 2400 powder and 75 years later it is still a favorite propellant. Custom stocks are by Keith Brown.

Taffin is a firm believer in the philosophy of a "Pair and a Spare" as exhibited by these 5" Model 27s. The 5" is one of the handiest barrel lengths. Custom stocks are by BearHug and BluMagnum.

Before 1957 Smith & Wessons were known simply as the ".357 Magnum" and these two from the early 1950s are pre-27s. Custom stocks are by Keith Brown.

Barrel lengths in order of preference were 6-1/2", 5", 6", 8-3/4", 3-1/2" and 4". In 1939 Smith & Wesson dropped the registration procedure and barrel lengths were standardized at 3-1/2", 5", 6", 6-1/2" and 8-3/8", not necessarily in order of preference. All of these guns had a beautiful high bright-blue finish (nickel was an extra option) with a fine-line checkering on the barrel rib, top strap and rear sight assembly. Both the backstrap and the frontstrap were serrated and the first grips/stocks were the small old-style found on all N-frames since late 1907. The .357 Magnum was the first Smith & Wesson to be fitted with Magna stocks, which were soon offered as an option. These filled in on both sides of the grip frame to the top of the backstrap.

Of course, production of the .357 Magnum and all other firearms stopped at the beginning of WWII as machinery was geared up for wartime production. After the war, it would be December of 1946 before another .357 Magnum would be produced, and only 142 were manufactured through 1949. One of these went to President Harry Truman. Obviously, .357 Magnums were hard to find.

Debut Of The Short Action

In 1950 the long action of the .357 Magnum was changed to the current short action, which allowed a shorter distance for the hammer to travel. Skeeter Skelton often remarked how hard it was to find a .357 Magnum in the 1950s. When I started really getting interested in gunshops in 1956, I don't recall ever seeing any. In fact, I saw the .44 Magnum first.

In 1956, the upper sideplate screw was deleted and the "5-screw" .357 Magnum became a "4-screw" with three screws in the sideplate and one in the front of the triggerguard. One year later, this magnificent revolver, which had been known only as the .357 Magnum since its inception, now became a number instead of a name: the Model 27. Four years later, the screw in the front of the triggerguard was eliminated and the Model 27 became a "3-screw" sixgun.

In 1994 the unbelievable happened, and the .357 Magnum, the Model 27, was dropped from production. However, it was not forgotten and just before the end of the 20th century a new Model 27 appeared. This Performance Center gun bears little resemblance to the original with an 8-shot cylinder and a heavy tapered underlugged barrel. It is a good sixgun, but simply not the same. Just recently, in their Classic Series, Smith & Wesson reintroduced the Model 27 in time for its Diamond Anniversary.

The .357 Magnum, as mentioned, was a beautifully finished revolver, so beautiful in fact, some were reluctant to

In the beginning, the .357 Magnum was considered the ultimate big-game revolver. Here, Col. Doug Wesson of S&W and the moose he took with his .357 Magnum in 1935.

19! In 1963 a 6" version was introduced for the Model 19, followed by a 2-1/2" in 1966. In 1970, the Model 19 was produced in stainless steel with the same barrel lengths, and was called the Model 66. In 1999, the Model 19 was dropped, and the Model 66 received the same fate in 2005. Long before they disappeared, they had basically been replaced by the stronger L-Frame, heavy under lugged–barreled Models 586 and 686.

Prior to World War II, Colt chambered their New Service, Shooting Master and Single Action Army in .357 Magnum. Production ceased in 1940. However, in 1954 Colt introduced their .357 Magnum followed by the Python, their Cadillac of revolvers, in 1955, and in 1956, the Colt Single Action Army returned in .357 Magnum.

Ruger's first centerfire sixgun was the .357 Blackhawk in 1955. This was a true outdoorsman's sixgun with adjustable sights, a heavy top strap and a Colt-sized grip frame. Since that time, both companies have introduced several other .357 Magnums, including the underrated Ruger GP100 and Colt King Cobra, and we have also seen .357s from manufacturers such as Freedom Arms, Dan Wesson and Taurus.

The .357 Magnum remains extremely popular and is probably the most powerful revolver most shooters can handle really well. We have a long list of revolvers chambered in the original Magnum available today. However, my heart still belongs to the old classics, and especially to the original .357 Magnum. With the Lyman/Thompson 158-grain gas-checked bullet over 14 to 15 grains of 2400 loaded in any of the above, life is quite pleasurable. Happy 75th anniversary to the Smith & Wesson .357 Magnum. **GUNS**

carry it as a duty gun. In 1954, to answer this "problem," Smith & Wesson brought out a special version of the .357 Magnum known as the Highway Patrolman. This was a basic no-frills .357. No high polish here as the finish was a matte blue, and also gone was the fine checkering on the top strap. Barrel length was 4" or 6" and Magna stocks were standard. The first new Smith & Wesson I ever purchased was a 4" Highway Patrolman. In 1957 the Highway Patrolman became the Model 28.

Now we had a less fancy .357 Magnum for duty and outdoor use. What's next? Bill Jordan began petitioning Smith & Wesson to produce a lighter weight .357 Magnum using the Military & Police .38 as the basic platform. In 1955 Smith & Wesson unveiled the .357 Combat Magnum. Using the K-frame .38, a full-length .357 Magnum cylinder was installed matched up with a 4" bull barrel. The result was a revolver Bill Jordan called "The Peace Officers Dream." Weighing a full 1/2-pound less than its older brother and with a smaller cylinder diameter, the Combat Magnum was much easier to carry all day.

In 1957 the Combat Magnum became the Model 19. Somehow, .357 Magnum, Highway Patrolman and Combat Magnum stir the sixgunning soul a whole lot more than 27, 28 and

THe M&P15-22
S&W fields their own unique rimfire AR.

Smith & Wesson fans, you're going to like the M&P15-22. Most of us were caught off guard a few years ago when S&W stepped forward with their very own AR-15, the M&P15. It was the right product at the right time. Demand for ARs was insatiable, prices were at scalper levels, and the supply pipeline for factory-finished ARs had dried to a trickle.

Smith &Wesson not only stepped up to the plate in a timely fashion, but their product immediately earned them high marks for the fit, finish and accuracy built into the M&P15 line. If you're looking for a high-quality, traditional AR, it's hard to beat the quality and price of the Smith & Wessons.

And then the .223 ammunition supply dried up, seemingly overnight. Whispers were it was conspiratorial, something like the earlier primer shortage. The fact was the United States was involved in two wars, and the ammunition plants were running 24/7 just to meet the needs of the troops. Ammunition and components are in short supply anytime a war is being waged.

There was no better time for AR makers to develop a rimfi e clone and understudy for the centerfi e ARs

The dual aperture, adjustable rear sight can easily be removed and replaced with optics.

resting in the rack. With the brilliance of American industry, we now have dedicated rimfi e ARs from Smith & Wesson, Colt and Ruger.

Each maker has taken a different tack to bring an AR rimfi e on line. Colt licensed Carl Walther in Germany to build all-metal versions of the AR. Ruger took the guts of their 10/22 and surrounded it with an AR wrapper. Smith & Wesson went to the drawing board and designed a rimfi e AR that makes maximum use of synthetics to capture the overall design and essential operating features of their M&P15 centerfi e rifle .

The Smith & Wesson rimfi e line currently consists of four models. The basic differences among them are the degree to which they are compliant with existing, ridiculous, state-by-state regulations/restrictions. For

Most of the USA can get the M&P15-22 with a 25-round detachable magazine. A 10-round mag is available for states with "restrictions."

example, the S&W model that can be sold in Connecticut, Massachussets, Maryland, New Jersey and New York can't have a 6-position, collapsing stock or a 25-round magazine. No, the stock has to be fi ed and the magazine reduced to 10 rounds. The California "compliant" model can have a 6-position stock but only a 10-round

Accurate and dependable, S&W's M&P15-22 is a great rimfire understudy to the full-size .223 AR-15. "M&P" is a standard designation in S&W lines, standing for "Military & Police."

Smith & Wesson's M&P15-22 exhibits excellent lines and attention to detail. The stock is fully extended. The quad rail Picatinny fore-end has enough space for sights, lasers and lights.

magazine. For the rest of the country, there are two models, both have a 6-position collapsing buttstocks and 25-round magazines but one sports an A1-style compensator on the end of the muzzle and the other, not.

When comparing the M&P15-22 design to the centerfire line, its overall design comes closest to the centerfire model M&P15T, with its extended, Picatinny, quad-rail fore-end.

Examining the M&P15-22 more closely, the upper and lower receivers are formed from a high-strength polymer, reinforced where necessary with steel inserts. Sounds like the composition of an M&P pistol lower doesn't it? And it is. The blowback bolt

rides on steel rails inside the polymer receiver, and a match-grade barrel is threaded and screwed into a steel breech unit housed in the forward end of the upper. The texture and tone of the polymer provides the whole gun with a matte black appearance. It's a pleasing finish and appropriate to the line.

Comparing the controls on the rimfire to the centerfire model, they're in the right place. The M&P15-22 does sport a fully-functioning charger handle, a two-position safety under your thumb on the left side, a bolt hold-open latch and release on the left side and a recessed-magazine release on the right.

The 6-position collapsing stock rides on a mil-spec polymer tube. Collapsed, the overall length of the M&P15-22 is 30.5" and fully extended, 33.75". What's particularly nice about a telescoping buttstock is it permits shooters of all ages and physical size to adjust the rifle to their physique. Also, when the stock is fully collapsed, the M&P15-22 is easy to store and easy to handle in close quarters. The stock functioned perfectly in all six positions, but there was just enough up and down and side play in the unit to be noticeable. The tolerances between the tube and the stock need to be tweaked a bit at the factory, and while the buttstock

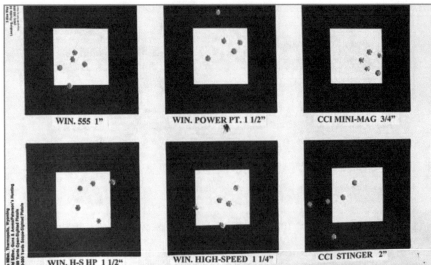

WIN. 555 1"   WIN. POWER PT. 1 1/2"   CCI MINI-MAG 3/4"

WIN. H-S HP 1 1/2"   WIN. HIGH-SPEED 1 1/4"   CCI STINGER 2"

incorporates a rear-sling swivel, there is no complementary forward-sling swivel.

The Picatinny, quad-rail fore-end is 10" long and mates nicely with the Picatinny rib forming the fl ttop of the receiver. The 4-sided Picatinny fore-end is cool looking, and just begs to be tricked out with scopes, red dots, lasers, flashlights and anything else you can hang on a Picatinny.

Accuracy

How did the M&P15-22 shoot? Averaging 7 pounds on a Lyman Electronic gauge, the single-stage trigger is a little on the hefty side but breaks cleanly. Functioning during the 5-shot, 35-yard tests was fl wless with a variety of high-speed, standard and target velocity ammunition.

I fi ed and averaged 12 different loads. In the high-speed arena, CCI Mini-Mag HP was the clear leader with groups hovering around 3/4" but PMC's Sidewinder was not far behind at 7/8". The more I shoot CCI's Mini-Mag HP in a variety of rimfi es, the

The M&P15-22 performed well across the velocity and ammunition cost spectrum.

Made in Springfield, Mass., the M&P15-22 features the right controls in the right places for its role as "AR understudy."

Collapsed, the 6-position buttstock is easy to store and handy in close quarters. Locked into one of six positions, the buttstock can fit shooters of all ages and physiques.

SMITH & WESSON M&P15-22	
**MAKER: SMITH & WESSON
2100 ROOSEVELT AVE.
SPRINGFIELD, MA 01104
(800) 331-0852
WWW.SMITH-WESSON.COM**	
ACTION TYPE:	Semiauto blowback
CALIBER:	.22 Long Rifl
CAPACITY:	10, 25
BARREL LENGTH:	16"
OVERALL LENGTH:	30.5" +collapsed, 33.75" (extended)
WEIGHT:	5.5 pounds
FINISH:	Black matte polymer
SIGHTS:	Rear, adjustable dual aperture, front, A2 adjustable post
STOCK:	6-position CAR
PRICE:	$569

more impressed I am. In the bulk-pack league, Winchester's "555" HP did best at 1-1/8". In target loads, both Wolf's Extra Match and RWS Target averaged 3/4". Frankly, it's nice to own a rimfi e that performs equally well across the velocity and price spectrum.

The M&P15-22 is a real fun gun and an excellent understudy to a real M4/M16, assisting the shooter to develop and hone their muscle memory so handling and shooting any of the AR models becomes subliminal and automatic. GUNS

THE RESURRECTION
SMITH & WESSON'S MODEL 58 .41 MAGNUM.

CLINT SMITH

As part of the continuing program of resurrecting older and popular models of Smith & Wesson revolvers, the Model 58 .41 Magnum has been brought back into production. Addressing and hopefully appeasing what is often considered a somewhat cultist group of shooters, the .41 Magnum, in fact, might have been singled out by a sharp group of individuals who saw and continue to see the advantages of this mid-size caliber handgun.

The lineage of the .41 Magnum includes (from top to bottom) the Model 57 with blue finish, Model 57 nickel finish and the original Model 58 with Spegel grips.

Introduced in the mid '60s, the .41 Magnum was considered by some to be the optimum self-defense cartridge and load for American law enforcement use. Historically, it can be traced to a wildcat cartridge called the .400 Eimer, which was on the drawing boards as early as the 1920s. In its initial introduction, the Smith & Wesson .41 Magnum was brought on the market in 1963-64 in the form of the named cartridge mated to the Smith & Wesson Model 57. The Model 57 was an adjustable sighted, 6-shot, large N-frame revolver. Shortly afterward, the factory folks at Smith & Wesson introduced a beefed up Model 10 fixed-sight version numbered the Model 58 that might be one of the best examples of a true fighting handgun—if there is such a thing.

Often with dismal results, the .38 special was for many years a pretty universal cartridge for the law enforcement community. Its failures are well noted and early attempts, such as the 200-grain .38-44 Super Police load, still did not bring the .38 to acceptable standards of stopping power. The .357 Magnum was the upgraded version of the .38, but it still lacked cross-sectional density, which is always helpful in a fighting handgun cartridge.

The .44 Magnum was, in fact, too much gun for general police use and the closest it came to solving the problem was the Remington 240-grain mid-range load. The .41 Magnum gave better cross-section density than the .38 Special and the bullet weight at 210 grains could be an attention getter to the misbehaving.

Two factory loadings were available. The barnburner was the 210-grain jacketed softpoint, which ran the gates at a smoking 1,500 feet per second declared and a probably true 1,400 fps. The second load was a 210-grain lead semiwadcutter cruising across the chronograph at a nominal 1,150 fps declared, but was in reality probably closer to 900 fps in the factory loading. It was plenty of load with plenty of projectile for the average shooter, and probably on the verge of too much.

I think one of the key ingredients to the failure of the .41 Magnum to achieve general acceptance in the law enforcement communities was the unclear boundary between the two loads and knowing the difference between the two. Probably if the truth was known, had the .41 Magnum been loaded to a nominal 850 to 900 fps with a 210-grain lead wadcutter from the get go I believe it would have been force to be reckoned with.

At 10 yards free hand, no rest, I shot CorBon DPX 180-grain hollowpoints for the test and the Model 58 placed them (with me attached) inside a nominal 1.5". Moving at 1,300 fps, the 180-grain DPX projects a true 676 foot-pounds of energy downrange. CorBon is one of the few who actually load what they say they are loading on the box. The rounds were stout and impacted steel had a distinct sound not often heard when 9mm or .40 S&W calibers are used on plates.

As mentioned before, this revolver is part of the program to bring back into the market older revolvers and this Model 58 falls into that category. The

Clint shot the test target (above) at 10 yards with the current production Model 58 using .41 Magnum ammunition made by CorBon. The current production Model 58 (below) has the 4th sideplate screw like earlier models. This is part of the program in producing newly made older-style revolvers. The grips are handsomely made and fit well.

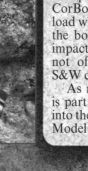

moDel 58	
maker: Smi Th & weSSon 2100 r oo Sevel T ave. Sprin Gfiel D, ma 01104 (800) 331-0852 www .SmiTh-we SSon. Com	
aCTion:	Double-action revolver
Caliber:	.41 Magnum
CapaCiTy:	6
barrel len GTh:	4"
weiGhT:	41 ounces
finiSh:	Blue or nickel plated
SiGhTS:	Fixed
Grip S:	Checkered wood
priCe:	$1,090

new Model 58 has a 4" barrel and fixed sights like its predecessor. The gun I had has the old-style cylinder latch and square butt, which is, of course, correct and true to the gun's linage.

The stocks are nicely done wood with silver Smith & Wesson medallions inlaid. This grip style and these stock panels are a good candidate for a Tyler T-grip filler for anyone who actually wants to carry and shoot the gun. With the filler or larger stocks the gun is a bit of a knuckle buster with full-power loads, which was the whole point of the exercise.

Total original production was a nominal 20,200 made during the years of 1964-1977.

The gun may be an example of a dud or, in reality, it may have been a gun and caliber ahead of its time. Either way, people who want one or wanted one to shoot, now have the chance thanks to the new Smith & Wesson Model 58 .41 Magnum being brought back online. **GUNS**

hol STer
5 ShoT l eaTher ll C
18018 n. l iGerwoo D CT.
Colber T, wa 99005
(509) 844-3969
www .5Sho Tlea Ther. Com

ammuni Tion
Cor bon/Gla Ser
p.o. box 369, S Tur GiS, SD 57785
(800) 626-7266
www .Dako Taammo.ne T

CuSTom S ToCkS
Crai G SpeGel
p.o. box 387, nehalem, or 97131
(503) 368-5653
www .Crai GSpeGel. Com

Tyler mf G.
p.o. box 94845
oklahoma Ci Ty, ok 73143
(800) 654-8415
www .T-Grip S.Com

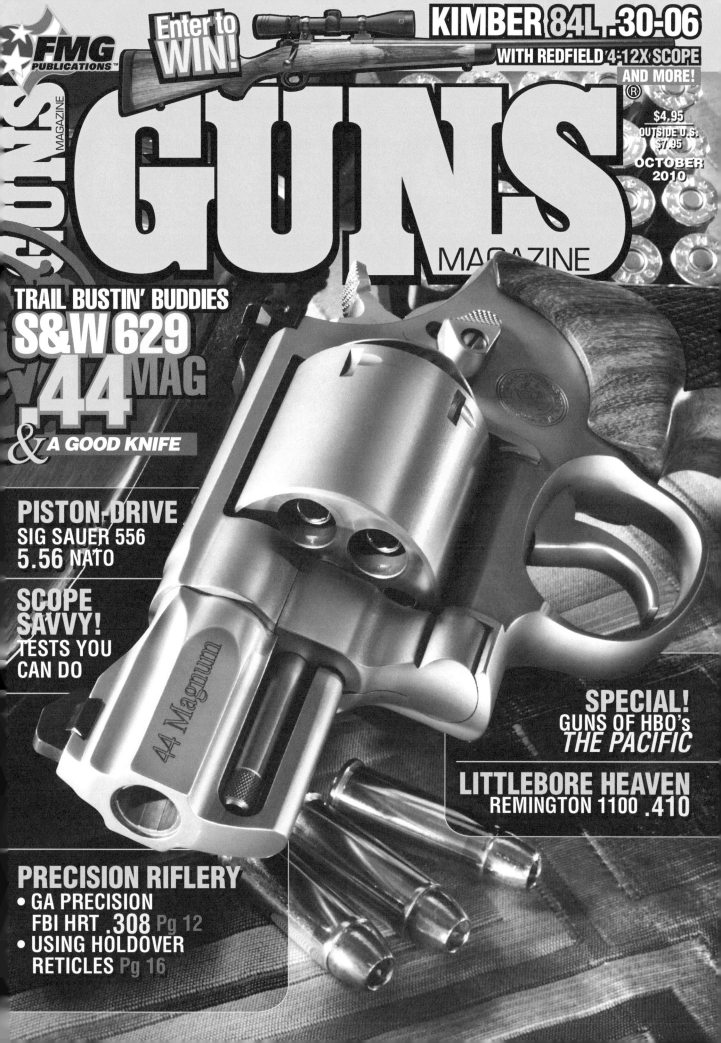

KIMBER 84L .30-06
WITH REDFIELD 4-12X SCOPE
AND MORE!

Enter to WIN!

FMG PUBLICATIONS™

GUNS MAGAZINE
MAGAZINE

$4.95
OUTSIDE U.S.
$7.95
OCTOBER 2010

TRAIL BUSTIN' BUDDIES
S&W 629
.44 MAG
& A GOOD KNIFE

PISTON-DRIVE
SIG SAUER 556
5.56 NATO

SCOPE SAVVY!
TESTS YOU CAN DO

SPECIAL!
GUNS OF HBO's THE PACIFIC

LITTLEBORE HEAVEN
REMINGTON 1100 .410

PRECISION RIFLERY
• GA PRECISION
  FBI HRT .308 Pg 12
• USING HOLDOVER
  RETICLES Pg 16

TRAIL BUSTIN' POWER

SMITH & WESSON'S MODEL 629 BIG-BORE PERSONAL PROTECTION .44 MAGNUM.

John Taffin   Photos: Joseph R. Novelozo

Today we have all manner of chopped and channeled sixguns and semi-automatics as well as a large selection of excellent leather for concealed carry. Semi-autos, having a much flatter profile, are normally easier to conceal than a big-bore sixgun with a 6-shot .44 or .45 cylinder. There is simply nothing to be done to downsize a 6-shot cylinder, however, both the barrel and the grip frame can be reduced considerably in the size.

The ejector rod housing is relieved on both sides of the sculpted 2-5/8" barrel.

If my memory is correct, sometime in the 1980s custom sixguns arrived taking up where Colt's Fitz had left off (see sidebar) with custom sixgunsmiths offering roundbutted, short-barreled revolvers with modified ejector rod housings to go below the 3-1/2" length of the original short-barrel .357 Magnum of the 1930s.

In recent years Smith & Wesson has reached back into history to offer many of the old Classic sixguns such as the original .357 Magnum, .44 Magnum and .44 Special of the mid-20th century. They have been resurrected and built to 21st-century specifications and requirements. At the same, time S&W is offering lightweight Night Guard revolvers in .44 Special, .357 Magnum and .44 Magnum, and the short-barreled, easier to conceal, all-steel, big-bore sixgun has not been forgotten; it has now arrived as a custom Model 629 from the Performance Center.

The original prototype .44 Magnum Smith & Wesson was built in 1954 on an existing 1950 Target Model, which had been chambered in .44 Special. The engineers at Smith & Wesson fitted a new, specially heat-treated cylinder to the 6-1/2" barreled 1950 Target, which had a weight of 39 ounces. The sixgun performed fine, however, the recoil was so fierce the engineers deemed it prudent to add more weight in the form of a heavy bull barrel and full-length cylinder, which brought the weight up to an even 3 pounds. This latest .44 Magnum from the Smith & Wesson Performance Center weighs the same as the original prototype. In the past 55 years, since the advent of the .44, Magnum sixguns have gotten bigger and and heavier to tame the recoil of heavier loads, and a 39-ounce .44 Magnum is going to kick fiercely with regular full-house .44 loads.

The original .44 Magnum was built with the hunter in mind. This one is aimed at those who want a big-bore sixgun for personal protection, a term that covers a lot of territory. Since what we have to be protected from depends on just where our wanderings happen to take us. By going with a powerful big-bore chambering such as the .44

HISTORY OF "BELLY GUNS"

John Taffin

It always looks so easy in the movies especially those wonderful old cowboy and gangster films of the 1930s and 1940s. The hero or villain is dressed in a tailored double-breasted suit and at the proper time reaches his left hand in below his breast pocket and pulls out a full sized Colt Single Action Army or 1911, which is somehow carried magically with nary a bulge detected. It is movie magic at its best, however, in reality it is not easy to carry and conceal a big-bore sixgun or semi-automatic.

The first Colt sixguns were not easily concealable but by the time the 1851 Navy and 1860 Army arrived, enterprising individuals found a way to make them more easily concealable. It wasn't long before barrels were chopped short and the big-bore pocket pistol had arrived. With the advent of the Colt Single Action Army, some enterprising types even removed the barrel altogether to make it fit easily into a pocket. Colt began offering short-barreled Store Keeper Models in the SAA as well as the new Lightning and Thunderer double actions of the 1870s.

In more modern times (well at least in the 1920s), John

Taffin found the short-barreled S&W 629 very accurate shooting at 10 yards offhand (left and right) with CorBon's DPX ammo. The chosen load for this test, CorBon's 225-grain DPX .44 Magnum ammo, delivered 1,200 fps from the Smith & Wesson's 2-5/8" barrel. Photos: John Taffin.

Henry Fitzgerald, "Fitz" of Colt, looked at the large Colt New Service chambered in .45 Colt and saw a pocket pistol. He shortened the barrel to 2", roundbutted the grip frame and, to make it even faster on the trigger, removed the front of the triggerguard. He was able to easily conceal a pair of these in the somewhat voluminous pockets of the trousers of that era.

Up to this point in time Smith & Wesson was making some of the finest large-frame, double-actions sixguns in existence especially their .44 Special and .38/44 Heavy Duty. By 1935, the .38/44 had evolved into the .357 Magnum with the first examples being outfitted with 8-3/4" barrels with the hunter and outdoorsman in mind.

To make the new .357 appealing to law enforcement Smith & Wesson cut the barrel as short as possible without interfering with the ejector housing. The result at 3-1/2" was not only one of most business-like looking revolvers ever produced, it was also carried easily in a Tom Threepersons-style holster under a suitcoat where it may not have been exceptionally comfortable but it was at least concealable.

When Smith & Wesson introduced the .357 Combat Magnum in 1955, they used the M&P .38 Special frame with its slightly smaller cylinder and added a 4" bull barrel to come up with what Bill Jordan called the Peace Officer's Dream. Then in the 1960s the Combat Magnum/Model 19 came out in a version with a roundbutt and a 2-1/2" barrel making it much easier to conceal and carry all day than the original .357 Magnum. **GUNS**

TRAIL BUSTIN' POWER

SMITH & WESSON'S MODEL 629 BIG-BORE PERSONAL PROTECTION .44 MAGNUM.

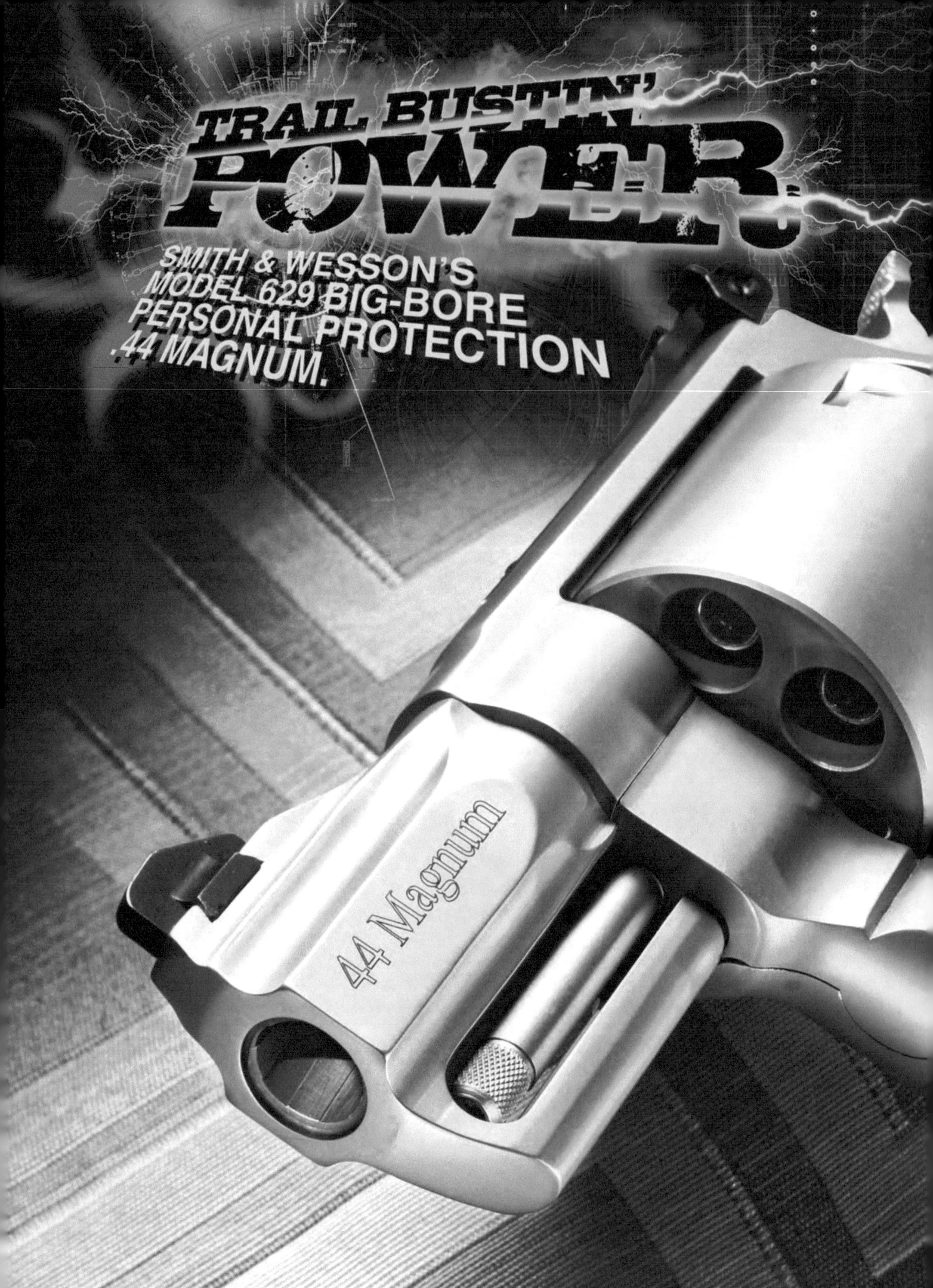

44 Magnum

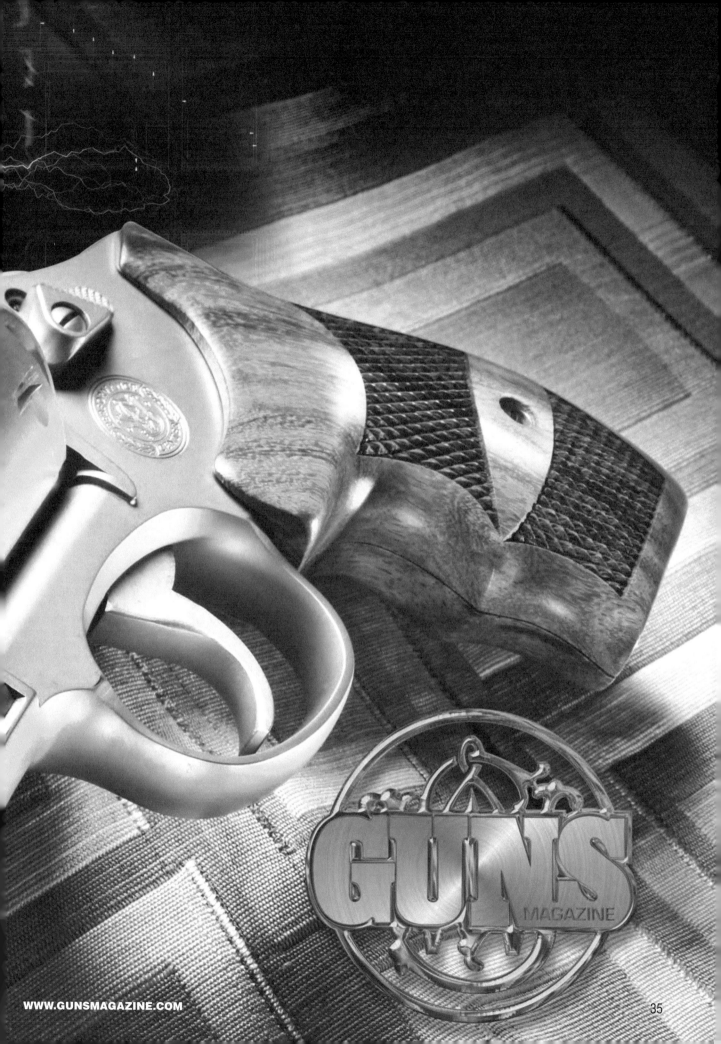

Magnum with proper loads, we are set for self-defense against the nastiest of creatures no matter how many legs they may have, well at least short of the big bears of Alaska.

There has been a noticeable trend in recent years, especially in this first decade of the 21st century to once again offer short-barreled big-bore sixguns. This is not Smith & Wesson's first short-barreled, all-steel offering as I have an older 3" Model 29 with the same roundbutt and un-fluted cylinder as this current offering. Smith & Wesson Night Guards are lightweight revolvers, while this new 629 is all steel.

The 3-1/2" N-Frame .357 Magnum and 2-1/2" .357 Combat Magnum are two of the most business-like looking pistols ever devised. Now we can add this new 629 to this select group. With its 2-5/8" barrel it fits right into the "Serious Looking Sixgun" list. It not only says serious, but it is also one good-looking sixgun! The major parts of this "little" .44 Magnum, barrel, cylinder and frame, are matte stainless steel while the hammer and trigger are hard-chromed steel.

The hammer has a most attractive teardrop shape, which is larger than a standard hammer spur but not quite as large as a target hammer. The trigger is non-target size with a smooth face making it easy on the trigger finger and it has a built-in trigger stop on the back. This is the one thing I do

PERFORMANCE CENTER MODEL 629	
MAKER: S&W	
2100 ROOSEVELT AVE.	
SPRINGFIELD, MA 01104	
(800) 331-0852	
WWW.SMITH-WESSON.COM	
ACTION TYPE:	Double-action revolver
CALIBER:	.44 Magnum
CAPACITY:	6
BARREL LENGTH:	2-5/8"
OVERALL LENGTH:	7-5/8"
WEIGHT:	39.6 ounces
FINISH:	Matte stainless steel
SIGHTS:	Adjustable rear, ramp front
GRIPS:	Checkered walnut
PRICE:	$1,185

not like about this .44 Magnum. I do not believe trigger stops belong on anything except a target pistol. For my use I would either remove it or file it down. I just do not want to take the chance of it ever backing out to the point the trigger will not go all the way rearward. It would probably never happen, but we all know what Murphy says.

The sights are excellent with a standard adjustable white outline rear sight matched up with a ramp-style front sight with a red insert. The front sight is also set in a dovetail should you need more windage than afforded by the rear sight or if a taller or shorter blade is desired. The ejector rod housing is cut all the way through making the ejector rod visible from both sides. Instead of the typical front locking feature of Smith & Wesson double-action revolvers, this one has a ball detent lock up with a ball on the front of the yoke fitting into a slot at the bottom of the ejector rod housing.

Grips are always, well almost always, a sore spot with me on factory double-action revolvers, but it's not the case here. These grips are exceptionally good looking, appearing to be of nicely grained walnut and are well shaped and designed for maximum concealment. They are checkered above and below the grip screw for a good secure feeling. The left grip is slimmed down at the top so as not to interfere with the ejection of cases, and both panels taper toward the bottom of the grip frame making them fit the hand quite comfortably. The grip frame itself has been roundbutted, which allows the use of such smallish grips.

There is a wide array of .44 Magnum ammunition available in weights from 165 grains up to 340 grains. I don't

HELTON
CUSTOM KNIVES

Roy Huntington

Since moving to the country outside of Joplin, Mo., I've found a wealth of local craftspeople. From custom furniture makers, weavers, potters and painters, to tractor restorers, blacksmiths and now—a sterling knifemaker.

An *American Handgunner* reader, Ms. Yvette, sent me an e-mail and simply said, "You need to meet this young man and feature him in your magazine." I phoned Billy Helton, and discovered he lives in Claremore, Okla., about an hour from me (the home of Will Rogers, by the way). I found him to be typical of the country people around here—polite, hard-working, modest-living and the kind of fellow whose handshake is a promise not to be broken. His hand-forged knife-work immediately took me, showing old school "hands-on" hard work, blending with an obvious creative enthusiasm for design and innovation. I immediately bought three knives from him.

I slated Billy to be featured in *American Handgunner's* Nov/Dec 2010 edition, and the work showcased in that article is stunning indeed. A dramatic leap in talent for someone who only began to make knives a few short years ago. His work, done in his small shop at home, shows the kind of care and attention you can only find in a hand-made knife. Each knife Billy makes comes with a letter of authenticity. In it, Billy describes the knife and signs it showing he made it personally. But what caught my eye is one line in that letter:

"*I believe that quality is the measure of a man's success, and I apply that to each*

The Helton knife features a blade almost as long as the overall length of the S&W 629. This pair would make serious traveling companions and earn the title of "Trail Bustin' Buddies."

and every knife."

The featured knife is a hand-forged bowie with bronze and copper fittings and an ironwood handle. While it is a one-off knife, Billy can make a dream come true for you too. And the prices begin at a very modest $250 for hand-forged work, and only $75 for a simple, stock removal model for everyday carry. **GUNS**

BILLY HELTON
18633 S. FERN PL., CLAREMORE, OK 74019
(918) 341-0263, WWW.HELTONKNIVES.COM

A) The 2-5/8" barrel is well sculptured and nicely crowned. Rather than having a second locking point at the end of the ejector rod, a ball detent locks the cylinder crane to the frame. B) The front sight is set into a dovetail and has a fluorescent red strip for high visibility. C) As with all modern S&W revolvers, the firing pin in mounted in the frame. The hammer is given a nice teardrop shape and is well checkered. Both hammer and trigger have been hard chromed. Note the fully adjustable white outline rear sight. D) The cylinder is unfluted to add a little weight to this otherwise lightweight sixgun. No matter how you cut it, a 6-shot .44 Magnum cylinder makes for a big revolver.

want to even contemplate setting off some of the latter in this little sixgun, nor even 300 grainers, or 240s or 250s for that matter. CorBon offers just about anything a .44 Magnum user would want including 165- and 180-grain hollowpoints as well as their 225-grain DPX. To go with the Smith & Wesson Performance Center .44 Magnum CorBon sent along several boxes of their DPX .44s.

DPX bullets are designed for Deep Penetration while the extremely large hollowpoint matches the penetration with maximum expansion. In the very short barrel of the Model 629, the 225-grain DPX bullet clocks out right at 1,200 feet per second. Recoil

is substantial, though not punishing, and the grips do a really good job of controlling felt recoil. All shooting was done at a "combat/self-defense" distance of 10 yards. It didn't take much concentration to put all six shots in one hole at this distance. For me, the typical red ramp insert washes out in sunlight or when shooting indoors. The red front sight of this .44 Magnum is a florescent strip extending the full length of the rear sight and shows up brightly for me even when shooting indoors.

Life is always full of trade-offs. If we want the most the .44 Magnum can offer we will opt for a long-barreled, long-cylindered version built to handle

the heaviest bullets. This type of sixgun is normally very large, very heavy and recoils tremendously. The Model 629 from the Performance Center is at the other end of the spectrum and what we give up in maximum performance is made up with ease of carrying and concealing while at the same time being able to deliver a respectable payload quite accurately at a reasonable distance. For anyone who roams off the beaten path this Model 629 could be a veritable lifesaver. GUNS

COPTALK

Massad Ayoob

The Rise of the S&W MILITARY & POLICE

Manual thumb safety, working like a 1911's, is an option on service and compact M&Ps in all calibers.

Ambi slidelock/slide release lever; integral light rail; tapered slide for easier holstering; extended tang; and ambi-safeties are available. www.smith-wesson.com

S&W revolvers had ruled U.S. police handgun sales until the sea-change to semiautos pistols began in earnest in the 1980s. S&W took a while to recognize polymer police pistols were here to stay, and they were not particularly quick to catch up. In 1993, S&W introduced Kevin Foley's design, the Sigma. Some departments adopted it, but it never really caught on in LE, instead finding its niche as a low-price, entry-level consumer pistol. A few years later, the company Americanized the Walther P99 into the SW99. A few cops liked them and still carry them today, but the SW99 didn't really catch on, either.

In-house, Joe Bergeron — a brilliant engineer who had begun his career in Gun Valley "down the road" at Colt's — was put in charge of a design team tasked with creating an all-new S&W handgun for this market. The result was the first semiauto pistol in decades to bear a name instead of a model number. That name was a hallowed one in the halls of S&W: "Military & Police."

Quick Acceptance

Test sample M&Ps started going out to writers and select police departments in 2005, and the pistols were in mainstream commerce by early 2006. The .40 S&W came first, followed in order by 9mm, .45 ACP and .357 SIG. Early on, Cincinnati and Columbus, Ohio adopted the M&P, in 9mm and .40 respectively, and Iowa State Patrol became the first state law enforcement agency to adopt the M&P, choosing the .40.

Early brush fires were quickly extinguished. It became apparent from the beginning the ambidextrous slide stop lever was too small to function effectively as a slide release lever; Bergeron and company acted quickly to rectify that. A few early feed problems, such as malfunctioning due to limp wristing, were cleared up with careful tweaks.

In the few short years since, acceptance has grown greatly. Iowa State Patrol was followed by five other state police agencies in adopting the M&P. These include Colorado (.40 S&W), New Mexico (.357 SIG), New Hampshire (.45 ACP), and most recently, the North Carolina Highway Patrol (.357 SIG) and Washington State Patrol (.40), according to Ian O'Donnell of S&W's law enforcement sales division.

Major municipal police agencies have been adopting the Military & Police, as well. Detroit, Michigan and Milwaukee, Wisconsin recently announced adoption of the M&P in .40, in both cases for department-wide adoption. Tampa, Florida and Atlanta, Georgia have also adopted the .40 caliber Military & Police pistol as standard issue; ditto Raleigh-Durham, North Carolina. Hartford, Connecticut issues the M&P in .45.

New Chicago Police Superintendent Jody Weis has indicated he wants all 13,000 or so CPD officers to carry the same uniform pistol, and if should come to pass, it's a contract I'm sure S&W will go after with alacrity. At this writing, the NYPD is testing the M&P for possible approval as an optional 9mm for its estimated 35,000 officers, who also buy their own duty weapons from an approved list.

WHY COPS BUY M&PS

S&W's critics and competitors say only dyed in the wool S&W departments are buying these guns. That's not entirely true. New Mexico troopers switched from Glocks, as did Milwaukee and Detroit, and NCHP and NHSP transitioned from SIG SAUERs.

Individuals accustomed to buying guns that fit themselves don't always appreciate the "one size fits all" needs of LE agencies, especially large ones. Alone among the big three makers of polymer police pistols (though the XD offers the feature in the M-series, and Glock may offer the option soon), all M&Ps from the beginning have come with small, medium and large interchangeable backstraps to adjust for grip girth and, most important, trigger reach. This has proven to be a huge selling point for the M&P, particularly with firearms instructors and department lawyers.

Whatever backstrap is installed, the grip tang goes out over the web of the hand more than the competition. Some find this just feels more solid in the hand, but a tiny percentage of cops have hands so big they need this to keep the slide from contacting their hand during firing, particularly when wearing gloves. The compact models don't have the extended grip tang.

Manual thumb safeties are available only on the .45 ACP version of the XD, and not at all on factory Glocks, but are optional now on all calibers of M&P, from service size to compact. More than one department has chosen the M&P with manual safety because of its proven life-saving capability if a bad guy disarms the officer by force. Neither of the other brands offers a magazine disconnector, it's an option on all M&Ps. According to S&W's Ian O'Donnell, some 40-percent are going out the door in that configuration. I know of one state police agency and one city department that mandated this on their M&Ps because it had already saved their officers' lives in earlier struggles for guns, when the embattled cop deliberately pressed the magazine button as he felt the attacker gaining control of his weapon.

M&P round count equals Glocks in three of the four calibers offered, when comparing service size pistols. That's 17+1 in 9mm, and 15+1 in .40 S&W and .357 SIG. It does come up short in .45 ACP, with 10+1 in the standard magazine M&P45 versus 13+1 in the Glock 21 or the XD45.

The bottom line? The S&W M&P autolo has made a "positive entry" into the US police pistol market. It's a race worth watching.

HANDGUNNER

AMERICAN HANDGUNNER

MAY/JUNE 2010

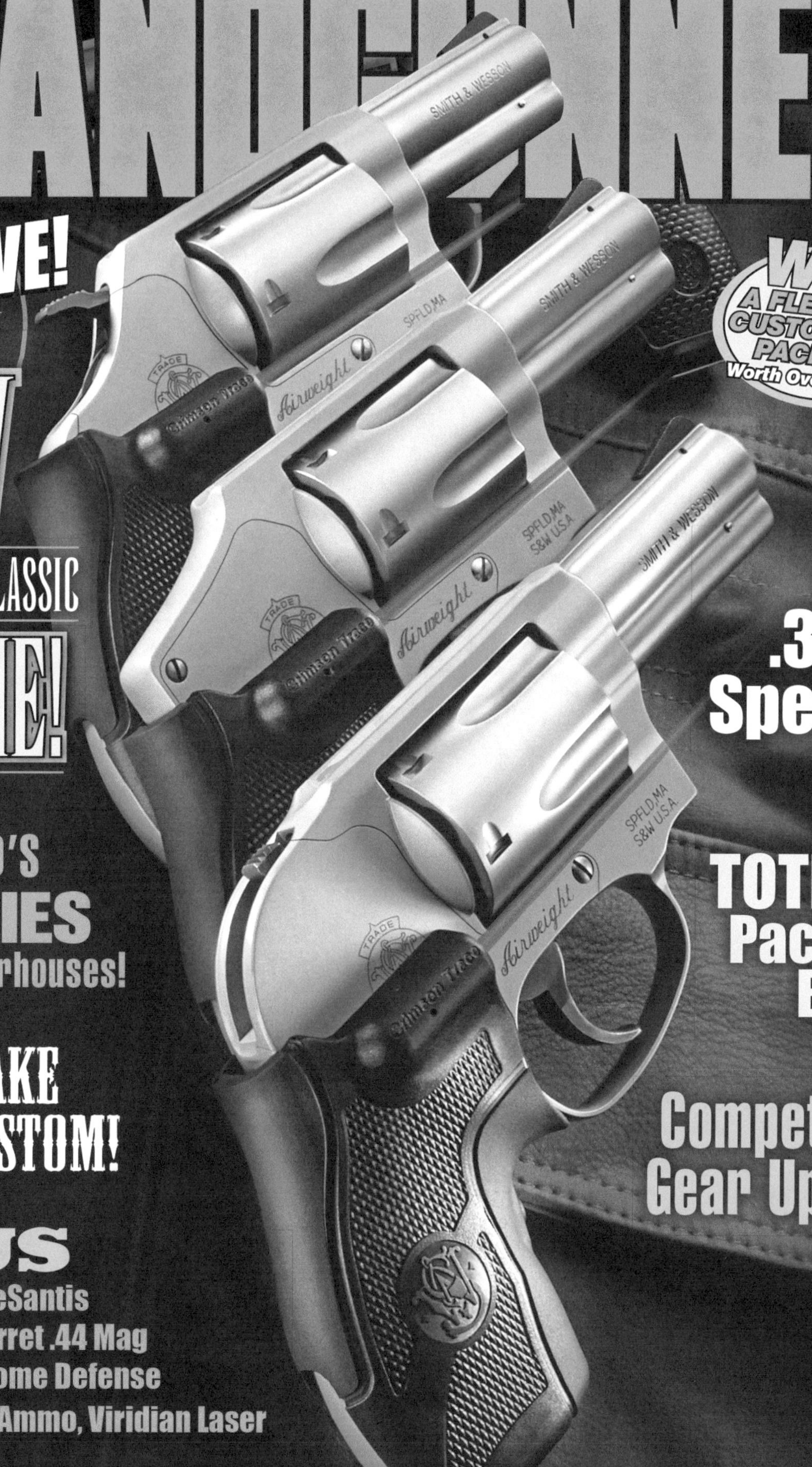

EXCLUSIVE!

S&W
UPDATES THE CLASSIC
J-FRAME!

**SPRINGFIELD'S
XD SERIES
Polymer Powerhouses!**

**TAFFIN: MAKE
MINE A CUSTOM!**

**WIN
A FLETCHER
CUSTOM 1911
PACKAGE
Worth Over $3,000!**

**The
.38 IS
Special**

**TOTE IT!
Packs &
Bags**

**Competition
Gear Update**

FOCUS
**Carry Options: DeSantis
Handloading: Garret .44 Mag
Reality Check: Home Defense
Gunny Sack: ICC Ammo, Viridian Laser**

S&W'S MOST POPULAR HANDGUN GETS A FACELIFT

The mighty X-frame revolvers and the gorgeous handguns of their Performance Center notwithstanding, the single most popular handgun Smith & Wesson makes today is the J-frame revolver. Now in its 60th year, it's probably our most ubiquitous "everyday" handgun. While the classic service revolver has largely been relegated to the police museum, the J-frame outnumbers even baby Glocks in the backup holsters of America's police. Many concealed carry instructors find it the most common gun for newbie students to bring to class. When *American Handgunner* polled its staff writers on their carry guns a couple of years ago, the one most constant factor was one or another permutation of the J-frame in almost everyone's "carry rotation."

They're handy, they're simple, and they're dead-nuts reliable. Their slim barrels and rounded butts make concealment easier in pocket holsters, ankle holsters, belly bands and even inside the waistband holsters. You can get

them as light as 10.5 ounces (the Model 317 Titanium 8-shot .22 LR) and 12 ounces (the Model 340 PD Scandium .357 Magnum 5-shot); and with barrel lengths from 1⅞" (nominally 2", and still the most popular), to 5" (the Model 60 .357 variant introduced in 2005). Calibers over the years have included .22 LR, .22 Magnum, .32 Long, .32 H&R Magnum, .327, .38 S&W, .38 Special, .357 Mag, 9mm and even the short-lived .356 TSW. Of them all, though — from the first Chief Special of 60 years ago, to the single best-seller today, the Model 642 — their most enduring and most popular format has been that of a 5-shot, snub-nosed .38 Special.

A Brief History

The year was 1949. Carl Hellstrom had taken over as CEO of S&W, and didn't like the fact that arch-rival Colt had possessed a monopoly on small frame, short barrel .38 Special revolvers since introducing the Detective Special circa 1927. He ordered his engineers to beef up the small I-frame revolver, hitherto the core of S&W's .22 Kit Gun and small .32 and .38 S&W pocket revolvers, so it could be manufactured in .38 Special. This required length-

ening the frame and the cylinder. The new revolver was introduced at the 1950 national conference of the International Association of Chiefs of Police in Colorado Springs, and was dubbed the Chief Special. (Or "Chiefs Special" according to S&W historian Roy Jinks, or "Chief's Special" according to the authoritative *Standard Catalog of Smith & Wesson* by Jim Supica and Richard Nahas). The little revolver was an instant hit, and the die was cast. The new paradigm of the hideout revolver would, forever after, be a 5-shot .38 Special on a stretched .32-size frame.

There are three primary configurations of J-frame, and that was set in stone within the first five years of the line's existence. In 1952, at the request of the already famous Col. Rex Applegate, Hellstrom blended the Chiefs Special platform with the enclosed hammer and grip safety features of the top-break New Departure Safety Hammerless, an 1880s design. Because 1952 marked S&W's hundredth year in business, they called the new "hammerless" the Centennial. Then, 1955 would see a third option. Reacting to Colt's introduction of an optional bolt-on hammer shroud for their small frame revolvers

MASSAD AYOOB
Photos: Chuck Pittman, Inc.

The 2.5" barrel affords much longer ejection stroke, seen here with a Pro-Ported Chief.

Photo: Gail Pepin

Katherine Rutledge shows the effectiveness of the new Pro Series Model 60. Group was fired all double action from ten yards.

Photo: Gail Pepin

"THE J-FRAME WOULD BE A TEST BED FOR S&W INNOVATION."

circa 1950, S&W designers created a Chief with a built-in hammer shroud and dubbed it the Bodyguard. The tip of its specially-shaped hammer created a "cocking button" that allowed easy-trigger single action firing, but retained the snag-free nature of the Centennial.

The J-frame would be a test bed for S&W innovation. In 1952, the first aluminum-framed Airweight to leave the production line was a Chief's Special, a variant that would later become known as the Model 37 when S&W went to numerical designations in 1957. So was the first all stainless steel revolver by S&W (or anyone else), the Model 60, introduced in 1965. The first Titanium Smith & Wesson was yet another J-frame, the .22 caliber Model 317 of 1997. When Scandium first made its way into Smith & Wessons at the turn of the 21st Century, those were J-frames, too.

Picking Your Format

Shooting paradigms change, and tastes of shooters change with them. The Chief and the Bodyguard have been in continuous production in one form or another since their introduction. The Chief, of course, is a traditional look double/single action revolver with exposed, spurred hammer, though it has been produced for NYPD and others with the hammer "bobbed." The Bodyguard looked different enough that some purists thought it ugly, and from the beginning Smith fans nicknamed it "the humpback," a term you'll see at the excellent S&W Forum *(www.smith-wessonforum.com)* to this day.

The Centennial was a different kettle of fish, and quickly found itself on the hind teat of J-frame sales. In the mid-20th Century, many shooters preferred to cock their wheel-guns to single action, and considered double action shooting

to be something they would do only in a rare, fast-breaking emergency. The grip-safety put them off, too. The Bodyguard was just as snag-proof coming out of a pocket or shoulder holster, so what the heck was the point of the Centennial? Circa 1974, S&W put the Centennial out of its sales misery and out of the catalog.

Somewhere in the background, one could almost hear the choir singing, "You don't know what you got, 'til it's gone." By the mid-70s, people were growing savvy to the fact that if you were carrying the gun for those "rare, fast-breaking emergencies," that's what you should be practicing for by shooting it that way all the time, so who needed *single* action? Suddenly, demand for Centennials on the used gun market skyrocketed, and so did their prices.

Along about then, folks were figuring out that because the "horn" on the backstrap rose higher on the frame of a Centennial than other J-frames, the shooter could get the firing hand higher on the gun, lowering the bore axis and significantly reducing muzzle rise. A clamor arose for the reintroduction of the Centennial. Circa 1988, I was at a conclave of writers hosted at the S&W factory by then-CEO Steve Melvin. He told us he wanted to reintroduce the Centennial, this time without the superfluous grip safety. We endorsed it heartily, to a man, and the "hammerless" was soon back in the line as the Model 640 — a stainless .38 Special in all steel in its first iteration, with traditional 1⅞" barrel, *sans* grip safety, and marked +P+ on the frame. It sold like the proverbial hotcakes. Fifteen years after its discontinuance, the Centennial's time had finally come in the marketplace.

Today, S&W's head of revolver production, Jim Unger, says the Centen-

nial is the strongest seller in the entire line. The Chief Special with traditional spurred hammer, is second. He tells me the Bodyguard is experiencing something of a resurgence in popularity and biting close at the heels of the Chief for second place honors. The single best-selling handgun in the whole S&W catalog is the Model 642. That's the classic-look Centennial in .38 Special, with stainless barrel and cylinder and "stain-less-look" aluminum Airweight frame. Weight is just under a pound, unloaded. In sales by caliber, according to Jim, the old standby .38 Special remains number one, with .357 Mag second and the .22 rimfires third. In 2009, the company responded to dealer demand and began offering the J-frame chambered as a six-shot .327, which of course will also fire .32 H&R Mag and .32 S&W Long.

The choice between Chief, Bodyguard and Centennial is among the first of many branched paths you take when you enter the vast domain of S&W J-frame options. Each has pros and cons. It goes kinda like this:

Details

Good news: Easy to cock if that's how you like to shoot, particularly with something like the longer barrel 317 .22 carried as a trail gun. Potential snag of hammer can be overcome by drawing with thumb on hammer, turning your thumb into a "human hammer shroud." Keeping finger off trigger and thumbing hammer back just enough to drop the bolt and free-up the cylinder allows a cylinder rotation check to make sure there are no high primers that are going to jam the gun in firing. If something *does* make the cylinder bind, the Chief gives you the most leverage of the three designs to force the hammer back and get a shot off.

Bad news: Too-small, too-smooth,

old-style stocks (or too weak a grasp) allow the gun to roll up in the shooter's hand. In rapid fire, that can quickly allow the spurred hammer to contact the web of the hand, which will block its motion and prevent the gun from firing. The hammer spur, even the reduced profile on the currently produced models, is still "shaped like a fish hook" as NYPD Inspector and firearms authority Paul B. Weston used to say, and can snag on something and stall your draw in an emergency. If fired through a coat pocket, it is possible for a fold of pocket lining to get caught between the face of the hammer

and the frame, jamming the gun and preventing firing.

Bodyguard

Good news: That ugly hump of the hammer shroud acts as a "catch point" against the web of the hand to make it much less likely that the gun will roll upward in your grasp upon recoil sufficiently to impair your ability to fire the gun. It is totally snag free. You can thumb the hammer back for an easy single action pull for a "precision shot" if need be. You can safely perform cylinder rotation checks, as with a Chief.

Bad news: Dust collects inside

the hammer shroud, and you'll need to take a pipe cleaner or Q-tip to it regularly, particularly if you carry in the pocket. With just the tiny stub of the cocking button to work with, *un*-cocking the hammer can become a nightmare, and that problem increases exponentially when you have to do so with hands that are covered with sweat, shaking from adrenaline, and numb from fight-or-flight-induced vasoconstriction, or from winter cold.

Centennial

Good news: It has the best control in a J-frame because you can get your

J!

SMITH & WESSON

S&W'S J-FRAME

ting mean with serious ammunition. By the time it hits .357 Magnum with full power loads in the 12-ounce variation, it turns into something close to a torture device. It wants to move in your hand, and your hand just wants it to move *away.* A few tips from an adult lifetime of teaching folks to shoot these things might be in order about now.

Hold the gun *hard.* Whomever it was that said "hold your gun with 40-percent strength in your dominant hand, and 60-percent strength in your support hand, and above all, just relax" had never fired a light J-frame with +P or, God help us, full-power .357 Magnum. The harder you hold it, the less it will move upon recoil. The harder you hold it, the less it can come back and whack the web of your hand with the upper part of its backstrap, or your middle finger with the back of its trigger guard. And the harder you hold it, the less the ten-*ounce* gun can move off point of aim as you exert a ten-*pound* trigger pull upon it, suddenly and swiftly.

Unless you have extra-long stocks, which kinda get in the way of the whole hideout gun concept in the first place, curl your little finger tightly under the butt. This makes the other fingers sympathetically stronger, and also creates a block against the gun rolling backward and muzzle upward/butt downward in your grasp upon recoil.

S&W has equipped these guns with at least four different cylinder latch configurations over the years. The one least likely to slice your thumb firing right-handed, and will still allow you to open the cylinder quickly, is the current production version, which is sort of a checkered semi-oval shape.

From the beginning, these guns were cursed with tiny .10" wide front sights, with correspondingly tight rear sight notches, which were almost useless under less than perfect conditions. They've gotten better. The replacement fixed sights from Bill Laughridge at Cylinder & Slide Shop are so good that S&W put them on their larger framed Night Guard snubbies. Dave Lauck at D&L Sports came out with a great retrofit that I have on my 11-ounce Model 342 Titanium Centennial, and just love. Hamilton Bowen of Bowen Classic Arms also does a sterling job with his sights. At Smith, the humongous Tritium XS 24/7 sight with correspondingly large rear U-notch gives a superb combination of speed and accuracy. It's found only on the Model 340 M&P .357 at this time, and is the primary reason I bought that gun and carry it most of the time as a backup.

Consider Crimson Trace LaserGrips. I have them on multiple J-frames. Particularly on the older models with less-

hand so high and the bore axis so low. Even with the super-light .357 Mags, which come back into the hand brutally, you can keep all shots on target fast because the muzzle doesn't rise as much. *You* will stop hurting when you stop shooting. This won't be true for the bad guy on the other side of your gunfire. You have absolute freedom from snag in any kind of draw.

Bad news: There is no safe way to do a cylinder rotation check on the fully loaded Centennial, because the trigger will have to be pulled slightly back for the bolt to release. We've tried all sorts of "stick another finger behind the trigger" and all that, and it's just too awkward. With the Centennial, you have to have your double action trigger pull skills down pat, and you have to *know* the chambers are clean and won't keep a fresh cartridge from seating fully, and you have to inspect and *know* your carry rounds have no high primers.

Shooting The J-Frame

By the time your J-frame reaches .38 Special caliber, the recoil starts get-

perfect sights, they make *huge* sense. They're now available as S&W factory options on many J-frame models.

Latest Developments

One shortcoming of the J-frame snub has always been incomplete ejection. Between the 1⅞" barrel and the traditional ejector rod lug, the ejector rod became necessarily stubby and just didn't have enough stroke. That has been changed of late, and you can thank *American Handgunner* editor Roy Huntington, a long-time J-frame fan.

Roy explains, "After a comprehensive shoot at Gunsite with S&W's Paul Pluff and about 30 J-frames of all flavors, I came away with the firm conviction a slightly longer barrel and ejector rod would be more efficient. I chatted at length with Jim Unger at S&W, and he was very open to improvement ideas. Some months later during a meeting at a trade show, Jim said, 'Wait until you see what we have out later. I'm sure you'll like what you see!' It turns out the newest offering in the J-frame line-up does indeed have slightly longer barrels and ejector rods. I'm impressed Jim listened to what we learned at the shoot at Gunsite. The guns should offer more reliable ejection and a bit more sight radius to make hitting easier. On a side note, I was not surprised to see many of us regularly hitting 100 yard steel silhouettes, even with the 2" guns. These guns are indeed accurate in the right hands, solidifying my trust in the J-frame."

Having shot several of the new 2.5" J-frames, I can tell you Roy's predictions have come true. The 5/8" difference in sight radius becomes significant in a gun as short overall as the J-frame snub, and probably most important, ejection of spent casings is much more positive. Plucking partially ejected brass out of the chambers does not make for a "speed reload," it makes for a "slow reload." This longer rod definitely helps. Barrel profile is dramatically changed, of course, but Jim Unger tells me that DeSantis and Galco are already on line with holsters to fit the new-length "J," with more to come from other makers. The 2½" guns are available in Airweight Chief Model 637, Airweight Bodyguard 638 and Airweight Centennial 642 configurations. All weigh 16 ounces with the slight added barrel heft, and all carry a suggested retail of $640 with standard "rubber" grips, and $924 with Crimson Trace LaserGrips.

Also available from the list are J-frames with an integral recoil reduction port ahead of the muzzle. These are in the Pro Series, S&W's line of upscaled handguns designed and engineered in

S&W J-FRAME
Continued from page 57

the Performance Center but built in main-line mass production to reduce cost to the buying public. Upward jets of expanding gases at the instant of the shot do indeed help keep the muzzle down, but they also pose a danger of burning powder debris striking the shooter's eyes and face if fired from a close-to-the-body retention position. Tailor your choice to your particular defensive manual of arms. My own favorite in the crop is the Pro Series Model 60 .357 with flat-sided 3" barrel.

And More To Come

By the time you read this, S&W will have introduced their 2010 new products list, in which the J-frame line is richly represented. We will see the return of the all-steel .22 Kit Gun, the stainless Model 63, now in a 3" barrel/8-shot cylinder format.

And, speaking of .22 Kit Guns, remember the Model 43 Airweight Kit Gun in .22 LR, and the Model 51 Kit Gun in .22 Magnum? Well, 2010 will see the Models 43C and 351C. The "C" stands for Centennial, and we're talking about eleven-ounce "hammerless" .22s to duplicate the feel of today's most popular pocket revolver. The 43C will hold eight .22 Long Rifles, and the 351C, seven .22 Magnum rounds. Sights will resemble the excellent high-visibility models seen on the M&P 340 in .357.

The J-frame Smith & Wesson's 60 year history encompasses both evolution and revolution — and that history is far from over.

More Here:
americanhandgunner.com

a Special that

mike "duke" venturino
photos: yvonne venturino

These are Duke's current .38 Special revolvers, out of the dozens he's owned in the past 40 years. Left to right: S&W Model 442, S&W Military & Police (aka Model 10), and S&W Outdoorsman (aka Model 23).

the Redoubtable .38 S&W Special

a few issues back I wrote a piece in these pages titled "The .44 Special Ain't So Special" (*July/Aug 2009*). Some might be surprised I received as many "atta-boys" for that piece as I did death threats! Now I want to tell you I think the .38 Special is indeed *special*. It does exhibit the inherent accuracy often mistakenly attributed to the .44 Special. It can be loaded hot in suitable handguns, and it can be loaded very light for paper target shooting. It's equally adaptable to tiny snub nosed 5-shooters or large frame 6-shooters. It's even been chambered in at least one auto pistol, the S&W Model 52. Factory ammo comes in so many styles, types and weights it's impossible to keep track of them all. It's also a handloader's delight: easy to load and with a vast amount of suitable components available.

First off, let's look at some dimensions. Of course, most of you know the .38 Special isn't a .38 caliber. It's actually a .35 caliber, with the bullet diameter being .357". It was preceded by the .38 Long Colt which had a case length of 1.03". Then the .38 Special came out with a 1.16" case. It was succeeded by the .357 Magnum with a 1.29" case. All .38 Special revolvers can safely fire .38 Long Colt cartridges. All .357 Magnum revolvers can safely fire both .38 Long Colt and .38 Special cartridges. Just so you know.

Just about anybody can be taught to shoot a .38 Special with enough proficiency to defend themselves. In fact when someone asks me what would be a good home defense handgun, yet they don't show signs of becoming avid shooters, I tell them to get a mid-size frame, 4"-barreled, .38 Special revolver. There are plenty of them still being made today, and there have been millions made in the 110 years of .38 Special history.

110 Years?

Does that 110 surprise you? The following information comes from *U.S. Cartridges And Their Handguns 1795-1975 by Charles R. Suydam*. The Union Metallic Cartridge Company made the first .38 Specials early in 1899 to go with S&W's brand new First Model Hand Ejector revolver. Original loads held 18 grs. of black powder with 158 gr. roundnose bullets. In June of 1899 the powder charge was increased to 21.5

RCBS S&W M-23 + 11-2400 1½"

grains with the same bullets. Smokeless powder loads came about in September 1899. Suydam says initial smokeless powder loads were "probably" with 3.6 grains of Bullseye. And here's another little tidbit from Suydam's book. The official name is .38 Smith & Wesson Special, not just .38 Special.

Anyway, if the .38 Special has had an albatross hung around its neck in its history it was that 158 grain roundnose bullet. It was a notoriously poor man-stopper. I've actually made solid hits on tiny ground squirrels at no more than 10 feet with that bullet and had them run off to their holes. Now swallow this: I've done the same thing with 255

Above: With only a little in the way of load development, Duke's S&W Outdoorsman (aka Model 23) .38-44 began shooting groups like this.

S&W came out with this scandium Model 360 a few years back chambered as a .357 Magnum. What they really had without knowing it was a fine .38 Special — and a miserable .357 Magnum.

The evolution of .38s: (left to right) .38 Short Colt, .38 Long Colt, .38 S&W Special and .357 S&W Magnum.

Duke figures just about any lead alloy .357/.358" bullet with a flat nose is fine for .38 Special reloading. From left to right: Oregon Trail 158-gr. SWC, Lyman 158-gr. gas check SWC (mould #358156), RCBS 158-gr. RN/FP (mould #38-158CM) and Lyman 158-gr. RN/FP (mould #358665).

grain roundnose .45 Colt bullets and likewise the ground squirrels ran off to their holes. That the ammunition factories stubbornly clung to roundnose revolver bullets for virtually all calibers decade after decade has to be one of the great mysteries of the gun world. By the time somebody shook them up enough to start loading semiwadcutter bullets and even hollowpoints, the .38 Special's reputation was tarnished almost beyond salvation.

Sometimes It Worked

Here's one time it did not fail, however. In the book *The Lions Of Iwo Jima* by Major General Fred Haynes (USMC-retired) and James A. Warren, Hayes relates a happening on the morning of March 3, 1945 on Iwo's hill 362A. He and another officer were observing the terrain ahead when a Japanese soldier charged from a cave with a bayoneted rifle. The other officer's runner, Wenton Yates drew his non-issue .38 revolver from a shoulder holster and dropped the

attacker with one shot.

Although the .38 Special's greatest reputation was as America's predominant police cartridge for at least a half century, it did serve America's military in an official capacity during World War II. Model 1911 .45 autos were in short supply so naval and marine aviators were often issued Smith & Wesson "Victory" model revolvers. Those were Parkerized K-frames with either 4" or 5" barrels. They were also issued .38 Special tracer rounds so they could signal search and rescue planes if they were in life rafts at sea. Also the US Government bought a number of Colt Commando .38 Special

This photo shows the large and small of .38 Special cylinders. At left is the 5-shot J-frame S&W Model 442. At right is the 6-shot cylinder of the large N-frame S&W Outdoorsman (aka Model 23).

Duke figures his S&W Model 442 .38 Special makes a fine hip pocket revolver.

Duke has lived happily for over 40 years reloading his .38 Specials with these three smokeless propellants.

This is the .38-44 cartridge introduced circa 1930 as a forerunner of the .357 Magnum. It looked just like any other .38 Special factory load but was too high pressure for any revolver but those built on a large frame.

Some of the many different types of .38 Special factory loads past and present. From left: 158-gr. RN, 148-gr. WC, 200-gr, RN "Super Police" 130-gr. RN tracer (military load) 158-gr. SWC-HP +P (Blazer with aluminum case), 125-gr. JHP +P and 158-gr. RN/FP (cowboy load).

revolvers to arm homeland defense industry guards.

Beginner Loading

My handloading career — and I'd bet the handloading careers of many of you — started with the .38 Special. Mine began in December of 1966 and I cast my own bullets from the very first day. My .38 Special handloading was for an S&W K-38 target revolver, and I loaded and fired thousand upon thousand of cartridges for that handgun. As would be natural for any 17/18 year old I yearned

During World War II the US government bought thousands of Colt Commando .38 Special revolvers. Mostly they were issued to defense industry guards.

Right: Despite the fact S&W intended their Heavy Duty (aka Model 20) as a vehicle for the hot .38-44 loads, it was still stamped simply ".38 S&W Special."

instead for a .357 Magnum. When I got one in 1968 it only took a few shots with those ear splitting .357s to convince me shooting .38 Specials was more my game. That .357 was a 4⅝" Ruger Blackhawk. I've owned dozens more .357 Magnum revolvers is the 40 years since that first and likewise have fired far more specials in them than magnums.

Let's back up to 1967 though. As a senior in high school the only friend I

had with the slightest interest in firearms was named Mike Bucci. (Pronounced Butch). His father coincidentally was our town's chief of police. So that his son could go shooting with me, he gave him one of his spare revolvers. When first showing me his .38 Special Butch felt a bit slighted because it had fixed sights compared to my K38's target sights. When he handed me that massive revolver for the first time my jaw dropped. It was an S&W Heavy Duty .38-44 with 5" barrel. I had seen photos of them but that was the first one I'd ever encountered. Butch perked up when I told him his .38 would handle far hotter loads than my .38 because it was built on S&W's large N-frame and mine was on the medium-sized K-frame. In short order I handloaded him some .38-44 velocity rounds. At the range I set

These three large-frame revolvers were perfectly adequate for the hot .38-44 loads. From left: S&W Outdoorsman (aka Model 23), Colt SAA and S&W Heavy Duty (aka Model 20).

up a brick at about 20 yards and popped it with my standard .38 Special loads. It just fell over. Then I told Butch to whack it with one of his .38-44s. It shattered to pieces and Butch loved that old handgun from then on. Sadly, my friend Butch died of cancer at age 21.

More Fun

The .38-44 was the precursor of the .357 Magnum. Smith & Wesson brought it out in 1930 to give cops something more powerful with which to fight gangsters of that violent time. It was probably not the best ammunition idea to come down the pike. Factory loads had those same old roundnose 158 grain bullets but they moved at 1,150 fps compared to 850 fps for normal .38 Specials. No way those .38-44s should ever find their way into an ancient K-frame Hand Ejector, and heaven forbid that someone stick them in a tiny J-frame 5-shooter.

Speaking of those J-frame revolvers, I've owned a bunch of them, such as the Model 36 Chief's Special and similar variations. They are great for sticking in a hip pocket. A few years back I acquired an aluminum frame, "hammerless" Model 442 that goes almost everywhere here in Montana.

A couple years ago some bright light at Smith & Wesson conceived the idea of making a small frame, 5-shot .357 Magnum, and to make it even more punishing they decided it had to be a scandium frame to boot. That made it weigh a mere 12 ounces. They named it the Model 360. I love mine. But if you actually consider it a .357 Magnum you're nuts! It only took one .357 Magnum full bore factory load from it

to convince me its really a .38 Special.

On the other end of the spectrum from those hot .38-44 loads are light .38 wadcutters. As factory ammunition they have 148 gr. bullets popping out at about 700 fps. Given a good handgun, they can be exquisitely accurate. I once did some extensive machine rest testing with Remington 148 gr. .38 Special wadcutter loads from my old 1940s vintage S&W Military & Police revolver with 5" barrel. After a couple dozen 5-shot groups were fired at 25 yards, the average was not much over 1".

A Weighty Choice

In between heavy .38-44s and light wadcutter loads there have been scores of various .38 Special factory loads. They have lead alloy or jacketed bullets and can be of normal pressures or +P types. There are even "cowboy" .38 Specials for that action shooting sport. Bullet weights have ranged from 95 to 200 grains, and that can present a problem for many .38 Special revolvers. Most of them, past and present have fixed sights; mostly that's a groove down the frame's topstrap and some sort of blade type front sight. And most of them are factory sighted for bullets weighing 150-160 grains. Fire 95 gr. bullets in them and point of impact is way low from point of aim. Fire 200 gr. bullets in them and they hit way high. How to cope with that? Simply stick with the bullet weights that hit on for your sights, which will likely be 150 to 160 gr. ones.

Early on in my love affair with the .38 Special I hit upon three handloads suiting all my purposes. The main one used for all recreational shooting is 3.0 grains of Bullseye under any lead alloy

150 to 160 gr. bullet. My opinion is that any with a flat nose are best. Next is the load I keep in a .38 Special if it's kept around for defensive purposes. That's 4.5 grains of Unique and ditto for the bullets. And lastly is the load *I only use* in large frame revolvers such as my S&W Model 23 Outdoorsman, which was built for the .38-44 loading described above, or in Colt SAA .38 Specials. That's 11.0 grains of 2400 and again ditto for the bullets. In the same order and from 4" to 5" barrels and depending on exact bullet weight, those loads will give about 750 fps, 900 fps and 1,150 fps.

Turn your nose up at the old .38 Special if you want — I don't. There are hotter, newer, flashier and much bigger handgun cartridges about. But, in terms of simple practicality none are more *special*.

This is just a sampling of the many different types of current .38 Special factory loads that Duke found on his shelves.

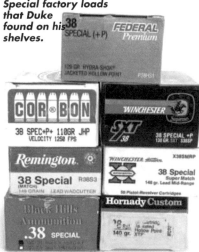

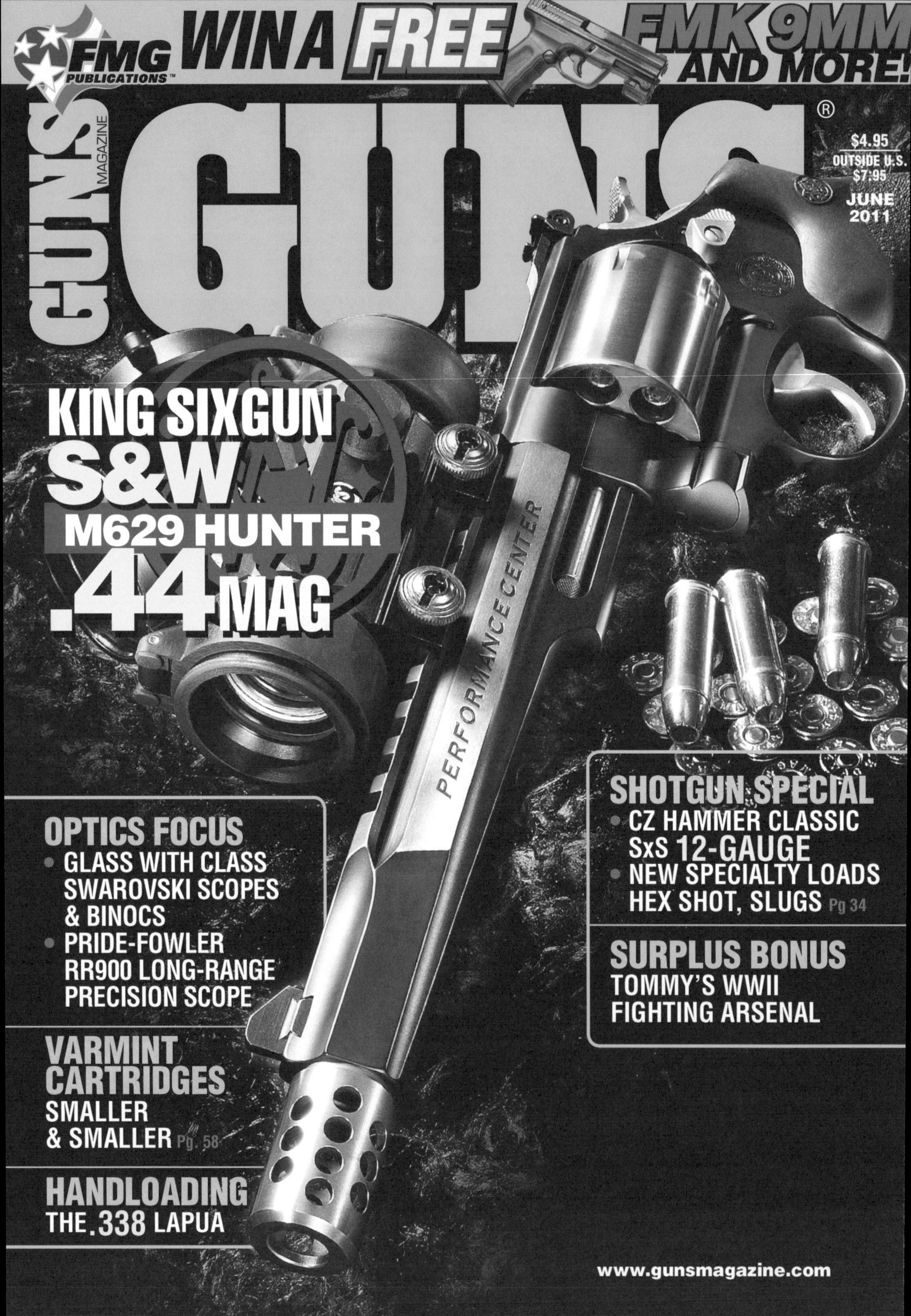
FMG PUBLICATIONS™
WIN A FREE FMK 9MM AND MORE!
GUNS MAGAZINE
GUNS®
$4.95
OUTSIDE U.S. $7.95
JUNE 2011
KING SIXGUN
S&W
M629 HUNTER
.44 MAG
PERFORMANCE CENTER
OPTICS FOCUS
• GLASS WITH CLASS SWAROVSKI SCOPES & BINOCS
• PRIDE-FOWLER RR900 LONG-RANGE PRECISION SCOPE
VARMINT CARTRIDGES
SMALLER & SMALLER Pg. 58
HANDLOADING
THE .338 LAPUA
SHOTGUN SPECIAL
• CZ HAMMER CLASSIC SxS 12-GAUGE
• NEW SPECIALTY LOADS HEX SHOT, SLUGS Pg 34
SURPLUS BONUS
TOMMY'S WWII FIGHTING ARSENAL
www.gunsmagazine.com

Load more content anytime.

THE KING OF S

John Taffin

Photos: Joseph R. Novelozo

If the truth be told, I would not be afraid to bet there are more .44 Magnums sold than all the rest of the more powerful sixguns combined. The .44 Magnum has been used to cleanly take all big game including Alaskan brown bear, polar bear, African elephant, Cape buffalo and African lion. And since we are being truthful I would also be willing to bet the .44 Magnum is the most powerful sixgun the vast majority of shooters can actually handle. It may not be regarded as awesome as it was in 1956; however, it is just as powerful now as it was then, actually more so with all the different ammunition choices now available. More than once I have called the .44 Magnum the King of Sixguns; I see no reason to change that in the twilight years of my life.

I have to admit I have not been enamored with all the creations emanating from the Performance Center, but the current model is not only one of the best looking Smith & Wesson big-bore sixguns I've ever seen, it also has a function matched up perfectly with its form. It handles the .44 Magnum with ease while visiting a minimum of felt recoil upon the

S&W PI

XGUNS

shooter without being overly heavy and cumbersome. They did it right!

The basic platform for the .44 Magnum Hunter is the Model 629, stainless steel version. Actually, it does not look like a normal stainless steel sixgun as the frame is matte black, as is the barrel. The 2-tone effect comes from the polished stainless steel cylinder, and the flats on both sides of the barrel. The 7-1/2" barrel itself is not of the heavy underlugged variety, but closer to the original configuration of 1955. The flat on the left side is polished, and inscribed, "PERFORMANCE CENTER" while the right side says, ".44 MAGNUM HUNTER" with with quite bold and exceptionally attractive lettering. It appears to have been cut with a laser. The hammer and trigger are both of the target style and are plated carbon steel.

The rear sight is the standard Smith & Wesson adjustable, matched up with a red ramp front sight in a dovetail. As supplied by the Performance Center, the .44 Magnum Hunter comes with a Leapers red-or-green-dot 1X scope mounted on the barrel. This is an entry-level scope, which provides out-of-the-box performance for the hunter while at the same time not adding much to the cost. With the Leapers there are five choices of red-dot intensity and five also of green. The reasoning for this low-priced scope is many will opt to provide their own choice of optics, whether red dot or traditional pistol scope. My choice for anything, other than up close hunting in deep cover, would be a traditional 2X or 4X LER scope. The head of the Performance Center, Tony Miele, was thinking boar hunting and this red/green-dot scope appears to be a perfect choice for such applications.

When compared to all the double-action .44 Magnum revolvers that have come after the original Smith & Wesson .44 Magnum, the latter is quite a bit lighter resulting in heavier felt recoil. To combat this Smith & Wesson has done two things with the Magnum Hunter. First we have a muzzlebrake added to the end of the barrel, it appears not to be removable, and is drilled with holes

RFORMANCE CENTER'S
.44 MAGNUM HUNTER

THE KING OF SIXGUNS

SCP-RD40RGW

Leapers

PERFORMANCE CENTER

The M629 Hunter comes with traditional fully-adjustable iron rear sights in addition to the Leaper's red/green-dot sight.

Like all modern S&W revolvers, the firing pin is now mounted in the frame. The top of the hammer is wide and sharply checkered for easy cocking for single-action shooting.

The barrel (above) is fitted with a muzzlebrake and, combined with the revolver's 57-1/2 ounce weight makes for a pleasant shooting .44 Magnum. A backup iron front sight is dovetailed into the barrel. The swing-out cylinder (below) is unfluted and left unblackened in contrast with the frame and barrel.

Fine Pedigree

The .44 Magnum in its original form from Smith & Wesson is one of the finest, perhaps *the* finest sixgun to ever come from the Springfield factory. Starting with the 1950 Target .44 Special as the basic platform, the cylinder was lengthened to fill out the frame window, the barrel was changed to a bull-barrel configuration as found on the 1955 Target .45 introduced earlier in the year, special heat treating was applied, a target trigger and hammer along with target stocks were utilized, and the sights consisted of a white-outlined, rear-adjustable sight matched up with a red ramp front sight. All in all, it was a most magnificent sixgun!

I have recounted in the past my first experience with the S&W .44 Magnum. The local gun range rented a 4" version with six rounds of ammunition to anyone brave enough to try. My teenage friends and I tried, almost cried, and then we lied and said it wasn't bad. It would take several years before I could even come close to handling the .44 Magnum. In the ensuing years I did a lot of growing up.

The .44 Magnum cartridge in its original form used a 240-grain bullet, at the same muzzle velocity as the 158-grain .357 Magnum from 20 years earlier. Elmer Keith said the recoil would not bother a "seasoned sixgun man" and was actually less than a .38 Special J-Frame. He also called it the greatest revolver and ammunition development in his lifetime. Major Hatcher of the NRA said shooting the new Smith & Wesson was like getting hit in the hand with a baseball bat. Colonel Askins, always one to try to stir up controversy, said he thought the good Major probably had lace on his panties. A few years later Askins would say the .44 Magnum should have been stillborn.

With the introduction of the .44 Magnum and the tremendous power it gave to sixgun hunters, there were still detractors who said: "Yes, but it's not a .45!" It is simply impossible to please some people. Since the introduction of the .44 Magnum there has been a long list of more powerful cartridges chambered in factory sixguns. In fact, while Smith & Wesson was developing the .44 Magnum, Dick Casull was working on what would become the .454 Casull. Just over 25 years after the introduction of the .44 Magnum, Freedom Arms started manufacturing the .454 which allows the use of a 300-grain bullet 200 fps faster than the original .44 Magnum. Over the past 1/4 century the .44 Magnum has also been overshadowed, at least in some minds, by the .445 SuperMag, .475 and .500 Linebaughs, .480 Ruger, .500 Wyoming Express and even two more S&W Magnums, the .500 and .460.

Smith & Wesson's original .44 Magnum was available in blue and nickel finishes with barrel lengths of 4", 6-1/2" and 8-3/8" cataloged along with a special run of 500 5" sixguns in 1958. All were magnificent sixguns. *But* since we are being truthful I will admit today's sixguns are better built with tighter tolerances, better steel and they mostly shoot better. They just aren't "classic." I think that is an attitude that comes with being a "seasoned citizen."

During the heyday of long-range silhouetting in the 1980s, there was also a 10-1/2" model with special sights. The original .44 became known as the Model 29 in 1957 and then was joined by a stainless steel version, the Model 629 in 1979. Although we learned to handle the recoil of the S&W .44 Magnum that had so intimidated us in the early days, the reality of heavy recoil did change. In the early 1990s, Smith & Wesson addressed this by the introduction of the Endurance Package, which lessened the stress of interior parts against each other and added weight with the heavy underlugged barrel. In the beginning decade of this still relatively new century, the Smith & Wesson Performance Center began offering special editions of their revolvers. The latest is the Model 629 .44 Magnum Hunter. **GUNS**

for the full 360 degrees. At the other end we have recoil-reducing rubber fingergrooved grips. Rubber grips are never attractive but their lack of form is highly overshadowed by the great function they perform. Add in the weight of the red/green-dot scope and we have a .44 Magnum that is quite comfortable to use.

Ten factory loads weighing from 180 to 300 grains were fired in the Performance Center .44 Magnum Hunter. It performed well with all loads and when sighted in with 240-grain bullets, as expected, shot slightly high with the 300-grain bullets, and slightly low with the 180-grain loads. Of the 10 loads tried, nine were jacketed while one was a gas-checked hollowpoint cast bullet, "The Deer Magnum" from Buffalo Bore. The Magnum Hunter shot the latter just as well as it shot jacketed bullets. The average group size for five shots at 25 yards using the red-dot scope was less than 1-1/8". Looking at both ends of the spectrum, Hornady's 180-grain XTP-JHP grouped into 5/8" for five shots while the 300-grain version did 7/8". That is excellent performance for

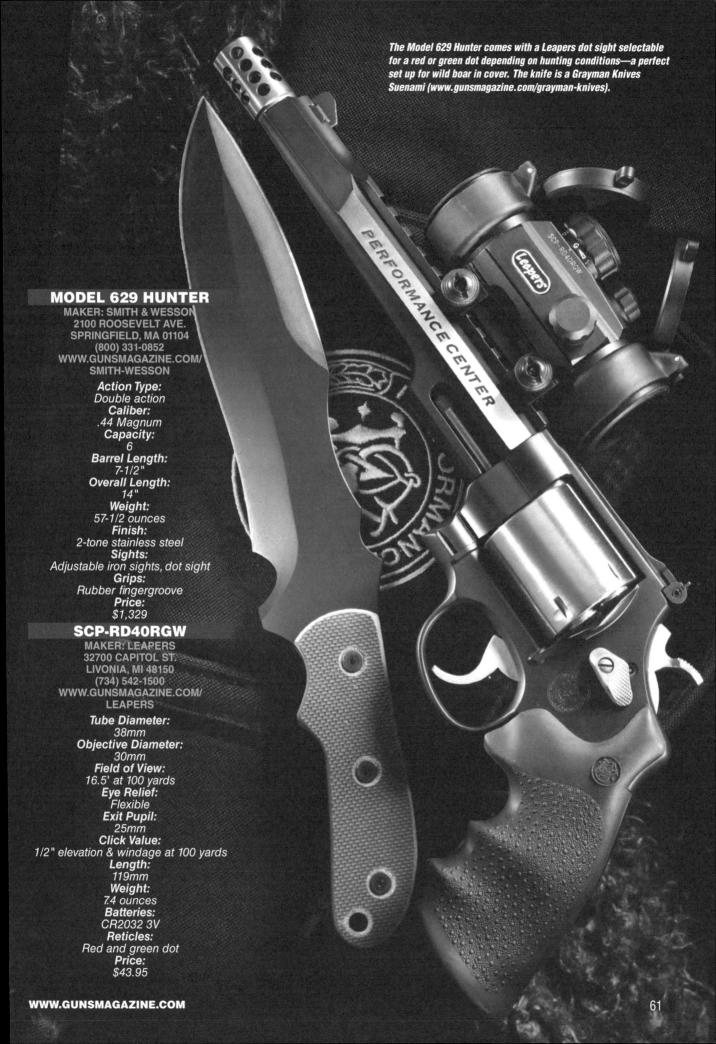

The Model 629 Hunter comes with a Leapers dot sight selectable for a red or green dot depending on hunting conditions—a perfect set up for wild boar in cover. The knife is a Grayman Knives Suenami (www.gunsmagazine.com/grayman-knives).

MODEL 629 HUNTER

MAKER: SMITH & WESSON
2100 ROOSEVELT AVE.
SPRINGFIELD, MA 01104
(800) 331-0852
WWW.GUNSMAGAZINE.COM/
SMITH-WESSON

Action Type:
Double action
Caliber:
.44 Magnum
Capacity:
6
Barrel Length:
7-1/2"
Overall Length:
14"
Weight:
57-1/2 ounces
Finish:
2-tone stainless steel
Sights:
Adjustable iron sights, dot sight
Grips:
Rubber fingergroove
Price:
$1,329

SCP-RD40RGW

MAKER: LEAPERS
32700 CAPITOL ST.
LIVONIA, MI 48150
(734) 542-1500
WWW.GUNSMAGAZINE.COM/
LEAPERS

Tube Diameter:
38mm
Objective Diameter:
30mm
Field of View:
16.5' at 100 yards
Eye Relief:
Flexible
Exit Pupil:
25mm
Click Value:
1/2" elevation & windage at 100 yards
Length:
119mm
Weight:
7.4 ounces
Batteries:
CR2032 3V
Reticles:
Red and green dot
Price:
$43.95

The Complete Collection Of

GUNCRANK DIARIES

by John Connor

In Paperback Or Kindle Version

Available at amazon

"Like fine wine, Connor's insights age well. More please." ~ Doc H

The complete series of excuses, alibis, pithy observations and general ephus now in a new book.

Order at Amazon.com search for Guncrank Diaries

Forever Changed

Sixgunning was forever changed with the introduction of the Smith & Wesson .357 Magnum in 1935. Up to this point the most powerful factory loaded cartridge available was the black powder, (yes, black powder) .45 Colt. The .357 Magnum used a 158-grain bullet at over 1,500 fps from an 8-3/4" barreled sixgun; this was unheard of power in a revolver.

However there were those who looked at the .357 Magnum and said, "Yes, but it's not a .44 Special." Those devotees of the .44 Special had already been loading heavy .44 Specials for nearly 10 years and, led by such experimenters as Elmer Keith, John LaChuk and members of the .44 Associates, they continued to push for a factory loaded heavy .44 Special. They finally got even more than they asked for and the result in the waning days of 1955 was Smith & Wesson's .44 Magnum with ammunition developed by Remington.

GUNS

.44 MAGNUM FACTORY AMMO PERFORMANCE

LOAD (BRAND, BULLET WEIGHT, TYPE)	VELOCITY (FPS)	GROUP SIZE (INCHES)
American Eagle 240 JHP	1,395	1
Black Hills 240 JHP	1,276	1-1/2
Buffalo Bore 240 Cast-HP Deer Magnum	1,586	1-1/4
CorBon 225 DPX	1,391	1
Federal 225 Barnes HP	1,398	1-3/8
Hornady 180 XTP-JHP	1,704	5/8
Hornady 200 XTP-JHP	1,312	7/8
Hornady 240 XTP-JHP	1,437	1-1/8
Hornady 300 XTP-JHP	1,126	7/8
Winchester 250 Platinum Tip HP	1,385	1-1/4

Notes: Groups the product of best 5 of 6 shots at 25 yards.
Chronograph screens set at 10' from muzzle.
Temperature: 35 degrees F.

the ammunition, sixgun and this very well seasoned shooter.

Over the past year, I've written up several Performance Center Smith & Wessons for both this magazine and our sister publication *American Handgunner*. For the latter it was the .500 S&W Bone Collector, and for *GUNS* it was my pleasure to do both

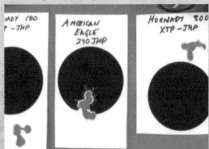

John found the Smith & Wesson Performance Center Model 629 .44 Magnum Hunter (above) a pleasant shooting and pleasantly accurate sixgun. These targets (below) were shot with 180-, 240- and 300-grain bullets. Notice the different points of impact.

a Packin' Pistol .44 and a Hunter Model .44. The latest version is my favorite of the four. I also think it's the most attractive of the four big bores. In talking with Tony Miele of the Smith & Wesson Performance Center, I found the idea behind this latest creation was his concept of the perfect sixgun for hunting wild boars. Of course, it is not confined to that as it also will work just fine for any other hunting application a .44 Magnum might be called upon to perform. Set up as it came from the Performance Center, it is just about perfect for deep woods use.

I have been a fan of Smith & Wesson sixguns seemingly forever. My first in 1957 was a WWI Model 1917 in .45 ACP. Virtually every one of us teenagers had such a Smith & Wesson, as well as a surplus 1911 and a Springfield 1903-A3. They were the cheapest guns available. In 1958, I purchased my first new Smith & Wesson, a 4" Highway Patrolman, and then for our first Christmas together in 1959, Diamond Dot gave me a 1950 Target .44 Special. My first .44 Magnum from Smith & Wesson was purchased in 1963. Over the following years there have been many Smith & Wessons in all the various chamberings, including a dozen or more .44 Magnums. The N-Frame Smith & Wessons are simply my favorite double-action revolvers. **GUNS**

OUT of the BOX

MIKE CUMPSTON

The S&W Bodyguard 380 (above, middle) compares favorably in size to the FN Model 1910, also in .380 ACP (above, top) and the .25 ACP Baby Browning. The disassembly lever of the 380 is hard to unlock, but after it is down, the pistol strips easily (below).

THE SMITH & WESSON BODYGUARDS

Your choice of pocketsize semi-auto or revolver comes complete with an integral Insight laser sight.

About a half-century ago, Smith & Wesson began numerical designation of the growing range of handgun models largely abandoning the familiar cognomens of the early 20th century. Handgun enthusiasts took this in stride and soon became walking encyclopedias of model numbers and the dash-numbers appended to designate variations.

As of late though, purpose-oriented model names have reappeared in the line. The demographic of gun users has undergone a profound shift. Practicality rather than enthusiasm is the motivating factor for many gun purchasers today. The name "Bodyguard" may speak to such buyers much more clearly than a mere number.

Responding to the demand for lightweight concealment arms of the smallest practical size, Smith & Wesson fields the J-frame 5-shot .38 Special and a pocketable .380 semi-auto with a maximum capacity of 7 rounds. Both are products of 21st century design making use of plastic, aluminum alloy and stainless steel. Both models were co-designed with the Insight Laser Company and are equipped with dedicated, fully adjustable laser sights. The provided Laser Adjustment Table is superior to most laser sight instructions.

The semi-auto Bodyguard is a double-action-only, concealed hammer, locked-breech design with features common to full-sized pistols. These include positive slide lock, a left-side safety as well as a passive firing pin block internal safety and the favored grip-mounted magazine release. Held up next to similar-sized Ruger LCP and Kel-Tec, it appears to be the same size, though measurement shows it is about a 1/4" longer and a 1/2" taller than the LCP. The difference is insignificant in terms of concealability though the taller grip proved advantageous in terms of shooter comfort. The sights, compared to other pistols of this size, are highly visible; both front and rear are dovetail mounted and driftable for windage adjustment.

I had a comprehensive supply of Buffalo Bore .380 ACP loads on hand, including standard- and high-velocity loads. Tim Sundles, the CEO of Buffalo Bore, anticipated the recent ammunition shortage and by laying in components well in advance, managed to keep .380 ammo in stock throughout the crisis. The Bodyguard was 100-percent functional with all of these rounds and perhaps, incidentally, they all struck usefully close to the same point of aim.

I shot the pistol through the Texas

Teresa Gold was very impressed with the Bodyguard 380. The moderate felt recoil and smooth trigger function translated to a tight, evenly spaced group at close range.

The gun-buying frenzy of recent months has subsided, but the demand for compact, lightweight and economical handguns is stronger than ever. In the spring of 2011, the Smith & Wesson Bodyguards (above) —particularly the .380 ACP—are flying off gunshop shelves. The Bodyguard 38 revolver (below) utilizes an innovative double-ratchet cylinder rotation complex.

Concealed Handgun Proficiency Demo which includes timed fire at 3, 7 and 15 yards using a mix of the Buffalo Bore loading. Forty-five of the 50 rounds landed in the 10- and X-ring with the outliers being very tight 9-ring hits. While some shooters complain about the long and heavy trigger pull, I considered it just about right for a pistol possibly carried with the mechanical safety disengaged. I handed the pistol off to friend Teresa Gold, who found the trigger quite manageable. Her hits on the B-27 target were well centered and free of the vertical stringing normally signaling difficulty with trigger control. Pocket .380s have a reputation for being uncomfortable to shoot. Neither Teresa, nor the

BODYGUARDS

MAKER: SMITH & WESSON
2100 ROOSEVELT AVE., SPRINGFIELD, MA 01104
(800) 331-0852, WWW.GUNSMAGAZINE.COM/SMITH-WESSON

Bodyguard 380	MODEL:	Bodyguard 38
.380 ACP	CALIBER:	.38 Special
6+1	CAPACITY:	5
2.75"	BARREL LENGTH:	1.9"
DAO semi-auto	ACTION:	DAO revolver
11 pounds	TRIGGER PULL:	10.5 pounds
Ramp front, notch rear	SIGHTS:	Fixed, ramp front
5.25"	LENGTH OVERALL	6.6"
11. 25 ounces	WEIGHT:	14.3 ounces
Polymer & stainless steel	MATERIAL:	Stainless steel, aluminum alloy, polymer
Matte black	FINISH:	Matte black
$399	RETAIL:	$509
Notes: Both Bodyguards have an integral Insight laser factory installed.		

other shooters who fired this pistol experienced discomfort from recoil.

The laser sight activation is via an ambidextrous switch on the front of the unit. Activation is best accomplished with the thumb of the support hand and requires significant pressure. Pressing the button twice puts the laser in strobe mode with a third press shutting it down. The unit automatically switches off after 5 minutes and is rated for 3 hours maximum use from a pair of fresh No. 357 silver oxide batteries. Sighting in is via a supplied Allen wrench and adequately covered in the owner's manual. We found the laser to be completely invisible in bright or overcast midday conditions regardless of distance to the target. It is very bright indoors and could be very useful in low light given the time to activate it.

Some of the first Bodyguard 380s were prone to spontaneous partial disassembly due to unseating of the disassembly lever. The problem has been corrected though it now requires considerable pressure to rotate the lever to 6 o'clock for removal. The plastic toe of the magazine extension is useful for this. To reassemble the pistol with the barrel and takedown pin in correct register, it is very advantageous to align the slide/barrel assembly onto the frame as it would appear in final assembly and partially insert the takedown lever before drawing the slide to full lockback and fully snapping the lever into place.

To all appearances, the Bodyguard 380 is a very sturdy example of new-tech craftsmanship. It is built for the long haul with recoil bearing surfaces of stainless steel securely bolted to the polymer elements of the frame. The entire package is configured to deliver significantly better accuracy, range and shooter comfort than the general

run of pocket pistols.

While superficially resembling traditional J-frame revolvers, the current Bodyguard 38 is a complete departure from earlier models. The barrel and cylinder are of stainless steel—both encased in an alloy frame, which is rigidly bolted to the polymer grip frame. The cylinder rotates clockwise in the Colt revolver pattern. The cylinder locks up on two points: the cylinder bolt and an odd circular breech-mounted ratchet that engages with the cylinder "star."

This element replaces the hand and rotates with trigger pull to advance the cylinder. The cylinder latch is on the top of the grip frame accessible to both thumbs, though the shooter would have to be a juggler to enjoy the benefits of any ambidexterity this might afford. The firing pin is of the inertia-type, reminiscent of the very early S&W Safety Hammerless Revolver. The Bodyguard does not have the once-ubiquitous key actuated lock. The Insight laser is mounted on the right rear of the frame and has the same features as the one on the

Much more user-friendly than most of the sub-compact .380s, the S&W Bodyguard produced a perfect score for Mike on the Texas Concealed Handgun Proficiency Demo. This 3", 25-yard bench group from the Bodyguard .38 Special (below) is well within the accuracy standards set forth in the owner's manual. Point of impact is significantly leftward of the sight picture.

.380. The activating button is easily accessible to either the shooting or support hand.

Our sample revolver worked perfectly when dry cycled. In live fire however, after the initial shot, it required two pulls of the trigger to rotate the cylinder and discharge subsequent rounds. Apparently the ratchet elements were being knocked out of sync by recoil. Two identical revolvers available locally functioned perfectly and we acquired one of them to complete our evaluation. Bench rest accuracy was in the vicinity of 3" at 25 yards, but the groups were centered 5" left of point of aim and as much as 7" high, depending upon the load in use.

The trigger pull was smooth and produced good on-target results as long as we put the correct bias on the sight picture. With both standard- and high-velocity loads from Buffalo Bore, the Smith's grip arrangement moderated recoil noticeably more

.380 ACP BUFFALO BORE FACTORY AMMO PERFORMANCE

LOAD (BULLET WEIGHT, TYPE)	VELOCITY (FPS)	ENERGY (FT-LBS)
90 JHP	979	192
95 FMJ	810	138
95 JHP+P	1,039	278
100 cast FP	915	186
100 cast FP+P	1,046	243

.38 SPECIAL BUFFALO BORE FACTORY AMMO PERFORMANCE

LOAD (BULLET WEIGHT, TYPE)	VELOCITY (FPS)	ENERGY (FT-LBS)
125 Low Flash Powder	942	246
125+P	1,036	298
150 Wadcutter	923	284
158 SWC HP	852	255
158 SWHP+P	1,020	365

These bullets were recovered from water after passing through raw beef brisket. They are the standard pressure/low-flash/short-barrel loads from Buffalo Bore loaded with bullets carefully selected to perform at such velocities. The .38 Special 158-grain lead hollowpoint from Rim Rock (left) performs well at the standard and HV level. The .38 Special 125-grain Gold Dot load (middle left) produced mild recoil and full expansion. Both the Buffalo Bore .380 ACP loads feature the 90-grain Sierra JHP.

effectively than other snub revolvers of similar weight. Unlike many short-barrel revolvers, the Bodyguard has sufficient ejector length to positively clear fired cases from the cylinder.

The .38 Special revolvers with nominal 2" barrels are quite popular and Buffalo Bore ballistics are based on performance from the snubs. Notably, those loads designated "standard pressure," record velocity and energy stats normal from revolvers with 4" to 6" barrels. Both the standard and high velocity loadings of the Rim Rock 158-grain gas-check hollowpoint have gathered a significant following and have proven effective "on the street." The standard pressure loading of the 125-grain Gold Dot produces very mild recoil and the full expansion expected of that bullet. All of the rounds display a very prominent roll crimp and none were prone to recoil/inertia bullet pull from the lightweight Bodyguard.

The Bodyguard 38 has good potential as a comfortable and unobtrusive concealment arm. HKS J-Frame Speedloaders are just right for the Bodyguard revolver. Owners are reporting that some J-Frame Holsters will accommodate the laser sight but others will not. I found my Fobus Kydex Paddle Holster for my Ruger SP-101 is a perfect fit. **GUNS**

BUFFALO BORE AMMUNITION
P.O. BOX 1480
ST. IGNATIUS, MT 59865
(406) 745-2666
WWW.GUNSMAGAZINE.COM/BUFFALO-BORE

RIM ROCK BULLETS
103 MAIN ST. S.W.
RONAN, MT 59864
(406) 676-3250
WWW.GUNSMAGAZINE.COM/
RIMROCK-BULLETS

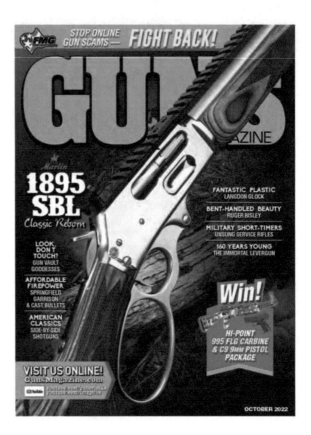

THE SIXGUNNER John Taffin

The .500 S&W Special

Cor-Bon's factory loads for the .500 Special with Jack Huntington's custom .500 Special Ruger Bisley Model — maybe a perfect match?

In 2003, Smith & Wesson went directly to the top of the heap and introduced their .500 S&W Magnum. This cartridge is basically the same length as the .500 Linebaugh Long, however it differs in that it uses .500" bullets. It is a brutal recoiling cartridge, yet it is manageable to a point in the Model 500 Smith & Wesson revolver, weighing in excess of four pounds. I can't even fathom what it would be like shooting this cartridge in a "normal" 2½-pound sixgun.

THE BIG GUYS

For the past several decades I've done a lot of work with the heaviest sixgun cartridges beginning with the .44 Magnum and progressing through the Heavy .45 Colt, .454 Casull, .445 SuperMag, .475 and .500 Linebaughs, .475 and .500 Linebaugh Longs, .480 Ruger, .460 and .500 S&W Magnums, and the .500 Wyoming Express. During this time I have received numerous requests for full house loads for all of these cartridges. I still get many requests for loading data for all of them, however a strange thing has happened. Rarely does anyone ask

Four shots fired at 20 yards from the Huntington custom .500 Special!

The Cor-Bon .500 Special loads proved accurate in the S&W Model 500 S&W Magnum.

anymore for full house loads; instead, in their words, they are looking for loads that are powerful but yet pleasurable to shoot.

All of these cartridges in their full house loadings are good choices for really big game, but what about the other 99.9 percent of hunting endeavors? If we need the power it is there, but for most sixgunners big-game hunting consists of deer, and deer are not all that hard to bring down. A heavyweight bullet at 900 fps in any of the above cartridges will give total penetration on a deer-sized animal. Even

larger animals such as bison cannot stand up to a 400-grain bullet at 1,100 fps; with a broadside shot my bullet went in one side and out the other and I had a beautiful trophy bull.

Awesome is a totally overworked word, however the factory .500 S&W with a 400-grain bullet at 1,675 fps is definitely an awesome load. That is nearly 400 fps more from a sixgun barrel than a standard .45-70 from a rifle barrel. Apparently a lot of folks have found the .500 S&W Magnum more than they want to handle and it has now been downsized to the .500 Special.

Top: The Barnes 275 DPX and Sierra 350 JHP are excellent choices for reloading the .500 Special. Left: The .500 Special compared to the 500 Magnum.

Modest Loads

Corbon offers two loadings for the .500 S&W Special, a 275 gr. Barnes DPX rated at 1,350 fps, and a 350-grain Sierra JHP at the same velocity. These may be "Special" loads when compared to the original .500 S&W Magnum, however they are not light loads by any means.

The case length of the .500 Special is approximately 1.28" while the .500 Magnum has a corresponding length of approximately 1.6"; this means the .500 Special bullet has to jump an extra .3" in that long cylinder. Sometimes Special loads shoot accurately in a Magnum cylinder; other times they don't. Every sixgun is a law unto itself when it comes to this.

Both Corbon factory loads were test fired in a S&W Model 500 Magnum with an 8⅜" barrel. I was most pleasantly surprised at the accuracy.

SIXGUNNER

The 275 DPX round clocked at 1,195 fps (1,005 fps in a 4" Model 500) and the heavier 350 JHP came in at 1,285 fps (1,160 fps in a 4" Model 500) with both rounds placing five shots in 1¼" at 25 yards. Again both of these loads are more than adequate for anything short of elephant/rhinos/Cape buffalo/big bears. For any of these I would still want the heaviest possible hard cast or flat-nosed bullet for maximum penetration. It's been a long time since an elephant or Cape buffalo was spotted in Idaho so I feel well served with the .500 Special loads.

Reloading

Next it was time to go to work at the reloading bench to come up with loads for the .500 Special. I found it necessary to modify the RCBS .500 Magnum dies to accommodate the shorter cartridge. The expander button extends too far into the Special case and the Special case was too short to reach the crimping shoulder of the seating die; both were shortened appropriately. For powders I chose some of the same propellants I normally use to produce every day working loads in large capacity sixgun cartridges, namely Hodgdon's TiteGroup and Winchester's 231. My goal was to come up with relatively easy shooting loads in the 1,100-1,200 fps range using bullets from the Barnes 275 DPX up to the Cast Performance Bullet Co. 400-grain LBT Gas Check.

For bullets I could choose from the Barnes 275 DPX, Sierra 350 JHP, BRP's 380 designed for the .50AE as well as a 370-grain .500 hard cast bullet, the CPBC 400-grain hard cast LBTGC, and a couple of hard cast bullets of unknown origin weighing in at 325 and 335 grains.

With the Barnes 275 DPX over 10.5 grains of TiteGroup, muzzle velocity is 1,170 fps from the 8⅜" S&W Model 500, basically duplicating the Corbon factory loading, with a 25 yard group for four shots of 1¼". With the Sierra 350 JHP over 11.5 grains of TiteGroup, muzzle velocity at 1,150 fps is about 125 fps slower than the Corbon factory load, however it shot into a very pleasing 7/8".

Compact Wheelgun

With the arrival of the factory loaded .500 Special and brass available from Starline it is only natural to look for a much more compact and easier to pack sixgun. Life is full of trade-offs and the Model 500 is easier to shoot than a sixgun weighing a pound and a half less, however it is not something one would normally want to pack all day, day after day. The ideal sixgun for the .500 Special is a 5-shot single action of approximately the same size as a Ruger Blackhawk. Gunsmith Jack Huntington was able to provide me with just such a vehicle.

Jack's answer for a home for the .500 Special is one of the most attractive and practical packin' pistols I have ever come across. Starting with a stainless steel Ruger Bisley Model, Jack fitted a 5-shot un-fluted cylinder, modified the grip frame to make it smaller and rounder at the butt end, and then topped everything off with a 4" Colt Anaconda barrel re-bored to .500. This sixgun epitomizes everything a Perfect Packin' Pistol should be; lightweight, compact, and certainly powerful. CPBC's 400 grain LBTGC over 11.0 grains of WW231 clocks out at 950 fps from this short-barreled .500 Special with four shots in 1⅛" at 20 yards, while the Sierra 350 JHP over 11.5 grains of TiteGroup places four shots in 1⅜" with a muzzle velocity of 1,055 fps. Either of these loads suits me just fine.

DRIFTING BACK TO IRON

The pronghorn doe slowed and cut a tight loop. The buck followed then paused at 90 yards. I crushed the trigger. At the whip-crack report he raced ahead...

READ FULL ARTICLE

HEAVY LEVERAGE

It's not too much of a stretch to say there are certain similarities between the first Winchester leverguns and modern ARs. They both gained large

READ FULL ARTICLE

AN ULTIMATE FIGHT STOPPER

I finally found it. This is the one. After years of evaluating guns and writing about them I've finally located the long gun of my dreams. It's in .300...

READ FULL ARTICLE

WANT MORE?

RUGER 10/22 CUSTOM COMPETITION
A NEW EDGE FOR THE BREAD-AND-BUTTER RIMFIRE

READ MORE

THE NIGHTHAWK CUSTOM AGENT 2
SAVE THE PLANET... AND LOOK GOOD DOING IT

READ MORE

THE ESSENTIAL OPTIC
BINO-TRUISM: MORE MAGNIFICATION ISN'T ALWAYS BETTER

READ MORE

IL-BOSSIN' TRAPPERS

READ MORE

Click Here:
gunsmagazine.com

URUS .357 MAGNUM RAGING HUNTER
NEW LEVEL OF REVOLVER ACCURACY DEFINED

READ MORE

WHY GUNS BLOW UP

CAN WOMEN OUTSHOOT MEN?

N WOMEN OUTSHOOT MEN?

howed in 1955 the answer was yes. And it's still true Here's a fun look back at K. D. Curtis' five-page article July 1955 issue of GUNS...

FULL ARTICLE

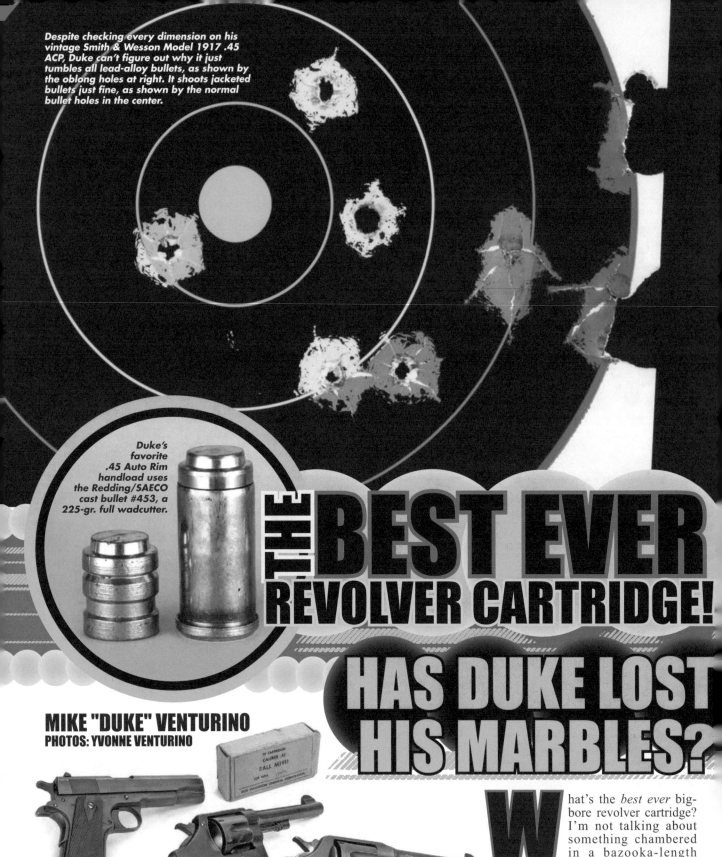

Despite checking every dimension on his vintage Smith & Wesson Model 1917 .45 ACP, Duke can't figure out why it just tumbles all lead-alloy bullets, as shown by the oblong holes at right. It shoots jacketed bullets just fine, as shown by the normal bullet holes in the center.

Duke's favorite .45 Auto Rim handload uses the Redding/SAECO cast bullet #453, a 225-gr. full wadcutter.

THE BEST EVER REVOLVER CARTRIDGE!

HAS DUKE LOST HIS MARBLES?

MIKE "DUKE" VENTURINO
PHOTOS: YVONNE VENTURINO

The .45 ACP became a revolver cartridge because in 1917 the US Army did not have enough Model 1911 pistols for WWI and so prevailed on S&W and Colt to adapt their big-frame revolvers to it.

What's the *best ever* big-bore revolver cartridge? I'm not talking about something chambered in a bazooka-length revolver fitted with a bipod like I saw at SHOT Show 2011. Nor am I talking about the sort of revolver and cartridge you would want in order save yourself from being eaten by some critter or another. The sort of revolvers I'm talking about are ordinary sized ones you might have in a holster or in a drawer by the bed at home.

In these pages I've not hesitated

70

Smith & Wesson recently recreated their Model 1917. At left is an original version, with the new on right.

Revolvers chambered for .45 ACP can be very accurate, as this group fired with a Smith & Wesson Model 25 (aka Model 1955 Target) shows.

to point out what I think are not the greatest revolver cartridges ever, despite the genuflecting some people do at the mere mention of them. Those are namely the .44 Special and .45 Colt. Both are good old calibers for which I own several handguns each. But the best ever? No way! Now its time to point out what I do think is the very best, all around revolver cartridge. Are you ready?

Huh? What?

It's the .45 ACP! That's right, the .45 Automatic Colt Pistol (ACP) is the very best ever round for ordinary, everyday revolvers. Its case capacity is correct for its bullet weight and ballistics, with no tiny charges of powder floating around in a huge case meant originally for black powder. It was the first revolver cartridge used in "speed-loaders," otherwise known as half-moon clips. And now there are full-moon clips too. And, it's capable of fine accuracy from some guns. It's one of the easiest and most versatile cartridges for reloaders, and it has a stepbrother identical except for having a rim on the case, if that trips your trigger instead of fiddling with clips. That, of course is the .45 Auto Rim.

In 1917, when the United States stuck its nose in a European war, it did

"CCI'S .45 ACP SHOTSHELLS WARNED, DO NOT FIRE IN REVOLVERS. I TOOK THAT AS A PERSONAL CHALLENGE AND DID SO."

The Smith & Wesson Model 22 (aka Thunder Ranch Revolver) is a versatile .45 ACP revolver because it can be loaded with .45 ACP rounds in half-moon or full-moon clips or with .45 Auto Rim rounds in standard speed loaders.

All that's required to load both .45 ACP and .45 Auto Rim cases with a standard set of .45 ACP dies is a different shell holder.

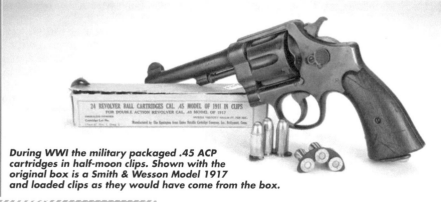

During WWI the military packaged .45 ACP cartridges in half-moon clips. Shown with the original box is a Smith & Wesson Model 1917 and loaded clips as they would have come from the box.

WHICH GUN

is right for you?

TURN HERE

for help

americanhandgunner.com

BEST EVER

it without having enough weapons for its army. In regards to pistols, we were sorely shot of Model 1911s. Smith & Wesson and Colt already had big bore revolvers, so it was a simple matter to make them for .45 ACP, except there was no rim for the star-type extractors for case ejection. Hence half-moon clips came into existence. Together, over two years, those handgun manufacturers turned out nearly a third of a million US Model 1917 revolvers for the American government.

Mating the .45 ACP with big-frame revolvers was such a good idea that post WWI both companies kept them in their catalogs: Colt until 1944 and S&W until — well until now, with some recesses along the way. Besides 1917s, S&W's versions have been Models 22, 25 and 26. They had names instead of numbers prior to 1957. The S&W '17s and Model 22s have been fixed sight "service revolvers" while the Models 25 and 26 have been intended for paper punching and had proper adjustable sights for such. Along the way I've owned them all. Colt's only .45 ACP revolver was their New Service, along with a target-sighted version called Shooting Master. While I've owned several Colt 1917s, I've never even seen a Shooting Master .45 ACP. I don't know vintage prices on the Smith & Wesson .45 ACP revolvers, but an original 1935 Colt catalog says their fixed sight New Service cost $34 while the target-sighted version was $52.50.

Auto Rim

About 1920, the Peters Cartridge Company responded to shooter demands for a .45 ACP case with a rim, and so the .45 Auto Rim was born. Because .45 ACP revolvers were engineered to include the thickness of half-moon clips in their headspacing, the rims of .45 Auto Rim cases look like they have mumps. In other words they are far thicker than any other revolver cartridge rims. Of course that means a .45 Auto Rim-specific shell holder is necessary. Otherwise it can be reloaded with ordinary .45 ACP dies.

When Remington absorbed Peters they kept the cartridge going until relatively recent times. To the best of my knowledge Black Hills, CorBon, Buffalo Bore and DoubleTap are the other makers producing .45 Auto Rim now. Whereas .45 ACP factory loads have always used jacketed bullets, in the past .45 Auto Rims were loaded with the same, but eventually roundnose lead ones became their standard.

Normally the idea of lead-alloy bullets goes hand in hand with revolvers, except for one factor. The US Model 1917s by both S&W and Colt were cut with fairly shallow rifling because they were first and foremost intended for FMJ military ammunition. And that led me to one of those conundrum thingies.

For my collection, I've purchased Colt and S&W 1917s. The former shoots even fairly soft lead alloy bullets like a champ. The latter keyholes all lead alloy bullets, even very hard ones poured of Linotype. And I have checked all its dimensions and cannot find a reason why that happens. It shoots jacketed bullets perfectly adequately. This also adds to the conundrum. My new S&W Model 22 Thunder Ranch revolver, and the 1917 recreation S&W sold a few years back, both have rifling appearing very shallow. They shoot lead-alloy bullets nicely.

Some Particulars

A great portion of my reloading efforts these past few years have been with .45 ACP, greatly spurred because I bought a couple of submachine guns as part of building a World War II firearms collection. Most of that reloading has been with 220- to 225-gr. lead alloy roundnoses. Powered by either 5 grains of Bullseye or 5.4 grains of HP38, those bullets slide right through the full autos and 1911s. They do fine in the sixguns too. Except that contrary S&W '17! I won't take up a lot of space with a load chart. Suffice it to say the above two powder charges with 220- to 225-gr. lead bullets give 800 to 825 fps from the 5½" barrel of a Colt '17, whereas some 1966 dated military surplus 230-gr. FMJs gave 843 fps from the same Colt.

However, when loading just for the revolvers there is one bullet head and shoulders above all others. That is Redding/Saeco's cast bullet #453 for a 225-gr. full wadcutter. Drive that thing to about 860 fps with 4.7 grains of Red Dot in either ACP or Auto Rim case and it strikes like the hammer of Thor.

Shooters of .45 ACP revolvers have available all the vast array of that caliber's factory ammo, plus the few .45 Auto Rim loads still around. But here's a tip: CCI's .45 ACP shotshells warned, *"Do Not Fire In Revolvers."* I took that as a personal challenge and did so. A wooden mallet was required to hammer open the cylinder of my rare and valuable Model 1950 Army!

In the 45 years I've been buying handguns, I've owned scores of revolvers chambered as .44 Special, .45 Colt and .45 ACP/.45 Auto Rim. So, I'm speaking from experience here. Unless you want to shoot black powder, or have a big case of nostalgia, the .45 ACP/.45 Auto Rim will serve you best. Let the letters begin. Sorry Your Editorship!

HANDGUN HUNTING

J.D. Jones

The S&W X-frame revolver — excellent sights, trigger and accuracy — and a real handful to boot.

The shorty .500 with a dot sight, my favorite.

MONSTER MAGNUMS

Monster size, weight, power, penetration, muzzleblast, recoil, accuracy and great fun are at-hand, as it were, for those capable of using these beasts. Make no mistake, the traditional 97-pound weakling shouldn't even think of shooting them. The .500 is the "baddest," closely followed by the .460. Strength of the individual shooting them is important. If you aren't strong enough, hold the gun steady while squeezing off an off-hand shot accurately; they are little more than a serious handicap to the hunter.

Weighing in at around 72 ounces, it takes a strong individual to hold them and squeeze off a shot. Add a scope and the weight goes up. But without a scope, few are capable of matching the inherent accuracy of the guns. Physical strength in handling the recoil — particularly the .500 with heavy bullets and max loads — is important. Taking a hit to your forehead during recoil from one of these guns is an extremely unpleasant and often costly experience, likewise, eating an improperly mounted scope. You have to be a match for the gun physically, and more than a match for it mentally. Any tiny fear creeping into your mind about what is going to happen after the fuse is lit and I guarantee a screw up of one sort or another is in the make.

WHY?

Their real purpose is plain and simple: killing big game effectively, as well as being profitable and increasing the status of the manufacturer. Do we need them for deer? Hell no, but they work fine on them, and the power and exceptional revolver accuracy factor adds range to a revolver's effectiveness. When heavy, big-boned animals are the targets, then big, heavy, strong, high-velocity bullets come into their own. The .500 won't kill them any deader than a .44 Mag, but generally will do it a lot quicker and more effectively. Figure elk and the bigger bears are where the Monster Magnums come into their own. African game such as kudu, similar sized and larger critters, including the big five, have all fallen to these guns. Certainly

The .460 and .500 beat any variety of .30-30 for punch, and possibly headaches.

this is not unexpected, as the .44 and others have taken them too.

Herb Belin, Director, Emerging Technology, is the most visible of the folks at S&W, behind development of the X-frame revolver. Peter Pi, owner of CorBon, was the ammunition guy. Jamison made the first cartridge cases. I believe the first test barrels came from SSK, in the form of Encore pistol barrels used in initial load development. The first animal killed with the .500 S&W was a cow elk I pulled the trigger on. It was a short-range shot and was instantly effective. I wish I could show the photo of the exit in the offside rib cage — with my fist *not* filling the hole.

.460

Call the .500 a fat boy and the .460 a skinny lad. Everything else being equal the X-frame picks up a bit of weight, as not quite as much metal is carved out of it. Generally speaking, the fat boy runs out of velocity quicker than the skinny, faster .460. The .500 packs a bigger punch up close, and the .460 has a longer reach. Using lighter bullets, the .460 is more pleasant to shoot than the .500, but a touch more demandinwwg of bullets. On truly big game, the .500 has the edge, with the .460 (if loaded with correct bullets) a close second.

Both put out around 3,000 FPE at the muzzle, which is a somewhat misleading way to compare cartridges, but puts both of them in the muzzle energy class of .270 Winchester, .308 and .444 Marlin rifles. Obviously, the ballistic inefficient pistol bullets simply cannot compete with the vastly more efficient rifle bullets at any distance, although, at close range the larger diameter handgun bullets may well be more effective. Both cartridges are very versatile, even in sub-sonic, suppressed rifles with heavy bullets.

If you want a bit of history on the Monsters, go to *www.john-ross.net*. That will get you to John's website and to the best information I can recommend on the history, development and loading of the Monster Magnums. I firmly believe John Ross knows more about the .500 S&W ammunition than anyone. You also might recognize him as the author of *Unintended Consequences*!

MICHAEL JANICH

COL. REX APPLEGATE:

"In 1947, after retiring from the regular army and moving to Mexico City, I formed a Mexican sales company for representation of American firearms and allied lines. During this period I carried a Fourth Model .38 S&W Hammerless with a 2" barrel, either in my pocket, or when in southern Mexico, in the hotter tropical climate, in a Myers special belt-attached upside down holster that was a very practical system, particularly when wearing an open bottom shirt as was customarily worn.

Just prior to one of my regular trips to the states around 1950, I had been in southern Mexico, near the Guatemalan border, in the area of Salina Cruz in the company of a Mexican Army officer. On this particular evening the officer and I encountered a very drunk, machete-wielding Indian who seemed bent upon decapitating us both. The officer carried his .45 Automatic in a U.S. Army holster. While he was frantically trying to get it into action, I was successful in drawing my Safety Hammerless from the Myers holster, from under my sport shirt and dropped the machete wielding Indian after putting five slugs into his torso. He finally fell to the ground about five feet from me, just as I was getting ready to throw the empty gun at him. Due to the Mexican army connection, there were no repercussions.

I mentioned this incident to W.H.B. Smith when I next met him in New York, prior to our trip to the S&W plant, and complained about the lack of stopping power. We both began wondering why it was not possible, and advisable, for S&W to consider the production of a model similar to the Safety Hammerless, using the Chief Special frame in the more potent .38 Special caliber. We discussed this at some length with Carl Hellstrom [then president of Smith and Wesson].

On my next trip to the plant in the fall of 1951, Carl Helstrom presented to me a prototype model of one of the first Centennials. This is one of my most prized firearms and one which I will always treasure. I cannot help but think that, especially due to the urging of W.H.B. Smith and perhaps myself, that we were at least partially responsible for convincing Hellstrom to produce the Centennial Model."

- Col. Rex Applegate, June 1990

The above passage is an excerpt from an unpublished work called *The Guns of Famous Shooters* written by the late Col. Rex Applegate. Intended to document the stories behind the most significant guns in his extraordinary personal collection, it also provides great insight into the genesis of one of the most popular personal defense guns ever produced, the S&W Centennial Model.

When I had the privilege of working with Col. Applegate in the late 1990's, he shared this story with me and showed me the original S&W Safety Hammerless he used in the incident. He also

The Model 442 after receiving its black-and-tan coating from Iron Ridge Arms. Also shown is a companion Spyderco Sage 2 that received the same coating treatment.

showed me the "Myers" holster referenced in the passage and explained why it was one of his all-time favorite carry rigs. In another letter included in *The Guns of Famous Shooters,* dated January 1992, he explains, "When operating in warmer areas such as coastal

or southern Mexico and in central Mexico, I used a special belt-suspended upside down holster (left side) that enabled me, with either hand, to draw quickly and unnoticed from the gun-butt down position when wearing an open bottom sport shirt."

As both a fan and a student of unique concealed-carry rigs, I was fascinated with the Colonel's Myers rig and always wondered why the design had never gained broader acceptance or made it into the market. I also knew the "lemon squeezer" .38 (so called because it possessed a grip safety)

Col. Rex Applegate's original .38 S&W Hammerless and the unique Myers carry rig he used during his post-WWII years in Mexico.

Col. Applegate's classic "lemon squeezer" .38 (a break-top) he used to shoot a machete-wielding attacker in Mexico. It, and the performance of the .38 S&W cartridge, ultimately inspired the Centennial model.

Carry rigs then and now: Colonel Applegate's original carry rig and the author's modern DIY Kydex version.

ORIGINS OF THE S&W CENTENNIAL REVOLVER

that he allowed me to examine was undeniably a significant piece of firearms history.

The Colonel's Guns

After the Colonel passed away in 1998, the S&W Safety Hammerless and Col. Applegate's Fitz Special .45 were purchased from his estate by my then-employer, Peder Lund, of Paladin Press. Lund maintained them in his collection for several years before deciding to sell them. I immediately jumped at the offer, even though I was unsure I could actually muster the asking price. After several months passed without a defined price, Peder came into my office with both guns in a plastic bag and handed them to me.

He stated that "I couldn't think of anyone the Colonel would rather have own these guns. If you keep them, they're yours. If you sell them during my lifetime, you owe me part of the sale." Needless to say, that was one of the greatest honors I've ever received, and those two guns are the most treasured pieces in my collection.

Although I still get a thrill every time I pull them out of the safe and handle them, it always seemed a shame that guns that were bred explicitly for use as personal-defense weapons were relegated to

Mounted butt-up, the Centennial drew smoothly from the SERPA, but required an open-front cover garment.

Col. Applegate's Myers rig in action. Held in place against the hip by the belt, it basically functions as a shoulder holster without the harness.

"safe-queen" status. That got me thinking. Since the S&W Hammerless was in fact the inspiration for the Centennial model, what if I took that inspiration a bit further and created a modern expression of the Colonel's Mexican carry rig? "Genius" may be a bit of an overstatement, but the idea was too cool to pass up.

Got Gun?

The first step in the process was to secure a S&W Centennial, the Model 442. Out of the box, this 5-shot J-Frame revolver boasted a factory matte black finish and black synthetic grips. For

a stock carry gun, this combination was perfectly serviceable; but for this project, I wanted better. My first step was to take the gun to my friend Oliver Mazurkiewicz, owner and proprietor of Iron Ridge Arms in Longmont, Colorado. Iron Ridge is one of the premier suppliers of Class II and Class III firearms in the Rocky Mountain region. In support of these services, Iron Ridge has also become a leading source of aftermarket firearm finishes and coatings.

After talking with Oliver, I decided

on a two-tone black-and-tan finish. For the frame I chose a coyote tan Cerakote ceramic finish. For the cylinder and trigger group, I opted for a black Teflon coating ofering both durable protection and enhanced lubricity of the moving parts. I left the gun — as well as a companion Spyderco Sage 2 folding knife — in Oliver's capable hands and turned my attention to the other requirements of the project.

Get A Grip

Col. Applegate's greatest contribution to the field of close combat was his work on handgun point shooting. The core elements of his method were based on an in-depth understanding of the physiological effects of life-threatening stress, most notably the loss of near-vision acuity and the tendency to naturally focus on the threat trying to kill you. Although the Colonel was very traditional in many ways, he also was amazingly progressive when it came to useful advances in gun technology — like laser sights. Since lasers put the sight picture on the target, where you will naturally be focused under stress, they are an outstanding tool for combative shooting. Crimson Trace were very intrigued with my project and were kind enough to provide samples of all three styles of J-frame LaserGrips they produce.

The Holster Platform

Next I turned my attention to the carry platform for the Applegate-inspired Centennial, which proved to be much more of a DIY project than the gun itself. I remembered Col. Applegate had mentioned "wearing out" several of the original carry rigs because the humid climate in Mexico quickly took a toll on the leather. With that in mind, I started with a BlackHawk J-frame SERPA holster. This popular injection-molded holster features the SERPA retention system, which automatically provides positive retention when the gun is inserted.

Since no commercial platforms for the Colonel's style of carry are available, I decided to "roll my own" by heat-forming a panel of tan Kydex around a rolled carpet. With a little experimentation, I got the contour just right so it would tuck tightly against my pelvis when inserted under a belt. To simplify the design and make donning and doffing of the platform easier, I skipped the traditional belt loops and installed two "frogs" made from Chicago screws and rubber washers. And, while the Colonel's original platform carried extra ammo in classic cartridge loops, I took a quantum leap forward and molded a Kydex double speed-loader pouch that also acts as a shelf to support the platform's weight.

Putting It All Together

To put it simply, the work Iron Oak did on the 442 turned out beautifully. The frame is a handsome matte-finished coyote tan, contrasted by the deep black of the cylinder, trigger, ejector rod and cylinder latch. The companion Spyderco knife I chose for the project received identical treatment, with tan Cerakote on the titanium handle and black Teflon on the blade. Aesthetically, both were perfect.

With all the component parts complete, I couldn't wait to put them all together and "test-drive" the whole package. I first practiced drawing from the rig to get comfortable with it. Initially, I mounted the SERPA holster in a butt-down position to replicate the original; however, I found drawing from this position required a very precise angle and the gun would sometimes bind in the holster. Re-mounting it in a muzzle-down, shoulder-holster position promoted a much more positive draw from the SERPA. Although this position makes the rig inconsistent with carry under a closed-front garment, it's still much more comfortable than a traditional shoulder holster, and easily concealed under a jacket or even a vest.

With very little practice, I was able to achieve very quick and consistent draws from the carry platform. The positioning of the speed loaders also turned out to be ideal, making them easily accessible to my left hand for quick reloads.

The final step of the project was to take the gun to the range and wring it out with the Crimson Trace grips. With a friend along, we spent a great day on the range putting several hundred rounds through the gun. We also tested all three styles of LaserGrips on the gun and struggled to determine a favorite. While the longer LG-305 was the easiest to shoot, I ultimately chose the polymer LG-105 as the best balance of control and concealability for me. Once zeroed, LaserGrips make quick, accurate shooting with the Centennial a breeze, and are must-have accessories for all defensive snubbies in my opinion.

Working with Col. Applegate was an incredible privilege and an amazing learning experience. Similarly, his personal guns and carry systems are not only priceless pieces of history, but ongoing insights into the realities of close-quarter gunfighting. I hope he would consider this project a fitting tribute to his Mexico carry rig, and a worthy evolution of the concepts behind it.

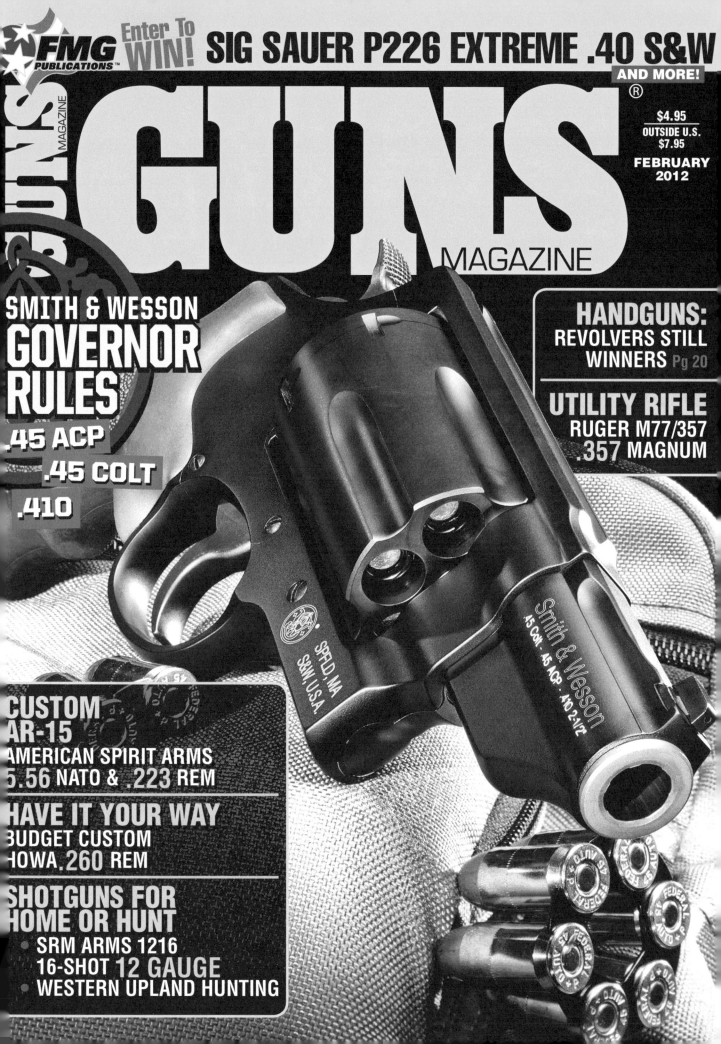

The Governor is a large handgun but well-balanced, and accepts a wide variety of ammunition for personal defense. The Governor's tritium night sight is a real plus for typical self-defense scenarios.

S&W's new revolver shoots .410, .45 Colt and .45 ACP.

Holt Bodinson
Photos: Robbie Barrkman

Who would have thought that a personal sized blunderbuss would turn out to be one of the hottest selling handguns of the 21st century? In a short decade, we've gone from the pot-metal, cap-gun looking Thunder Five (look that one up on the web) to its more classy sequel, the Taurus Judge and now Smith & Wesson, roars out with their own version, or should we say, "elects" its own version, the "Governor."

Well, the model name *is* sort of corny. Taurus started it, but the Smith & Wesson Governor-elect goes to the head of the class because he's a 6-shooter!

Believe me perps, do not mess with the hand holding a Governor if it's loaded with six Winchester PDX .410 shells. Or if the owner is of a more experimental persuasion of mind, the Governor might be loaded with two Winchester PDX .410 shells, two .45 ACPs and two .45 Colts. Yes, this little blunderbuss is a meat grinder.

I admit that more S&Ws occupy the stalls in my stable than any other handgun—from the old Centennial my grandfather used to shoot coyotes and jacks with from the window of his Model T, to the AirLite Titanium that rides my shoulder holster every morning when exercising the dog, to the latest, an M&P9 fitted with Crimson Trace grips and a SureFire X300 weapon light. I like the pull of their double actions better than Colt's, and the quality and reliability built into S&Ws, generally, have been outstanding. The new Governor follows that tradition.

When you finally have one in your hand, you'll realize the Governor, in spite of its stubby 2-3/4" barrel, is a large revolver—not heavy, but large—yet stylish. Much of its size is dictated by the long, stainless steel, 6-shot cylinder that accommodates 2-1/2" .410 shells. Anyway, the Governor is 8-1/2" long, 5-1/2" high and 1-3/4" wide. It will be interesting to see what the holster makers cook up for open and concealed carry of the big Governor. I like to think of it in the role of an unholstered home and car gun.

THE GOVER
GOVE

GUNS

MAGAZINE

Smith & Wesson
.45 Colt · .45 ACP · .410 2-1/2"

SPFLD, MA
S&W, U.S.A.

WINCHESTER
PDX1
AMMUNITION FOR
PERSONAL DEFENSE
2 1/2 INCHES   12 PLATED BB's
3 PLATED CYLINDER PROJECTILES

WINCHESTER
PDX1
410
AMMUNITION FOR
PERSONAL DEFENSE
410   2 1/2   12 PLATED BB's

WARNING: Keep out of reach of children. Read all warnings on package.
AVERTISSEMENT: Gardez hors de la portée des enfants. Lisez tous les avertissements sur l'emballage.

6 FEET
.410 PDX1

12 FEET
.410 PDX1

18 FEET
.410 PDX1

25 FEET
.410 PDX1

The Governor is devastating (above) when fed Winchester's 2-1/2" .410 PDX1 personal defense load. The Governor handles .45 ACP and .45 Colt just fine, too (below).

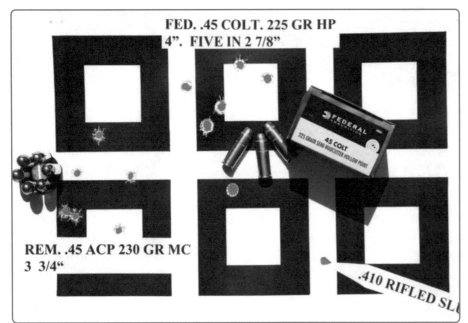

FED. .45 COLT. 225 GR HP
4". FIVE IN 2 7/8"

REM. .45 ACP 230 GR MC
3 3/4"

.410 RIFLED SLU

The Brownells moon-clip stripper tool is an essential part of the Governor's tool kit.

The frame itself is composed of that great, lightweight, heat-treated alloy, S&W calls "Scandium" which lends strength and reduced weight to a number of handguns in the S&W line. On my Sunbeam scale, I weighed the Governor unloaded and loaded to see where it ranks in the handgun world, given its choice of three possible ammunition types. Unloaded it weighs 1 pound, 13 ounces. Loaded with six 230-grain .45 ACPs, it goes up to 2 pounds, 2 ounces; with six 225-grain .45 Colts, it weighs 2 pounds, 3 ounces; and with six Winchester PDX shells, 2 pounds, 4 ounces. Not exactly an air weight but still nicely portable. There's just enough mass there to be comfortable in your hand.

Because the Governor has an omnivorous appetite, S&W has come up with a neat idea for the .45 ACP. Included with the Governor are standard 6-round moon clips and a unique 2-round clip. The 2-round clips enable you to load the cylinder with either two or four rounds of ACP in any arrangement thought effective.

S&W's 6-round moon clips are something else entirely. You can load them, but I dare you to unload them with finger power. Once that S&W clip snaps onto a case, it hangs on for dear life. I've loaded and unloaded a jillion moon clips for 1917s and Webleys with no problems whatsoever. The solution to the S&W problem is Brownells ".45 ACP Moon Clip Stripper Tool," part No. 352-197-000. Denise Murphy of Murphy's Gun Shop in Tucson, Ariz.,

GOVERNOR

MAKER: SMITH & WESSON
2100 ROOSEVELT AVE., SPRINGFIELD, MA 01104
(800) 331-0852
WWW.GUNSMAGAZINE.COM/SMITH-WESSON

ACTION TYPE: Double-action revolver, **CALIBER:** 2-1/2" .410 shotshell, .45 ACP, .45 Colt, **BARREL LENGTH:** 2-3/4", **OVERALL LENGTH:** 8-1/2", **WEIGHT:** 29.6 ounces, **FINISH:** Matte black, **STOCKS:** Synthetic, **PRICE:** $679 (with laser grips: $899)

The cylinder can hold a mixed fruit pudding of .410 2-1/2" shotshells, .45 Colt or .45 ACP. Stoked with 6 rounds of Winchester .410 PDX1, it is indeed a formidable self-defense revolver.

turned me on to this wonderful, little tool. It not only pops loaded or fired rounds out of those S&W moon clips with no effort at all, but stores them in its hollow handle. If you're going to own a Governor, buy the Brownell tool, too.

The sights are fixed but clean and clear. S&W anticipated an essential need in the Governor and put a tritium night sight on the end of the barrel. It's a blessing in low-light environments, and taking night fighting a step further, S&W offers the Governor with factory installed Crimson Trace laser grips as well.

The trigger is smooth, measuring 4.1 pounds in single-action mode and 11.5 pounds in double action. These are average values generated using a Lyman electronic gauge.

How does it shoot? Winchester's Supreme Elite "PDX1" ammunition is made for the Governor. This new .410 personal defense load consists of three plated, 70-grain, disk-like projectiles and 12 plated, hard BBs. Shooting at center of mass, you can see how lethal that load is from the Governor at 6', 12', 18' and 25'. The PDX1 does have a little bit of a kick to it, but recoil is soaked up with the Governor's shock absorbing grip.

Switching over to conventional handgun ammunition, the Governor at 25 yards will keep six rounds of .45 ACP and .45 Colt in 2-1/2" to 4". I also had a brilliant idea to test some Brenneke .410 slugs in the Governor. Don't bother. The Brenneke brand is a top performer, but the first shot landed 10" low and several inches off in windage, so I called it a day.

Above all, the Governor is fun to shoot with .410 shotshells. It's a quality Smith & Wesson handgun, and offering one more shot than the competition, the Governor has just taken over the State House. **GUNS**

The Governor is a large handgun but well balanced. The Governor's tritium night sight is a real plus for typical self-defense scenarios.

BROWNELLS
200 S. FRONT ST.
MONTEZUMA, IA 50171
(641) 623-4000
WWW.GUNSMAGAZINE.COM/BROWNELLS

CRIMSON TRACE
9780 S.W. FREEMAN DR.
WILSONVILLE, OR 97070
(800) 442-2406
WWW.GUNSMAGAZINE.COM/CRIMSON-TRACE

Mas found the 6" S&W 586 very controllable in rapid fire.

RETURN OF A CLASSIC

RECOGNIZING SOME PREFER BLUE STEEL AND WALNUT, S&W BRINGS BACK THE L–FRAME 586 .357.

Massad Ayoob

Thirty-some years ago, stung by complaints from law enforcement that their K-frame service revolvers weren't holding up to steady training diets of the ferocious 125-grain .357 Magnum load rated for 1,450 fps muzzle velocity, Smith & Wesson introduced their L-frame revolvers. The K-series had basically been ".38-frame" guns, and the big N-size models, ".44-45 frame." The L models were in essence ".41-frame" guns, and their resemblance to the Colt Python was inescapably stark: all they failed to copy was the ventilation cuts in the barrel rib. No matter: the L-frame was an instant hit.

Speedloads went smoothly into the 586 (the stocks are cut to allow loaders). This is Herman Gunter about to run an IDPA stage with the 4" 586.

The Model 686 in stainless came first, in 1980, augmented the following year by the Model 586, made of carbon steel and offered with traditional blue or nickel finish. Stainless was still "The New Thing," and a very practical thing at that, and from the beginning the 686 far outstripped the 586 in sales. Both revolvers came with S&W's Micro adjustable rear sight, and except for special order, a ramp front with a colored insert. Catching some demand for a fixed sight variant, they introduced the stainless 681 and the chrome-moly 581, but the 686 remained the clear-cut star of the L-frame show.

Within a few years, double-action autoloaders including S&W's own would swamp the revolver in police sales (followed by a tsunami of polymer-frame pistols, but that's a tale for another day). The fixed sight L-frames faded first. The 681, except for special orders from distributors and some Performance Center variations, was discontinued in 1992. The 581 lasted but 7 years, from '81 to '88. The handsome, sweet-shooting target/service grade 586, introduced in 1981, was discontinued in 1999.

The 686 lived on, remaining one of the most popular revolvers in the S&W line. Outdoorsmen, like cops, appreciated its rust-resistant stainless construction. The introduction of a 7-shot variation helped it greatly. A short run of 2,000 blued 586s were produced on special order for the Dick's Sporting Goods chain midway through the first decade of the 21st century, and were quickly snapped up. These, to my knowledge, were the only 586s produced with 7-shot cylinders.

Meanwhile, gun collectors and

S&W lovers pined wistfully for the lost 586. It had all the excellent shooting characteristics of the 686, but it also had... that look. Those of us who frequented the firing lines couldn't help but notice that the 686s we saw were generally wearing one or another flavor of neoprene grips... but the 586s we ran across, more often than not, wore wooden stocks. There's just something about blue steel and walnut....

Smith & Wesson tries to keep a close touch on the pulse of the shooting public. They picked up on that vibe. They'd had successful sales of their Classic lines, the "guns of our youth" from the Smith & Wesson catalog, resurrected in modern dress.

For 2012, at the SHOT Show in Las Vegas, S&W unveiled their latest in the Classic series: the Model 586 in all its blue steel and walnut glory.

S&W's Tony Miele shipped me a pair of the new-iteration 586s, one with 4" barrel and one with 6". When I opened the boxes, the first thing that hit me was—you guessed it—blue steel and walnut.

I was very pleased with the blue, and the polish beneath it that makes

Using the 4" S&W 586 test gun, Herman Gunter won the Stock Service Revolver division at an IDPA match in Jacksonville, Fla.

it "happen." Holding it to the light on an angle, there was none of the ripple effect we saw in the sad early '80s days of S&W workmanship. Just good polish, and that sweet, dark blue we Ancient Ones associate with the S&W logo. The kind of blue Clint Smith has likened to looking into a pool of oil, that John Taffin so eloquently said you can see your ancestors in.

The stocks are cut in the new style: not the S&W Target stocks of The Old Days, but nice in their own

right. These two guns had wood with pleasing grain, left panels well matched to right, with acceptable fit to the gun. Fit to the hand wasn't bad, either: they're slim amidships, and let you get a good hold on the revolver. Still, if the purpose is a Classic line, I wish they'd do something else. They could go into that cool little museum they have right there at 2100 Roosevelt Avenue in Springfield, Mass., and pull a pair of "Cokes" off of, say, an old 1955 .45 Target revolver. Nicknamed

The S&W Classic 586s came out at the same time as Tim Mullin's excellent new book, Magnum: The S&W .357 Magnum Phenomenon.

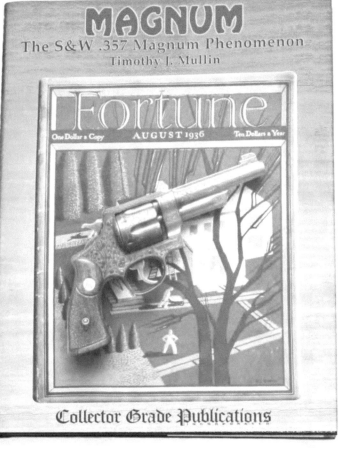

Winchester .38 Special RNL (above) gave the best 25-yard accuracy from the 4" 586. The large bullet hole is a tight double. This tight double in the 25-yard group is better seen on exit side of target (below).

Remington's economy 125-grain Magnum hollowpoint grouped well from the 4" 586 at 25 yards.

that by S&W aficionados because there's a very slight palm swell that reminds shooters of the distinctive old Coca-Cola bottle, true duplicates of these would gladden the hearts and hands of countless thousands of S&W revolver buffs, and put the "classic" back in their Classic line.

Trigger pulls were tested on a Lyman digital gauge procured through Brownells. On the 4" gun, double-action weight averaged 10 pounds, .6 ounces, and single action averaged 4 pounds, 9.22 ounces. On the longer barrel test sample, pull weight averaged 10 pounds, 2.5 ounces in DA and 4 pounds, 3.4 ounces in SA mode. On the 4" gun, the trigger rolled in true S&W fashion with no stacking in one sweet, smooth stroke from first touch to break of shot, no matter what the speed of pull.

The action of the 6" 586 was very subtly different. Run at any sort of speed, it felt like the shorter gun, but if you did a slow-roll of the trigger, it was easier for a new shooter to "stage" or "trigger-cock," and then apply the last bit of pressure to drop the hammer. Both guns "pre-timed," a desirable thing. That is, the cylinder locked in place well before the hammer had completed its rearward arc prior to its fall. It's just that this was a little more palpable through the trigger on the longer-barreled 586.

For decades, S&W's "service/target grade" revolvers came with an integral trigger stop built into the gun. It turned out that a clumsy amateur could adjust it so poorly that it could keep the gun from firing. Back "In The Day," S&W developed the policy of leaving that feature out of such guns sold to police departments. It is absent entirely from the Classic 586, and frankly, this writer thinks it's just as well.

On The Range

With a Caldwell Matrix rest on a concrete bench at 25 yards, I selected three different loads suitable for different applications of a 4" revolver chambered for .38 Special/.357 Magnum in this day and age. There's plinking, there are certain specific sporting disciplines, and of course, self-defense.

PMC Bronze 132-grain full metal jacket is a good exemplar of "plinking"—informal target practice—ammo in .38 Special. The 130-grain FMJ is what a plinker is likely to find in Wal-Mart, and the regular gun dealers I prefer to do business with tell me the soft 130-grain FMJs are their best selling .38 Special practice load. It also meets the power factor for Stock Service Revolver competition in the International Defensive Pistol Association (IDPA) matches, since that was lowered as of January 2011. It can also serve in a pinch for protection: last summer, I spoke for a woman who was charged with manslaughter after killing a man who violently attacked her as she was leaving an informal range from a plinking session. The death wound was caused by a single, perfectly placed 132-grain PMC Bronze FMJ .38 Special bullet. She was totally acquitted at trial.

From the 4" 586, firing single action, this load finished with a 5-shot group measuring 3.45". However, the best three of those were under an inch, in a group that went .85" center to center. That "best three" measurement, I discovered long ago, takes enough unnoticed human error out of the picture to give a very good prediction of what the same gun and ammo would have done with all five shots from a machine rest.

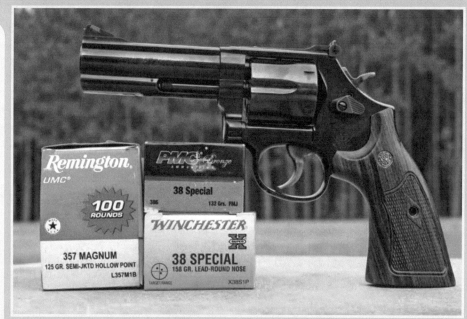
The 4" Model 586 was tested with these three loads for 25-yard accuracy.

Accurate

The next load was Winchester's "standard line" gray box 158-grain roundnose lead .38 Special. This sort of round is the load of choice for NRA PPC Service Revolver matches, and was from a lot that had won the last such match I shot with it out of an early '80s S&W 686 tuned by Bob Lloyd. The Winchester took the accuracy honors for the day with the short 586. The group consisted of two "doubles," one so tight it looked like a single .40-caliber bullet hole, and a single hole a bit above the others. All five shots gave a 1.25" measurement, and the best three were within 8/10". Given that the 10- and X-ring on an NR B-27 Police target is an oval that's about 3" high by just over 2" wide, it's obvious to me Winchester 158-grain RN .38 Special in that 4" S&W 586 Classic would be a winning combination in an NRA Police Service Revolver match.

Oddly, the 6" sample was not as accurate with the test .38 RNL load as the 4" at 25 yards.

You can't test an L-frame .357 without running the load it was built around: the 125-grain, 1,400 to 1,450 fps Magnum round that beat K-frames so savagely it forced the L-frame's creation. The final test cartridge was Remington-UMC 125-grain .357 Magnum, its hollowpoint bullet semi-jacketed with copper in the scalloped configuration Remington made famous. This is the loading one researcher called "the king of the street" back in the day.

On police departments like Indianapolis PD and the surrounding Marion County Sheriff's agency, and state patrols from Kentucky to Indiana to Texas, the 125-grain SJHP Magnum earned an awesome

Mas got best 25-yard accuracy from the 6" with Buffalo Bore Heavy topped with a Barnes bullet in .357 Magnum.

reputation for rapidly stopping violent encounters. Within a law enforcement agencies, the details of each shooting would spread, and create either confidence or insecurity. In this case, it was confidence. More than one Kentucky trooper called that round a "magic bullet" in my presence, and more than one member of the Texas Department of Public Safety was known to speak of the "lightning bolt effect" when the 125-grain .357 Magnum hollowpoint hit a man who was trying to kill a trooper.

Five scallop-jacket bullets produced a 1.90" group, with the best three in 1.40", measured center to center. Bearing in mind that this green-and-white box UMC ammo is Remington's economy line, positioned under their

MORE GUNS HERE

every month!

"standard grade" Express ammo in the green-and-yellow box, this means that we still had a less than X-ring size group at 25 yards with relatively low-priced ammunition. I for one thought this spoke very well for both the Remington-UMC ammo, and the Classic 586 Smith & Wesson revolver with the "service-size" 4" barrel.

Different Results

With the 6" version, I went more toward field Magnum loads on the theory this configuration appeals more to the outdoorsman. However, it's also the barrel length of choice for PPC Distinguished Revolver, and the relatively new bull's-eye revolver games at the National Championships at Camp Perry (their version of Distinguished Revolver, and the Harry Reeves Match). The standard pressure 158-grain .38 Special is the load of choice in all three of those games, so I tried the Winchester roundnose lead again. The most accurate in the 4" 586, it proved the least so in the 6". The five shots went into a 3.00" group, stringing vertically. Four were in 2.80", though the best three measured 1" on the nose, all measurements being taken to the nearest .05". Go figure.

Accurate & Powerful

An outdoorsman looking for .357 Magnum field loads at the Monster Mart will probably end up with one or another flavor of 158-grain semi-jacketed generic softpoint. I chose Federal's low priced Champion round. This delivered a 5-shot group measuring a much more pleasing 1.60", and the best three were under 1" by 15/100". Much better accuracy that I've seen with, for instance, Federal Champion 9mm practice ammo.

In a hollowpoint for hunting, you want something heavier than the 125-grain anti-personnel load, for more penetration. I selected what Buffalo Bore lists as their Heavy 140-grain load, using the all-copper Barnes XPD hollowpoint bullet. Buffalo Bore's headman, Tim Sundles, lists this load at 1,550 fps nominal velocity, and 747 foot-pounds of

The S&W Classic 586 has the current-style cylinder latch, internal lock, and generous speedloader cutout in the stock.

energy at the muzzle. Distinctly louder than the 158-grain .357 Magnum we had just fired, and snappier, these high-tech bullets punched five holes in a 1.45" group, with four of them under an inch at .90" center to center, and the best three in .65". The Buffalo Bore was far and away the most accurate load in the 6" 586 Classic.

There's no better (or safer!) way to test a "combat revolver" than in a "combat shooting match." My plan was to take the 4" 586 Classic to an IDPA event, but a 10-day bout with a bum ankle kept me out of running-and-gunning during the test period. So, I tag-teamed my shooting buddy Herman Gunter, III, who sighted in with just a few gun-loads of Speer Lawman 158-grain +P FMJ ammo, and took it to a 103-shooter match at the First Coast IDPA Club in Jacksonville, Fla.

A regular winner in the revolver divisions there, he captured First Place overall in Stock Service Revolver with the test 586 Classic, drawn from a Galco Yaqui Slide holster and refilled via Safariland Comp III speedloaders, which slid easily and smoothly past the generous cutout that's carved out of the Classic's left stock panel for just that reason.

Herman found the gun smooth and sweet, so much so that Monday morning after the Saturday match, he picked up the telephone and ordered a 586 Classic 4" for himself.

After that, what more can I say? Only this: thanks, Smith & Wesson, for bringing this cool symphony of blue steel and walnut back, to sing its song again for us many fans of traditional double action revolvers. **GUNS**

MODEL 586

MAKER: SMITH & WESSON
2100 ROOSEVELT AVENUE
SPRINGFIELD, MA 01104
(800) 331-0852
WWW.GUNSMAGAZINE.COM/SMITH-WESSON
ACTION TYPE: Double-action, **CALIBER:** .357 Magnum, **CAPACITY:** 6, **BARREL LENGTH:** 4", 6", **OVERALL LENGTH:** 9-1/4" (4"), 11-1/4" (6"), **WEIGHT:** 40.9 ounces (4"), 46.3 ounces (6"), **FINISH:** Blue **SIGHTS:** Adjustable white outline rear, red ramp front, **GRIPS:** Checkered walnut, **PRICE:** $809

CAMPFIRE TALES

BY JOHN TAFFIN

John hopes the "Modelo de Tres Candado" will shoot a little better when he tries bigger bullets.

MODELO DE TRES CANDADO

Spanish Three Lock model.

For more than 100 years Colt and Smith & Wesson competed with each other to see who could come up with the most modern model first. Of course, Colt had started in 1836 with the first truly workable revolver, the percussion Paterson. In 1857, S&W introduced the Model 1, a 7-shot, tip-up .22 which was the first successful cartridge-firing revolver.

Then 1869 saw the first big-bore centerfire sixgun with the S&W .44 American and then Colt countered in 1873 with the first solid frame—the .45 Single Action Army. While Colt was on a roll they went double action with the 1877 Lightning followed by the 1878 Double Action. S&W came-right back in 1881 with the double action version of their single-action New Model 3.

Before the close of the 19th century both companies were ready to look to the future and Colt introduced the Army, Navy and New Service Models,

all double actions with swing-out cylinders. By 1899 S&W had the .38 revolver which would become known as the Military & Police. All of these double actions locked only at the rear of the cylinder, however S&W soon added a second lock under the barrel in front of the ejector rod. At this point only Colt had a big-bore double action revolver with a swing-out cylinder. That was about to change.

The Triple Lock

In late 1907, S&W brought out their first big-bore modern double action

with the New Century. The competition was the Colt New Service which only locked at the rear of the cylinder and had an exposed ejector rod. The New Century was the first of what would become the N-Frames and was chambered in a somewhat modernized version of the excellent .44 Russian cartridge. It was lengthened slightly, about 2/10" to become the .44 Special, however the ballistics stayed basically the same. S&W countered the single lock/exposed ejector rod of the Colt by not only using a lock at the end of the ejector rod but also completely enclosing said rod. However S&W engineers did not stop there.

The New Century, also known as the .44 Hand Ejector First Model, would soon be known to all those who really appreciated it as the Triple Lock. Not only was this new sixgun chambered in a new cartridge using an enlarged Military & Police frame, improved with the use of the shroud to enclose the ejector rod which protected the rod, and also improved the looks of the S&W revolver. And S&W did not stop there, either.

The Triple Lock got its name because of a third lock brilliantly machined in the front of the frame at the yoke and barrel junction to solidly lock the cylinder in place. Even to this day many sixgun lovers will tell you the S&W Triple Lock is the finest revolver ever produced. Alas, it didn't last very long. By 1915 the third lock as well as the enclosed ejector rod were gone. Why did S&W drop the .44 Special Triple Lock? Could it have been too expensive to produce? It can't be for that reason as the Second Model of 1915 only sold for $2 less; for a measly $2 what may have been the finest sixgun ever produced disappeared.

Actually the blame probably rests upon the British. They were at war in Europe and ordered 5,000 Triple Locks chambered in .455 for use in the trench warfare of the time. The precise fitting of that extra third locking feature as well as the enclosed ejector rod was an object of concern when matched up with the muddy trenches. If either the lock or ejector rod housing became caked with mud the revolver would be out of commission until thoroughly cleaned. Removing both features resulted in what they thought was a firearm better suited to the conditions.

Was the third lock even necessary? In their book *S&W 1857-1945*, authors Robert Neal and Roy Jinks say, "Most authorities believe that the third lock provided on this model was put there by S&W more as an example of the ultimate in precision machine work than as a necessary item for extra strength. Even with S&W's normal two locks they provided twice the locking strength of any Colt Hand Ejector arm then produced, along with the extra accuracy of the forward lock in keeping the cylinder in line with the barrel." Why was the third lock there? Because it could be.

The Triple Lock was very popular with peace officers especially those in the Southwest and along our southern border. The pre-WWII S&Ws are usually referred to as having long actions, which were particularly good for shooting double-action style. As new peace officers came along a demand arose for a return to the Triple Lock or at least an enclosed ejector rod housing. S&W did not feel the demand warranted such a return until Wolf & Klar of Fort Worth, Texas, placed an order for 3,500 .44 Specials in 1926. The shrouded ejector rod was back but the Triple Lock was never to be seen again, or at least I thought so. The Triple Lock did come back but not through S&W.

In the August 1979 issue of the *American Rifleman* there is a picture of what was then a new Triple Lock. Built with a 4" barrel with a ventilated rib and smooth Roper-style grips, this Triple Lock was produced by Rossi and chambered in .44 Magnum. No one seems to know whatever happened to it; however, there may have been two of them made.

Spanish Connection

For all these years as far as I knew there were no other Triple Locks ever produced. Then I got a phone call from my good friend J.D. Jones telling me he had found a Modelo Silo Nuevo, a Spanish copy of the Triple Lock or, if you please, a Candida Triple. J.D. was going to buy it himself but figured I would appreciate it much more since

I am so enamored and captivated by the .44 Special. He gave me the name of the Ohio gunshop which I immediately called and for $300 plus shipping I had a Spanish Triple Lock. Where in the world did it come from?

The answer comes from the late Dan Shideler. We all know, if we've been around handguns very long, that Spain had been copying both S&W and Colt revolvers since the frontier days. This particular revolver came from Trocaola, Aranzabal y Cia (or TAC) of Eibar, Spain. This company began in 1905 and by the time of the Spanish Civil War in 1936 was out of business. Unlike many other Spanish revolvers there is no way these could be classified as junk and in fact Great Britain not only purchased .455 Triple Locks from S&W for use in WWI they also bought Webley copies from TAC.

The original S&W Triple Lock was never adopted as US military issue, however the Spanish version is officially known as the Modelo Militar. The Spanish considered revolvers with adjustable sights as target guns while fixed-sighted versions were considered military-style revolvers. TAC was obviously proud of their "Candado Triple" as they made no attempt to pass it off as a S&W. Many of those other S&W-style revolvers had such a misleading mark on the barrel as "For the SMITH & WESSON cartridge." Many years ago, I answered an ad in the local paper and went to look at a pair of "Smith & Wessons" for sale. When I told the seller they were not S&Ws but actually Spanish copies, she became very indignant and practically threw me out of the house. However, the following week they were advertised in the paper once again for a lot less money.

Will the real Smith & WessonTriple Lock please stand up? It's the bottom one (above). Only the front sight placement is a giveaway. The third lock (below) can be seen at the front of the yoke and at the back of the ejector rod shroud.

My new Triple Lock seems to be very well-made, looks exactly like a 6-1/2" fixed-sight S&W Triple Lock and is finished in bright blue with excellent checkered walnut stocks. Case colors on hammer and trigger are both still quite brilliant. The only down side is the fact the chamber mouths are well over size at .437". The only loads I had made up for test-firing with bullets even close were .432"; next spring I will try some larger bullets and hope I can do better than the 2" groups I am now getting.

While there is no attempt to pass this off as a genuine S&W it is somewhat humorous to read what it says on the barrel. On the left side we find: "FOR 44 SPECIAL AND U.S. SERVICE CTG" (I don't know of any US service cartridge which will fit in a .44 Special). Then on the top we find: "BEST AMERICAN CARTRIDGES ARE THOSE THAT FIT BEST THE TAC REVOLVER." At least they're not warning labels! At my age discovering something new is pretty rare. This Candado Triple from Spain is worth much more than the price of admission to me. Thanks J.D. [GUNS]

HAMMER OR... "-LESS?"

Debate rages over which is better: "hammerless" or "thumb-cocking" S&W J-frame models.

Grant Cunningham with the J-frame he feels is the smoothest, the Centennial.

Along about 1950, S&W introduced what would become the most popular concealment revolver in the world in the J-frame .38 Special. The original Chiefs Special had a conventional external hammer and could be fired double or single action. In 1952, firearms authority Rex Applegate convinced S&W to make the same gun with the sleek internal hammer design of the old top-break New Departure Safety Hammerless revolver of 1887. Since it was introduced in the year Smith & Wesson was celebrating its 100th anniversary format, this "hammerless Chief Special" was dubbed the Centennial. In 1955 came a third variation, the Bodyguard. This was the company's answer to the removable hammer shroud that had grown in popularity since their archrival Colt introduced it for their small-frame snubs in 1950. On the Bodyguard, the shroud was integral to the frame and looked sleeker, but still left a nub of hammer spur exposed for single-action cocking.

We all have our preferences. For my needs, I'm inclined toward the Centennial hammerless. Here's why.

The "hammerless" model's most obvious advantage is its snag-free profile. The great police weapons authority of the past, Paul B. Weston, described the conventional hammer spur as found on the Chief Special as a "fish-hook" that tended to snag on clothing and stall a fast draw. Even so, bobbing the Chief's hammer can eliminate the snags, or choose the Bodyguard which has a smooth-drawing shape fans affectionately call "the hump-back."

One thing the Centennial offers that its siblings can't is a higher grasp. The shape of its frame allows the shooter's hand to get all the way up that high "horn" of its backstrap. This puts the bore axis proportionally lower to the wrist than either of the other styles, and affords significant leverage to the shooter. Muzzle rise is less, allowing a faster rate of accurate rapid fire. This is a very significant advantage to the Centennial, and is the main reason I so often carry one while my Chiefs and my Bodyguard lie neglected in the gun safe.

The rationale of the dual single-action/double-action capability is the option of cocking the hammer for an easy single-action trigger pull, "for a precision shot." The thing

Note the higher hold afforded by Centennial (right), which lowers the bore axis more than the Chief (left).

of it is, "precision shots" are rarely taken with these pocket-sized guns, which are generally seen as reactive close-quarters weapons. Double action is faster. If you do need a precision shot, a slightly slower roll of the double-action trigger will get you there. Double action also gives a shorter hammer fall, improving lock time, and probably more important, doesn't require you to break your hold and thumb your hammer back.

There's also the matter of cases where the cocked revolver went off unintentionally, with fatal results (New York vs. Frank Magliato, for example) or when it was falsely alleged that this had happened, to create an element of negligence after a justified shooting (Florida vs. Luis Alvarez, to name one). Both avenues of legal attack against you are road blocked with a gun that can *only* be fired double action. And that's before we get into de-cocking a revolver that has been cocked by sweaty, trembling human hands in a high-stress situation.

My friend Grant Cunningham, master wheelgun-smith and author of

Centennial (Model 642, left) can only be fired double action, while Chief Special (Model 60, right) can be cocked to fire single action if desired.

the excellent *Gun Digest Book of the Revolver,* writes the following at his blog at www.grantcunningham.com: "… the Centennial models simply have better actions! The enclosed hammer Centennial models have slightly different sear geometry than do the exposed hammer models, which gives them a pull that is more even— more linear—than the models with hammer spurs. For the savvy shooter it's a noticeable difference, making the Centennial a bit easier to shoot well."

Grant continues, "The Centennials also have one less part than the other models: since they have no exposed hammer, they don't have (nor do they need) the hammer-block safety common to all other 'J' frames. That part, which is quite long and rides in a close-fitting slot machined into the sideplate, is difficult to make perfectly smooth. Even in the best-case scenario, it will always add just a bit of friction to the action. Not having the part to begin with gives the Centennial a 'leg up' in action feel. (In fact, at one point in time a common part of an 'action job' was to remove this safety, in the same way that some 'gunsmiths' would remove the firing-pin block on a Colt Series 80 auto pistol. Today we know better!) So, if your criterion is action quality, the choice is clear: the enclosed hammer Centennial series is your best bet!" GUNS

S&W
2100 ROOSEVELT AVE.
SPRINGFIELD, MA 01104
(800) 331-0852
WWW.GUNSMAGAZINE.COM/SMITH-WESSON

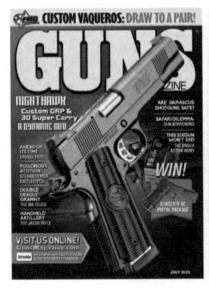

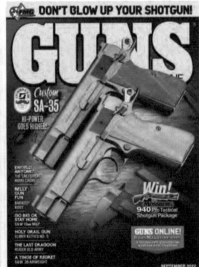

.22 MAG VS. .38 SPECIAL

VELOCITY VS. BARREL LENGTH	BARREL LENGTH			
CARTRIDGE/BULLET WEIGHT (GRS.)	1⅞"	3½"	5½"	20"
Hornady Critical Defense/45	1,001	1,137	1,298	1,680
Speer Gold Dot/40	1,086	1,252	1,385	1,850
Winchester HP/40	1,084	1,243	1,351	1,813
Remington HP/40	1,016	1,205	1,365	1,852
Remington Premier/33	1,095	1,277	1,473	1,918
Winchester Supreme/30	1,305	1,495	1,770	2,190

(Velocities in fps, average of 10 rounds.)

YES? NO? MAYBE?

Smith & Wesson has a couple of very light J-frames in .22 Magnum. The model 351PD with 1⅞" barrel weighs just over 12 ounces loaded. Compared to similar .38 Special/.357 Magnum models they offer increased cartridge capacity (seven rounds vs. five), along with much lighter recoil and a milder report. The theory, and it's not an unreasonable one, is it's better to hit with a .22 Magnum than to flinch and miss with a .38 or .357.

As a small-game/varmint cartridge in a rifle the .22 Magnum is one of my favorites. There's no questioning the round's effectiveness in a rifle. What about in a handgun? Both Hornady and Speer have .22 Magnum loads intended specifically for short barrels. The Hornady Critical Defense round has a 45-gr. bullet rated at 1,000 fps. The Speer Gold Dot short-barrel/personal-protection load has a 40-gr. bullet rated at 1,050 fps. These velocities are from sub-2" barrels. Both loads delivered the advertised velocity in our tests. I did find a 3½" barrel provides a pretty good velocity increase, from around 150 to 200 additional fps. Check out the chart. I wouldn't mind seeing S&W offer the option of a 3 – 3½" barrel on the 351PD.

I didn't have a 2" .22 LR on hand but did run some high-speed .22 LR (36-gr. HP) through a couple of 4" revolvers (S&W 34 and Ruger SP-101). Velocities were around 200 – 250 fps slower than those of the .22 Magnum in similar barrel length.

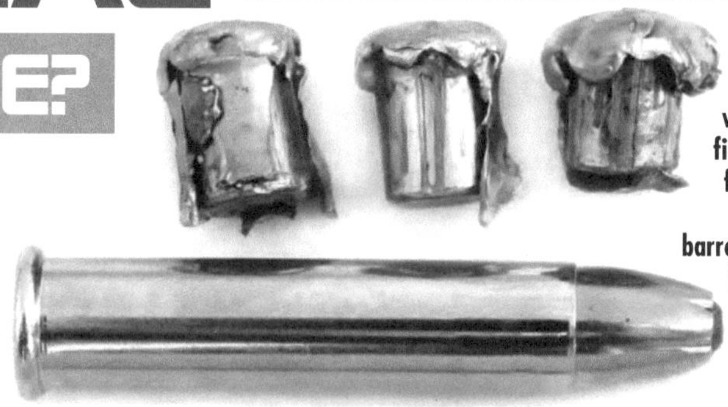

Hornady Critical Defense .22 Magnum with 45-gr. FTX bullet, fired into paraffin block from (L-R) 1⅞" barrel, 3½" barrel and 5½" barrel. The Speer load performed similarly, with both loads holding together well.

CONSISTENT & RELIABLE

I've read these two loads from Hornady and Speer use a powder especially suited to short barrels. Could be, though velocities were no better than other loads using similar bullet weights. Personally, I don't think the magic, if any, is in the powder; it's in the bullet. The bullets appear to be designed to provide expansion, weight retention and good penetration even at moderate velocities. To get some sense of bullet performance I fired them from various barrel lengths into paraffin blocks. I won't pretend this is as informative as using ballistic gelatin but it is at least consistent.

Both the Hornady FTX and Speer Gold Dot bullets performed splendidly in this medium. Even from the short barrel there was bullet expansion, increasing as velocities increased in longer barrels. Penetration was consistently around 5" to 6" regardless of barrel length. It seemed, as velocity increased, greater expansion slowed bullets down more quickly, and they ended up with about the same penetration as slower bullets.

The Gold Dots seemed to expand a bit more violently, possibly because they are a bit lighter and faster, or maybe Speer is using softer jacket/core material. The Gold Dots also tended to lose a bit more weight as velocity increased.

My impression is this ammunition, from both makers, is superlative in quality. Both loads gave consistent velocities and both were extremely accurate. In a rifle they equaled the accuracy of the best load I've ever used, the Winchester 33-gr. Supreme. There's also a perception rimfire priming is inherently less reliable than centerfire primers. While I've had occasional misfires with .22 LR ammunition I have never had a misfire with .22 Magnum ammunition, over the course of firing many thousands of rounds.

A QUANDRY?

These .22 Magnum loads were made specifically for short barrels, though they performed splendidly in longer barrels as well, such as the 3½" barrel on my old S&W 51 Kit Gun.

So, do I carry a .22 Magnum handgun for personal defense? No, and for the same reason I don't carry a .32 or .380. For me, at least, there is no downside to using a .38 Special or 9mm (both +P). I have compact handguns available for these cartridges, easy to carry and conceal, and I can shoot them as fast and accurately as I can a .22. I often have a .22 Magnum revolver along during outdoor activities, but for small-game or varmint shooting rather than defense.

Is a short-barreled .22 Magnum as effective as a .38 Special or 9mm? No it is not. Is it better than a .22 LR? Definitely, with 20- to 25-percent greater velocity and greater ignition reliability. How about compared to a .380? There I'm on the fence. The best .380 loads provide similar velocities, with heavier bullets. On the other hand I prefer revolvers for pocket carry. The 12-ounce S&W 351 I borrowed from a friend is a mighty appealing little revolver!

S&W's M&P22

Note the collar on the muzzle of the M&P22's barrel, which protects a threaded portion of the barrel.

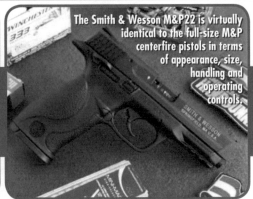

The Smith & Wesson M&P22 is virtually identical to the full-size M&P centerfire pistols in terms of appearance, size, handling and operating controls.

Smith & Wesson's M&P22 is a high quality pistol, a fine choice for plinking, small game hunting, casual target shooting and training. It's particularly suitable for shooters of the very popular M&P centerfire series. It's not quite a dead-ringer for the full-size centerfire model, but comes pretty close. Weight empty is similar to a full-size 9mm (both around 24 ounces). Loaded, obviously a magazine loaded with 17 9mm cartridges weighs more than one with 12 rounds of .22 LR. The MP22 doesn't have the interchangeable backstraps of the centerfire version.

But operating controls are in the same place, trigger pull is very similar, and the .22 even has the accessory frame rail for practice with lights/lasers. The magazine release button is reversible. The .22 version also has the same high quality components and workmanship as the originals.

Carl Walther in Germany makes the M&P .22. It has an ambidextrous thumb safety, which no doubt helped earn the points needed to be approved for import. The centerfire version is available both with and without a manual safety. A law enforcement buddy kindly loaned me his M&P 9mm duty gun so I could shoot the two side by side. His pistol has a manual safety, and allowed me to get a feel for shooting both guns.

500 Rounds Later

The M&P22 magazine holds 12 cartridges, with a 10-round magazine available for states that limit capacity. One magazine is provided, and for a plinking/hunting .22 I can get by with one magazine. For training purposes, a shooter really should have two magazines for use in reloading drills. Currently, extra magazines in either 10- or 12-round versions are listed as being available at $32.

I really enjoyed shooting the M&P22, and running around 500 rounds through it — mainly CCI MiniMags, some Federal and Winchester match, plus value pack cartridges from Remington and Winchester. This was without disassembling for cleaning, though I did use a boresnake at about 250 rounds. I had one failure to feed (frankly, not uncommon with a .22 auto); otherwise function was flawless. Trigger pull was consistent and fairly smooth with weight-of-pull at 6¾ pounds.

Disassembly for routine cleaning is fast and simple. Remove the magazine and check the chamber to be certain the firearm is unloaded. With the slide forward, rotate the takedown lever to point down and pull it about ½" out from the frame. Then retract the slide, lift the rear of slide, and move it forward off the frame. There's no need to pull the trigger on the empty chamber prior to takedown. In fact, the hammer should remain cocked throughout.

FINAL COMPARISONS

The M&P22 barrel comes threaded to accept an adapter, so a suppressor can be fitted. As delivered, the threaded portion has a thread protector tightly screwed in place. Those who don't use a suppressor can just leave it as-is. For those who do, a wrench to remove the thread protector collar is provided.

The rear sight is adjustable for elevation, and both the front and rear sight can be moved in their dovetail cuts to adjust windage. As delivered, the pistol on consignment shot several inches to the left. The front sight was off to the right rather than centered in the slide, so I used it to adjust for windage. Groups (five shots at 25 yards) averaged a whisker unde 2".

Compared to the 9mm, trigger pull was very similar in terms of both weight of pull and trigger movement to fire and reset. While a .22 understudy is a useful training aid, it obviously is cannot completely substitute for centerfire training, especially in terms of learning recoil management and timing.

On the other hand, a .22's lack of recoil lets the shooter concentrate on technique, with less chance of learning bad habits (such as flinching and blinking), and at considerably lower cost. Searching on the Internet I see 9mm practice ammunition priced around $12 for 50, or 24¢ a shot. Yet, .22 LR ammo can be found for around 5¢ to 7¢ a shot. The savings from four or five bricks of .22 ammo would pay for the gun, and teach a lot about shooting in the process.

Top is a full-size S&W M&P 9mm, bottom the M&P22.

The M&P22 lacks the tritium night sights and interchangeable backstraps of the 9mm, and adds a magazine safety.

THE INSIDER ™

ROY HUNTINGTON

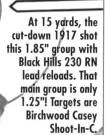

New S&W 1917 on top with Roy's snubbie project gun below. He built it on a Brazilian contract 1917 in the early 1980s and found it shoots as well as the new one.

At 15 yards, the cut-down 1917 shot this 1.85" group with Black Hills 230 RN lead reloads. That main group is only 1.25"! Targets are Birchwood Casey Shoot-In-C.

BIG-BORE CUT DOWN

Maybe a benefit of the shallow rifling is it doesn't tend to throw birdshot all over. The 3" gun delivered this tight group from a CCI .45 ACP shot round at about 3 yards. Perfect snake, rat or who knows what medicine?

I n the late 1970s I spotted a cut-down S&W 1917 .45 ACP revolver in a gun book that really caught my eye. This was long before there were any factory short-barreled big-bore revolvers, so if you wanted such a thing, you had to make one. Someone had taken a beater military 1917, cut the barrel to about 2.5", then hard-chromed it. They put a set of those early Pachmayr rubber grips on it, and to my eyes, had a perfect serious big-bore revolver for self-defense. Plus, it just looked cool. But in those days, even beater 1917s were hard to come by, and I moved on in life without making that dream come true.

Then the angels sang, and in the early 1980s, someone advertising in

Shotgun News started to bring in Brazilian S&W 1917 contract revolvers. As I recall, they were made by S&W for Brazil in the 1930s, but don't hold me to that. They were cheap too, around $150. They didn't "grade" them so you took your chances. I bought three. One was fairly nice, one was okay and one was pretty tired, with pitting on the cylinder and outside of the barrel. But, the bore was shiny and the action decent. Looking them over, I decided my gunsmithing skills warranted I experiment on the beater — and save the better ones for later projects.

While the gun giving me the idea had a 2.5" barrel, it also meant a good deal of work to make that happen. After measuring, I found if I nipped the barrel off right in front of the front ejector rod locking bolt housing (on the underside of the barrel), it would measure right at 3" to the rear of the forcing cone. Good enough for me, and saved me no-end of work shortening the ejector rod, welding the housing back on and such. A minute or two with a hacksaw and the "pocket" .45 started to happen.

I've been a life-long hobby gunsmith and have amassed a good selection of tools. Even back then, I had a bead-

blaster, jewelling tools, drill press, belt sander/grinder and plenty of other hand tools. So, with some judicious thought, and even more careful handwork, it came together. The front sight was a problem, but I scrounged a generic one, filed/sanded it to fit the barrel contour, then silver-soldered it to the barrel. I also put a screw in it to fill the screw hole, just for looks. I also carefully widened the rear groove, squaring it up to fit the front blade width.

I slicked up the action (note the amateur jewelling on the hammer and trigger ... just had to try that), used different grits of wet or dry paper to work out some of the pitting (but most were too deep so stopped before I got into trouble), then bead-blasted the frame and parts. I was experimenting with doing Parkerizing then, thanks to chemicals from Brownells (it's actually easy to do — you should try it), so the blasted gun went into the pot. About ten minutes later everything was grey.

After reassembling it I hefted it and thought, "Hey, this is just as I imagined it would feel." I opted to leave the smaller standard grips, but when fired, it does tend to bite at the web of your hand. After some test firing and lowering the front sight some, my new .45 ACP pocket-pounder was done.

While you can shoot .45 ACP without moon clips, it's easier to use Auto Rim cases or moon clips so you can eject the empties.

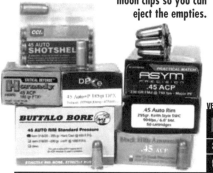

LOAD	185 Hornady FTX	Buff. Bore 255 LSWC AR	DT 255 LSWC AR	CorBon DPX 185	ASYM 230 FMC	Blk.Hills 230 LRN
VELOCITY IN FPS						
3" BBL	919	841	687	977	716	846
5.5" BBL	977	887	761	1,049	727	877

I promptly gave it to my old friend, Don Hacklander (owner of San Diego Police Equipment Company), who needed it worse than I did. He "guarded" it for me for the next 28 years or so, until only recently gifting it back to me when I told him how much I wished that old gun was still around. "Hell, I still have it. It's been my bed-table gun, I'd be proud to give it to you." Just like that my first big-bore project gun came home.

I dug it out for this column and fired it a bit, along with a brand new S&W 1917 (5.5" barrel). I honestly forgot how good that little-big gun shot. I'm not sure why, but for some reason, it shoots under 2" at 15 yards all the time, and some groups chase 1.25"! The new gun actually shot about the same, with a 1.65" being one of the better groups. Interestingly enough, after firing six loads through them, an old box of Black Hills 230-gr. lead RN reloads delivered the winning groups. I've often heard 1917s don't like lead due to the shallow rifling in the bores, but these two liked it just fine. This also allowed me to compare some velocities of .45 ACP loads from a shorter-barreled revolver and a longer one. I thought we'd learn something, but actually the difference was barely noteworthy.

If I did this project again I'd round the butt, de-horn the edges, bevel the front of the cylinder, nip the hammer spur off and maybe do a Hi-Viz front sight. Oh, and some different grips would help with that biting in the web of my hand. If you have the urge, and some basic tools, don't be afraid to tackle a project like this yourself. But don't try anything you're not confident you have the skills to manage. And practice on old broken guns first! As Clint Eastwood said, "A man's gotta' know his limitations."

ADD IT UP

473,479
Semi-auto production in 2010 by Ruger.

352,969
Semi-auto production in 2010 by S&W.

266,316
Semi-auto production in 2010 by SIG.

85,991
Semi-auto production in 2010 by Kimber.

29,331
Semi-auto production in 2010 by Colt.

2,285
Semi-auto production in 2010 by Wilson's Gun Shop.

1,876
Semi-auto production in 2010 by Ed Brown Products.

2,817,377
Total handguns (all types) produced by all makers in 2010.

...friend and contributor to our magazines, Peter T. Tomaras, has published *Resistors*, his action/adventure novel featuring an erstwhile Huey door gunner and federal air marshal who entangles himself with skyjackers, CIA operatives, Palestinian terrorists, an Aussie mercenary, the Israeli Navy and two women (one a covert commando) in Cyprus, Crete and the States. Read about multiple firearms and other goodies, and locales stretching from Sparta, WI to the Middle East. A real page-turner! Well done, Peter! Check out *Resistors* as a paperback or an e-book at *www.amazon.com*

That's Chuck in the middle, with other battle-weary Marines on an island in the Pacific.

MEMORIES OF CHUCK

You might remember us featuring Tom Ables an issue or two ago posing at his battle station aboard a battleship; first as a young sailor and then, recently, some 65 years later, in the same spot aboard the U.S.S. Alabama, now a museum. Tom's family has a history of service, and we wanted to note with honor the passing of Tom's 91-year-old brother, Chuck. According to Tom: *"He was my mentor, coach and inspiration. An Eagle Scout in his youth, Chuck joined the Marines right after Pearl Harbor and was in all those famous island battles, from Guadalcanal to Iwo Jima. He never came home until the war ended. After the war, Chuck joined the San Diego Park and Recreation Department where his design skills resulted in wonderful parks people still enjoy today. My favorite, which I treasure every time I drive by, is the very special Mission Bay Park. When Tom Brokaw created the absolutely correct term, 'The Greatest Generation' I always wondered how it was he knew my brother Chuck, who personified that generation."* Chuck was buried with appropriate Marine Corps honors at Fort Rosecrans. Thanks for telling us Tom, and thanks to Chuck for his heroic service. Rest easy old Marine.

BEAR OPS BOLD ACTION KNIFE

This is a genuine, 100 percent made in the USA knife, done-up by Bear in its plant in Jacksonville, Ala. So, if that's important to you, there you go. With a 3" blade of premium-quality CPM-S30V stainless steel (.115" thick), it's heat-treated to a Rockwell

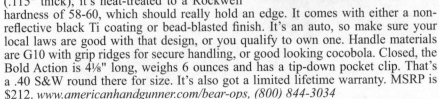

hardness of 58-60, which should really hold an edge. It comes with either a non-reflective black Ti coating or bead-blasted finish. It's an auto, so make sure your local laws are good with that design, or you qualify to own one. Handle materials are G10 with grip ridges for secure handling, or good looking cocobola. Closed, the Bold Action is 4⅛" long, weighs 6 ounces and has a tip-down pocket clip. That's a .40 S&W round there for size. It's also got a limited lifetime warranty. MSRP is $212. *www.americanhandgunner.com/bear-ops*, (800) 844-3034

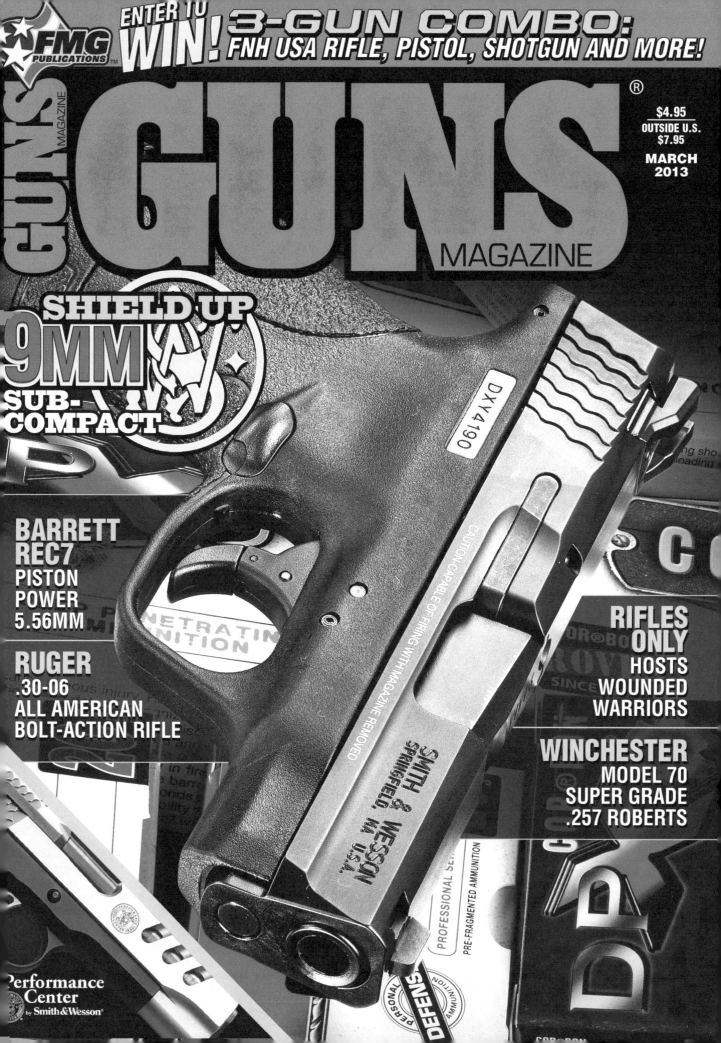

ENTER TO WIN! 3-GUN COMBO: FNH USA RIFLE, PISTOL, SHOTGUN AND MORE!

FMG PUBLICATIONS™

GUNS MAGAZINE®

$4.95
OUTSIDE U.S. $7.95
MARCH 2013

SHIELD UP 9MM SUB-COMPACT

BARRETT REC7 PISTON POWER 5.56MM

RUGER .30-06 ALL AMERICAN BOLT-ACTION RIFLE

RIFLES ONLY HOSTS WOUNDED WARRIORS

WINCHESTER MODEL 70 SUPER GRADE .257 ROBERTS

CAUTION-CAPABLE OF FIRING WITH MAGAZINE REMOVED

SMITH & WESSON SPRINGFIELD, MA U.S.A.

Performance Center™ by Smith & Wesson®

THIS 9MM IS "JUST RIGHT!"

JOHN CONNOR

SMITH & WESSON'S NEW SUBCOMPACT M&P SHIELD

You remember the fairy tale, Goldilocks and 3 Bears right? Goldilocks invades the home of three innocent bears. She tries out their porridge, chairs and beds, finding two out of three of each too hot or too big, too cold or too small, but one is just right. Today, she would be busted for burglary and vandalism, but that's another story. Anyway, that was my impression the first time I picked up our test-and-eval S&W's Shield 9mm: Not too small, not too big, but *just right.* It snuggles nicely in a coat pocket, but shoots like a belt-gun.

It's no secret that I don't like little-bitty guns, especially the 9.5-ounce teensy .380s. They almost seem alive as they squiggle around in my oversized mitts,

and when I present 'em, it's like I'm pointing my truck key. Then comes their *bite* when I pull the trigger, which seems out of any reasonable proportion to their terminal effect.

I realize they fill a niche, and I often carry one as a backup. I have no illusions about the .380 ACP cartridge. It ain't a .45, but I wouldn't want a 10-year-old boy thrusting a sharpened stick into my gut or face, either—especially if he does it a half-dozen times, as hard as he can. Still, I would be more comforted with the power of a 9mm Parabellum round, and a frame I can get a firm and certain grip on. I've tried a handful of undersized 9s and found them lacking in reliability, pointability, and/or stability in the hand. The Shield fills the bill for me beautifully, and it might do the same for you.

NEXT GEN

This latest addition to the "next-generation" M&P family is S&W's smallest to date, and the Shield faithfully replicates their proven mechanics and best features, just in a coat-pocket-friendly size. No parts are interchangeable with the other family members, and the Shield really had to be reengineered to assure reliability and longevity using a powerful round in such a small format. It wasn't just a matter of reducing all dimensions. Let's do a walk-around, OK?

UNDER THE HOOD

Despite its diminutive dimensions, the Shield's sights are big-gun size, highly visible 3-dot types set in dovetails, and dot-to-dot sight radius is maximized

WARNING: Improperly hand-loade
loading should only be attempted afte
M&P
9 SHIELD
20
CARTRIDGES
ammunition ca
attempted after
SAFE
FENSE
AMMUNITION
NETRAT
MUNITIO

WWW.GUNSMAGAZINE.COM • MARCH 2013

THIS 9MM IS "JUST RIGHT!"

SMITH & WESSON'S NEW SUBCOMPACT M&P SHIELD

Take a Shield to the range and you'll have plenty of volunteers to "help" with testing. Here, Ken, a gunsmith, declares it "Sweet, smooth and straight-shooting! Can I buy this one?" *NO!*

for its 6.1" overall length. Many sights on small pistols are miniscule and kind of an afterthought; not these. They're low profile and anti-snag, too. If I can keep this sample, I may install a bright fiber optic front sight, but the white dot is more than adequate.

Both the slide and the 3.1" barrel are stainless steel with a tough, corrosion-resistant Melonite finish. The signature M&P wavy slide serrations provide excellent control without being tough on fingers or clothing. The recoil spring is a dual-captive-type wrapped around a real steel guide rod, so you get staged spring pressure in just the amount needed at the right points in cycling, and, you don't have to worry about "springs-'n'-things" rocketing around the room when disassembling the piece.

There's a loaded-chamber indicator "peephole" in the barrel hood, so you *should* be able to look down and see the brass glint of a chambered round. Personally, if I peep and see brass, I assume a round is chambered. If I don't see brass, I assume a round *might* be chambered! In my book, there's only one way to know for sure….

The frame is Smith & Wesson's proven polymer with internal chassis design, resembling other M&Ps in

Where the Shield shines: Six shots in under 6 seconds (above), 1-handed at 7 yards, using Hornady TAP FPD 124-grain ammo.

general shape with excellent surface texturing. A singular departure is the lack of interchangeable backstrap inserts. Smith & Wesson did this to keep the width and overall grip circumference as compact as possible. The frame is only 0.95" at its widest, but we had shooters with a broad range of hand sizes report it provided a very sure and comfortable grip.

A full set of controls is on the left side, including a takedown lever, slide lock, and a thumb safety. The safety, I'm glad to say, is just prominent enough to engage/ disengage with certainty, but not exaggerated. I suspect many concealed carriers will elect not to engage the thumb safety except in static or storage situations, relying on the trigger safety and the relatively long, heavy trigger pull—but it's nice to have on tap. None of these controls present potential snag problems, and all are suitably grooved.

The magazine release, like the manual safety, is thankfully not too big or too small either. I'd call it "appropriately prominent" without being "protuberant." We didn't experience any surprise mag releases from incidental handling, but when properly punched, the release dropped mags reliably. The magazines themselves—you get *two* with each Shield—appear well made, and we had no magazine issues. One mag, a 7-rounder, fits flush with the frame base, while the

The S&W Shield disassembles easily into its major components. The captive recoil spring ensures you won't be chasing springs around the room.

M&P9 SHIELD

MAKER: SMITH & WESSON
2100 ROOSEVELT AVE.
SPRINGFIELD, MA 01104
(800) 331-0852
WWW.GUNSMAGAZINE.COM/SMITH-WESSON

Caliber: 9mm Parabellum, **Magazine capacity:** 7 and 8, **Barrel Length:** 3.1", **Overall length:** 6.1", **Overall height:** 4.6", **Frame width:** 0.95", **Slide width:** 0.98", **Weight:** 19 ounces, **Price:** $449

Full-size 3-dot sights are provided. The rear sight is nicely sculpted to decrease snag points for concealed carry.

second, my top choice, is an 8-rounder with a "sleeve" which melds with the grip frame. Folks with smaller hands can get a good grip with the 7-rounder, while those with big paws like mine will be tickled to get a full 3-fingered grip with the 8-rounder. The bigger mag adds less than 1/2" to the Shield's 4.5 height, but the extra bit of grip pays big dividends in control.

The segmented trigger with its incorporated safety is pretty broad and comfortable. The pull is longish, as is appropriate for a pocket pistol, and the weight measured in at slightly less than 7 pounds. After the takeup, the break is firm and fairly crisp, and the reset is tactile and audible, which will help a trained trigger finger better manage rapid fire. If you're not tuned in to managing the reset, you can just "roll" the trigger as you would with a double-action revolver and you'll be just fine. It's definitely not a target trigger, but it's not supposed to be, and as defensive triggers go it's excellent.

Disassembly is "typical M&P pistol," meaning it's easy and non-complex, with no "wiggle it this way, not that way" elements, and cleaning is a snap. I recommend lubing it according to the manual, just a tad heavier on the slide rails and barrel at first, during break-in shooting. The instructions are well written, with no 2-semester course needed.

Our test Shield is a 9mm; a .40 S&W model is forthcoming. Smith & Wesson recommends initial shooting of the Shield be done with the lowest power, lowest velocity, lightest weight slug available in the weapon's chambering. We plunged right in with full-power loads in a range of weights from 95 to 147 grains. They further caution that +P ammo may affect wear characteristics or exceed the margin of safety, and +P+ ammo must *not* be used in Smith & Wesson firearms. There are lots of excellent 9mm "standard" loads out there!

IT'S RANGE TIME!

Simply put, shooting the Shield was pure pleasure, and it won a lot of instant fans on the range, me being the first. It points naturally, handles recoil better than

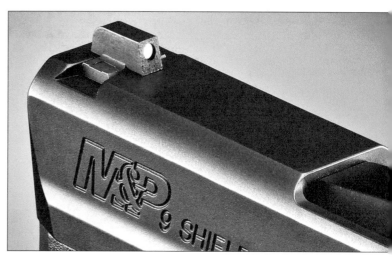

The front sight (above) is set into a dovetail and is adjustable for windage if necessary. The Shield gives a good easy to pick up sight picture for such a compact pistol. The 7-round magazine reduces the overall height (below) yet still allows for most hands to get a firm grip. Note the magazine release button is big and recessed slightly so it is not one easily pressed by mistake.

9MM FACTORY AMMO PERFORMANCE

LOAD (BRAND, BULLET WEIGHT, TYPE)	VELOCITY (FPS)	GROUP SIZE (INCHES)
Hornady 115 Critical Defense FTX	1,014	1.72
Speer 147 Gold Dot HP	924	1.58
CorBon 95 DPX	1,292	2.29

Notes: Hornady's Critical Defense FTX is another solid deep hollowpoint with a sure-feeding synthetic tip producing excellent penetration through typical barrier materials while assuring rapid expansion in tissue. Speer's street-proven 147-grain Gold Dot ammo is extremely accurate. It produced the most felt recoil but was still highly controllable. The CorBon 95-grain DPX load is spanky-new and a real zipper. Very comfortable to shoot, it's a Barnes all-copper solid, with a radical deep hollowpoint—a very promising round. Five-shot groups were measured 8 feet from the muzzle with a ProChrono Chronograph from Competition Electronics.

I had any reason to expect, and does *not* show the slightest tendency to want to fly out of your hand. Cycling was smooth and sure, and its overall performance and feel promotes confidence.

We experienced one failure to go completely into battery with the first round of a magazine upon release of the slide, then two more failures to go into battery upon cycling. All three occurred in the first three magazine-loads fired. After that, there were no failures or malfunctions of any kind during the remainder of testing— over 300 rounds. My conclusion is, break the Shield in right, stretch its legs and clear its throat, and it should deliver fine reliability. If I can buy this one, I'll bet my life on it with confidence.

The Shield is clearly a defensive pistol intended for use in encounters, which tend to be close, fast and violent. In the gravest extreme, it is more likely to be employed at 10" to 10 feet than at 7 to 10 yards. Still, we had to check its accuracy under polite social conditions, which we did at 10 yards, using a 2-handed hold, seated, with arms rested on a counter. If you're threatened by stationary goblins the size of a beer bottle, and you can sit comfortably and rest

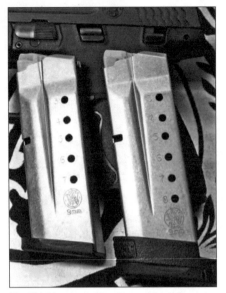

The Shield comes with a 7-round flush-fit mag (left) and an 8-round extended mag (right).

your hands on a solid surface, your odds of survival are terrific! But, at least it proves the Shield can deliver accurate fire.

I'm much more impressed with the results we got shooting the Shield free-standing, 1-handed, cadenced at about one shot per 3/4 second to 1 second, at a range of 7 yards. We wanted to do closer, faster work, but a surly Range

Safety Officer was hovering, waiting to smack us with a 2-pound Range Rules book. Strings of five and six shots ran from 4" to 5-1/2" at 15 yards, similar strings stayed well within 10 disks. That's very good gunfighting performance from a little 19-ounce pistol.

The real character of the Shield becomes evident when you present it from concealment and rapidly engage multiple targets at close range. Its combination of grip ergonomics, natural pointing, quick sighting, propensity to allow good trigger control, minimizing felt recoil effects, and ability to recover and reengage on targets tells the tale—and it's a very good tale indeed.

Smith & Wesson wisely distributed molds on a confidential basis for the Shield to many holster makers long before its announced debut, so there's no lack of carry options available. LaserMax jumped right in with a variant of their sleek, ultralight frame-mounted CenterFire laser. Sadly, Shields are very hard to find as I write this in October. Smith & Wesson had produced a good stockpile of Shields before the first ad ran, but demand has so far outstripped supply that they're scrambling to fill back-orders. Best advice? Get on a list; it will be worth the wait. Connor *OUT*

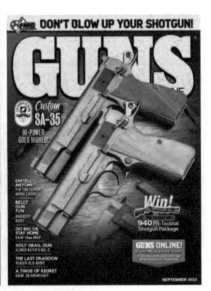

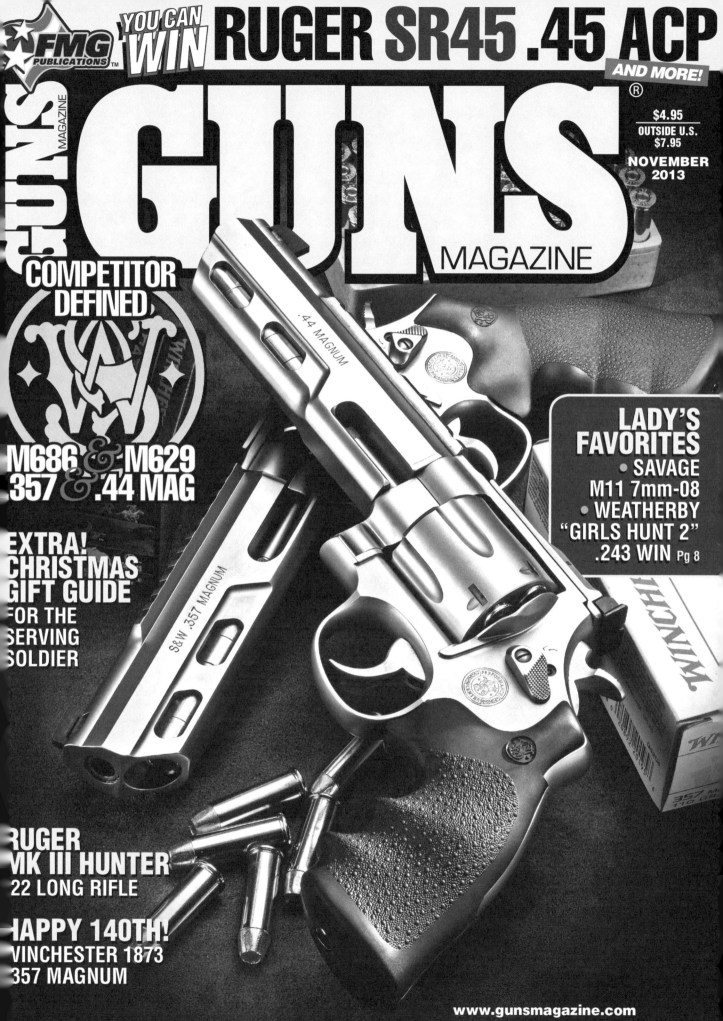

YOU CAN WIN **RUGER SR45 .45 ACP** *AND MORE!*

GUNS MAGAZINE

GUNS
MAGAZINE

®

$4.95
OUTSIDE U.S.
$7.95

NOVEMBER
2013

COMPETITOR DEFINED

M686 & M629
357 & .44 MAG

EXTRA! CHRISTMAS GIFT GUIDE
FOR THE SERVING SOLDIER

.44 MAGNUM

S&W .357 MAGNUM

LADY'S FAVORITES
- SAVAGE M11 7mm-08
- WEATHERBY "GIRLS HUNT 2" .243 WIN Pg 8

WINCHE
357 M

RUGER MK III HUNTER
22 LONG RIFLE

HAPPY 140TH!
WINCHESTER 1873
357 MAGNUM

www.gunsmagazine.com

M629 COMPETITORS M686

THESE VERSATILE, ACCURATE, RELIABLE REVOLVERS ARE AN EXCELLENT CHOICE FOR TARGET SHOOTING OR HUNTING.

MARK HAMPTON
PHOTOS: ROBBIE BARRKMAN

It seems whenever life floats leisurely by and the years seem to pass all too quickly, our ideas and opinions about things sometimes adjust themselves. What was a strong belief regarding certain firearms and cartridges long ago, now appear in a different light. Like many of you, especially those of us with a touch of silver in what hair we have remaining, I appreciate truly fine guns. That wasn't always the case.

Today I enjoy and cherish shooting top-shelf firearms more than ever before. There is just something special about a truly high-quality firearm regardless if the platform is rifle, pistol, or shotgun. So, whenever the opportunity comes knocking to test and review such a custom firearm, I look forward to the endeavor. Recently I had the pleasure of testing two Performance Center revolvers from Smith & Wesson: the Model 629 and Model 686 Competitor. And the results were nothing short of my expectations.

When I first opened the new boxes the "wow" factor hit me between the eyes. I own both a Model 629 and Model 686 in their original form so I had a preconceived idea of what these Competitor models would look like. But these Performance Center revolvers have a touch of modern technology I was not expecting. While they originate from their standard design, they certainly have been blessed with the ultimate expression of rugged simplicity. Apparently both models have enjoyed a steady regime of steroids. They are beefed-up versions of their counterparts. The glassbead finish is aesthetically pleasing and contrasts well with Hogue's black synthetic grip. Caliber designation is nicely etched on one side of the barrel, Competitor on the other.

Both guns are six shooters that can operate in single- or double-action mode. The front sight consists of a black Patridge in a dovetail that can be easily acquired in the notch of the black target-style rear sight both fully adjustable and removable. Even these aging eyes can see the sights well and settle-in on targets expeditiously. Both revolvers frames and cylinder are stainless steel. I guess the notable difference comes in the weighted 6-inch barrel. Five weighted inserts fit inside the authoritative looking underlug and can be removed or adjusted to accommodate individual needs or desires. By removing the Allen-head screw at the end of the underlug, you can remove one, two, or all of the weighted disks if needed. You can see the weights from the cutout portion in the underlug from both sides of the barrel.

All details in machine work and configurations of the barrel are streamline and easy on the eyes. The Model 629

Both competitors come with a weighted barrel system where the user can adjust the overall forward balance of the barrel and weight of the revolver by removing the supplied weights.

Modern swing-out cylinder revolvers such as these are safe to carry with all six charge holes loaded.

M686

The M686 .357 Magnum was topped with a Meopta M-RAD electronic sight with a 5-MOA dot. The bigger dot is fast to pick up, but Mark feels the smaller 3-MOA dot would be better for hunting.

M629

Winchester's 225-grain Beveled Profile Hollowpoint proved one of the more accurate .44 Mag loads tested in the M629 aided by mounting a Leupold 2X Long Eye Relief scope to the integral rail.

M629
COMPETITORS
M686

.44 MAGNUM

S&W .357 MAGNUM

meopta

Competitor tipped the scale a little over 57 ounces while the original Model 629 with the same barrel length weighs in at 45 ounces. The .357 Magnum version of the Model 686 Competitor weighs 53 ounces. That is nine ounces heavier than my personal 686 with a 6-inch barrel, which has been a constant companion in the home protection battery.

The Performance Center's tuned action was smooth and much what you would expect in a custom gun. Single action trigger pull was crisp with zero creep, no gritty feel, breaking around 3 pounds. The double-action mode was silky. Located on the backside of the hardchrome trigger was a trigger stop. This is one feature I appreciate especially shooting a revolver in single-action regardless whether I am shooting steel targets or handgun hunting. The serrated hammer was also finished in hardchrome. The overall fit and finish on both models were nothing short of first class. The barrel/cylinder

gap appeared tight and alignment true.

Both models featured integral mounting systems on their barrels. You can easily mount optics of your choice be it scope or red-dot-type optics. I wanted to use optics on both guns for accuracy testing and this feature made mounting a scope quick and easy. The integral mounting system did not detract from the eye-pleasing appearance.

So, what are these revolvers actually designed for? Smith & Wesson's Tony Miele informed me the Model 686 Competitor was originally made for PPC competition and they are still popular in Europe. I would only assume many of the PPC competitors here in the states are using semi-autos or perhaps their duty gun. The larger .44 Magnum could be used in bowling pin matches, steel plates, and many other competitive games. Full house magnum loads could be used effectively in the hunting fields.

Obviously .44 Special loads wouldn't

MAKER: S&W
2100 ROOSEVELT AVE.
SPRINGFIELD, MA 01104
(800) 331-0852
WWW.GUNSMAGAZINE.COM/SMITH-WESSON

MODEL 686 COMPETITOR

Action: Single-, double-action revolver, **Caliber:** .357 Magnum, **Capacity:** 6, **Barrel Length:** 6", **Overall Length:** 11.5", **Sights:** Fully adjustable square notch rear, Patridge front, **Weight:** 53 ounces, **Grip:** Hogue Synthetic, **Finish:** Glassbead stainless steel, **Price:** $1,389

MODEL 629 COMPETITOR

Action: Single-, double-action revolver, **Caliber:** .44 Magnum, **Capacity:** 6, **Barrel Length:** 6", **Overall Length:** 11.25", **Sights:** Fully adjustable square notch rear, Patridge front, **Weight:** 57.7 ounces, **Grip:** Hogue synthetic, **Finish:** Glassbead stainless steel, **Price:** $1,509

recoil as much as the magnum variety making them a viable option in other matches. Our very own Dave Anderson, who is kind of a competition guru, advised me both revolvers could possibly find use in ICOR (International Confederation of Revolver Enthusiasts), Steel Challenge, or USPSA in the revolver division.

Not being a serious competitor, I can see handgun hunters taking a liking to either revolver especially the "double four." I don't honestly think you have to be in competition to enjoy either of these fine wheelguns. (At least that is what I am trying to explain to my wife.) To get a better idea of what these Performance Center guns were capable of doing, I loaded the truck with a variety of ammunition in different bullet weights and headed to the range.

My shooting buddy, Joe, came along as he enjoys testing and reviewing different guns as much as I do. Joe is somewhat younger than me, and with his steady nerves and keen eyes it's always good to get his take on things during the evaluation process. The first day out we shot from 25 yards with open sights exclusively. We tested .357 Magnum ammo from Winchester and DoubleTap with both 125- and 158-grain bullets. During the .44 Magnum session, ammo from Hornady, Federal, CorBon, Black Hills, Buffalo Bore, and Winchester were used, all with 240-grain bullets. Joe had several groups fewer than 2 inches from a sandbag rest. My groups were a little larger.

We both agreed optics should be mounted on both guns to get a better idea of the accuracy potential. During this first session Joe and I both commented on the trigger. The crisp, clean break without tugging made shooting both guns enjoyable. It's difficult to shoot any gun with a terrible trigger, one that has creep or overtravel, and doesn't break without tugging until

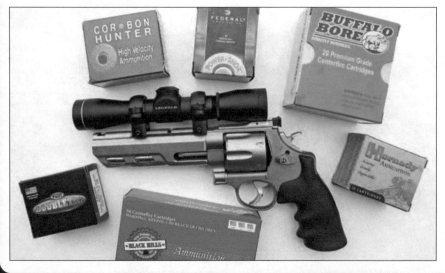

After shooting a variety of factory ammo, the M629 (above) showed it was not picky as it digested most brands with consistent accuracy. This .44 Mag would make an ideal hunting handgun. The S&W Competitor Model 629 (below) was tested with several brands of factory ammo. For testing, the Leupold 2X scope is mounted in low Burris Signature Zee Rings, which required the removal of the dovetailed Patridge front sight.

sweat pops out of your forehead. These good triggers actually made shooting these guns fun and definitely enhanced accuracy.

Another aspect we both noted was the lack of muzzle rise compared to revolvers without a weighted barrel. This makes getting off subsequent shots much quicker and easier if necessary. The additional weight of both guns also lessened felt recoil. I actually prefer a little heavier gun than most. Regardless if I have to shoot offhand or get to take advantage of a rest of some sort, I feel the added weight helps me with more precise bullet placement. All of our shooting consisted of single action. Next, we would mount optics on both guns and shoot from 50 yards and further.

With handgun hunting in the back of my mind, I mounted a quality Leupold 2X scope on the .44 Mag. After shooting Leupold scopes, both fixed power and variable, for over 30 years, I wasn't concerned about punishing recoil affecting the optic. Those Leupold fixed power models are built like a tank. The Leupold scope was mounted in Burris Signature Zee Rings. I like the Burris rings because they never leave a blemish on the scope tube. They also secure the optic firmly and I don't worry about them coming loose. I had to remove the front sight, which easily drifted out of the ramp. The integral mounting system on the Competitor made mounting the scope simple and painless.

As luck would have it, two new red-dot sights from Meopta landed on my doorstep. One of these babies would land on the 686. Meopta is no stranger in the optics arena. This company has facilities in the USA and Europe. They have been producing quality glass in both military and sporting versions for many years. Both of these red-dot sights were designed to aid quick target acquisition. Thanks to a locking, lever-activated, quick-release mount, I slapped Meopta's M-RAD reflex sight on the .357 Magnum. This sight comes in 3- or 5-MOA dot sizes. The sight conveniently incorporates eight levels of brightness adjustment for daylight shooting and another eight levels for nighttime activities. Shooters can fine tune the dot intensity for a variety of conditions. The matte-black body is machined from aircraft-grade aluminum alloy and built to withstand the rigors of battlefield conditions. It should do just fine on the .357 Mag.

After acquiring more ammo I was looking forward to the second range session with optics now added to the sixguns. I shot the .44 Magnum with a variety of factory loads including some .44 Specials, from 25 and 50 yards.

Mark found shooting the .357 Mag with Meopta's lightweight M-RAD sight (above) enjoyable. The .44 Mag would make a good choice for whitetail or boar hunting, especially with a good optic such as this 2X Leupold Long Eye Relief scope (below).

The additional weight on the barrel made shooting magnum factory loads comfortable. While going through seven different brands of ammo I was happy to see the Model 629 was not picky. Most magnum loads consisted of 240-grain bullets. With an upcoming hog hunt, it only seem fitting to try Winchester's new Razor Back XT offering in their 225-grain beveled profile hollowpoint. Groups were more than acceptable from most every manufacturer. The 5-shot, 50-yard group held much less than minute-of-deer. I ran a few .44 Specials through in double action, not against steel plates in an official heat of any kind, just rocks on the berm. The action is smooth although I seldom shoot in this manner; a few rocks got busted nonetheless. With the addition of the Leupold scope, I can clearly determine this would make a fine hunting revolver for close-range encounters. I liked the feel of the Competitor, it handles recoil well, and balances nicely. Dirty Harry would be impressed.

We shot the .357 Mag with Winchester, DoubleTap and Buffalo Bore ammo using 110-, 125-, 158- and 180-grain bullets. Our home-defense gun is loaded with Winchester's 110-grain JHP so I wanted to see how this personal protection ammo fared in the Competitor. My wife, Karen, mentioned she would like to shoot the 686. After running the first cylinder on the 25-yard target she commented, "That's a nice trigger." The added weight in the barrel made shooting targets comfortable.

The M-RAD reflex sight allows shooters to use both eyes making target acquisition quick. I ran some .38 Special loads through in double

The 686 performed well with the addition of Meopta's M-RAD red-dot sight. The big 5-MOA dot works fine for speedy target acquisition.

Winchester's 110-grain Personal Protection ammo shot well at 25 yards. This 5-shot group was made using the open sights.

Winchester's Razor Back XT load in .44 Mag utilizes a 225-grain beveled profile hollowpoint. A big mean hog wouldn't stand a chance.

action and getting back on target for multiple shots was a piece of cake. The M-RAD I was using had a 5-MOA dot size, which is fine for competition shooting against the clock at close range. For hunting purposes I prefer the smaller 3-MOA dot. The heavier frame of the 686 Competitor is easier for me to shoot more accurately than my original model. I finally had to tell Karen our ammo supply was on empty.

Are these Performance Center guns worth the coin? Well, if you happen to be a revolver aficionado with an inextinguishable desire for top-shelf six-shooters, the Competitors will be worthy of a position in your arsenal. You certainly do not have to be involved in competition games to appreciate the satisfaction from shooting a fine wheelgun. They are good looking guns and just as importantly, they shoot well too. Plus, they would make a stellar hunting handgun. What more can you ask? **GUNS**

Black Hills Ammunition
3050 Eglin St., Rapid City, SD 57703
(605) 348-5150
www.gunsmagazine.com/
black-hills-ammunition

Buffalo Bore Ammunition
P.O. Box 1480, St. Ignatius, MT 59865
(406) 745-2666
www.gunsmagazine.com/
buffalo-bore-ammunition

Burris
331 E. 8th St., Greely, CO 80631
(970) 356-1670
www.gunsmagazine.com/burris

CorBon
1311 Industry Rd., Sturgis, SD 57785
(800) 626-7266
www.gunsmagazine.com/cor-bon

DoubleTap Ammo
586 S. Main St. #333, Cedar City, UT 84720
(866) 357-1066
www.gunsmagazine.com/doubletap

Federal Premium Ammunition
900 Ehlen Dr., Anoka, MN 55303
(800) 322-2342
www.gunsmagazine.com/
federal-premium-ammunition

Hornady
P.O. Box 1848, Grand Island, NE 68802
(308) 382-1390
www.gunsmagazine.com/hornady

Leupold
14400 N.W. Greenbriar Pkwy.
Beaverton, OR 97006
(503) 646-9171
www.gunsmagazine.com/leupold-stevens

Meopta USA
50 Davids Dr., Hauppauge, NY 11788
(631) 436-5900
www.gunsmagazine.com/meopta-usa

Winchester Ammunition
600 Powder Mill Rd.
East Alton, IL 62024
www.gunsmagazine.com/
winchester-ammunition

THE 500 S&W:
TOO MUCH OF A GOOD THING?

Both by S&W. Standard 4" and the 5" John Ross limited edition version.

I first became aware of the cartridge when Pete Pi (owner of Cor-Bon) called to discuss the cartridge and the possibility of a test barrel for it in an Encore, as the revolver was not yet produced. Pete supplied the reamer and SSK made the first 500 S&W barrels. The second went to Pete and I still have the first. A pressure test barrel went to S&W at the same time.

Initially I used bullets intended for the .50 AE, and Barnes bullets furnished by Pete. Frankly, the S&W was very impressive compared to larger .50-caliber cartridges I had experience with. It worked with less case capacity and higher pressures to achieve very impressive ballistics, accuracy, muzzle-

blast and recoil. It was obvious this cartridge was going take a monster of a revolver to handle it. Incidentally the first animal taken with the 500 was a cow elk which Ed Brown videoed for me. Short shot, maybe 40 yards, with an instant down and tremendously impressive damage. My fist would go through the hole in the rib cage exit. Since then, the big S&W has taken literally every big game species.

My first shot with the revolver was from a 4" model loaded with the 440-gr. Cor-Bon max load, while stooped-over in a small test tunnel. At the shot, I wondered what the hell I had done. The awkward position and enclosed tunnel magnified the blast and recoil characteristics —which don't really need magnifying.

The full-size S&W is a real handful.

Left: An extremely wide variety of bullets exist for the big 50. These are for Lehigh; Barnes, Sierra and Speer.

HANDLOADING

The long-barreled revolver is massive in size and weight but consistent with its power and recoil. The 4" version is just as massive, but shorter and a little lighter. John Ross (author of *Unintended Consequences*) is the most knowledgeable individual on the 500 revolver and loading for it (*john-ross.net/handloading.htm*). Other reliable sources are the load manuals by recognized sources of published loading manuals. I've seen some internet data I would be very leery of. For non-handloaders, a very wide variety of ammo is marketed. For handloaders you probably won't live long enough to try everything.

JR liked the revolver enough to have S&W make a 500-gun run of a special model for him which he sells. It's really a relatively lightweight 5"-barreled gun without a brake. Frankly, I find

it better balanced than the 4" factory version and really can't see any difference in recoil between the two with the loads I've tried. The recoil of the max loads are probably in excess of my ability to detect the differences between the two guns. Frankly, I like it better than the factory versions, but it is still a real handful with heavy loads. JR has developed cast bullets up to a bit over 700 grains, and data for them, which gives good accuracy and relatively mild pressures and recoil.

NEEDS MUSCLES

We have three S&W revolvers in this caliber, and the Encore, all with a well-proven track record. We have 275-gr. Barnes bullets at over 1,800 fps from the 8⅜" — more from an Encore — and 725-gr. cast bullets at 1,200-1,300 fps from the revolver and good bullets at about 50-gr. steps between those limits.

So we have big heavy revolvers; the 8⅜" (combustion chamber length 9.75") weights in at 4.2 pounds; the 4" (CCL 5.5") at 3.6, the 5" (CCL 7.25") at 3.6 and an 11.25" (CCL 10.25") bull-barreled scoped Encore at 4.8 pounds. At those weights, it takes a lot of strength to hold and shoot them accurately. With the right loads the 500 revolver's accuracy will equal the best revolvers, and scoping them just seems awkward to me.

Is the weight and recoil too much of a good thing? It takes a lot of strength to hold and shoot all of them. How much

is too much? Only you can answer that. Some can't handle the recoil of a .357, while others are literally impervious to recoil. Interestingly, the 500-gr. Hornady at sub-sonic velocity in an SSK suppressed carbine is quiet, accurate and effective. Maybe that's where it all really shines.

Just because the barrel says ".44 Magnum" doesn't mean you need to shoot heavy loads. Roy found the 2-tone finish to be appealing.

Mag-Na-Ports patented porting system did help to tame muzzle flip.

Note the high visibility bright green front sight and additional lightening cuts made by Mag-Na-Port on the 329's barrel shroud.

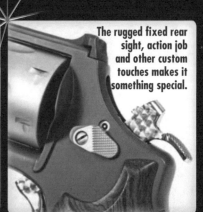

The rugged fixed rear sight, action job and other custom touches makes it something special.

MAG-NA-PORT'S CUSTOM
NIGHT GUARD

ROY HUNTINGTON

Mag-Na-Port turned a plain-Jane S&W Night Guard black revolver into something special. Roy felt the baked-on finish and 2-tone look makes it stand out.

I'll say it right up front: According to the S&W website, the .44 Magnum Night Guard is no longer in production. However, not only were they still available when we started this project, you can still find them at places like *www.gunbroker.com* and even your local gun store at times. Having said that, the real reason we did this project was to showcase the out-of-the-ordinary custom work Mag-Na-Port has become famous for doing. So keep in mind, you could apply the sorts of custom work featured here to *any* revolver. Be creative with *your* dreams. I just happened to like the concept of a lightweight, big-bore revolver.

And, if you ask me, I wasn't wrong about that idea,

A 4" Bowen Custom Arms Model 29 at top, the Mag-Na-Port Model 329 in the center and a classic J-frame Model 36 below for size.

While the 329 isn't as convenient as a J-frame, it does offer .44-caliber stopping power in a relatively compact package.

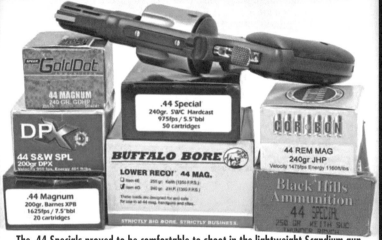

The .44 Specials proved to be comfortable to shoot in the lightweight Scandium gun, while most of the heavy .44 Magnum loads really rocked the boat.

Buffalo Bore's .44 Special Anti-Personnel load (a 200-gr. full wadcutter at 890 fps) shot into 2" at 20 yards from the 2.5" barrel. Roy said it will probably be his daily carry load.

especially after Ken Kelly at Mag-Na-Port was finished with his magic.

The Idea

There's something comforting about the .44 caliber in a handgun. Like a 1911 in .45 ACP, it makes you feel confident you're prepared for whatever may occur — even if it's not *exactly* true in the real world. But there's something to say for a confident feeling, so when I first saw the short-barreled .44 Magnum Night Guard series from S&W, I ordered one. And like many things in life, it needed a bit of improvement to meet what my idea of a "perfect" smallish, big bore should be. I know it's a bit of an oxymoron (small, big bore?), but next to a 6.5" all-steel Model 29, this one is darn near svelte.

I found the front XS Tritium 24/7 sight perfectly good for personal protection, but being a bit old school (and

Purdy Gear's custom "rough-out" field rig — called The Spartacus — has a few added features like the tooled stiffener sections and plated hardware. A practical and elegant rig for a practical and elegant revolver.

since this was going to be more of a field gun for me) I wanted a day-glow green ramped front, to match up with the very cool "fixed" rear Cylinder & Slide sight. If you have an adjustable rear on your S&W, you can order one of these from the Cylinder & Slide shop to replace it. It gives you a "fixed" sight that's tough as an old goat.

I also like a smooth-faced polished trigger, felt an action job was in order, and bet when shooting lighter, higher velocity .44 magnum loads Mag-Na-Port's legendary porting would help to contain things. And, being an old-school sort of guy, I've always like the way good old fashioned hard chrome looks and wanted a touch of that on the Night Guard.

Mag-Na-Port

Ken Kelly runs the shop at Mag-Na-Port and is an amazingly talented custom pistolsmith (rifles and shotguns too, by the way). Mag-Na-Port has come up with some signature "looks" over the years and the idea of a 2-tone gun, with interesting highlights is right up their alley.

"Roy, I love this idea!" said Ken on the phone. "We'll hard chrome any bits we can, do a bead blast of the stainless steel cylinder so it looks like it's hard chromed, slick the action, port it, and I imagine I'll come up with a few other touches just to make it fun. Oh, we'll

have to definitely polish and jewel the hammer and trigger while we're at it!" he laughed.

I hate being that transparent, but he was right about the jewelling part.

"Can you do something with the boring-black frame finish?" I asked.

"You bet, I've got access to some great colors, so what color do you want?" asked Ken.

At this point, I did what I like to do and simply said, "Ken, you're the expert, make it whatever color you think works. I told him this was going to be a field gun for me, something I'd wear on the tractor, working in the woods, to have when deer hunting, simply an all-around big-bore sixgun as near to what our own John Taffin calls a "Perfect Packin' Pistol" as I could think of.

"Leave it up to me," he said. I think I could hear him smiling on the phone.

The Concept

While we've explored the concept of big-bore, short-barreled revolvers before, I think when you chamber one of the lightweight guns in a caliber like .44 Special/Magnum, .41 Magnum, .45 Colt, even .45 ACP loaded correctly, it makes them much more carry-friendly than the same model in steel. You go from 39 ounces in stainless, to only 29 in Scandium. That adds up fast on your hip or in your pocket. Guess what gun I take when I feed chickens, check gates or mow pastures these days?

Since moving to the country, I've found the CCI shot cartridges to be

WHICH GUN
is right for you?

TURN HERE
for help

NIGHT GUARD

very useful. From field rats to snakes and sneaky squirrels on the patio, they make it easier to hit than even trying to use a .22 at times. Plus, you don't get the "carry" of a bullet, so taking a close shot at a squirrel on a branch is safe. And, I've found the .38-caliber shot rounds simply don't have the thump of the .44/.45 Colt versions. A .38 shot cartridge *can* work, but the bigger one simply shreds a venomous snake, and knocks Mr. Squirrel clean off the patio.

Where we live, wild boars are coming up from Arkansas and some have been seen as close as just a few miles. They travel along the rivers from what I under-stand, and we have plenty of those in Missouri. The Department of Natural Resources here have billboards saying, "Shoot On Sight And Report The Loca-tion" regarding wild boars. They are simply so destructive you can't let them get a hold. Also, we only recently had a cougar sighting just a half-mile from our land here. So (not counting any 2-legged miscreants who might cause trouble) having a big-bore revolver, loaded cor-rectly, makes sense.

The Final Result

Once the gun came back from Mag-Na-Port it proved I had made a good decision to go with their shop. And, while it was surprising at first, the sort of OD green finish (a baked-on type) grew on me fast. It looked serious and capable, and right at home in the woods or riding an ATV. The bead-blast finish on the stainless steel cylinder matched the hard chrome on the screws and cyl-inder release, and while you may or may not agree, I think the jewelling and high polish of the hammer and trigger act like a bit of lipstick on a pretty lady.

Ken did a great action job, the wood grips from Ahrends felt good (Ahrends sent me two sets, hence the two slightly different colors in some pictures), and Ken's porting and cosmetic cuts in the barrel were perfectly done. Ken also installed a bright-green front sight to help my aged eyes.

I'm a sucker for a crossdraw field rig, and since I had one I've been using from Purdy Gear, I reached out to Karla again for one to fit this gun, asking for something a bit lighter and more utili-tarian since it would likely live hard. In the spirit of ruggedness, I had asked for a "rough-out" leather look and a simple 6-cartridge loop setup. What she sent was certainly lightweight, but to call it utilitarian would be silly.

"I just can't do utilitarian," Karla confessed to me when I chatted with her about the holster. "You'll take what I send you." And I did.

Karla said she experimented with a slight polish or smoothing of the rough-out leather, and the added tooling on the stiffening piece on the holster and cartridge belt was just something I'd have to get used to she said. To keep things interesting, Karla asked Robbie Barrkman of Robar to coat the buckle and hardware on the belt with his Poly T2 Teflon polymer finish in a color matching the gun. A nice touch, and it takes the bling factor down a notch for a field rig.

Shooting

I had talked about how versatile the .44 is in a recent *Insider* column ("Those Fabulous .44s," July/Aug 2012) where I shot a cross-section of loads through different barrel lengths, including a rifle. Grab that issue (or go online to our dig-ital editions) and give it a read if you like. What I mostly learned then (I used the Mag-Na-Port gun during the tests since I had just received it), was how versatile the .44 caliber truly is. From low-level .44 Special cowboy-type loads from Black Hills, to hot .44 Magnum loads from Cor-Bon and others, you can pretty much tailor the ammo to meet your needs.

I also think I'll mostly be carrying .44 Special loads. The Buffalo Bore Anti-Personnel .44 Special load (a 200 gr. hard cast lead wadcutter) would be hard to beat in this revolver. It deliv-ered around 890 fps from the 2.5" barrel and was very controllable and accurate. Check out the 2" group at 20 yards in the picture. What a great defensive, or even ranch load.

If we do start seeing hogs though, I'll likely move up to the Black Hills 240 JHP .44 Magnum. It chronographed at an honest 1,045 from the short barrel, and unlike some other magnum loads I shot, didn't beat me to death with recoil and muzzleblast. Still, you'd never want to shoot anything out of this gun unless you had hearing protection on, unless it's a real emergency.

Build Your Own

This came together better than I could have hoped for. The final modi-fications make practical sense and look good too. Karla's holster and belt set make carrying the .44 a breeze, and it rides on a peg just as I step into the garage, making it a snap to strap on. I was once confronted by a feral dog by the chicken coop and I reached for the gun I *always* had in my pocket — and realized I didn't have it. A handy rake shooed him off, but I vowed never to have that happen again. And now it won't.

FMG PUBLICATIONS™

GUNMAN IN THE COURTROOM!

$5.95
OUTSIDE US
$9.50

AMERICAN
HANDGUNNER

JULY/AUGUST 2013

WIN
HK P30
.40 S&W!

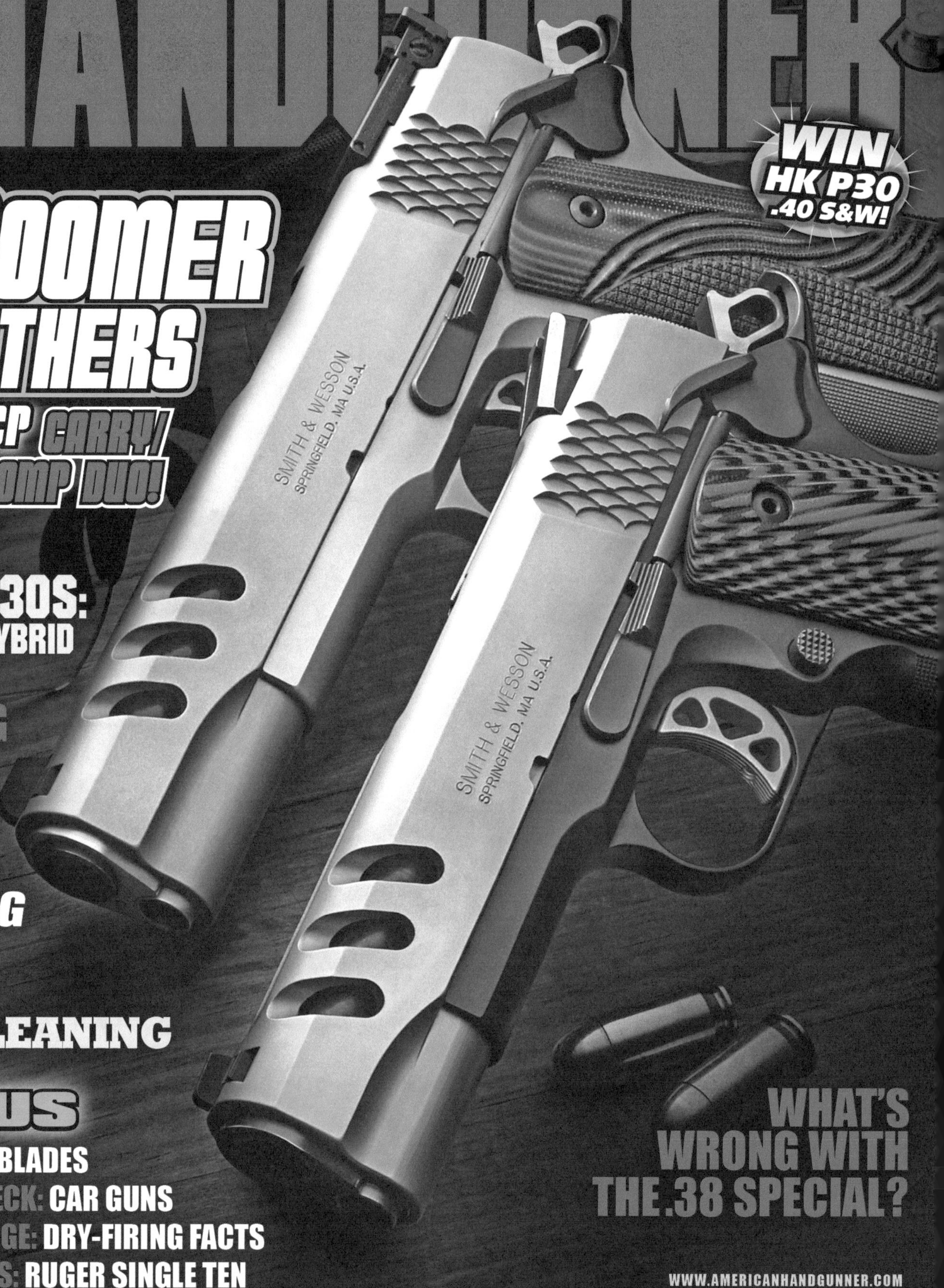

BOOMER
BROTHERS
45 ACP CARRY/
COMP DUO!

LOCK 30S:
5 ACP HYBRID

KINNING
MALL
AME

OADING
EAD

UN CLEANING

FOCUS

GHLIGHT: **BLADES**

EALITY CHECK: **CAR GUNS**

INNING EDGE: **DRY-FIRING FACTS**

FFIN TESTS: **RUGER SINGLE TEN**

WHAT'S
WRONG WITH
THE .38 SPECIAL?

WWW.AMERICANHANDGUNNER.COM

SMITH & WESSON
SPRINGFIELD, MA U.S.A.

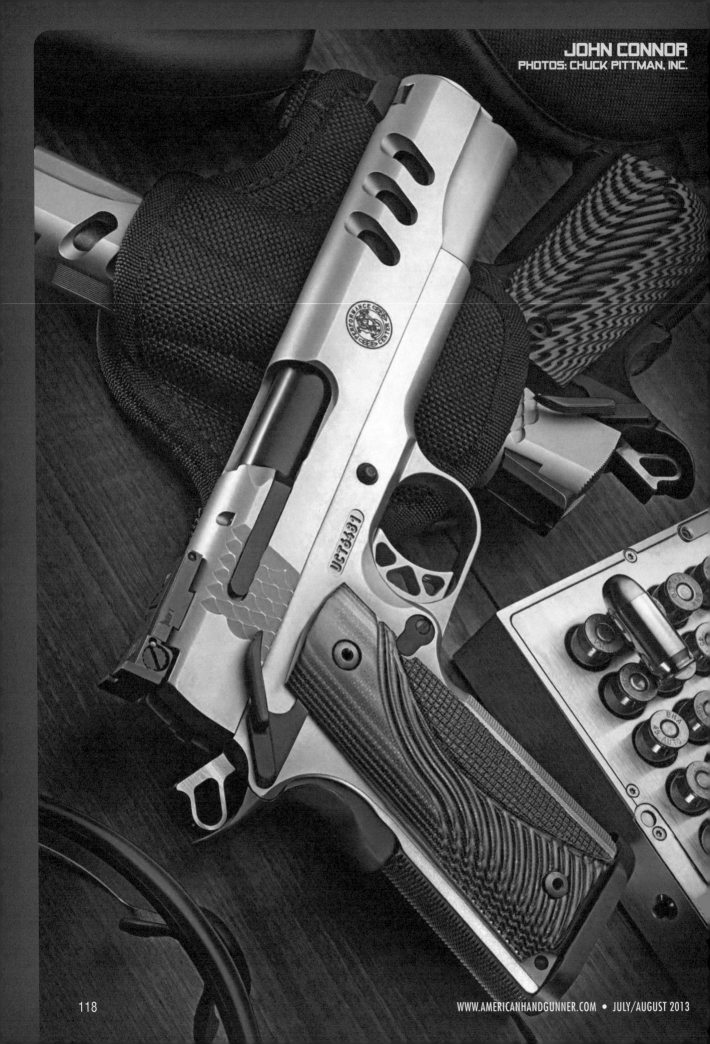

JOHN CONNOR
PHOTOS: CHUCK PITTMAN, INC.

THE BOOMER BROTHERS

HIGH-END CUSTOM MEETS AFFORDABILITY

Okay, settle down, folks; I know they're awfully pretty, but take a deep breath, let it out slowly, and let's clear the air, okay?

I suspect like me, many of you have developed a love-hate relationship with 1911 pistols over the past decade or so. Since everybody in the world with access to a machine or two have started making them, including outfits like *Fred & Earl's Fine Lawn Furniture & Firearms*, we've seen iterations of the classic which would make ol' John Moses weep with pride — and, in some cases, just plain *weep*. I'm no longer

anxious to examine "new" 1911s. I figure, like new model trucks, if they last a season without massive recalls and catastrophic failures, then I might check 'em out.

However, assignments are assignments, and for the first time His Illuminated Immenseness Roy-Boy wasn't even snickering or sneering when he said, "I think you might like these." He didn't sound medicated, either ... just sorta semi-normal. "Huh?" I thought.

With all the variances in quality I've experienced, pretty appearances don't count for much. But I can learn a lot from pickin' 'em up, pointing and

swinging them, racking the slide, shaking them side to side like a dog shakin' the water off, clickin' the controls and then carefully and repeatedly pressing their triggers. I liked what I learned.

The Boomer Brothers

Released simultaneously from Smith & Wesson's Performance Center, we have the *Custom SW1911,* an all-stainless 5"-barreled platform optimized for competition, and the *Round Butt SW1911,* a scandium alloy-framed lightweight packin' pistol with a 4.25" barrel and a trimmed backside that slides smoothly under garments.

SW1911
CUSTOM/ROUND BUTT DUO

PERFORMANCE CENTER CUSTOM SW1911

SKU: 170343 • CALIBER: .45 ACP
CAPACITY: 8+1 • ACTION: SINGLE
BARREL LENGTH: 5" • OVERALL LENGTH: 8.7"
WEIGHT: 40.5 OUNCES • GRIP: G10 CUSTOM WOOD
FRAME MATERIAL: STAINLESS STEEL
SLIDE MATERIAL: STAINLESS STEEL
FINISH: GLASS BEAD-BLASTED
PRICE: $1,539*

*SUGGESTED RETAIL; DEALER SETS ACTUAL PRICING

PERFORMANCE CENTER ROUND BUTT SW1911

SKU: 170344 • CALIBER: .45 ACP
CAPACITY: 8+1 • ACTION: SINGLE
BARREL LENGTH: 4.25" • OVERALL LENGTH: 7.95"
WEIGHT: 29.6 OUNCE • GRIP: G10 CUSTOM WOOD
FRAME MATERIAL: SCANDIUM ALLOY
SLIDE MATERIAL: STAINLESS STEEL
FINISH: 2-TONE • PRICE: $1,539*

*SUGGESTED RETAIL; DEALER SETS ACTUAL PRICING

Both are chambered in .45 ACP and share the full range of Performance Center upgrades.

Both have match-grade barrels with hand-cut chambers, appropriately throated, with hand-polished feed ramps, precision-crowned muzzles and Briley spherical bushings. The barrels have a sleek, slick, hard black finish unmentioned in the documents. I asked a Smith & Wesson executive about it. He said it's "…a stainless steel blacking process we call *Black Magic*" — and that's all I got. There are several goops and an oxide process using that name, but who knows? Hmm …

The slide and frame rails are hand lapped, with no wiggle, no slop; not even the faintest hint of inconsistent tightness throughout the full slide travel of both our test samples. Both have match grade hand-tuned triggers with over-travel stops, skeletonized speed hammers, gracefully upswept beavertail grip safeties dished to accommodate the hammers, ambidextrous thumb safeties, and angled lightening cuts in their slides. They also share oversized *external* extractors, visible loaded-chamber indicators, full-length solid steel guide rods, and we note that even the butts of the guide rods, like the grip safeties and several other parts, are gently radiused and smoothed.

Like all Performance Center firearms, the exacting tolerances are further enhanced by the personal attention of Smith & Wesson's master gunsmiths, producing expertly tuned actions and

precisely mated components.

An industry professional who can't be named because of his affiliation with other makers examined them and concluded, "Well, what you've got here is upwards of $2,500 worth of gun and custom shop work for about $1,500. A pretty fine deal, I'd say; the advantage of having a dedicated performance shop operation in-house."

Brothers — Not Twins

The slide and frame of the *Custom* (the big one) are bead-blasted for glare reduction and a nice matte appearance. The sights are bold and black, with the front sight's forward-angled face and the rear sight's big, rearward-angled surface horizontally fine-line grooved to minimize any reflection. The front sight is drift adjustable horizontally, and the rear is micro-adjustable both horizontally and vertically.

Distinctive fish-scale slide cocking serrations provide an excellent grasp. The lightening cuts, three diagonal ports on each side of the slide, are nice looking and serve their weight-reducing purpose, but I wouldn't use them for press checking. Their angle and position isn't right for that, and I'm sure

the Smith & Wesson engineers didn't intend them to be used that way. The ambi-thumb safeties are ample without excessive projection.

The frontstrap has extremely fine 30 LPI checkering from its base right up to where the middle finger snuggles under the triggerguard, where it's smooth and relieved. The flat mainspring housing has slightly more aggressive checkering, in exactly the right balance with the finer checkered frontstrap. The blue G10 grips are "decoratively functional"; smooth where the trigger finger and thumb need a little freedom, checkered toward the lower front and grooved toward the lower back, right where you need more and less firm purchase.

A black metal magazine well extension is generously flared and perfectly mates inside with the frame's flared mag well. It extends downward about one-quarter inch, and is open at the front. This brings the rubber base pad of the supplied magazines almost, but not quite, flush with the bottom of the extended mag well, and leaves the toe of the base pad available. The magazines, which are seamless stainless steel 8+1s, punched out smartly and dropped freely, but if one stuck you could pinch the protruding toe of the mag base pad and pull it out — a nice touch.

Inside, in addition to the polished feed ramp, the interior and exterior of

BOOMER BROS

the muzzle bushing is well polished, as are the locking lugs on the barrel, the lug recesses and the cocking surface of the slide. The result is a smooth, superb lockup, made even more consistent by the Briley spherical bushing.

The trigger pull is just outstanding for competition; no creep, virtually zero take-up, and a miniscule reset. Measured with a Lyman electronic gauge, the very crisp trigger pull was 3 pounds, 12 ounces.

Talk about attention to teensy little details: Y'know the slide-stop lever shaft, which protrudes slightly from the right side of the frame? I noticed there was a tiny flat machined on the end. Every one I'd ever seen was simply rounded. I had to ask my go-to gunsmith/consultant Kenny M about it. He fingered it and chuckled.

"It's the kind of thing only a nitpicky master 'smith would think of," he said. "See, if you ever had to put a punch to it, you'd have a nice flat surface to mate with, so there's less chance of slipping and marring the finish."

At 8.7" long and weighing 40.5 ounces dry and 49.5 ounces fully loaded with nine 230-grain rounds, it's not a candidate most might carry, but for match shootin', the heft, hold, balance and all the competition-oriented enhancements seem perfect.

The Feisty Little Brother

Oh, dudes, now we're talkin' *fighting pistol*! At 7.9", 29.6 ounces dry and 38.6 "wet," if the *Custom* is a lion on the firing line, the *Round Butt* is a saber-toothed tiger on the prowl. The difference in weight — attributable to the anodized scandium frame — and length, is only the quantifiable difference, and not as significant as the difference in balance, agility in the hand and fast pointing and handling; the essential determinants of what really distinguishes a carry-and-fighting pistol. The *RB* feels live, alert and wired, and points just like pointing my index finger.

Select a target, like a 4" circle at 10 yards or 2" at 5 yards. With the pistol in hand at low ready, focus on the target, close your eyes, point the pistol and open your eyes. How close are you to "on target," and more importantly, how straight and even is your sighting plane aligned? The *RB* is an ace for me; a natural pointer, and it moves from target to target, well, like it's wired. It's almost embarrassing, like I gotta ask myself, "Are you blowin' smoke up yer own skirt, dude?" Nope.

All the Performance Center enhancements are present on the *Round Butt* too; so let's examine the differences, from top to bottom. The sights are classic carry: a three white-dot system, low profile but highly visible, and quick on pickup. The front post is drift-adjustable, as is the rear sight, which is also secured with a setscrew. The top of the slide has a lowered and flattened track with fine, machined lengthwise grooves. Between lowering the reflecting surface and striating it, the effect minimizes glare. On either side of the skeletonized speed hammer, the butt-end sides of the slide are similarly grooved horizontally, again, to minimize glare. The top edges of the RB's slide are far more beveled and radiused than those on the *Custom,* lessening bulk, aiding a smooth draw, and gliding better under fabric.

I've had very little experience with rounded-butt 1911s, and they were briefly borrowed hand-built custom jobs way beyond my reach. But having handled this one and feeling the difference, I'm sold. Losing the sharply defined back corner of the frame tucks the butt a bit further into the meat of the heel of my hand, yielding more comfort, control, and I think it contributes significantly to the *RB's* superb pointability. I handled those custom round-butts a long time ago and memory fades, but it seems to me Smith & Wesson got the geometry just right with this one.

For most handgunners, I think all it would take is placing a traditional squared-butt 1911 side by side with the *Round Butt*, then alternately gripping and pointing them, simulating recoil effect by having someone reach over and cycle the slide. Whether you're in the market for a *Round Butt* or not, it can be a revealing experience. Trying it, an old shootin' buddy said, "It makes the grip feel more like my favorite round-butt revolver."

The *RB*'s G10 grips look like thin laminated sheets of orange and dark wood, and the flowing basically vertical grooves and dimensions promote a grip that's "sticky without stickin'," if you know what I mean. At centerline they are minimally thicker — a millimeter or two — than the *Custom*'s grips, but significantly more tapered down in the forward and rearward thirds. The bottom ends of the grips are well tapered and the mag well is adequately beveled, and leaves the mag base pad completely exposed for grabbin' — a good thing on a fighting pistol.

The crisp, fine-tuned trigger correctly has just a bit more take-up than the *Custom*'s, and broke clean at 3 pounds, 14 ounces to 4 pounds. Reset is short and sweet. *If* you're thoroughly accustomed to a short take-up, creep free, relatively light trigger pull, you'll love it. But if you're used to a longer pull and heavier press, this ain't a trigger to immediately start carrying

into possible lethal threat stress situations. Train that digit with lots of practice first, okay?

My highly technical and scientific assessment: The *Custom* makes you want to go out and punch some bull's-eyes with a smug, serene smile. The *Round Butt* makes you wanta blast the blazes outta multiple surprise pop-ups and smash a line of steels while grinnin' like a polecat.

Briley Bushing Brief

If you're not familiar with the Briley spherical bushing, I'm not an expert but I'll give it a shot: It's like a bushing within a muzzle bushing. Take a closely fitted muzzle bushing and machine a circular race into the inside surface just a tad back from the exit. Into that race, place a precisely machined ring of a steel alloy given a titanium nitride treatment. This produces a super-smooth extremely hard, virtually friction-free surface. Now your barrel rides on and is centered by the inner bushing while being stabilized longitudinally by the conventional bushing. Friction and wear is reduced, and the possibilities of play diminished.

There were no instructions on the Briley spherical bushing in the included manual. Smith & Wesson might fix that by the time you read this. Thankfully it's not hard to figure out. When the piece is disassembled, stick your finger into the bushing until you've got a light "compression hold" on that titanium-nitrided ring. Slowly and gently rotate the ring while applying light upward pressure. You'll feel the ring clear two recesses and you'll pull it right out. I asked my gunsmith pal what kinda fancy specialized tool he uses for that. He smiled and held up his trigger finger.

"Standard Index Digit, Mark I Mod Zero, Service Issue," he said. "Want the NSN number? Brownells carries it." *Smartass* ...

Reinsert the same way, gently rotating until the ring slips back into the race. I recommend sparingly lubing the end of the barrel and interior of the muzzle bushing (including very lightly wiping the interior of that race) with a high-quality, thin, light lubricant, because tolerances are precise. Don't worry about the ring poppin' out of its race under fire — it won't.

The Range Report

Do *not* buy a *Custom* unless you're really, really good, or purty dang good and trying hard for "really-really." Otherwise it will drive you screamin' bugnutz not being able to shoot up to the capabilities of this gun. There we were, the Rat Canyon Crew, less the "Over The Hill Gang" as in the *Dragged-Over-The-Hill Gang*, held shakily upright by bolts, staples and duct tape, tryin' to shoot like Camp

Perry competitors. I'm a service-issue gun guy, all about getting on target fast and shootin' *fast enough, good enough,* and the others?

"I don't shoot groups at 25 yards; I shoot *patterns,*" sez one, the other adding, "I shoot 1-hole groups — with one shot, maybe." We were cussin' ourselves and each other before it was over, only later realizing that first, for *us,* we were doin' great! — And second, we just weren't up to the gun.

We shot freestanding, no rest or bracing, 2-handed at 25 and 20 yards, 1-handed at 15. If you took out called flyers we woulda scored some 1.75" to 2.5" groups at 25. Yeah, I know: *woulda, coulda.* The pistol loved Hornady's HAP Steel Match 185- and 230-grain loads, with the 230s having a little edge over the 185s.

It was infuriating. Pop this puppy in a Ransom Rest or even into the hands of a Master Class shooter and I'll bet she'll tear single ragged holes. We did however get some nice groups at 20: a 1.25" group with Black Hills 230-grain ball, and a ragged 1-holer measuring an honest 1" center-to-center with AYSM 230-grain JHP Tactical XTP. Almost outta ammo at 15 yards, we got a sweet 1-handed 1.75" group with 230 HAP. Those let us sleep that night, but still … *Grrrr* ...

The *Round Butt* will probably shoot better than you can hold it too. Shot 2-handed at 15 yards firing "cadenced" at one to 1.5 seconds per shot, we got some 2" groups, and 1-handed at 7, we got one down to 1.10". We were shooting Federal HST Tactical 230-grainers, Black Hills 185-grain Barnes Tac-XP+P and CorBon 185-grain DPX; all ferocious butt-kickers, about equally accurate. Light as it is, the *RB* definitely has some torque with these loads, but thanks to the fine grip, it's surprisingly controllable.

Personally, I was most impressed with the *RB's* rapid-fire performance. Once you get used to the short reset on that light, crisp trigger, rapid doubles at 7 yards were only an inch apart. Cool, huh?

And by the way, there were *zero* failures to feed, extract or eject with either pistol, with any ammo — maybe not a surprise. But remember, even my group of less than steller hole-punching miscreants know how to provide a rock-solid platform for an auto, and even we have enough sense to use good maintenance techniques and good ammo. Do the same and I'you'll have equally reliable work out of this pair.

Okay; time to put this behind me and go back to my "Lance-Corporal-in-a-Mudhole-Class 1911." Connor *OUT.*

GET YOUR HANDS DIRTY

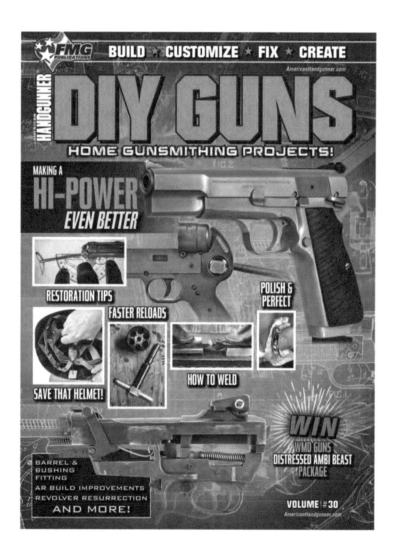

BUILD ★ CUSTOMIZE ★ FIX ★ CREATE

AmericanHandgunner.com

DIY GUNS

HOME GUNSMITHING PROJECTS!

MAKING A HI-POWER EVEN BETTER

RESTORATION TIPS

FASTER RELOADS

POLISH & PERFECT

SAVE THAT HELMET!

HOW TO WELD

WIN WMD GUNS DISTRESSED AMBI BEAST PACKAGE

BARREL & BUSHING FITTING
AR BUILD IMPROVEMENTS
REVOLVER RESURRECTION
AND MORE!

VOLUME #30
AmericanHandgunner.com

ORDER @ FMGPUBS.COM

KIT GUN COMMENTS

Three "magnum" S&W revolvers. From left, Model 57 .41 Magnum (1964); Model 19 .357 Magnum and a Model 51 .22 Magnum (1970s).

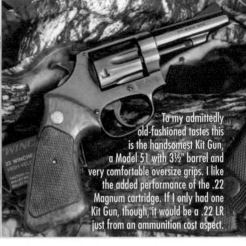

To my admittedly old-fashioned tastes this is the handsomest Kit Gun, a Model 51 with 3½" barrel and very comfortable oversize grips. I like the added performance of the .22 Magnum cartridge. If I only had one Kit Gun, though, it would be a .22 LR just from an ammunition cost aspect.

Back around 1910 dealer Philip Bekeart placed an order for a variation on the small S&W I-frame. He specified .22 LR, 6" barrel and adjustable sights. S&W shipped the first 292 revolvers in 1911. In 1915 Bekeart's design became a regular cataloged item. Collectors refer to them as the .22/.32 Hand Ejector, .22/.32 Bekeart and .22/.32 Heavy Frame Target (though at 23 ounces it was not very heavy).

By the mid 1930s target shooters wanted heavier guns on medium size frames, such as the Colt Officer's Target and the S&W K22. Sales of the lightweight .22/.32 languished. S&W fitted the I-frame with a 4" barrel with ramp front sight and adjustable rear sight. They called the result the Kit Gun, meaning a gun a hunter, fisherman, or camper could pack along with other outdoor gear in a kit bag. The concept proved very popular, and in fact Kit Guns are being built to this day.

There have been many variations, in .22 LR and .22 Mag, with 2", 3", 3½" and 4" barrels, with blued or nickeled carbon steel, stainless steel, aluminum alloy and scandium frames, with 6-shot and (currently) with 7- (.22 Mag) and 8-shot (.22 LR) cylinders.

By 1950 S&W felt there was a market for a small-frame, .38 Special revolver. The I-frame cylinder at 1.25" long was too short, so S&W designed a new size, the J-frame, with a longer cylinder and longer frame window. However I-frame production continued through the '50s, used in the Kit Gun and for .32 Long and .38 S&W models.

J-FRAME VARIANTS

In 1953 S&W introduced the "Improved I-frame" with a coil spring mainspring rather than the original leaf spring. These were used on the 1953 .22/.32 Kit Gun. The Kit Gun Airweight was built on an alloy J-frame, the same frame size as used on Airweight .38 Specials. The .22 Magnum version, introduced in 1960 as the Model 51, was made on the steel J-frame.

When the factory began using model numbers in 1957, the steel-frame version was assigned #34, the alloy-framed Model #43. Making two frame sizes, so similar the casual observer couldn't even tell them apart, wasn't very economical. In 1960-1961 S&W phased

A 1953 22/.32 Kit Gun on the improved I-frame.

A more modern compact 22, a Walther P22, formally distributed by S&W.

out the Improved I-frame in favor of the J-frame. The 43 and 51, already made on the J-frame, kept their numbers. The Model 34 remained, but with a -1 added.

I've owned or tested half a dozen Kit Guns and still have three. Personally I don't care for the 1⅞" models, except as a training understudy to a .38 Special. Inherent accuracy is fine, but the short-sight radius affects practical accuracy. Performance-wise the 4" barrel is best, though aesthetically the 3" and 3½" versions look "just right."

My most "collectible" Kit Gun is a 1954-era model on the Improved I-frame. The others are a 34-1 and a 51, both from the early 1970s. Actually the most practical Kit Gun is one I don't have, but which is still in production, the stainless-steel Model 63. Current Model 63s have a 3" barrel, adjustable rear and a HiViz fiber optic front sight. Handsomely proportioned, rust-resistant and tough as nails, the 63 is a darn near perfect outdoorsman's revolver.

SEMI-AUTOS TOO

If revolvers don't appeal to you there's nothing wrong with a pocketsize .22 semi-auto. It's strange S&W has never made what I'd call a good pocket .22 auto. The great Model 41 is my favorite target .22, while the 22A pistols are excellent for plinking, informal target shooting and small-game hunting.

Back around 1970 S&W made the Model 61 .22 for about 3 years. It was well enough made, but with a tiny misshapen grip, was hard to hold, much less shoot. I didn't think S&W was capable of making an ugly gun but they succeeded with the Model 61. More recently S&W has been the USA distributor for Walther pistols, including the P22. Initially, I heard of reliability issues with the little guns. Walther may have modified the magazines a bit, in any event, the sample I have has been reliable and provided good accuracy.

However as I write this the arrangement for S&W to distribute the P22 is winding down, though you may be able to find S&W-marked models on dealer shelves for a while. The fine M&P .22 will still be available from S&W, while Walther will set up its own facility for several other models, including the P22.

Right now S&W is working hard to meet demand for current models. Someday, I'd like to see an S&W compact .22 semi-auto with the same appeal as the Kit Gun. Long ago famed knifemaker Bob Loveless made a few "trail guns" on cut-down Model 41s. Something similar, using an alloy frame to save weight, would suit me just fine.

TAFFIN TESTS
THE SIXGUNNER HIMSELF: GUNS, GEAR & MORE
JOHN TAFFIN

.44 SPECIAL DA SIXGUNS

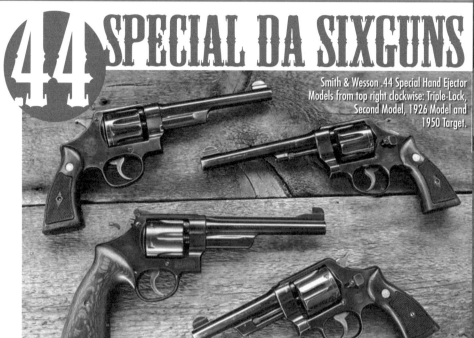

Smith & Wesson .44 Special Hand Ejector Models from top right clockwise: Triple-Lock, Second Model, 1926 Model and 1950 Target.

THE DO-EVERYTHING REVOLVER

I n the closing days of 1908 Smith & Wesson brought forth a new sixgun which was destined to have great impact for most of the 20th century. The same basic sixgun platform would go on to be chambered in .45 ACP, .38/44 Heavy Duty, .357 Magnum, .44 Magnum, .41 Magnum, and rarely .45 Colt. That revolver was the New Century, or First Model Hand Ejector, or as it's most commonly known, the Triple-Lock.

The first chambering was none of the above classic cartridges, but rather the Triple-Lock introduced the .44 Special, and the revolver itself was the first N-frame Smith & Wesson. As might be expected it was beautifully crafted, gaining its name from the fact the cylinder locked in three places, at the front of the ejector rod and at the rear of the cylinder, while a third lock was a magnificently machined between the back of the ejector rod housing and the yoke. Subsequently, historians have said the third lock was not necessary, but instead highlighted the extreme talents of Smith & Wesson craftsmen prior to WWI. The Triple-Lock was also the first Smith & Wesson double action sixgun with an enclosed ejector rod housing.

As beautiful machined as the Triple-Lock was it was to be short lived. In 1915, to save manufacturing costs, the enclosed ejector rod and the third locking feature were dropped as the Second Model Hand Ejector arrived with a retail price of $2 less than the Triple-Lock. A measly 2 bucks! The Second Model was still chambered in .44 Special, however the vast majority were made for the military use in WWI.

For the American Expeditionary Force the chambering was .45 ACP, while revolvers for the British chambered the .455. After the war, dedicated sixgunners began to petition Smith & Wesson to bring back the Triple-Lock but it never happened. However, thanks to Texas distributor Wolff & Klar the Third Model, or 1926 Model, returned the enclosed ejector rod housing. This model was produced side-by-side with the Second Model until the eve of WWII and even for a few years after that, when the final Hand Ejector, the Model of 1950, replaced it.

Smith & Wesson .44 Specials from the last quarter of the last century: Model 24-3, Model 624, Model 696 and the lightweight Model 296.

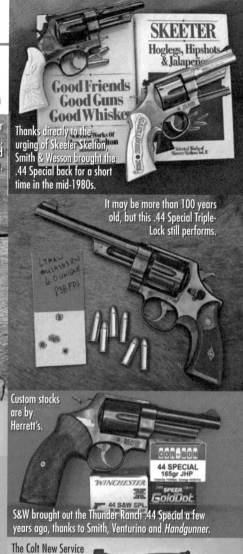

Thanks directly to the urging of Skeeter Skelton, Smith & Wesson brought the .44 Special back for a short time in the mid-1980s.

It may be more than 100 years old, but this .44 Special Triple-Lock still performs.

Custom stocks are by Herrett's.

S&W brought out the Thunder Ranch .44 Special a few years ago, thanks to Smith, Venturino and *Handgunner*.

The Colt New Service .44 Special is slightly larger than the S&W version.

STILL STRONG

M y first ever Smith & Wesson .44 Special was a 6½" 1950 Target. In the early 1960s that original .44 Special had to be sacrificed to buy groceries for my three young kids who insisted upon eating regularly. As usually happens, time healed the hurt and the 1950 Target, which was lost has been replaced several times over, with different models. These are simply some of the finest double-action .44 Specials ever produced.

Smith & Wesson dropped the .44 Special in the 1960s, however it was

TAFFIN TESTS

resurrected for a couple years in the 1980s as the blued Model 24-3 and stainless steel Model 624 with both offered in 4" and 6½ " versions. Just recently Smith also brought back the basic Model 24 in the Classic series. These are all excellent sixguns.

Thanks mainly to Clint Smith, Mike Venturino and *American Handgunner*, the 4" Military .44 Special was reborn as the Thunder Ranch Special. Smith & Wesson also offered the .44 Special in a 5-shot Model 696 L-frame along with a Model 296 lightweight fi ve-shooter. Both demand high dollar prices today.

A Taurus Model 681 5-shot .44 Special I have is prized as it has been worked over by Bill Oglesby. He added high visibility sights, smoothed out the action, dehorned the hammer, all of which turned it into a fi rst-class defensive double-action sixgun. I also have had Charter Arms Bulldog .44 Specials through the years, and still rely on the model today.

Working Loads

My every day working load with the Models of 1950 and 1926 is what most sixgunners know as the Skeeter Skelton Load, namely a 250-260 Keith bullet over 7.5 grs. of Unique, for 950 to 1,000 fps. The same results can be had with the same amount of Universal or 8.0 grains of Power Pistol. For the past half-century plus I have virtually fi red every revolver manufactured and chambered in everything from the .22 Long Rifl e up through the biggest of the big bores. I have said more than once I could quite easily fi ll out my remaining years with a good quality .44 Special, and the Keith Load will handle anything I am likely to hunt.

Colts

Smith & Wesson was not the only manufacturer to provide a quality double-action .44 Special sixgun. Colt's large frame, swing-out cylindered, big-bore, double-action sixgun actually arrived 10 years before Smith & Wesson's N-frame. Way back in 1878 Colt added a double-action mechanism to their Colt Single Action Army to produce their first self-cocker, and then before the turn of the century introduced the New Service. I would like to know who designed the grip of the New Service as it is defi nitely made for very large hands and at least for me is nowhere as comfortable to use as that of the Smith & Wesson.

This revolver was defi nitely made for heavy-duty use. During WWI, just as with the Smith & Wesson, it was chambered in .45 ACP for use by the troops. It was also selected in .45 Colt as the standard RCMP revolver and in .38 Spe-

cial was adopted by the Border Patrol. The Hand Ejector Models were all primarily chambered in .44 Special, while the New Service is mostly found in .45 Colt. However, Colt also chambered it in .38 Special, .357 Magnum, .45 ACP, .38-40, .44-40 and thankfully in .44 Special.

Any .44 Special, whether it's one of the Hand Ejectors or the New Service, normally demands collector prices. Just as I never expected to have examples of all the Smith & Wesson .44 Specials in excellent shooting shape, I figured the Colt New Services would be even farther out of reach. Again thanks to a reader I wound up with a 4½" Colt New Service .44 Special at a very reasonable price as it had some issues. The action was not quite right and someone had installed an S&W adjustable rear sight assembly while leaving the factory front sight intact. The result, of course, was a high shooting sixgun.

> ## "After the war, dedicated sixgunners began to petition Smith & Wesson to bring back the Triple-Lock but it never happened."

I turned it over to gunsmith Milt Morrison who totally rebuilt it, fitted a ramp front sight, and finished it off with one of his magnificently polished high bright-blue jobs. The addition of stag grips finished the project and I had my first New Service .44.

About 20 years ago at the Shootists Holiday, friend and fellow shootist Allan Jones, editor of the Speer Reloading Manual, shared his .44 Special Colt New Service Target Model with me. That old sixgun shot like it was equipped with radar and I lusted for it. Target Model Colts do not come cheap, however my patience was rewarded this year when I won an auction for a 1928-issued 7½" Colt New Service Target Model .44 Special and it shoots just like Allan's did!

Do-Everything Sixgun

Whether they bear the name Colt or Smith & Wesson on the barrel, I favor 6-shot, big-bore, large-frame, double-action .44 Specials. However, one easily takes first place in my sixgunning heart, and that is the 4" 1950 Target from Smith & Wesson. It packs easy, shoots superbly, and is capable of handling anything I need a sixgun for.

WHICH GUN
is right for you?

TURN HERE
for help

americanhandgunner.com

THE .32 S&W LONG & .38 S&W

2: This S&W Model 30 in .32 S&W Long was made around 1970 on the J-frame. Why a .32 when the .38 Special version is the same size? Some people wanted less recoil, plus the .32 cylinder holds six cartridges, the .38 holds five. Buffalo Bore offers two hardcast lead bullet loads to help get the most out of these old guns.

This S&W Regulation Police was made around '56-57, on the Improved I-frame in .38 S&W. Many quality revolvers such as this one were purchased for home defense. Since they were seldom carried or even shot much, they often show up in excellent condition.

Recently I acquired a handgun I'd rather not have. Barrie Gwillim, a shooting buddy and close friend, died last fall and left me a couple of handguns. The revolver is a S&W Regulation Police in .38 S&W made in 1956 or 1957, on the "Improved I-frame." The I-frame had a cylinder nominally 1.25" long and corresponding frame window. Production of I-frames continued during the '50s, with revolvers chambered for .32 S&W Long, .38 S&W and the popular "Kit Guns" in .22 LR. In 1960-61, S&W dropped the I-frame in favor of the J-frame, which could chamber the longer .38 Special.

Coincidentally about the time I acquired the Regulation Police, shooting buddy Steve Kukowski bought a Model 30, made around 1970. It's built on the J-frame with a 6-shot cylinder and chambered for the .32 S&W Long. It came from the collection of a long-time friend, Al Francis. Al tried to join the US Navy after Pearl Harbor. He was told the Navy just couldn't overlook one small problem — Al had been born with only one arm. What the Navy couldn't overlook the merchant marine could. During the war his ship hauled the vital materials ("beans, boots and bullets") to keep the armed forces supplied.

I went into the background of how these revolvers were acquired because they represent a current trend. A lot of quality guns from the post-WWII era seem to be coming on the market, some from collections, others found stored away in a dresser drawer.

EARLY GUNS

Before the .38 Special became ubiquitous, the moderately powered .32 S&W Long and .38 S&W were popular. Colt, reluctant to stamp the name of their primary competitor on their revolvers, called these cartridges the .32 and .38 Colt New Police. Many thousands of quality Colt and S&W revolvers were chambered for these cartridges. But, in the early 20th century many inexpensive break-top revolvers were also chambered for these cartridges. In old mail-order catalogs they were advertised for around $3 to $4. The "steel" was little more than soft iron, not heat treated, and they had delicate lock-work components. Most you find today don't function.

With so many old and weak revolvers floating around, factory loads in .32 and .38 S&W are modest. Currently the Winchester website lists .32 S&W Long with a 98-gr. LRN bullet at 705 fps. The .38 S&W load is a 145-gr. LRN at 685 fps (both from 4" barrels). Both are pleasant, low-recoil loads, fun for plinking, not to mention a good source of quality brass for reloading. As a defensive load, a LRN bullet at modest velocity is about as bad as it gets. I wouldn't shoot a skunk in a trap with such loads, much less count on them for defense.

The .32 Long enjoys some popularity as a target round — Federal offers a 98-gr. WC load at 780 fps. Though not intended as a defensive load, it's wadcutter profile would at least cut a hole rather than just push through. I'm not sold on the .32 Long as a defensive round but I'd use Federal's WC load to shoot a skunk in a trap — from a good safe distance!

NEW TECH

Buffalo Bore has developed loads for the .32 and .38 S&W to increase their defensive capability. They use hardcast lead bullets with flat profiles specifically designed not to deform on impact, but to cut and penetrate. Buffalo Bore feels an expanding bullet for these cartridges would be a mistake, as expansion would limit penetration. Hard lead bullets produce higher velocity than jacketed bullets, all else being equal. Buffalo Bore uses what they call "modern powders" to provide higher velocities than other factory loads.

It should be noted these are *not* "+P" loads. Pressures do not exceed standard SAAMI limits. Buffalo Bore rates them as safe to shoot in any solid-frame (i.e., *not top-break*) revolver, assuming, of course, it is in safe firing condition.

The chart shows chronographed velocities. The .38 S&W/125-gr. load interests me most, as in my 4" S&W velocities are similar to what most 125-gr. .38 Special loads produce in 2" barrels, around 956 fps. The Buffalo Bore 115 .32 S&W Long yielded about 771 from a S&W 2" barrel, while the 100-gr. WC delivered 852 fps. from the same gun.

With all loads tested recoil was moderate. Accuracy is limited more by short-sight radius than by ammunition, but I could keep most shots in the A-zone of a USPSA target at 25 yards. I'm not sold on anything under .38 Special/9mm Luger for personal defense, but if a .32 or .38 S&W is what you have, these Buffalo Bore loads are a good option. Just *not* in those cheap top-breaks!

"THE FINEST REVOLVER EVER MADE..."

S&W'S TRIPLE LOCK COMBINED MANY "FIRSTS" IN LESS THAN A DECADE OF PRODUCTION.

MASSAD AYOOB

When the Triple Lock was introduced, telephones looked like this.

"In 1907 Smith & Wesson brought out the Triple Lock, perhaps the finest revolver ever manufactured anywhere, at any time. Today no example of finer revolver making is to be had." Those words are found in the classic *Sixguns* written by the great Elmer Keith, who for many years served as Shooting Editor of *GUNS Magazine*. S&W had actually dubbed it the "New Century" revolver, and some collectors refer to it as the ".44 Hand Ejector, First Model," but Triple Lock was the name which stuck.

It was a rare compilation of "firsts." This was S&W's first large frame/large caliber revolver with a swing-out cylinder. It was their first double-action revolver with a barrel shroud protecting the ejector rod. It was the debut platform for the .44 S&W Special cartridge, basically a lengthened .44 Russian which would eventually inspire the .44 Magnum round. And of course, it had that eponymous feature, the third lock.

S&W already had the strongest of swing-out cylinder lockups, with their signature barrel lug securing in front of the ejector rod and the cylinder's spring-loaded axis locking up firmly at the rear of the frame window. The third lock took the form of a U-shaped block on the inside of the cylinder yoke (crane), mating with a stud protruding from the bottom rear of the ejector rod shroud. The frame itself was niched out to make room.

Was this extra lock needed for the .44 Special? Nah. After all, it was hardly more powerful than the .44 Russian, which had debuted in S&W's top-break revolvers in 1871. In its early black powder form and even in smokeless, .44 Special factory ammo wasn't as powerful as it might have been. Our own John Taffin, in his *Gun Digest Book of the .44,* quotes two great authorities saying S&W installed the third lock for another reason.

BECAUSE SMITH & WESSON COULD

In the book *Smith & Wesson 1857-1945* (Barnes, 1966) Robert Neal and Roy Jinks say, "Most authorities believe the third lock provided on this model was put there by Smith & Wesson more as an example of the ultimate in precision machine work than as a necessary item for extra strength."

If so—as seems likely—it would not have been the only time in Smith & Wesson's history they added a feature more cosmetic than intrinsically useful, simply to showcase the machining skill of which they were capable. In 1935, they checkered the top-strap of the frame of their deluxe .357 Magnum revolver, a feature continuing throughout what later came to be called their Model 27 series. The Triple Lock in 1907, and the Registered Magnum and the

Mas' early production Triple Lock .44 Special with 6.5-inch barrel, also sporting rare factory target sights.

Recoil of .44 Special Silvertip is mild in the big old Smith.

Model 27 later, were the flagships of the fleet: the finest, most expensive revolvers Smith & Wesson produced at the given time.

DETAILS

According to Jim Supica and Richard Nahas in *The Standard Catalog of Smith & Wesson,* the Triple Lock was primarily chambered in the round it was made for, the .44 Special, to the tune of 13,753 guns. Some were produced in .45 Colt (which Keith called the finest double-action revolver ever made in that caliber), though sources differ on the exact number so chambered. Much smaller numbers were made in other calibers, including

The third lock consisted of a block on the yoke (1) mating to a stud at the bottom rear of the ejector shroud (2). All three locks were unlatched by pushing forward on the cylinder release latch.

.44-40, .38-40 and even a very few allegedly in .22 Long Rifle. More than 1,200 were produced in .455 for the Brits, and therein lay the beginning of the end of the Triple Lock.

Embroiled in the trench warfare of WWI, England wanted more S&W .455s, but feared the ejector rod housing and the precisely-machined third lock would become a trap for gun-jamming mud. They ordered thousands more, but insisted those two features be done away with. They were, and the Second Model .44 Hand Ejector had neither, resembling an enlarged .38 Special Military & Police and becoming essentially the shape of the famous 1917 model. The change came in 1915, when the Triple Lock was discontinued. Popular demand would eventually bring limited production of the Third Model, the 1926 Hand Ejector .44 with the ejector shroud back, but the Triple Lock was gone for good. It would return in much different form, by different name, in the 21st Century with a ball-detent crane lock on the X-frame .500 and .460 revolvers.

In less than a decade of production the Triple Lock had set a high-water mark for revolver quality. In 1916 in Sweetwater, a Triple Lock saved the

Mas is comfortable firing modern .44 Special loads in the old gun's massive cylinder. This is Winchester Silvertip. The old Triple Lock is still accurate after more than a century.

life of famed Texas Ranger Frank Hamer, killing his assailant with a single .44 Special slug fired weak hand only because Hamer had been wounded in the gun-side shoulder at the opening of the ambush. Generations to come would thank the designers of the Triple Lock for paving the way for some of the finest handguns the world has ever seen. **GUNS**

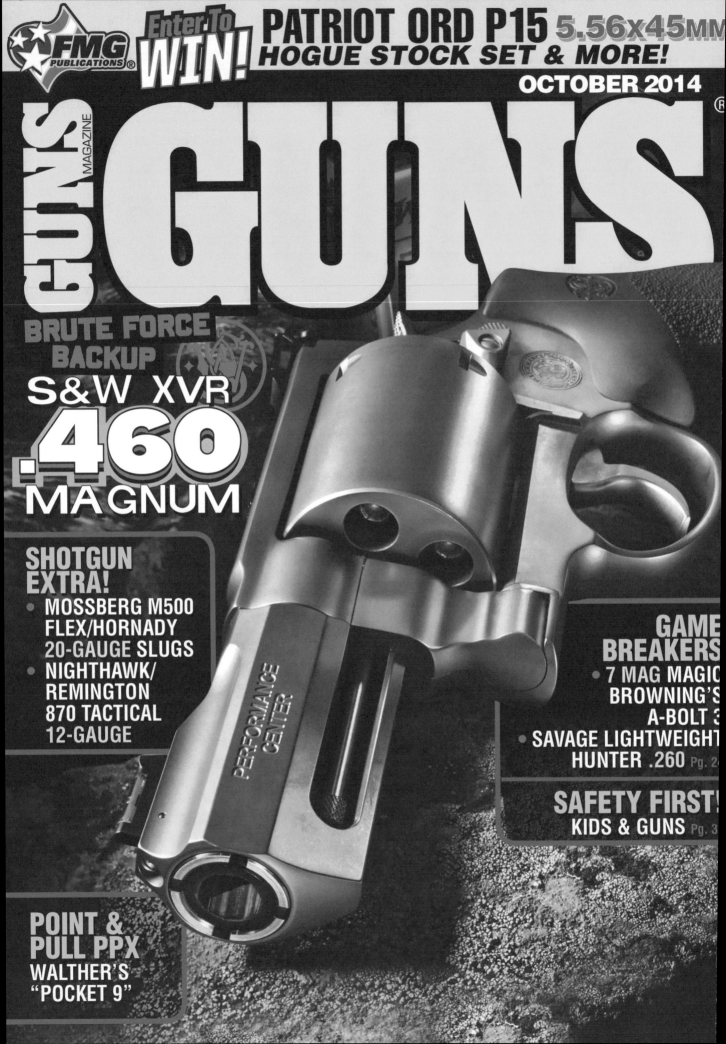

Enter To WIN!

PATRIOT ORD P15 5.56x45MM
HOGUE STOCK SET & MORE!

OCTOBER 2014

GUNS
MAGAZINE

®

BRUTE FORCE
BACKUP

S&W XVR
.460
MAGNUM

SHOTGUN
EXTRA!
- MOSSBERG M500
  FLEX/HORNADY
  20-GAUGE SLUGS
- NIGHTHAWK/
  REMINGTON
  870 TACTICAL
  12-GAUGE

PERFORMANCE CENTER

GAME
BREAKERS
- 7 MAG MAGIC
  BROWNING'S
  A-BOLT 3
- SAVAGE LIGHTWEIGHT
  HUNTER .260 Pg. 2

SAFETY FIRST!
KIDS & GUNS Pg. 3

POINT &
PULL PPX
WALTHER'S
"POCKET 9"

BRUTE-FOR

B

THE S&W .460 XVR OFFERS POWER APLENTY.

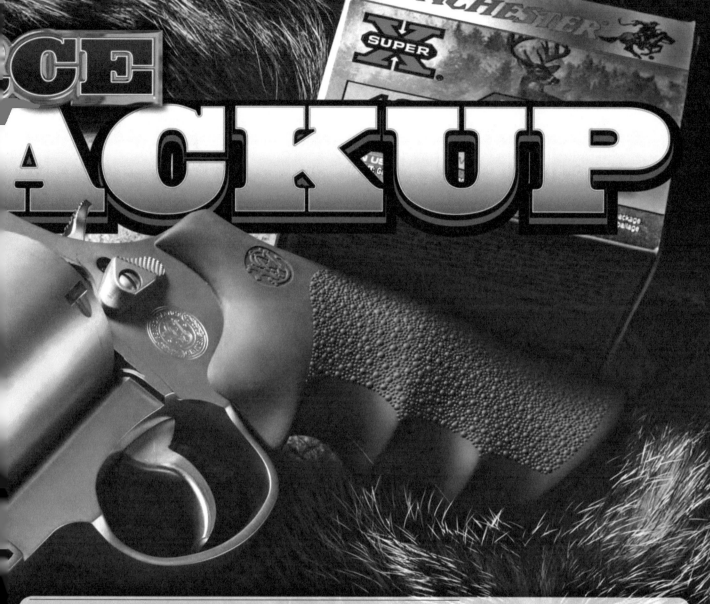

ACKUP

MARK HAMPTON   PHOTOS: JOSEPH R. NOVELOZO

The last time I went fishing in Alaska on the Naknek River we ran in to some problems. Bears! There weren't just a few bears wandering around our fishing camp, there were a bunch. Not black bears mind you—brown bears. Every evening around camp the bears would come looking for the remains of our fish cleaning.

While fishing one morning I had to start the motor and get out of the way of a large bear swimming toward our boat. Don't think he wanted to check our fishing license, but I wasn't crazy about the idea of him joining us. Another day we took our boat up in Big Creek, a tributary that dumps into the main river, trying to finesse one of those big king salmon with spinning gear. Wading up and down the creek searching for a big king, the sandbar was loaded with evidence we weren't the only ones fishing. Tracks were all over the sandbar. Large tracks! It's difficult to pay attention to your fishing technique when you're looking over your

shoulder every few seconds. I didn't have a gun.

Several years ago when I was much younger, feeling 10-foot tall and bulletproof, I was guiding a couple of bow hunters for bison. The first string-flipper launched an arrow perfectly in the heart of a bull bison. It was a textbook shot. The big boy ran 50 yards or so and we started the laborious task of field dressing and skinning.

Later in the day, our next archer wasn't so lucky. He made a bad shot. Then he made another bad shot. Followed by, you guessed it, another misplaced arrow. The particular bull was a big, mature bison tipping the scales around 1,800 pounds. My buddy

and I followed the bull for quite some time before all hell broke loose. I know you think a bison is a docile animal, tame enough for your kids to ride. Well, when several arrows miss the vitals and the buffalo loses his sense of humor, a personality change occurs.

He charged and for some reason, picked me as his target. I took off running like an Olympic athlete. At that time it didn't dawn on me the buffalo could possibly be faster than me. I didn't get any gold medal but in a matter of seconds, I won his horn in the back of my leg. He tossed me in the air like a rag doll. I hit the ground hard, knocking my glasses off and leaving me in a daze. Luckily he didn't finish me off! I did get a free ride to the hospital and was the brunt of jokes between my buddies. You guessed it—I didn't have a gun.

I'm only sharing a couple of these real-life experiences to say this…I should have had a gun! Well now I can honestly say what gun I will be carrying when the next round of excitement comes knocking on my door. From

WINCHESTER

SUPER X

DEER & BLACK BEAR

460 S&W MAG

BAD BLOOD

GUNS

MAGAZINE

BRUTE-FORCE
BACKUP

460 S&W MAGNUM

(Overleaf) Winchester offers a .460 S&W topped with a 250-grain JHP in the Super-X line of hunting ammunition. Mark took several Texas hogs with this ammo in the XVR. The knife is a Bad Blood/Kendrick Razorhoof Folder. The XVR (below) features a plain square-notch rear sight mated to a quick and easy-to-see Hi-Viz fiber optic front sight.

the Smith & Wesson Performance Center comes a 3-1/2-inch Model 460 XVR. This double-action revolver is chambered in the powerful .460 S&W Magnum.

Since the model's introduction back in 2005, there have been several permutations with longer barrels. Up until now, most of these models were specifically designed with the handgun hunter in mind. This model is purpose-built for dangerous game bent on clawing, goring or a taking a bite out of your hide. Perfect, when you stop and think about it, for a variety of circumstances. Like the Alaskan fishing adventure mentioned earlier, or following a wounded animal that could turn the tables on you during a normal, peaceful, fun-filled day.

This large-framed revolver is built on the same beefed up, double-action X-frame as the company's S&W 500 Magnum. It holds five rounds in a massive cylinder. My gun tipped the scales at a tad over 59 ounces and the weight is most welcome when you unleash one of those .460's. This is the most powerful .45 caliber revolver in production. The XVR stands for Xtreme Velocity Revolver and is capable of launching a 200-grain bullet over 2,300 fps (although from a longer barrel). The frame and unfluted cylinder are stainless steel, and the soft glass-bead appearance is eye-pleasing. Barrel length is 3-1/2 inches, nonported. The soft, green synthetic grips are very comfortable. The rear sight

460 XVR

MAKER: S&W
2100 ROOSEVELT AVENUE
SPRINGFIELD, MA 01104
(800) 331-0852
WWW.GUNSMAGAZINE.COM/INDEX

Action type: Double-action revolver,
Caliber: .460 S&W, **Capacity:** 5, **Barrel
length:** 3-1/2 inches, **Overall length:**
10 inches, **Weight:** 59.5 ounces, **Finish:**
Matte stainless steel, **Sights:** Hi-Viz
green fiber optic front, adjustable rear,
Grips: Synthetic, **Price:** $1,609

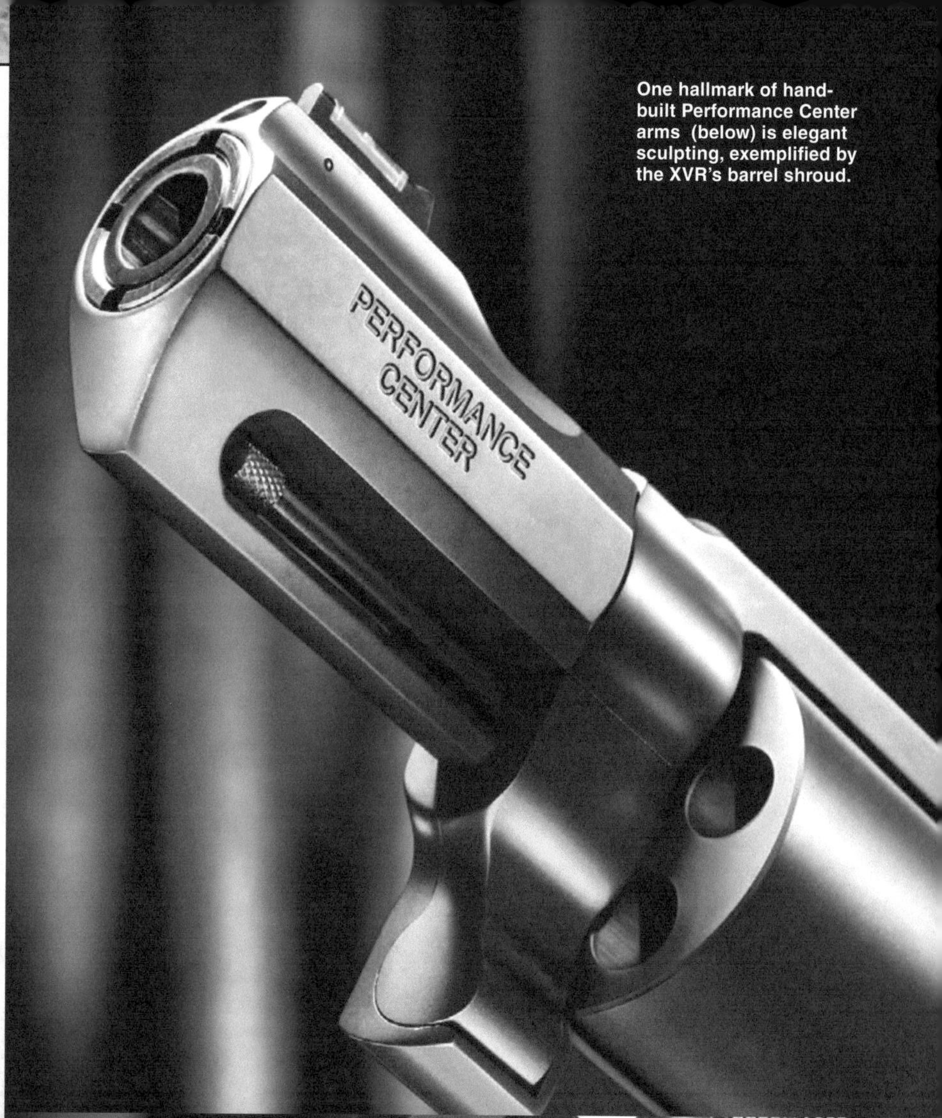

One hallmark of hand-built Performance Center arms (below) is elegant sculpting, exemplified by the XVR's barrel shroud.

is adjustable in the form of a black square notch. My aging eyes appreciated the Hi-Viz fiber optic front sight. That bright green post makes target acquisition quick and easy. If you want to complicate things a bit and decide to mount a scope; no problem, the 460 XVR is drilled and tapped just like their S&W 500 Magnum. The fit and finish on this revolver is typical Performance Center—superb.

The double-action pull was silky-smooth while the single-action pull dropped the hammer at around 3 pounds. No grit, no creep. I believe the single-action trigger is perfect for this gun, not too light but you sure don't have to tug all day long either. This is not an ankle gun by any means. It is however, a serious, well-built revolver intended to save you hide in an unexpected, cataclysmic encounter.

The .460 is a lengthened .454 Casull. As you already know, the .454 Casull is a stretched .45 Colt. If you don't want to shoot a steady diet of .460 S&W

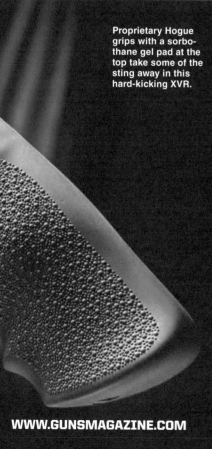

Proprietary Hogue grips with a sorbothane gel pad at the top take some of the sting away in this hard-kicking XVR.

The massive cylinder holds five rounds of .460 S&W ammo.

Magnum ammo, you have the option of shooting both .454 Casull and .45 Colt rounds. Just like a .44 Special is welcome in a .44 Magnum. This capability allows extended range sessions and provides enjoyable practice time.

AMMO CHOICES

At first I was a bit concerned about finding .460 ammo. Well those concerns were truly unfounded. It was relatively painless to procure a couple of different loads from Winchester including a 250-grain JHP and their 260-grain DJHP Bonded offering. Big Red's 250-grain HP is ideal for whitetail, boar or black bear. CorBon offers six loads from 200- to 395-grain bullets. I happen to have their 275-grain DPX along with a 325-grain FPPN. CorBon's 395-grain will handle just about anything on this planet. Buffalo Bore makes a 360-grain LBT-LFN and their 300-grain JFN. These are bear stoppers for sure. Federal hops on board with a 275-grain Barnes in their Vital-Shok line plus a 300-grain Swift A-Frame, and a 260-grain SP in their Fusion ammo. I'm currently shooting a 275-grain Barnes Expander. Grizzly Cartridge Company also makes a 260-grain BCFP and 300-grain LFNGC. DoubleTap ammo provides a 275-grain Barnes XPB. The 200-grain FTX from Hornady is another round for consideration. For deer-sized game, the 200-grain bullets work just fine and Hornady's FTX is a dandy. Lucky for us, there is a bullet weight and design capable of just about any application you may desire.

At the range I started out with .45 Colt rounds in the form of Winchester 225-grain JHP Bonded ammo. This was a very pleasant, well-behaved round quite enjoyable to pick rocks off the pond bank. Next I worked up to some Buffalo Bore 250-grain Barnes XPB in .454 Casull. You could tell this was an increase in horsepower. By no means was it uncomfortable or uncontrollable. I ended my first range session with Winchester's .460 250-grain JHP in their Super-X line. Honestly, it wasn't as bad as I expected. Those soft, finger-grooved rubber grips really help. I had to adjust the sights as it was shooting a tad high. For a short-barreled revolver, accuracy was acceptable. Winchester labels this ammunition suitable for whitetail and black bear. No doubt it will serve its purpose well.

When I hit the range again it was time for some high-octane rounds. To be perfectly honest, it does get your attention. What would you expect? This firearm is not designed for competition or casual plinking. Naturally, the heavier bullets do recoil considerably. The 460 XVR packs a lot of power in a fairly compact platform. Ergonomically,

For close range hunting opportunities, the S&W 460 XVR is a potent choice. Photo: Mark Hampton.

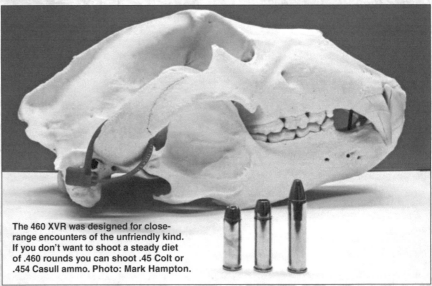

The 460 XVR was designed for close-range encounters of the unfriendly kind. If you don't want to shoot a steady diet of .460 rounds you can shoot .45 Colt or .454 Casull ammo. Photo: Mark Hampton.

the revolver is ready for action. If you should ever be so unfortunate to find yourself in a situation where an animal is trying to kill you, the recoil probably won't be noticed. I didn't have time to experiment with handloads but looking through Hodgdon's reloading data, there are plenty of options with a variety of bullet weights ranging from 200 to 395 grains.

As luck would have it, a hog hunt in Texas materialized right before closing time on this piece. I couldn't pass up an opportunity to chase a big mean hog behind a pack of hounds. Heck, I couldn't wait! This kind of action gets you up close and personal. Shots are usually close range affairs with this type of hunting. Grabbing a box of Winchester's 250-grain JHP ammo, my wife and I hit the road south for some Texas hog-hunting action. The XVR

was ready for a trial run, now if we can only get one of those big old boars to cooperate.

We met up with some real dog men near College Station. The bottomland country is ideal for hogs and there are far more than plenty. When the dogs were turned loose they worked their way toward a small, brushy creek. The heavy vegetation along the creek bottom provided ideal habitat for hogs. It wasn't long before the dogs found action. We headed toward the area where they were bayed but before we could get there the hogs broke and ran. One of the boars came flying past me and I tried to put a bullet in his boiler room, to no avail. The chase continued. Since there were several hogs, the canines got split up and were going in different directions. By the time we caught up with one particular dog, he was barking bayed, but the hog had other ideas and took off. If you think hunting behind a pack of dogs is easy or unsporting, think again. Luckily the dog handlers had put tracking collars on the dogs so we could eventually find them.

It was getting up in the day when we hiked for over a mile where another dog was barking. The hog was in the thickest jungle of undergrowth you could imagine. As I fought my way in to the gauntlet of briars and brambles, I could barely make out a dark shape in the impenetrable jungle. I fought my way a little closer and could scarcely see what the dogs were barking about. Unfortunately I couldn't make out the head from the tail and about that time the big hog busted out of his hiding place never to be seen again. We crawled our way out of the thicket, wiped the blood off from all the thorn punctures and headed a different direction.

I didn't have a holster made for the gun but that will soon change. Those across the chest rigs would work well for the XVR, keeping it close and readily available, yet non-restrictive. Leather-stretchers like Simply Rugged or Barranti Leather make a dandy system such as this and would be great for hunting or fishing in the backcountry where four-legged critters are a concern.

After a short break for lunch our luck changed for the better. Once again, the dogs had a pig bayed in a real thicket. I eased in this time with the hopes of dropping the hammer on some pork. By the time I scrambled

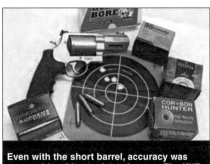

Even with the short barrel, accuracy was acceptable with a variety of ammo. The XVR wasn't finicky. It produced minute-of-bear groups with just about any ammo (above). There is a variety of quality factory ammo available for the .460 S&W Magnum (below). Photo: Mark Hampton.

through the vines and brush, sweat was running in my eyes so bad I could barely see. But I did see a big pig fighting the dogs. Carefully I got in a position for a shot. The distance was close. Heck, you couldn't see 15 feet! I wanted to make certain the dogs were clear before shooting. The big .460 slug could go clean through a hog and I sure didn't want to hit a prize dog on the other end. When a shot finally materialized, the mighty .460 performed as expected. The hog dropped on the spot and that chase was over. Those green fiber optic sights were an asset. Even though the thick jungle-like growth made for dim lighting conditions, it was easy to see the sights.

There are a lot different ways to hunt hogs but chasing a pack of hounds is sure a lot of fun. We hunted the rest of the day and took several hogs in the process. The S&W XVR worked like a charm. The Performance Center has once again concocted a superb revolver that performs like a champ. I can't wait to see what they come up with next. **GUNS**

Bad Blood Knives
P.O. Box 220, Kodak, TN 37764
(866) 583-3912
www.gunsmagazine.com/index

141

J-FRAME UPGRADES

THOUGH NOT WHAT YOU MIGHT WANT FOR A MATCH, THE UBIQUITOUS SMALL-FRAME S&W OFFERS IMPORTANT CARRY ATTRIBUTES.

MASSAD AYOOB

J-Frames have limited capacity improved by good reloading practice. Here Mas' cylinder is already closing (above) as the 5-shot Jetloader (arrow) falls away, during a Back-Up Gun match. The new Hyskore Compact Revolver Light, available through Cylinder & Slide, aids illumination for this S&W 340 PD .357.

A few years ago at our sister publication *American Handgunner,* editorial director Roy Huntington did a poll of his writers as to their preferred carry guns. The answers encompassed everything from Glock to 1911, but the one common touchstone was virtually all of us had at least one J-Frame Smith & Wesson in their carry rotation, whether as primary or backup.

Made in calibers including .22 LR, .22 WMR to .327 Federal Magnum and 9mm, the J-Frame is most commonly encountered as a 5-shot .38 Special or .357 Magnum on its extended .32-size frame. Since the introduction of the Chief Special circa 1950, it has been America's most popular "snubnose .38" and remains hugely popular for armed citizen concealed carry and police back-up and off-duty carry.

The tapered barrel and rounded butt make it faster when drawing from ankle holsters (presuming you don't have a snag-prone hammer spur), and quicker to access and clear from a pocket. The shrouded hammer models in particular allow firing at close range through coat pocket or purse. With hard muzzle contact against a belly-to-belly rapist or killer, most autos would come "out of battery" and fail to fire at all, but these snub revolvers will guarantee a shot for every pull of the trigger, with the muzzle blast significantly magnifying each wound at press-contact distance.

The downsides of the J-Frame are likewise well known: nasty recoil and hard-to-see sights, both of which impair hit potential, particularly as speed and distance increase. Fortunately, those shortcomings can be

significantly alleviated with careful attention to grips, sights, and planning.

STOCKS

Start with your choice of J-Frame. The "hammerless" Centennial style (Model 642, etc.) gets my vote because the shooter's hand can get higher on the backstrap, lowering bore axis and reducing muzzle rise. Next most controllable is the Bodyguard (Model 638, etc.) whose built-in hammer shroud acts like a recoil shield at the web of the hand to prevent the gun from rolling up on recoil, which can let a Chief Special (Model 637, etc.) hammer be blocked by the web. The original, tiny "splinter" stocks on early J-Frames tended to let the gun twist in the hand upon recoil. Pachmayr and Tyler-T (and now, BK) grip adapters helped, without changing the gun's concealability. However, decades ago, Craig Spegel designed his much copied Boot Grips which kept concealability, but filled the hand much better.

To decrease recoil discomfort you need to cushion the web of your hand, and many neoprene grips will do a good job of that. My own favorites in that respect are Pachmayr Compacs, which increase bulk more than I like for

J-Frame grip progression (from left) include the factory "splinter," Eagle "Secret Service," Herrett's, Pachmayr Compac and (below) the new Ergo Delta.

MORE GUNS HERE

every month!

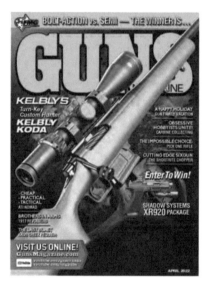

Better J-Frame sights include (left to right) the Crimson Trace Laser Grip, D&L sight set on Model 342 .38, XS Big Dot front and U-notch rear on Model 340 M&P .357.

pocket carry but are still concealable, and shaped to distribute the "kick" across the entire web of the hand. Of late, I've come to appreciate the new Ergo Delta grips, which seem to direct the recoil into the heel of the hand. The Ergo also has a Luger-like grip angle, locking the muzzle down to reduce muzzle rise, and I've found it acceptably sized for trouser pocket carry.

SIGHTS

In their early decades, J-Frames had tiny 1/10-inch wide front sights and equally Lilliputian rear notches notoriously hard to align in less than ideal conditions. Some prized the rare adjustable sight version of the Chief Special because the sights were at least visible. Most of us just painted the sights and hoped for the best, until S&W finally made them bigger. The best in the S&W catalog for my money are the XS Big Dot front with correspondingly large rear U-notch, found on the expensive-but-worth-it Model 340 M&P .357 snub. Of course, you can get larger Patridge sights from Dave Lauck at D&L Sports. Or, you can simply go laser. I've seen John Strayer win the Snubby Summit match in 2005 with a stock Model 642 and Crimson Trace LaserGrips against target-sighted 2.5-inch Model 19's and Colt Pythons, and Dave "the Blaze" Blazek with the same gear once beat night-sighted subcompact autos at Lance Biddle's Back-Up Gun Championship. The Crimson Trace Model LG-405 laser grip gets my vote for the best balance of concealment and control.

FIREPOWER

Five shots are often enough, but not always. Tuff Strips and Bianchi Speed Strips fit the "watch pockets" in jeans. My new favorite speedloader for the J-Frame is the Jetloader from Buffer Technologies. Snubby guru Michael deBethencourt turned me on to it. It's simply faster for me than anything else, and while longer than other speedloaders, it conceals

perfectly in the cell phone pocket of cargo shorts or upright in the outer corner of a hip pocket (a folding handkerchief holds it in place). Of course, the trusty New York reload—another loaded J-Frame elsewhere on your person—is faster still!

Training is key. The three best J-Frame courses I can recommend are taught by Michael deBethancourt in Massachusetts, Denny Reichard in Indiana and Claude Werner in Georgia. Google will get you to all of them.

The J-Frame S&W is like any other tool. Take advantage of its strengths, and shore up its weaknesses. The S&W 340 M&P, loaded with Speer's street-proven .38 Special 135-grain +P Short Barrel Gold Dot ammo, remains my single most often carried backup gun. **GUNS**

The Brownells' chamfering set allows you to optimize forcing cones and chamfer the chambers for easier loading.

GAUGES

J's with Spegel and VZ grips (left and top).

Little "J"ems

One of the nicest perks of my new gig here is that the boss and I get to spend a little time talking about guns and gunsmithing. We pick each other's brains and solve a remarkable number of the world's problems long distance. We recently discussed our mutual love of the J-frame S&W revolvers, which natu- rally led to a chat about the ways they can be improved.

The little J-frames — typically carried much and shot little — are often the focus of "What can I do to make my (fill in the blank) better?" questions. This becomes increasingly true as more and more gunsmiths specialize, narrowing their focus, with the goal of enhancing profitability. Hence, we see fewer and fewer shops willing or even able to do the little things many J-frames need to run well. The good news is some of the most beneficial modifications can be accomplished by a patient, determined gun owner — one with reasonable problem-solving skills, proper tools, knowledge and some common sense.

Who, ME?

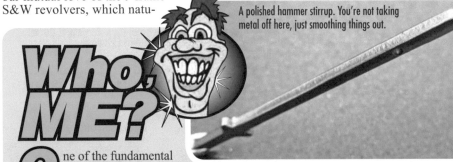

A polished hammer stirrup. You're not taking metal off here, just smoothing things out.

One of the fundamental principles of gun- smithing is the things that appear to be simple generally are not, and the things that appear complicated are, well … complicated. Attempting a full-blown action job on a J-frame's lockwork is best left to an experienced hand. But there are a few simpler modifications that can pay real dividends. If you're not familiar with basic disassembly procedures, you should first consult a reliable reference. The Kuhnhausen manual, available from Brownells, is a valuable tool, as are the books by our own J.B. Wood on take-down and assembly.

There are three things an owner can do on a newer J-frame that will improve the smoothness and "weight" of the trigger without major work. First, change the springs — especially the rebound spring. In the Brownells SWJ200 spring kit, there are three weights of rebound spring, in 13-, 14- and 15-pound versions. The 14-rated spring works best in my opinion.

When changing the mainspring, plan on testing your revolver with different types and brands of ammunition to ensure reliable ignition. Any light strikes and it's back to the factory mainspring.

The second "trick" helping to smooth things out is to polish the mainspring stirrup (actually the hammer strut). Newer models have a stamped, squared profile stirrup with sharp, square corners. Most will show chatter marks from contact with the inside surfaces of the spring. Carefully break these edges with a fine file, and polish them with fine abrasive paper. Don't get carried away here — there's no need to remove a lot of material. The difference is usually quite noticeable.

The third modification really isn't a modification at all. When you get things put back together, lightly lube any bearing surfaces you can see, and reattach the side plate. Then, and this is the secret part, simply dry fire the revolver — a lot. Of course, all safety considerations apply here. Roy and I both agree this simple step can be as important as any other in establishing a more comfortable relationship with your revolver. Plus, it really helps slick- up and settle things inside your gun.

GRIPS & CHAMFERS

A comfortable firing grip on a small revolver is another way to improve overall effectiveness. I'm not a huge fan of rubber grips, although they are an economical alternative. As an unrepentant wood lover, I've always favored Craig Spegel's beautifully crafted grips. They're not cheap, and you may have to wait a while, but they will not disappoint.

PISTOLSMITHING

Excellent-quality exotic hardwood grips are also available from Ahrends (through Brownells). Because choice is a good thing, now VZ grips is offering S&W grips made from synthetic mate-rials like Micarta and G10. They fi t very well, and since they have no added sur-face fi nish, they can be easily person-alized with nothing more than a little abrasive paper. The laminated layers create an almost "wood-like" appear-ance without any of the durability con-cerns of real wood.

There are three things an owner can do on a newer J-frame that will improve the smoothness and "weight" of the trigger without major work.

I'd feel derelict in my duties if I neglected to encourage the purchase and use of really cool tools. And honest, I'm not on the Brownells payroll, it's just that they have *so much* good stuff! Brownells' revolver chamfering sets allow us to chamfer chambers and opti-mize or restore forcing cones. They're available as complete multi-caliber sets, single-caliber sets and as individual components. A mild chamfer on the chamber mouths of any revolver will aid in smoothly loading that chamber, whether you're using speedloaders, strips or loading single cartridges.

As usual, it's important to be patient, go slow and check often, as with any gunsmithing procedure. While modifica-tions like chamfering are best undertaken by capable, experienced hands, the tools, along with Brownells' typically well-detailed instructions, put these processes into the hands of confident hobbyists. When cutting, insert *empty* fired cases into all the other chambers to keep the extractor properly aligned. Go light here, and remember to leave adequate support for the extractor to pull cases from the chamber.

Want to comment on this article? Let us know what's on your mind, and maybe tell us about your own experiences learning to gunsmith your own revolver. We can be reached at editor@americanhandgunner. com. RH

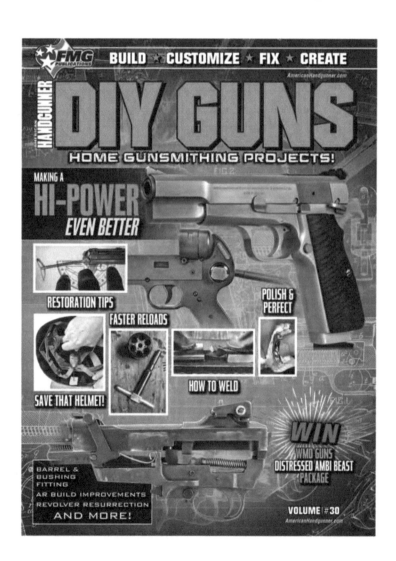

S&W .44/

Both S&W Competitor Models were fitted with optics for accuracy testing. The 2X Leupold and Meopta's reflex sight worked great, with zero problems.
Photo: Robbie Barrkman

MARK HAMPTON

HUNTING & COMPETITION!

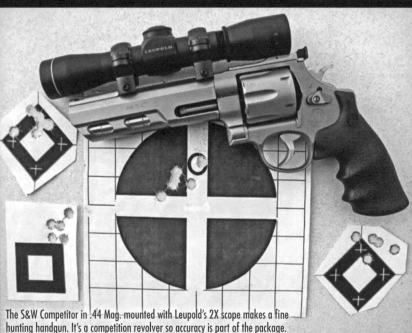

The S&W Competitor in .44 Mag. mounted with Leupold's 2X scope makes a fine hunting handgun. It's a competition revolver so accuracy is part of the package.

'll just say it: I'm a handgun hunter. I live it, breathe it, seek it out and engage in it whenever possible. When His Editorship assigned me to cover this duo, I balked. "But they're target revolvers!" I muttered. But then I saw them, and immediately thought of a better use for them!

Through the years I've seen many handguns designed for competition. Most of these purpose-built guns were highly modified with embellishments specifically designed to enhance the intended activity. Seldom are these custom creations suitable for other applications, especially hunting. Be that as it may, these Performance Center revolvers from Smith & Wesson are fully capable of multitasking. While the Model 629 and 686 Competitors were manufactured for competition, they are great all-around revolvers, easily doing double-duty as hunting handguns.

.357

Winchester's new Razor Back XT load with their 225-gr. beveled profile hollow-point shot great in the .44 Mag Competitor.

Left: The S&W Competitors (.357 lower) are both finely-tuned, accurate revolvers specifically made for target shooting disciplines. But, Mark found they make great hunting handguns too!

COMPETITOR MODELS

Although they originate from their standard 686 and 629 designs, the Competitors certainly have been blessed with classy, custom touches. Both models are beefed-up versions of their counterparts. The glassbead finish is aesthetically pleasing and contrasts well with the Hogue black synthetic grip installed. Caliber designation is etched on one side of the barrel, "Competitor" on the other, without looking like a neon sign. The front sight consists of a black patridge dovetail, easily acquired in the notch of the black target-style rear sight, which is adjustable and removable (more on that later). Their frames and cylinders are stainless steel.

The major and most noticeable difference comes in the weighted 6" barrels. These are, in actuality, target revolvers, and target shooters often like to custom-tune the "heft" of the barrel by adding or subtracting barrel weights. S&W enables that, but turned it into a design feature at the same time.

Five weighted inserts fit inside the massive underlug and can be removed to accommodate individual needs. By removing the Allen-head screw at the end of the underlug, shooters can remove one or all of the weighted disks if needed. You can see the weights from the cutout portion in the underlug; I

The .44 Mag. was not at all picky and shot all loads consistently. The weights shown here housed in the underlug can be removed if needed.

think it's all handsomely done.

All machine work and details of the barrel are streamlined. The Model 629 Competitor tipped the scales a little over 57 ounces, while the original Model 629 with the same barrel length weighs in at 45 ounces. The .357 Magnum version of the Model 686 Competitor weighs 53 ounces. That is nine ounces heavier than my standard 686.

Performance Center

The Performance Center's tuned action was smooth and much what you

would expect in a custom gun. Single-action trigger pull was crisp with zero creep, breaking around three pounds. The double-action mode was velvety. Located on the back side of the chrome trigger was a trigger stop. This is one feature I like shooting a revolver in single action, especially when I'm hunting. The serrated hammer was also finished in chrome. The overall fit and finish on both models were exactly what you would expect from a custom gun.

Both models featured integral

S&W COMPETITORS

mounting systems on their 6" barrels. You can easily mount optics of your choice, be it scope or red dot. I wanted to use optics on both guns for accuracy testing and this feature made mounting a scope quick and easy. For this old guy, employing optics would be the only way I could determine their accuracy potential.

But Target Guns?

What were these revolvers actually designed for? Smith & Wesson's Tony Miele told me the Model 686 Competitor was originally made for PPC competition, and they are still popular in Europe. I would only assume many of the PPC competitors here in the states are using semi-autos or perhaps their duty guns. PPC is a highly regimented target match requiring a high degree of accuracy from the hardware, and skill by the user. A PPC gun is a precision instrument and in the right hands can manage 1.5" at 50 yards — or better!

The larger .44 Magnum could be used in bowling pin matches, steel plates and many other competitive games. Our very own Dave Anderson, who is kind of a competition guru, advised me they possibly could find use in ICOR: International Confederation of Revolver Enthusiasts, steel challenge or USPSA in the revolver division. Not being a serious competitor, I can see handgun hunters taking a liking to the larger .44 Magnum, especially.

The .357 Magnum version offers modest recoil (maybe good for a smaller-statured handgunner) but would certainly be up to the task of taking a whitetail deer at realistic ranges. It's also a good revolver to "cut your teeth" on while learning handgun hunting.

In a nutshell, you don't have to be in competition to enjoy either of these fine wheelguns. To get a better idea of what these Performance Center guns were capable of doing, I loaded the truck with a variety of ammunition and headed to the range.

Learning The Guns

On my first trip to the range, I shot from 25 yards with open sights exclusively. Factory ammo tested included .357 Magnum from Winchester and DoubleTap with both 125- and 158-gr. bullets. During the .44 Magnum session, ammo from Hornady, Federal, Cor-Bon, Black Hills, Buffalo Bore and Winchester were used, all with 240-gr. bullets. Groups were acceptable from all brands, but honestly, optics needed to be mounted on both guns to get a better idea of the accuracy potential. One of the first things I noticed was the nice trigger. The

crisp, clean break without tugging all day made shooting both guns enjoyable. It's difficult to shoot any handgun with a terrible trigger, one having creep or over-travel and doesn't break without a struggle. These Performance Center triggers had been tuned perfectly.

Another notable aspect was the lack of muzzle rise compared to revolvers without weighted barrels. This makes getting subsequent shots off much faster and easier if needed. The additional weight of both guns also lessened felt recoil. I actually prefer a little heavier gun than most. Regardless, if I have to shoot offhand or get to take advantage of a rest of some sort, I feel the added weight helps me with more precise bullet placement.

Optics

With handgun hunting in the back of my mind, I mounted a quality Leupold 2X scope on the .44 Magnum using Burris Signature Zee Rings. I prefer Burris rings because they never leave a blemish on the scope tube. They also secure the optic firmly and I don't worry about them coming loose. I had to remove the front sight which is easily drifted out of the ramp. The integral mounting system on the Competitor made mounting the scope quick and painless.

Two new red-dot sights arrived just in time from Meopta. This company is no stranger in the optics arena. Meopta has facilities in the US and Europe. They have been producing quality glass, in both military and sporting versions, for many years. Both of these red-dot sights were designed to aid quick target acquisition.

Thanks to a locking, lever-activated quick release mount, I slapped Meopta's M-RAD reflex sight on the .357 Magnum. This sight comes in 3- or 5-MOA dot sizes. The sight conveniently incorporates eight levels of brightness adjustment for daylight shooting and another eight levels for nighttime activities. Shooters can fine-tune the dot intensity for a variety of conditions. The matte-black body is machined from aircraft-grade aluminum alloy and built to withstand the rigors of battlefield conditions. It'll definitely survive your next handgun hunt!

With optics now in place and a fresh supply of ammo, a second trip to the range was in order. I shot the .44 Magnum with a variety of factory loads, including some .44 Specials, from 25 and 50 yards. While going through seven different brands of ammo, I was happy to see the Model 629 did not discriminate. All magnum loads consisted of 240-gr. bullets, except for Winchester's new Razorback XT offering a 225-gr. beveled profile hollowpoint.

Groups were more than acceptable from most every manufacturer. Several 5-shot, 50-yard groups held much less

than minute-of-deer. I ran a few .44 Specials through in double action "against" some rocks on the embankment. No steel plates, but allowed me to get an idea of what faster DA work might be like. I busted some rocks due to the slick action — even though this type of shooting is not my cup of tea. With the addition of the Leupold scope though, this would make a fine hunting revolver for deer, hogs or bear. I liked the feel of the Competitor. It handles recoil well, and balances nicely.

> "It they're target revolvers!' I muttered. But then I saw them, and immediately thought of a better use for the!"

I will probably have a custom leather company like Diamond D Custom or 7X Leather make a holster for this scoped revolver. Both of these holster companies provide an across-the-chest rig ideal for the S&W Competitor.

The .357

My wife, Karen, and I shot the .357 Mag. with Winchester, Doubletap and Buffalo Bore ammo using 110-, 125-, 158- and 180-gr. bullets. After running the first cylinder on the 25-yard target she commented, "That's a nice trigger!" I ran some .38 Special loads through in double action, and getting back on target for multiple shots was a snap. The M-RAD we were using had a 5-MOA dot size, which is fine for competition but for hunting purposes, I prefer the smaller 3-MOA dot. The 686 Competitor was just plain fun to shoot. The heavier frame is easier for me to shoot more accurately than my original model, and Karen also had fun shooting the .357 Mag. with Meopta's reflex sight. The added weight and lower recoil really makes it a fun gun.

If you are searching for a first-class hunting revolver, the Competitors bear consideration. While these revolvers were made specifically for competition, they will make fine hunting handguns. Whether stalking whitetail in the woods or sneaking up to a big mean hog, the Model 629 Competitor will be a reliable friend. The .357 Magnum version is a perfect companion piece to the .44, and would allow training, new-shooter introduction to handgun hunting, and with lighter-bulleted loads, would make a fun varminter!

WINNINGEDGE
SOLID ADVICE TO KEEP YOU AHEAD OF THE COMPETITION
DAVE ANDERSON

HISTORICALLY IMPORTANT: S&W'S MODEL 39

In 1946 Carl H. Hellstrom was elected president of S&W. An enthusiastic and energetic man, Hellstrom immediately set S&W on a course toward improved production facilities and the development of new models. Favorably impressed with the Walther P38, he wanted S&W to have a double-action 9mm semi-auto.

S&W's chief designer, Joe Norman, had a prototype, serial number X46, ready on October 28, 1948 — the first American-made, DA 9mm. Oversimplifying a bit, the design combines the receiver of a P38 with the slide/barrel assembly of a 1911. The receivers of the P38 and the S&W are so similar the magazines will interchange. Although P38 mags won't lock in a S&W receiver because they lack the cut in the magazine body for the magazine catch.

Rather than the dropping block lockup of the P38, S&W stayed with the proven Browning-designed tilting barrel, controlled by a cam as on the Browning Hi-Power. The front of the barrel fits a bushing in the front of the slide, similar in concept to the 1911.

The prototype used an alloy frame. Wanting to cover all bases, in the early '50's the factory forged 1,000 steel frames. They also designed a single-action variation. Samples were provided to the US military for testing. About this time the military decided to stay with the pistols on hand. It would be another 30 years before a new pistol was adopted.

Walther P38, the first 9mm DA service pistol (bottom). S&W's 39 combines the DA feature of the P38 with the Browning tilt-lock system (center). A 3rd Gen. S&W 6906 follows the 39 design but in compact size, high mag capacity and stainless construction.

COPS FIND IT

In 1954, with no military contracts in sight, S&W decided to release the alloy-framed model for commercial sale. Uncertain about how the DA feature would be accepted, in 1954 to 1955 they made 10 DA and 10 SA production models.

There proved to be virtually no interest in the SA version, and in fact little enough in the DA model. No more SA's were built, and only a total of 797 DA models were made to the end of 1956. In 1957 the DA version was assigned model number 39. Total production in 1957 was just 426 pistols.

The SA version was designated model 44. The model 44 remained in the catalog until August 1959 in the hope of getting some orders, which never happened. No additional SA's were made, and none of the few produced were ever stamped with the model number 44.

Another "phantom" model number is the 39-1. The US Army Marksmanship Unit had developed a semi-rimmed version of the .38 Special they called the .38 AMU. At the request of the AMU, S&W made 87 alloy-framed pistols for the cartridge, intended to be named the 39-1.

When the frames were completed, to avoid confusion with the 9mm pistols, S&W decided instead to stamp the frames model "52." When the AMU dropped the project S&W released the remaining pistols for commercial sale — but to avoid confusion with their steel-framed, .38 Special model 52, they restamped the alloy versions as model 52-A. Yep, no confusion there.

Remember those 1,000 steel frames forged in the early '50's? In 1966 the factory decided to finish machining the 927 steel frames still on hand, assemble completed pistols on them and release them for commercial sale. These were marked model "39" and sold along with the alloy framed version, in three s/n ranges: 35,000 between 60,000-64,000 and 80,000.

GROWING PAINS

As interest in centerfire semi-autos grew in the '60's, sales of the model 39 slowly picked up. The biggest boost came in 1967 when the Illinois State Police adopted it as their duty sidearm. More extensive use revealed some weaknesses. A shorter, spring-loaded extractor, heavier duty barrel bushing and a reshaped feedramp resulted in the model 39-2 introduced in 1971.

Dave's 39 is handsome, displaying excellent workmanship.

Several other police agencies also adopted the 39 and its high-capacity version, the model 59, released in 1971. As Massad Ayoob reported in the J/A 1978 issue of *Handgunner*, several of these agencies soon transitioned back to revolvers, usually stainless-steel .357's. Problems reported were an unacceptably high rate of malfunctions, especially with bullets other than FMJ-roundnose and concerns with 9mm stopping power. There was still a lot to be learned about bullets and semi-autos.

S&W put the lessons learned to good use in developing its 2nd generation (3-digit model numbers) and 3rd generation (4-digit numbers) semi-autos. These proved successful, as police transitioned en masse to semi-autos during the 1980's. Available in more models, variations and cartridges than I have space to list, they remain exceptionally fine pistols.

For collectors, the model 39 has many variations. Blue steel and nickel plating, 39's and 39-2's, alloy and steel frames, pre-model numbers, .30 Luger versions (500+ made for sale in Italy), and you can dream of someday coming across a SA model or a 52-A. And don't overlook the 2nd generation models 439, 539 and 639.

Mine is a blued 39-2. It's completely reliable with every JHP load I've tried. The grip frame is very comfortable, it's adequately accurate, handles beautifully and is light and compact. To my eye it's one of the handsomest pistols ever made, and a historically important model.

S&W'S M&P22 COMPACT

A .22 LR HEIR TO THE LEGENDARY "MILITARY & POLICE" DESIGNATION, THIS SLICK LITTLE AUTO IS STATE-OF-THE-ART.

HOLT BODINSON

For training purposes, Holt set up the scaled down M&P22 Compact (bottom) like his full-sized M&P9 (top).

Some companies know how to keep secrets. After signing a 4-page, non-disclosure agreement, having my mug shot taken, my background checked, passing through a "photo badge mandatory" outdoor turnstile and two interior metal detection stations, I was in the promised land—Smith & Wesson's impressive manufacturing facility in Springfield, Mass. With 3,000 employees and 480,000 square feet of manufacturing space, it is, in a word, *big*. Lined from one end to the other are numerically controlled machines going 24/7. The company's firearm design process is now so sophisticated, engineers send their specifications from CAD computers directly to a 3D printer, which builds a replica model of the gun to be examined, analyzed and tweaked until the design is finalized and ready for production.

The plant tour was a lead-in to my reason for being there. There was something S&W's director of marketing communications, Paul Pluff, wanted to share. But for day one, the focus was on S&W's 2014 introduction of their Crimson Trace laser-equipped M&P Bodyguard .380 auto and .38 Special revolver. Both are great handguns for daily concealed carry, but the real surprise came in the traditional blue box on day two.

Smith & Wesson's recent Military & Police line of handguns and AR rifles have set a new standard and are engineered, manufactured and tested to professional standards. "Reliable, durable and accurate" is a good description of S&W's M&P products. Years ago I was a confirmed Glock guy until I began shooting S&W's full-sized M&P9. I've been shooting M&P's ever since.

The M&P line has included a previous .22 rimfire, the M&P22, produced for S&W by Walther of Germany (the relationship is dissolving on an amicable basis). The replacement product was the secret Pluff had been teasing us with for 24 hours—the M&P22 Compact.

This rimfire "tactical" featured pistol took the engineering design team 18 months to perfect. In size, it's an 87-1/2 percent scale version of my full-sized M&P9. The proportions are ideal—the M&P22 is compact without being skimpy. I have large hands, and when I grip the Compact, my pinky finger doesn't drift off the bottom of the magazine well.

The Compact is also well balanced, weighing 18 ounces (including its fully-loaded 10-round magazine) with an overall length of 6.7 inches. When I asked the engineering team how difficult that reduction in scale had been, I got an earful. It turned out to be much more of a challenge than I had expected.

The cartridge was the determining factor by defining the size of the magazine well. When the height of the full-size M&P was reduced, the feeding angle for the .22 LR round became an issue (as did the striking energy of the internal hammer because the arc-of-rotation was changed). The engineers did tell me how invaluable the in-house 3D printer had been for the fabrication of prototypes along the development path.

Like its centerfire big brother, the Compact is a mix of polymers and steels. Pluff told us S&W recently went out and purchased an entire injection molding company because "we knew how to cut metal, but not how to work polymers."

Anyway, the frame is made from a high-strength polymer, the slide from tough, 7076 T651 aluminum, and the barrel from 4140 carbon steel. Every part in this new model is American-made.

The Compact is a single-action, hammer-fired, blowback design featuring an articulated trigger with a drop safety/activated firing pin block, an ambidextrous thumb safety, a

Holt found the M&P22 Compact's trigger to be little short of terrific.

M&P22 COMPACT

MAKER: SMITH & WESSON
2100 ROOSEVELT AVE., SPRINGFIELD, MA 01104
(800) 331-0852
WWW.GUNSMAGAZINE.COM/INDEX

Action Type: Blowback, semi-auto, **Caliber:** .22 Long Rifle, **Capacity:** 10, **Barrel length:** 3.6 inches, **Overall length:** 6.7 inches, **Weight:** 18.1 ounces, fully loaded, **Sights:** 3-dot, fully adjustable, plus rail, **Stocks:** Polymer, **Finish:** Black, **Price:** $389

The 3-dot sight system (above) is fully adjustable for windage and elevation. The grasping grooves on the slide (below) are elegant and effective.

loaded-chamber observation port, and an internal lock activated by turning a supplied key. I can't think of a safer model on the market. The Compact would be an ideal plinker for the entire family to enjoy.

TACTICAL TOUCHES

When I used the term "tactical" to describe the M&P22, I wasn't exaggerating. The first feature that catches your eye is the Picatinny-style rail up front, just begging for some lights and lasers. My M&P9 is stocked with Crimson Trace LaserGrips, and I ended up mounting a complementary Insight white light unit on the Picatinny rail. To duplicate that package and controls on the Compact, I mounted a Streamlight Model TLR-4 green laser/white light unit on the front rail. It's a pretty cool tool, offering light only, laser only or light/laser combined at the flick of your finger.

I spoke with Mike Faw from Crimson Trace, who was at the factory as well. He told me the trend is definitely to green lasers, pointing out the fact green is more visible in daylight. It also projects a larger beam, but at the cost of more energy and bigger batteries. Faw also said since most confrontations occur at night, the advantage of green lasers isn't always significant. Whether a green dot in the middle of an assailant's chest will have the same calming effect as a red one remains to be seen.

Speaking of being a tactical design, the muzzle of the Compact is factory threaded for a suppressor. It's not obvious because the threads are concealed by a protective nut. The barrel thread form is 3/8-inch-24 threads, so a 1/2-inch-28 thread adapter will be required to mount most current rimfire suppressors. No big deal. They're readily available; however, because of its threaded barrel and trigger pull weight, the Compact cannot be sold in Massachusetts, Connecticut or California.

One of the nice features of the M&P22 Compact is the sighting system. It's a three white-dot setup with the rear sight being adjustable for windage and elevation. Being able to adjust your zero is an outstanding asset with a .22 handgun because no two .22 LR brands ever seem to have the same point of impact.

With a pull weight of only 5.8 pounds and a reset of only 0.150 inch, the Compact's factory trigger is sensational. Both at the factory and home on the range, I shot hundreds of rounds through it. The only type of ammunition that failed to cycle was Federal's Gold Medal target load. All other brands, whether standard or high velocity, solid or hollowpoint, fed and functioned fine.

I love the stainless steel magazines supplied with this gun. They drop right out when the reversible magazine catch is punched. They're tough enough to take the fall on a rapid reload without lip deformation. There's a big, soft, slide button for your thumb to lower the follower when charging the magazine (two of them come with the gun).

At 15 yards from a Caldwell pistol rest, my best overall group was 1-1/2-inches with Federal Champion. What surprised and intrigued me were the 4-shot groups turned in by Federal 550 and Winchester 555—those big-box store, 500+ round bulk packs we *used* to be able to buy. I hope we can

The slide is removed from the frame by first lowering this takedown lever (above). The M&P22 Compact is fully "tactical" and has a suppressor-ready, threaded muzzle featuring a protective nut (below).

again soon! There's some magic lurking there.

Field-stripping the Compact is simply a matter of switching the takedown lever down and removing the slide. The process can be seen at www. smith-wesson.com/mp22compact.

The M&P22 Compact story wouldn't be complete without mentioning S&W's accessory program. The company has arranged with holster makers (De Santis and Triple K), laser and flashlight firms (Crimson Trace, Streamlight, LaserMax and Laserlyte) and optics mounting system maker, UM Tactical, to have M&P22 Compact accessories available.

In short, Smith & Wesson's M&P22 Compact is a well-designed, quality pistol, worthy of the M&P designation, with a wealth of tactical features. **GUNS**

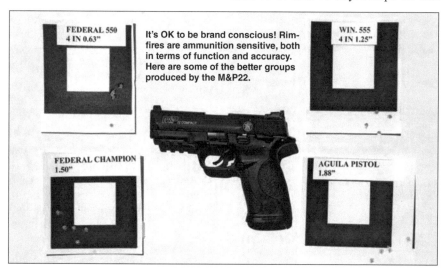

FEDERAL 550
4 IN 0.63"

WIN. 555
4 IN 1.25"

It's OK to be brand conscious! Rimfires are ammunition sensitive, both in terms of function and accuracy. Here are some of the better groups produced by the M&P22.

FEDERAL CHAMPION
1.50"

AGUILA PISTOL
1.88"

A SPECIAL PURPOSE WHEELGUN

YES, EVEN AN 8-SHOT 9MM N-FRAME HAS ITS NICHE.

MASSAD AYOOB

The crane is locked by a ball detent (arrow), replacing traditional the S&W front lug and providing solid lockup.

Smith & Wesson's Performance Center recently introduced an 8-shot N-Frame revolver chambered for the 9mm Luger cartridge. Its barrel with tapered underlug is almost 7 inches long counting the removable recoil compensator at the muzzle, it weighs 44.2 ounces, it's more than a foot long overall, and it carries a suggested retail of $1,189.

And from beyond the grave, I can hear the voice of Col. Jeff Cooper shouting… "Why?"

Why buy a 929 when a turn of the page (or a click of the mouse) of the S&W catalog will bring you to the M&P SHIELD, a very compact semi-automatic pistol holding the same eight (7+1) 9mm cartridges (and you can order mags that hold one more) but less than half the weight, length, and cost of a Model 929?

The answer would, first and foremost, be action revolver competition. It's a signature model of Jerry Miculek, and when the man I consider the world's best double-action revolver shooter puts his name on a gun, that carries weight with me. For the revolver division in the United States Practical Shooting Association (USPSA), the Model 929 makes huge sense. I'm told the 929 has already made its bones, a pretty deep pile of 'em, in that game.

It's also a solid choice for the Open Division or, with comp removed, the Limited Division of the International Congress of Revolver Enthusiasts (ICORE). In fact, the 929 appears

The big S&W was fired with three relatively inexpensive brands of 9mm FMJ ammunition.

to have been purpose-built to help the shooter dominate these games. There's another niche, too: Some folks are fine for double-action trigger pull and significant gun weight, but have palsied hands. The weight can dampen the tremors and make such people shoot better, even in home defense work.

PERKS & QUIRKS

For one thing, you don't want to shoot this gun without the cartridges in moon clips. Those of us who have shot .45 ACP Smith revolvers with loose ACP round know that they will reliably go bang if you have a stock mainspring, but you may have to punch the empties out by hand because the ejector star can't grab "rimless" cases. Headspace does not appear to allow that with 9mm ammo in the 929, however. I stuffed eight random 9mm ball rounds into the chambers, and pulled the double-action trigger eight times. The result was four unfired cartridges with untouched primers, two with tiny needle-like dings on the primers, one shallowly indented primer… and a single fired round and empty casing with its primer impressively smeared. The phrase, "Don't try this at home, kids" comes to mind.

So, you'll need the moon clips… but that's not really a knock on the gun,

The sole Miculek's moon clip for Miculek signature 8-shot 9mm was easier to both fill and empty than .45 ACP moons.

because moon clip capability is part of this revolver's *raison d'etre*. If you need 13 to 16 shots to complete your stage in an ICORE match and you're running this 8-shooter, you'll only need to reload once but the sixgunners will have to reload twice, and the unforgiving clock runs at the same pace for all. On a long assault course, you might only need three reloads where the six-shooter folks require four.

Bad news: The 929 comes with the internal lock S&W aficionados love to hate. Good news: the lock never screwed up, and on big N-frame, it doesn't uglify the classic the way it does on smaller S&W's.

Double-action trigger pull was smooth but heavy, a tad over 12 pounds, with the single-action press

Winchester 9mm 147-grain FMJ delivered sterling accuracy at 25 yards from the bench.

The lighter weight American Eagle 9mm 115-grain ammo also delivered excellent accuracy at 25 yards from the bench.

MODEL 929
MAKER: S&W
2100 ROOSEVELT AVENUE
SPRINGFIELD, MA 01104
(800) 331-0852
WWW.GUNSMAGAZINE.COM/INDEX

Action type: Double-action revolver, **Caliber:** 9x19mm, **Capacity:** 8 (moon clip necessary), **Barrel length:** 6-1/2 inches, **Overall length:** 12-1/4 inches, **Weight:** 44.2 ounces, **Finish:** Stainless steel, **Sights:** Fully adjustable, **Grips:** Synthetic, **Price:** $1,189

going about 4 pounds on the nose, crisp and backlash-free thanks to the trigger-mounted trigger stop. Due to headspace issues with springy moon clips, heavy pulls are standard on auto-caliber revolvers, but judicious custom gunsmithing can bring it down.

GREAT SHOOTER

Accuracy testing was done with affordable factory ball, all hand-held from a Matrix bench rest at 25 yards. Remington-UMC FMJ 115-grain put five shots in 3.15 inches, the best three in 1.90 inches. Federal's American Eagle 115-grain FMJ delivered 2.05

inches for all five, and 1.15 for best three. Winchester Winclean 147-grain delivered the same 2.05 inches group for five shots with a pleasing 0.70 best three cluster.

If the above makes me sound cool toward the 929, I may not have expressed myself well. This revolver speaks to me. What it says is, "Don't send me back to Smith & Wesson! Keep me here, where I can shoot ICORE and win for my shooter!"

I think I'm going to listen to that voice. And if they ever hold a National Pistol Whipping Championship, well, this big ol' 8-shot 9mm revolver should do nicely for that, too.

HOLT BODINSON

SMITH & WESSON'S MODEL 52 .38 MASTER

THIS CLASSIC BULL'S-EYE SEMI-AUTO PISTOL IS CHAMBERED FOR THE .38 SPECIAL MID-RANGE WADCUTTER.

A micrometer adjustable target sight (above) matched up with a Patridge front sight (below) provided high definition and zero backlash.

The Model 52 magazine (above) held only 5 mid-range, .38 Special flush-mouth wadcutters. Over-travel of the light, crisp trigger of the Model 52 (below) was controlled by a stop screw.

It was a pistol target shooters could only dream about—a .38 Special autoloader that held its groups into 2-inches or less at 50 yards. Yes, there had been prior 1911-frame-based .38 Special automatics before the S&W Model 52's debut in September 1961, but they were the handcrafted creations of gifted gunsmiths like James Clark with his .38 Conversion and the gunsmiths of the US Army Marksmanship Training Unit at Fort Benning, Ga., working with their unique .38 AMU ammunition, a semi-rimless, .38 Special round designed for enhanced stacking and feeding from an autoloader magazine.

The introduction of the Smith & Wesson Model 52 chambered for .38 Special, mid-range, wadcutter ammunition was a stunning first—the first successful, factory, .38 Special target autoloader ever launched, and it took the target shooting community by storm.

The story really begins in 1946 when C.R. Hellstrom took over the reins as President of Smith & Wesson. Hellstrom was intrigued by Germany's P-38, double-action, 9mm pistol. Sensing there might be large military and a police market interested in an American-designed, American-made, double-action, 9mm pistol, Hellstrom assigned the design task to master mechanic, Joseph W. Norman, head of the Experimental and Product Development Department.

Norman designed what would eventually become known as the Model 39. Interestingly enough, two lines of 9mm chambered prototypes were made for distribution and testing by the military and law enforcement communities—a single action, designated the Model 44, and a double action, given the Model 39 moniker. The Model 44 single action failed to generate any market enthusiasm. The Model 39, on the other hand, was enthusiastically received, and the alloy frame model was put into full production in 1957.

In 1960, the US Army Marksmanship Training Unit requested that S&W build them both steel and alloy framed Model 39's chambered for their .38 AMU cartridge for testing and evaluation as competitive target arms. S&W complied, but the USAMTU decided not to go ahead with the wholesale adoption of the design.

Now for a little collector's story. The initial model designation given those USAMTU prototypes was the Model 39-1, but then it occurred to S&W that the unsold Model 39-1's chambered for the unique .38 AMU cartridge might one day become confused with the standard Model 39 in 9mm Luger. The alloy frame Model 39-1's still in inventory were then stamped with the designation, Model 52. In 1964, three years after the successful introduction of the Model 52 .38 Master, S&W decided to release the Model 52 (formerly the Model 39-1 in .38 AMU caliber) into the marketplace. Once again they had to differentiate the USAMTU Model 52 from the Model 52 .38 Master so they stamped an "A"

The Model 52 had to pass an accuracy spec at 50 yards before it was shipped.

after the USAMTU model number, making them Model 52-A's. If you ever find a Model 52-A in the serial number range 35,850-35,927, it's a very rare bird since less than 87 were ever released, but it could be worth up to $3,000 if authenticated.

Their experiences with the US Army Marksmanship Training Unit and steel framed Model 39's in .38 AMU caliber certainly galvanized S&W to develop a commercial, target grade, centerfire, autoloader as a companion piece to their highly successful Model 41 rimfire target model. The qualities they were pursuing in the new autoloader were high accuracy, functional reliability, balanced handling, a competition grade trigger and target quality sights.

The decision was made to chamber the new pistol for conventional, mid-range, .38 Special ammunition featuring a wadcutter bullet seated flush with the end of the case. The initial Model 52 .38 Master, introduced in 1961, used the lockwork of the Model 39, which was modified to single action only by the addition of a setscrew.

S&W's claim for each Model 52 released was 10-shot, 10-ring accuracy at 50 yards from a machine rest. The 50-yard pistol target's 10-ring measures 3.39 inches. In his book, *The History of Smith & Wesson,* Roy Jinks, the official S&W historian, states, "… to insure the accuracy of the pistol, extra-rigid inspection was incorporated by having the Model 52 machine rest tested at 50 yards to assure that the pistol would shoot 5-shot groups having a maximum spread of two inches. Any pistol that could not meet this standard was returned to production for reworking."

Five-shot, 2-inch-or-less groups at 50 yards from a factory autoloader are simply otherworldly.

One of the secrets of the Model 52 is in the fit of the barrel to the model's unique barrel bushing. There is an enlarged ring at the muzzle end of the

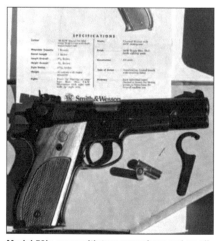

Model 52's came with two magazines and an all-important barrel bushing wrench.

MODEL 52 .38 MASTER

MAKER: SMITH & WESSON
2100 ROOSEVELT AVE
SPRINGFIELD, MA 01104
(800) 331-0852
WWW.GUNSMAGAZINE.COM/INDEX

Action: Single-action autoloader, **Caliber:** .38 Special, mid range wadcutter, **Magazine Capacity:** 5, **Barrel length:** 5 inches, **Overall length:** 8 5/8 inches, **Weight:** 41 ounces, **Sights:** 1/8 inch partridge (front), Micrometer adjustable (rear), **Sight radius:** 6 15/16 inches, **Stocks:** Checkered walnut, **Finish:** Blue, **Value:** $950 (*35th Edition of the Blue Book of Gun Values by S.P. Fjestad*)

barrel, which is closely fitted to the barrel bushing by tightening and locking the notched barrel bushing in place with a special spanner wrench. Another secret is a target trigger measuring only 2-3/4 pounds on my Lyman electronic gauge, and another secret is the competition quality target sights fully adjustable and without the least hint of backlash.

Because of tight tolerances and rigid inspections of the Model 52, only 90 pistols were built in 1961. Production in 1962 was only 1,078 for this flagship model. Total production for the original Model 52 made from 1961 to 1963 was 3,500 units.

Complaints about the M-39 double-action trigger modified to single action poured in from competitors and, in 1963, S&W designed a completely new and dedicated single action, target trigger and hammer. The newly configured model was designated the Model 52-1, which was produced from 1963 to 1971. In 1971, the factory installed an improved, coil spring tensioned extractor developed originally for the Model 39, giving it the new designation of Model 52-2. The Model 52-2 was the last variation of the Model 52, and it was the last of its breed, being discontinued in 1993.

The last retail for the Model 52-2 (with two, 5-shot magazines, its unique barrel bushing wrench, cleaning rod and brush) was $908. It was always an expensive handgun.

Model 52's are not uncommon on the used market and on Internet auction sites but be prepared to pay $1,000 or more for a gun in good condition with two magazines and that ever-essential Model 52 barrel-bushing wrench.

The development of the S&W Model 52 .38 Master is one of the great stories in the world of competition handguns. In the hands of marksmen like Bill Blankenship, it went on to win world championships, and it is as competitive today as it was 54 years ago. **GUNS**

History of Smith & Wesson by Roy Jinks, hardcover, 290 pages ©1977, out-of-print.

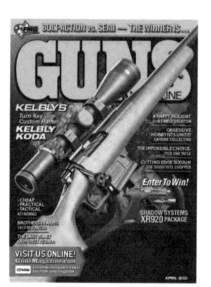

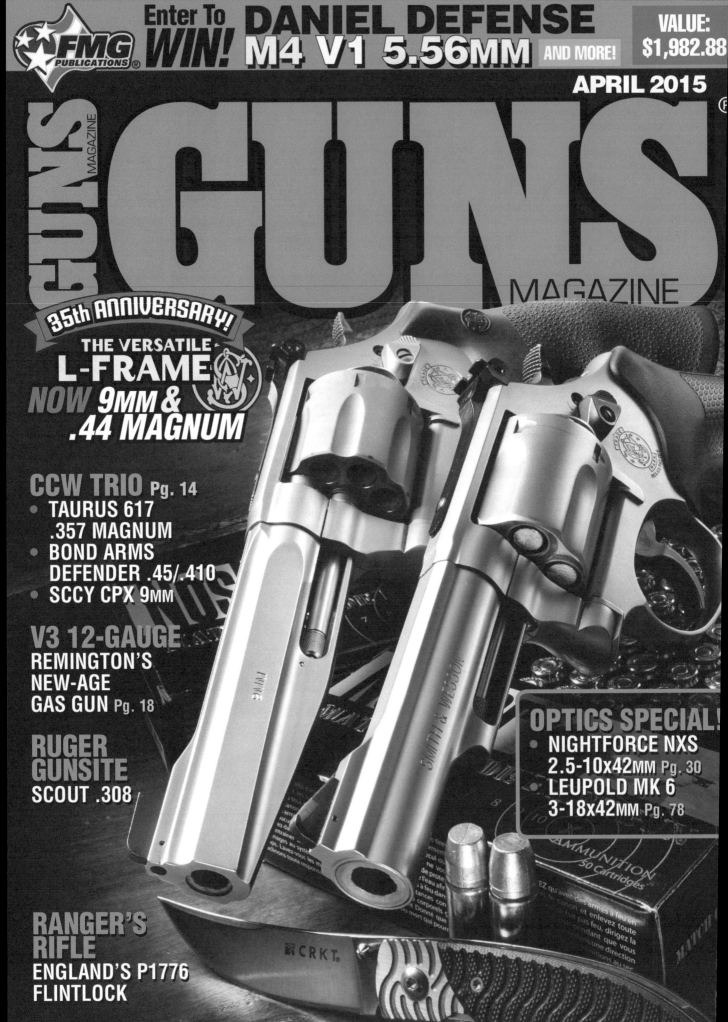

APRIL 2015

GUNS MAGAZINE

35th ANNIVERSARY!

THE VERSATILE L-FRAME
NOW **9MM &** **.44 MAGNUM**

CCW TRIO Pg. 14
- **TAURUS 617 .357 MAGNUM**
- **BOND ARMS DEFENDER .45/.410**
- **SCCY CPX 9MM**

V3 12-GAUGE
REMINGTON'S NEW-AGE GAS GUN Pg. 18

RUGER GUNSITE
SCOUT .308

OPTICS SPECIAL!
- **NIGHTFORCE NXS 2.5-10x42MM** Pg. 30
- **LEUPOLD MK 6 3-18x42MM** Pg. 78

RANGER'S RIFLE
ENGLAND'S P1776 FLINTLOCK

Happy 35th Anniv S&W L-

9x7= A Different Spin. S&W's Pro Series Model 986 is an upscale take on the 9mm revolver concept.

MASSAD AYOOB   PHOTOS: JOSEPH R. NOVELOZO

Introduced in 2014, the Pro Series 986 L-Frame is very much a niche gun, but it actually fills more niches than you may think. In the Open Class of ICORE action revolver shooting, many would prefer the 8-shot moon clips of the bigger N-frame version of this gun, the 929. However, weighing about the same as a 4-inch K-Frame .357 Combat Magnum and fitted with a 5-inch barrel, the 986 seems to track faster between targets. For some, that's worth losing a shot for.

Some folks just don't trust autos and cleave to the revolver for personal defense, but appreciate the relatively low price of 9mm practice ammo. Because a moon clip is generally faster than a speedloader, a 9mm revolver comes into its own in a crisis. And of course, there's the very mild recoil of the 9mm in a relatively hefty L-Frame.

One reason some of us cherish our .45 ACP S&W revolvers is that every now and then, our reload recipes for our .45 autos come out too short or too light in the powder charge to cycle our square guns. So our revolvers make a handy garbage disposal for those reloads (and it's a lot more fun than disassembling ammo). The same will be true for 9mm revolver/auto owners.

My friend Roger Clark has made his Bill Pfeil-tuned 986 his daily carry gun in a hip holster made by a local craftsman. Roger is tall, so he conceals the gun well and appreciates its light recoil, fast reloading, excellent handling and reliability.

Roger Clark wields his Bill Pfeil-slicked S&W 986. He's very happy with it.

MODEL 986 9MM

FRAME!

The Perfect Packin' Pistol is the Smith & Wesson's Model 69 .44 Magnum.

JOHN TAFFIN

Over the past 35 years Smith & Wesson has mostly offered L-Frame sixguns in .357 Magnum and, most notably, a 5-shot .44 Special including the Model 696 and the Mountain Light Model 396. Now Smith & Wesson has introduced the L-Frame M69 revolver, which to my way of thinking is just about the most Perfect Packin' Pistol double-action style ever offered by Smith & Wesson.

The Smith & Wesson .44 Combat Magnum was tested with a variety of factory .44 Magnum loads, and John found during shooting the M69 .44 it earned high marks as a "Perfect Packin' Pistol."

A Perfect Packin' Pistol was defined by yours truly too many years ago as an easy carrying sixgun, either double or single action, with a barrel length of 4 to 5-1/2 inches, and chambered in a cartridge which would handle anything likely to be encountered. Of course, the chambering would depend upon where the PPP was being carried and could be anything from .22 Long Rifle up to one of the really big-bore magnums.

Smith & Wesson has reach the epitome of Perfect Packin' Pistols with the Model 69 Combat Magnum chambered in .44 Magnum. This is a stainless steel, 5-shot, 4-1/4-inch double-action sixgun. Sights are typical S&W adjustables with a white outline rear sight matched up with a red ramp front sight. The frame screws, hammer, trigger and cylinder release as well as the front and rear sight are matte black finish and contrast nicely with the matte stainless steel of the rest of this excellent big-bore revolver.

The front of the cylinder is chamfered for easy entrance into a holster and the muzzle has a deep concave crown, which protects the rifling. The right side of the barrel is marked in two lines with ".44 Magnum" and "Combat Magnum." The grips are wrap around fingergroove-style, pebble-grained rubber. Single-action trigger pull is

4-1/4 pounds while the double action measures 14 pounds. The cylinder locks at the front of the frame with a modernized version of the Triple-Lock set up instead of locking at the front of the ejector rod. Since this is a 5-shot .44 Magnum the locking bolt notches on the cylinder are in between chambers so there is no weak spot on each chamber.

Test firing of this .44 Combat Magnum began with .44 Special loads

MODEL 69 .44 MAG

Happy 35th Anniversary
S&W L-FRAME!
9MM & .44 MAG

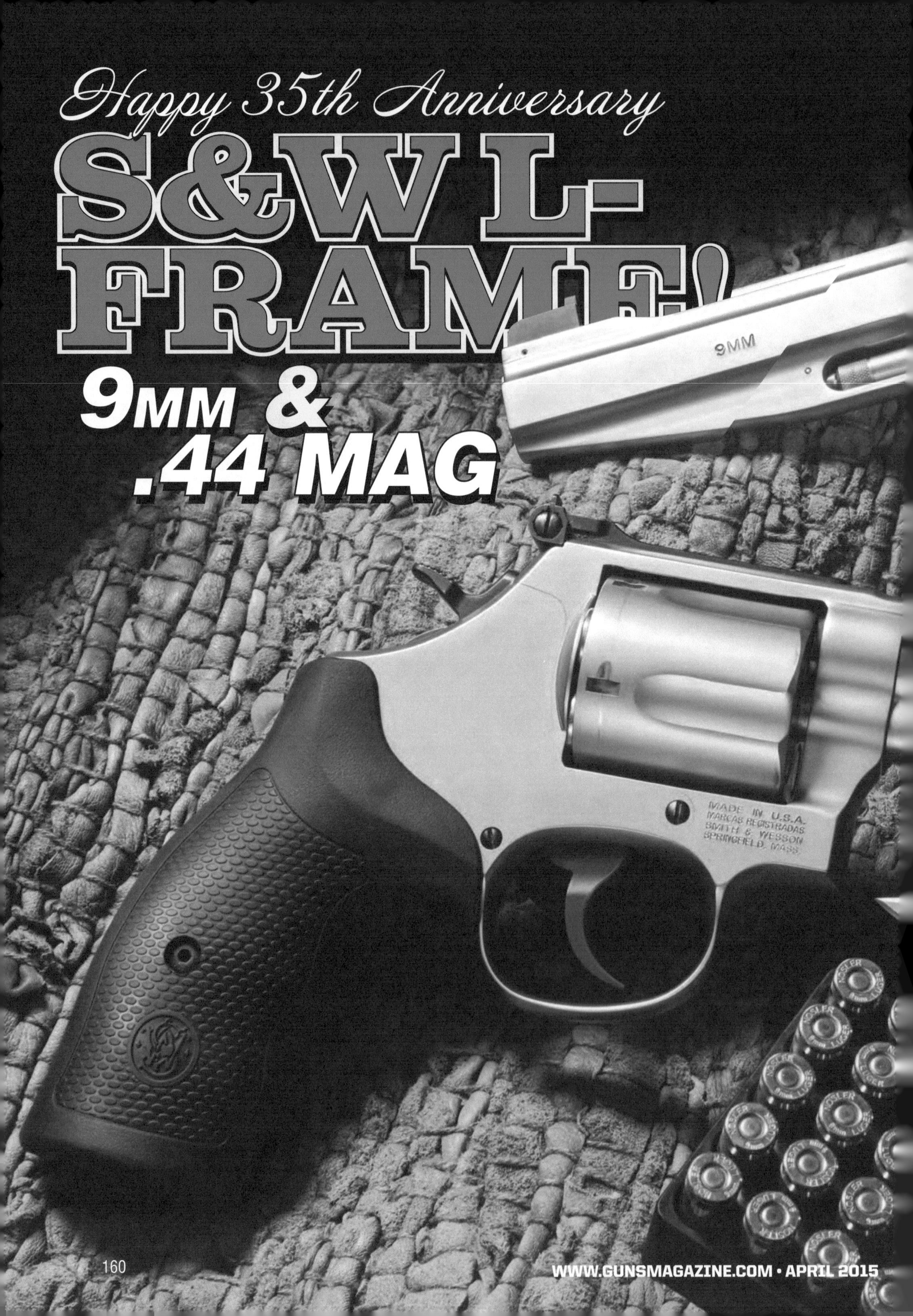

GUNS®

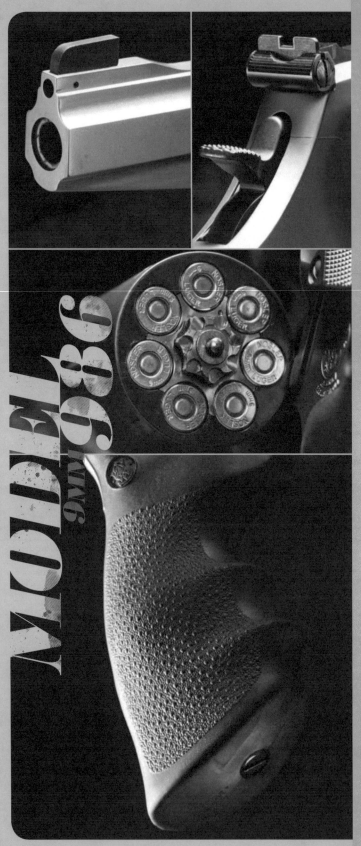

MODEL 986 9MM

MODEL 69 .44 MAG

It's subjective, but I love the S&W Performance Center's signature barrel style on this gun. Gracefully tapered, it pleases both the eye and the hand with exquisite balance and fast handling. The light titanium alloy cylinder is a help here. And given the range of 9mm loads, its standard S&W adjustable sight is almost a necessity.

with muzzle velocities in the 800 to 1,000 fps neighborhood. Results were most gratifying and especially so because of the fact my utility loads assembled with 7.5 grains of Unique under the Oregon Trail 240-grain SWC delivered 900+ fps and grouped into just over 1 inch. I then switched to .44 Magnum handloads using 15 different loads with muzzle velocities in

S&W 686 MEMORIES

MASSAD AYOOB

1980. The sea change to autos was still just over the horizon, and the big thing in police service revolvers was the switch from .38 Special to .357 Magnum, with full Mag loads in training. The latter was more than the K-Frame Combat Magnum was designed for, and S&W introduced the 586 (chrome-molybdenum steel in blue or nickel) and its stainless twin, the 686 on a ".41-size" L-Frame. Dimensions including weight almost exactly duplicated the Colt Python, but at a much lower price. The 686 was an instant hit, and remains one of Smith & Wesson's best-selling revolvers to this day.

I liked it, but already having Pythons didn't own one until Andy Cannon and I collaborated on his "Street-L," with enhanced action and an integral expansion chamber recoil compensator he machined out of the S&W barrel itself, which only slightly reduced velocity but hugely reduced Magnum recoil and muzzle jump. I carried it on duty sometimes, and one year fitted it with Jarvis barrel weight and Pro-Point red dot optic, and shot it at Bianchi Cup.

Over the years I acquired a 2.5-inch 686 (ideal for PPC "snubby" events) and a 6-inch Mag-na-Port Custom 686-Plus 7-shooter I won at Second Chance. However, the one I've spent most time with is a 4-inch stock configuration with shaved cylinder latch, bobbed hammer, and superb action job by Bob Lloyd. It was the gun I used when I shot Stock Service Revolver at the IDPA World Championships, and it won a few state and regional IDPA championships for me. For roughly 3-1/2 decades, the Smith & Wesson Model 686 .357 Magnum has served me well, and I'm one of the many who consider it a modern classic.

In Phoenix, Mas wins the 2011 South Mountain Regional IDPA Championship in Stock Service Revolver with a Bob Lloyd-tuned 4-inch 686 shooting smoky .38 Special 158-grain lead ammo.

FIRST ENCOUNTERS WITH THE L-FRAME

JOHN TAFFIN

More than 25 years ago I was assigned a comprehensive article on the history and use of the .357 Magnum. I already had several .357's including the K-Frame Model 19 Combat Magnum and the Model 27 N-Frame. The assignment gave me an excuse to add the newest Smith & Wesson .357 Magnum at the time, the L-Frame. The Model 19 when fully loaded was nearly 1/2-pound lighter than the Model 27 and was also less bulky. However, by the 1980's, some Combat Magnum Model 19 shooters as well as those using its stainless steel counterpart, the Model 66, were complaining the K-Frame would not hold up to modern ammunition.

MODEL 986

MAKER: S&W
2100 ROOSEVELT AVE.
SPRINGFIELD, MA 01104
(800) 831-0852
WWW.GUNSMAGAZINE.COM/
SMITH-WESSON

Action: Double-action revolver, **Caliber:** 9mm Parabellum, **Capacity:** 7, **Barrel length:** 5 inches, **Overall length:** 10.5 inches, **Sights:** Fully adjustable rear, Patridge front, **Weight:** 34.9 ounces, **Grips:** Synthetic, **Material:** Stainless steel frame, titanium alloy cylinder, **Price:** $1,149

MODEL 69 COMBAT MAGNUM

MAKER: S&W
2100 ROOSEVELT AVENUE
SPRINGFIELD, MA 01104
(800) 331-0852
WWW.GUNSMAGAZINE.COM/INDEX

Action Type: Double action, **Caliber:** .44 Magnum, **Capacity:** 5, **Barrel Length:** 4-1/4 inches, **Overall Length:** 9-3/4 inches, **Weight:** 37 ounces, **Finish:** Stainless steel, **Sights:** White outline adjustable rear, red ramp front, **Grips:** Finger-groove rubber, **Price:** $849

This early 1980's S&W 586 .357 Magnum set the stage for 35 years of success for the revolver. Lately, the platform has grown into the Model 69 .44 Magnum and Model 986 9mm.

Border Patrol Inspector Bill Jordan originally devised the K-Frame Magnum as one to be practiced with using .38 Specials and fed .357's for serious business. When shooters started pushing thousands of rounds of Magnum ammunition through the 19/66 some problems developed with forcing cone wear and guns shooting loose. Since the vast majority of my loads for my Model 19 had been assembled with cast bullets I had not experienced any of these problems. Nevertheless I ordered a blue 4-inch L-Frame Model 586 which was known as the Distinguished Combat Magnum. I found it weighed just 1-ounce less than the original Model 27, however, the weight was in the heavy underlug barrel and increased size at the forcing cone.

Shortly after receiving my L-Frame I was invited to take part in the qualification course with the local Sheriff's Department. At the time the duty weapon was the 4-inch Model 586 equipped with target stocks. I soon discovered several women deputies were having a difficult time with the Model 586 because the grip was much too large for their hands. I was able to show them what could be done by either slimming down the factory grips or fitting their revolver with much smaller custom grips which fit their hands. It made a huge difference in their ability to shoot well. Currently my L-Frame .357 consists of a nickel-plated 6-inch Model 586 which handles any .357 load with ease, while my original 4-inch Model 586 has been converted to .41 Special.

Overleaf: Sharing the spotlight with the pair of S&W revolvers is the CRKT Jernigan Persian frame-lock folder featuring a 2.71-inch blade & G10 scales.

The double-action trigger pull was a reasonably smooth 14 pounds. Heavy is necessary here, because springy moon clips create headspace and ignition issues, requiring a hard smack of the hammer. The single-action pull weight was a bit over 4 pounds and very crisp.

As with the N-Frame 929 9mm 8-shooter, you can't just drop rimless cartridges into a 986's chambers and fire away, punching the empties out with a pencil or plucking them out with a fingernail. We hand-fed 7 rounds into the 986's chambers, stroked the trigger seven times, and got seven clicks with no "bangs." The firing pin barely touched a couple of primers and never touched most. Obviously, moon clips are necessary with the 986.

To find out how the 9mm would handle the jump from a revolver's firing chamber to the forcing cone, across the velocity-bleeding barrel/cylinder we ran four of our accuracy-testing loads over an Oehler chronograph (see chart). For a good home defense load, I chose 115-grain Federal 9BPLE, a +P+ jacketed hollowpoint. Although my 5-shot group measured 3.30, with the best three in 1.65 inches. This load pretty much "shot to the sights," point-of-aim vis-à-vis point of impact.

Hunting with a 9mm revolver does not seem to compute, but if it's all you've got, it's better than a sharp stick. For dangerous game, we'd want something like the Buffalo Bore 124-grain Penetrator round, loaded to +P+ pressure with a

Mas runs the 986 over an Oehler chronograph. There was never a misfire with moon-clipped 9mm rounds of any flavor in our test 986. The tapering barrel and fiber-optic front sight of the 986 are useful touches.

9MM FACTORY AMMO PERFORMANCE

LOAD (BRAND, BULLET WEIGHT, TYPE)	VELOCITY (FPS)	GROUP SIZE (INCHES)
Federal +P+ 115 JHP	1,227	3.3
Winchester/USA 115 FMJ	1,039	5.0
Buffalo Bore +P+ 124 Penetrator	1,166	3.0
Remington/UMC 147 FMJ	891	2.2

Notes: Group size is the product of 5 shots at 25 yards.

solidly jacketed flatnose bullet which the 986 grouped slightly above the other loads, but right to point-of-aim. Ejection was sticky, and we had to hammer the ejector rod to get the spent moon clips out. Probably not the best load for our test sample.

As the test approached deadline, we received two flavors of Nosler's excellent Match Grade ammo, both JHP's. We did not have time to chronograph them, but the 115-grain was factory spec'd for a sedate 1,170 fps, while the 124 is loaded to a nominal 1,200 fps. With the 115-grain load we got 3.45-inch groups (best three

in 1.95). The 124 grain gave us 2.65 (best three in 1.05).

Back in the 1970's, I debriefed Illinois Trooper Ken Kaas, whose department was the only state police agency issuing semi-auto's instead of 6-shot revolvers at the time. He got into a gunfight with a bad guy who opened fire on him with a semi-automatic shotgun from behind hard cover, and was smart enough to keep track of his opponent's shots. As Kaas fired his sixth round, the gunman jumped up and rushed toward Kaas, who promptly dropped him with a bullet through the liver. Later, in custody at a hospital, his attacker was heard to tell his lawyer, "He (the trooper) fired all six!" April Fools! Trooper Kaas had a seventh round waiting in his issue S&W Model 39.

I shot the late, lamented Second Chance bowling pin match from the mid-1970's until the last one in the late '90's. I lost count of how many revolver shooters had left one pin standing after their six shots were expended, and had to take time to reload or go to another gun, when one more shot would have stopped the stopwatches and allowed them to clear the table with a prize-winning shot. And at Bianchi Cup, I saw one LAPD pistol team member who was in the lead lose the title when he short-stroked his S&W .38 Special on one shot, and didn't have time to run through the cylinder again before the moving target disappeared behind its impenetrable barricade.

So, yes, my revolver brothers, the 7th shot *does* bring value to the table. GUNS

This ain't your daddy's auto-caliber revolver. Without moon clips, cartridges seat to different levels in the chambers (above, left). *Don't shoot the 986 without moon clips!* Seven pulls of the trigger later, none of the rounds chambered without moon clip fired, some were untouched and some only very slightly dented by firing pin. Remington-UMC 147-grain 9mm ammo gave this fine 5-shot group (above, right) at 25 yards from the 986.

MODEL 69

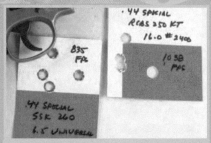

Modestly powerful .44 Special handloads in the Smith & Wesson Model 69 were accurate and pleasant.

Shooting with .44 Magnum handloads in the Smith & Wesson Model 69 show how accurate the new revolver is.

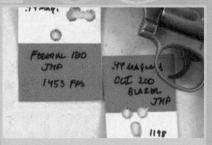

Targets shot with .44 Magnum factory loads in the Smith & Wesson .44 Combat Magnum show fine performance.

the same range as my .44 Special loads. Results also were quite gratifying with many loads in the 1-inch category. My .44 Magnum utility load also using the Oregon Trail 240-grain SWC this time over 8.0 grains of Universal clocked out at 1,000 fps and grouped just as did the .44 Special load. I got the same results with the RCBS 44-250KT bullet over 17.0 grains of 2400. For everyday use any of these loads will handle 99 percent of my needs.

I put it off long enough. Now it was time to try .44 Magnum loads. I was not looking forward to shooting full-house loads in this relatively lightweight pistol, however the grip proved to be exceptionally capable of reducing felt recoil. Normally, I prefer to fit custom grips to any of my sixguns, however these factory grips are about as perfect as one is likely to find for handling recoil of the .44 Magnum.

Six different .44 Magnum factory loads were put through the S&W .44 Combat Magnum with all loads shooting right into the 1-inch category or less. These loads consisted of everything from Federal 180-grain JHP's at 1,450+ fps to Garrett Cartridges of Texas 310-grain Hard Cast Hammerheads at just under 1,000 fps. This load is especially designed for use in 4-inch sixguns providing maximum penetration against critters—most notably bears—which can scratch, claw and bite.

My most used hunting .44 Magnum load over the last couple decades has been the Black Hills 240-grain JHP load using Hornady XTP's. I've taken 24 Texas whitetails and an Idaho cougar all with 1-shot kills using this load. In the Model 69 Combat Magnum it delivered just over 1,100 fps and groups of 1-inch. This was my first time to try HPR ammunition and their 240-grain JHP shot exceptionally well at just over 1,200 fps and a group under 1-inch. The most accurate load proved to be the CCI Blazer 200-grain JHP at 1,200 fps and a 3/4-inch group.

.44 SPECIAL HANDLOADED AMMO PERFORMANCE

BULLET (BRAND, BULLET WEIGHT, TYPE)	POWDER (BRAND)	CHARGE (GRAINS WEIGHT)	VELOCITY (FPS)	GROUP SIZE (INCHES)
RCBS 44-250 KT	2400	16.0	1,038	1-1/2
RCBS 44-250 KT	Universal	7.5	918	1-5/8
Oregon Trail 240 SWC	Unique	7.5	923	1-1/4
SSK 260 TC	Universal	6.5	835	1-1/4

Notes: Groups the product of best 4 of 5 shots at 20 yards. Chronograph screens set at 10 feet from muzzle. CCI 300 primers used in Starline brass.

.44 MAGNUM HANDLOADED AMMO PERFORMANCE

BULLET (BRAND, BULLET WEIGHT, TYPE)	POWDER (BRAND)	CHARGE (GRAINS WEIGHT)	VELOCITY (FPS)	GROUP SIZE (INCHES)
Oregon Trail 240 SWC*	Unique	6.0	815	2
Oregon Trail 240 SWC*	Universal	6.0	772	1-1/4
Oregon Trail 240 SWC*	Power Pistol	7.0	845	1
Oregon Trail 240 SWC*	AA5744	13.5	764	1-3/4
Oregon Trail 240 SWC*	HS-6	8.0	765	1-1/4
Oregon Trail 240 SWC	Bullseye	6.0	830	1-3/8
Oregon Trail 240 SWC	Red Dot	6.0	861	1-1/2
Oregon Trail 240 SWC	Universal	8.0	1,000	1-1/4
Oregon Trail 225 RNFP	4227	18.5	957	1
Oregon Trail 225 RNFP	WW452A	6.0	855	1-3/8
NEI 260.429KT	Universal	8.5	970	1-3/4
Lyman 429421KT	Power Pistol	9.0	899	1-3/4
RCBS 44-250KT	Power Pistol	9.0	904	1-3/4
RCBS 44-250KT	4227	20.0	915	1-7/8
RCBS 44-250KT	2400	17.0	1,036	1-1/4

Notes: Groups the product of best 4 of 5 shots at 20 yards. Chronograph screens set at 10 feet from muzzle. CCI 300 primers used in Starline brass.
*Bullets crimped over front shoulder.

.44 MAGNUM FACTORY AMMO PERFORMANCE

LOAD (BRAND, BULLET WEIGHT, TYPE)	VELOCITY (FPS)	GROUP SIZE (INCHES)
Federal 180 JHP	1,453	1-1/4
CCI Blazer 200 JHP	1,198	3/4
CorBon 225 DPX	1,246	1-1/4
Black Hills 240JHP	1,110	1
HPR 240 JHP	1,218	7/8
Garrett 310 Defender	980	1-1/4

Notes: Chronograph set at 10 feet from muzzle. Groups are 4 Shots at 20 Yards.

What all this shows is the amazing versatility of this 5-shooter with the ability to shoot everything well from lightweight to heavyweight bullets and from jacketed to hard cast.

My first Smith & Wesson .44 Magnum dates back to the early 1960's when I purchased a 4- and a 6-1/2-inch Model 29. Over the years I have added several more including examples of pre-29's and they are some of my most prized sixguns. This latest Perfect Packin' Pistol Smith & Wesson .44 Magnum has also become an instant favorite. It looks great and shoots great. Nearly everything about it is just

right. No wide hammer and trigger to get in the way of a real working sixgun and the trigger face is smooth for easy double-action shooting.

The red ramp front sight insert is a bother to my eyes in bright sunlight but this is a subjective problem easily cured. I can use it with everything from standard 750 fps .44 Special loads up to full house Magnum loads and it shoots accurately and handles well. I would call it the most useful .44 Magnum Smith & Wesson has produced since the original .44 Magnum Model 29 disappeared in the waning years of the last century. I like it. **GUNS**

SMITH & WESSON'S HAND EJECTOR 2ND MODEL

BORN IN WAR, THIS JEWEL IS OFTEN OVERSHADOWED BY THE 1ST AND 3RD MODELS.

MIKE "DUKE" VENTURINO   **PHOTOS: YVONNE VENTURINO**

When entering WWI, the United States was desperately short of military handguns so they also purchased Smith & Wesson's Hand Ejector, 2nd Model when altered to accept .45 ACP.

It seems like we older gun'riters are forever fawning over the legendary Smith & Wesson "Triple Lock" which incidentally is called Hand Ejector, 1st Model by collectors. Perhaps it is because besides being the very first of S&W's N-Frames sixguns, the Triple Lock was also the introductory vehicle for the .44 Smith & Wesson Special.

Then there is the Hand Ejector, 3rd Model also nicknamed Model 1926. Later the Hand Ejector 4th Model was introduced. It was divided into two variations with the names of 1950 Military for the fixed sight version and 1950 Target for ones with adjustable sights.

But what about the Hand Ejector, 2nd Model? It is seldom mentioned, never got a name and was just as good a revolver as the above mentioned ones and actually far more historical.

This particular handgun was introduced 100 years ago during World War I. The Brits got themselves enmeshed in Europe's continental war, and as usual, were short of weapons. They contracted with S&W to alter the Hand Ejector, 1st Model to accommodate their rather puny .455 Webley ammunition, but wanted changes. They said that battlefield mud and debris would foul its special 3rd lock and the ejector rod's protective shroud.

Perhaps more importantly S&W felt the Hand Ejector, 1st models were too expensive at $21. By removing the ejector rod's shroud and the intricately machined 3rd lock on the crane they could reduce retail price to $19.

And so was born the Hand Ejector, 2nd Model. For the American market the primary caliber offered was .44 Special. Also some were made as .38-40, .44-40 and .45 Colt but they numbered only in the hundreds each. According to Roy Jinks' *History of Smith & Wesson,* by September 1916 the company had produced 74,755 N-Frame revolvers in .455 caliber for the British. Of those, 69,755 were Hand Ejector, 2nd Models. The other 5,000 were Hand Ejector, 1st Models because the British didn't want to wait for the changes being made to the 2nd model.

All of those had 6-1/2-inch barrels, full blue finish except for the color case hardened trigger and hammer and a lanyard ring on the butt. Grips were checkered walnut and sights were S&W's trademark "half-moon" front with groove in the frame's topstrap for a rear. I have a sample in my collection that factory letters to the Canadian Government in 1916.

Even so, the military duty of Hand Ejector, 2nd Models was just beginning. Being almost as bad as the British for declaring war while lacking weapons, the United States entered WWI in April 1917. The US Army was desperate for handguns, so S&W was contracted to provide N-Frame revolvers altered to function with rimless .45 ACP cartridges—this was done by snapping the cases into little 3-round spring-steel clips. The Hand Ejector, 2nd Models were given the military designation of Model 1917. All were fitted with 5-1/2-inch barrels, lanyard rings and smooth walnut grips. Finish and sights were the same as for the Brit's contract revolvers.

Production of Model 1917's was

The first N-Frame was the Smith & Wesson Hand Ejector, 1st Model, often called the "Triple Lock" (left) and this one is a rare target model. It was replaced at the behest of the British during WWI with the Hand Ejector, 2nd Model, which never got a nickname. Both of these are .44 Specials.

The British persuaded Smith & Wesson to alter their N-Frame design for the .455 Webley and then bought thousands during WWI. This Hand Ejector, 2nd Model factory letters to the Canadian Government in 1916.

enormous. Jinks' book says 163,476 were made for the US Government in their own serial number range. Those are marked "United States Property" under their barrels as mine is. After WWI ended the company kept this model in their catalog until 1949 and produced about another 50,000. This order included 25,000 sold to the Brazilian Government in the late 1930's, with many of those returning to the United States for the surplus market in the 1980's. The commercially made Model 1917's had checkered walnut grips instead of the military's plain ones.

And that brings us back to the Hand Ejector, 2nd Model .44 Special. In nobody's world could it be called a big selling item. It was dropped from the S&W catalog in 1940, and again referring to Jinks' authoritative book, only 17,510 were sold in 25 years.

Barrel lengths offered were 4, 5 and 6-1/2 inches with full blue or full nickel for finish. Some were fitted with target sights but the vast majority had sights as described for the .455 variation. Grips were checkered walnut and lanyard rings were not standard. As interested as I have always been in N-Frame S&W handguns, I have never seen a Hand Ejector, 2nd Model in any barrel length but 6-1/2 inches, any finish but blue, any type of sights but fixed or any .38-40, .44-40, or .45 Colt chambering. (Original chambering that is. Many .455's were rechambered to .45 Colt in bygone years.)

Nigh on 20 years ago I wandered into a nifty little gun store on a trip to Los Angeles. To my utter amazement, in the handgun case was a Hand Ejector, 2nd Model .44 Special, blue finish with 6-1/2-inch barrel. I paid for it and made arrangements for it to be (legally) shipped back to Montana. It took me years to get around to factory lettering it but upon doing so I learned it had been sent to Charleston, W. Va., in 1929. Having been born and raised in that state, the provenance of this revolver dictates I keep it forever.

Besides, it shoots pretty good! GUNS

SPIN CLASS FOR BOOMERS

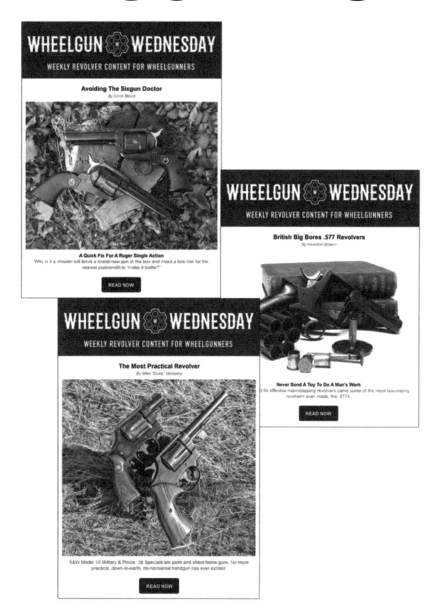

Just Enough
BARREL

MIKE "DUKE "VENTURINO   PHOTOS: YVONNE VENTURINO

Snubnose revolvers are usually loved or hated. The haters say they are hard to shoot accurately because of their short sight radius and claim a longer barrel on the same frame is just as easy to conceal. The lovers say they make perfect backup guns when carried concealed in ankle holsters or in the small of your back—locations prohibiting long barrels. And as for accuracy, snubnose lovers (fairly logically) claim at the distances they're needed, who *needs* pinpoint accuracy?

In the spring of my high school senior year, the local police chief got his son and me out of class to be "go-fers" for a special occasion. An FBI firearms instructor had come to town to teach basic marksmanship to all law enforcement officers in the county. The FBI guy started out with an eye-opening demonstration.

He ran the standard handgun course from 7 to 50 yards, firing double and single action—right and left handed—with a 2-inch .38 Special S&W Model 15 Combat Masterpiece. The cumulative group his 50 shots made could have been covered with a salad plate.

Yes, snubbies possess the inherent precision necessary to put bullets close together. The drawback is they are difficult guns to *do* it with. That FBI instructor I witnessed shoot so well probably put about a ton of lead through snubbies in order to achieve his level of skill.

The region of southern West Virginia where I grew up was a notoriously tough area. I attended Marshall University in Huntington but usually traveled back to my hometown for weekends where I could shoot and reload. Most of the driving to and fro was at night and breaking down—or running out of gas—on those lonesome roads wasn't advisable.

So I kept a snubbie of one sort or another in my car. Mostly they were Smith & Wesson .38's—a Model 36

Chiefs Special or a Model 10 or 12 Military & Police, but there was at least one S&W .22 Model 34 and one Charter Arms Bulldog .44 Special in the mix.

In those days carrying guns in a vehicle was illegal in West Virginia. But like I said, it was a tough area. After graduating and taking up residence in Montana, I didn't feel the need for a small concealable handgun because it was perfectly legal to toss a full-size one on the seat of my pickup. I also spent a bit of time in prime grizzly country. A big-bore magnum revolver was better suited to my needs, so whatever snubnoses I owned in West Virginia were soon sold, traded and forgotten.

One thing in life is for certain though. Situations

Duke gets back into the snubbie swing of things at 10 yards with his S&W Model 442, firing as quickly as he can reacquire the sights.

168

After decades of not owning a snubbie, Duke got back into them with this pair—an S&W Model 360 .357 Magnum (left) and an S&W Model 442 .38 Special (right).

S&W's K-Frame snubbies were six-shooters such as the M12 (above, left). Those on the J-Frame, such as the M442 (above, right), were 5-shooters. Snubbies have usually been offered with fixed sights such as the Colt Detective Special (right), but S&W has offered adjustable sights on a few models such as the M15 (left).

Snubbies employed different materials over the decades. At left is carbon steel Colt Detective Special, next is an aluminum alloy framed S&W M12, next is a stainless steel S&W M60 and at far right is a scandium-frame S&W M360.

Duke rediscovers the joys–and challenges–of snubnosed revolvers.

continually evolve. Now in my senior years I no longer spend time in Montana's mountains. My lifestyle keeps me well within civilization, so snubbies have once again become items of interest.

Smith & Wesson has produced a bewildering array of snubnose revolvers using both their J- and K-Frames. Back in my younger days the ones on the small J-Frame were 5-shooters if in .38 Special, but were sixshooters when in .22 Long Rifle. The K-Frames, however, were always sixguns.

Then there was the matter of sights—S&W made snubbies on both frame sizes with both fixed and adjustable sights. The fixed setups always consisted of a groove down the topstrap coupled with a simple blade front. When given fully-adjustable sights, the front sights have usually been ramp-type blades.

After decades without one, the first snubbie I acquired was a version I'd never previously owned—an S&W Model 442 .38 Special. It is a direct descendant of the old Model 40 first developed in the 1950's. The 442 has an aluminum alloy frame with a steel barrel and cylinder.

What is especially noticeable about the Model 442 is the hammer is totally enclosed by the frame—there's nothing to snag when worn under your clothes.

Of course it's a double-action-only proposition. In my younger days I avoided such revolvers because I preferred to shoot single action. Now with a half-century of shooting experience behind me, I realize that at snubbie distances, perfectly adequate shooting can be done double action.

BACK TO THE FUTURE

Because something called the "Space Age" came about, it was natural for handgun manufacturers to turn to exotic alloys. There are so many types—and combinations of types—used I haven't even *tried* to keep abreast of the technology. What I do know is the lightest handgun I've ever handled is my S&W Model 360, which is a Chiefs Special with a frame made of something called "scandium."

It only weighs 3/4 of a pound and is also the worst beast to shoot of any in my experience when used with

The S&W snubbie's two frame sizes include (left) the J-Frame M34 .22 LR, and (right) the K-Frame M15 .38 Special. Both have adjustable sights.

Duke fired three factory loads in these two .38 Specials to determine differences in velocity. The long-barreled one (top) is the S&W M14 with an 8-3/8-inch barrel, and (bottom) his prize 2-inch S&W M15 sporting a Tyler-T grip adapter.

The 6-shot S&W M12 (left) and Colt Detective Special (right) are a bit bulkier than the smaller Smith J-Frames. Both are in .38 Special.

ammunition for which it is labeled. This is because some dummy at Smith & Wesson decided it should be a .357 Magnum! I fired one .357 Magnum full-bore factory load in mine and then ejected the remaining four. The darn thing should be a .38, so I load mine with Black Hills Cowboy .357's, which are downloaded to .38 Special ballistics.

Seniors tend to look backwards and seniors who are gun folks focus on the firearms from their formative years. I am no different. The first snubbie to catch my attention was that long-ago FBI guy's K-Frame Model 15 with its target sights. It eluded me for nearly 50 years, so when I was at a gun show a couple of months ago, I saw one for sale and half-heartedly dickered for it. To my surprise, the seller took my offer.

When firing it for the first time with my standard velocity .38 Special handloads, the lack of recoil was evident due to the gun's weight, but it sure is loud compared to longer-barreled .38's. It shifted in my hand at every shot and had to be repositioned. I've never gotten along with S&W Magna-style walnut grips, so my Model 15 now wears an old Tyler-T grip adapter. It fills in the extra space behind the triggerguard perfectly. So now I'm prepared to try duplicating that FBI instructor's performance this coming summer. (That's a joke, but I *am* going to work on shooting my Model 15 as well as I can.)

SNUBBIE SEARCHING 101

Buying the Model 15 triggered something in me so I attended another Montana gun show a few weeks later with the intention of buying some more snubbies. To be specific, I was in the mood for a Colt Detective Special or Cobra—they're the same size, but the Detective Special is steel, the Cobra is aluminum alloy. Not only had I never owned a Colt snubbie, I had never even fired one.

Turns out I may as well have been looking for gold nuggets. There was not a single Colt snubbie in the house, so I satisfied my urge by buying another Smith & Wesson from my past—a Model 34 in .22 Long Rifle with a 2-inch barrel. It is, of course, a J-Frame, but one with adjustable sights. It's a fine little plinking pistol and since we have our share of rattlers in warm weather, perhaps it might substitute for one of my big-bore single actions for snake duty.

Still I had the Colt itch. One factor making my Colt snubbie quest more difficult was the fact I wanted a pre-1973 specimen. Why? After that year, someone at Colt decided that a shroud covering the ejector rod was a nifty idea. Let's think about that: We want a small, light revolver so let's add some *more* steel under the barrel! This doesn't make sense to me, but it's an academic point if you can't find one for sale anyway.

So I turned to my trusty gun-buying partner—the Internet—and soon had a 1961-vintage Detective Special .38 in hand. It had obviously been carried quite a bit judging by the finish wear and smoothness of the checkering on its walnut grips. But it hadn't been shot much as evidenced by its fine mechanical condition. I haven't had time to shoot it a lot, but I can say it hits high enough at 10 yards to make me think it was factory-sighted for 50. Time will tell as I get more trigger time with it.

S&W's M40 (right) right was the predecessor of Duke's M442 (left). Note the grip safety on the M40.

Duke used three .38 Special factory loads for his velocity measurements to determine dropoff between a 2-inch and 8-3/8-inch barrel. From left: Remington 148-grain wadcutter, Winchester 158-grain RN, Black Hills 158-grain SWC.

I've loaded tens of thousands of .38's since I started in 1966. What will go into my snubbies will be bullets from 148 to 160 grains in weight. They'll consist of lead wadcutters, semi-wadcutters, round-nose/flatpoints and even full RN's. If my velocities hit 800 fps then it means I'm getting too adventurous with powders, which, incidentally, will run the gamut from Bullseye to Unique in burning rate. I won't need anything fancy for these short-barreled revolvers.

Recently I also acquired an S&W Model 14 .38 with an 8-3/8-inch barrel. So for comparison I fired three factory loads in it as well as my 2-inch S&W Model 15. Remington 148-grain wadcutters hit 670 and 791 fps from the short and long barrel respectively. Winchester 158-grain RN's clocked 742 and 917 fps. Black Hills 158-grain SWC's hit 856 and 1,069 fps.

Comparable accuracy? Yes, the long-barreled Model 14 gave me much tighter groups at 25 yards, but the snubbie's groups at 25 were more than adequate. Am I done? Not hardly! I have a friend's Model 12 S&W snubbie here on loan and I'm trying to work up a trade.

And I'm *still* thinking about a Colt Cobra. GUNS

CAMPFIRE TALES™
BY JOHN TAFFIN

OLD STUFF IS STILL GOOD STUFF

YOU GOTTA RESPECT THE CLASSICS!

JOHN TAFFIN

We are trapped in an ever-changing world so much so it seems to be a fact the only thing that doesn't change is the fact everything changes. Fortunately, though only once in a while, the changes are sometimes actually positive. Such is the case here at *GUNS* as well as our sister publication, *American Handgunner.*

It takes hands, very good hands to create positive changes, and we have added some very good hands. One of those hands is Payton Miller. If you've been around gun magazines for a while you should recognize this name. I'd like to say I've been reading his stuff since I was a kid, however, that won't fly as I am much older than he is (it just seems like it's been a very long time).

In the March '14 issue Payton was introduced as our new executive editor. I think that just means he does everything else no one else does. I know Payton not only from reading his stuff for a long time as well as seeing him on TV gun shows, he is also the editor of my two latest, and probably last books, *Book of The .45* and *Double Action Sixguns.* So we have talked on the phone as well as exchanged emails and one major thing I found out about him is the fact he really knows stuff, including old stuff. He brought this out with his very first "GUNS Insider" column with "Old Stuff Is Good Stuff." I certainly could not have said it better myself. And as I turned the pages of the issue and

An all-original 1950 Model Military .44 Special compared to the same model customized with adjustable sights and a target barrel added. This former original 1950 Model Military shoots great, but would be worth a lot more money if left alone. John regrets doing so since only 1,200 Model 1950 Military revolvers were produced.

stumbled on his first column what should I see smack dab in the center of the page but a picture of a Smith & Wesson 1950 Military .44 Special. With his very first printed effort for us it went right to my sixgunnin' heart, soul and spirit.

He then went on to relate this particular Smith .44 belongs to editor Jeff who also subscribes to old stuff being good stuff. In fact if you check out both *GUNS* and *American Handgunner* you will find we are among very few publications which actually pay any attention to anything which is not black and polymer (yes, I believe black and polymer is good, however it is definitely not the do-all and end-all). So I not only thank Payton and Jeff but also Roy Huntington at *AH.* Some would call us dinosaurs. I think *open-minded* is more appropriate.

We do have to work on Payton a little as he confessed when Jeff "…was unleashing an S&W 4th Model Hand Ejector 5-inch in .44 Special that literally defined the term 'patina,' which to my way of thinking at the time was a desperate cry for a full-on rebluing job… I quickly learned rebluing was a dirty word as far as Jeff was concerned." Hallelujah!

I have very deep-rooted feelings for the .44 Special 4th Model. It brings up thoughts of Elmer Keith, Skeeter Skelton, and unfortunately some missteps both on my part and others. Let's take a look at a brief history of the S&W .44 Special. Smith & Wesson has come up with many firsts over the more than 160 years of producing quality firearms. In 1857 they were the first company to produce a workable cartridge firing revolver, namely the Model No. 1 a Tip-Up, 7-shooter chambered in the greatest cartridge ever, the .22 Rimfire. Other models came, the Model No. 1-1/2 and Model No. 2, and then three years before the 1873 Colt Single Action Army, S&W introduced the first successful big-bore cartridge-firing revolver with the top-break S&W

Model No. 3 American. Mainly chambered in .44 S&W it is also found rarely in the .44 rimfire cartridge used in the 1860 Henry rifle.

The Russians liked the S&W, however they made two changes. The grip frame was changed by adding a hump at the top and a spur on the bottom of the triggerguard to help with controllability. But the most important change was the cartridge itself. The .44 American cartridge used a 2-diameter bullet with the base being slightly smaller and fitted inside the case. The Russians wanted a bullet of uniform diameter with grease grooves inside the case and the result was the magnificent .44 Russian cartridge. S&W would go on to chamber this cartridge in the Model No. 3 Russian and New Model No. 3 and then in the 1880's their double-action revolver which was still of top-break design.

In late 1907 S&W did almost everything right with the introduction of their first swing-out cylindered big-bore sixgun, the 1st Model Hand Ejector (also known as the "New Century" and more lovingly known by sixgunners for over a century, as the Triple-Lock.) This revolver's cylinder locked at the back, at the front of the ejector rod, and a third lock beautifully machined at the front of the cylinder in the yoke/frame area. This was also the first S&W to feature an enclosed ejector rod, and most importantly the first S&W .44 Special. To come up with the .44 Special the .44 Russian was simply slightly lengthened. Smith & Wesson proved they really didn't know what they had as the ballistics of the .44 Special were the same as the .44 Russian and the first cartridges, even though we were now in the smokeless powder age, were loaded with black powder. It would remain for experimenters after WWI to begin to unlock the true potential of the .44 Special.

In 1915 the Triple-Lock was removed from production to be replaced by the 2nd Model Hand Ejector without the third lock and without the enclosed ejector rod. It was certainly a sad day for sixgunners who began to clamor for a return to the original or at least the enclosed ejector rod. The pleas fell on deaf ears at S&W; however, in 1926 Texas distributor Wolf & Klar placed a large order for what would become the 3rd Model Hand Ejector or the Model 1926. It came to be very popular with shooters and especially law enforcement officers in the Southwest. Both the 2nd Model and 3rd Model would be produced side-by-side by S&W until the beginning of WWII. After the War the 2nd Model was gone, however production of the 1926 Model was resumed and would last until 1949. All three of these Hand Ejectors were made with both fixed sights and target sights with the latter being rare and especially

rare in the 1926 Model. The 1926 Target Model, if it can be found, sells for approximately $8,000 to $10,000. I have lusted after one ever since I saw one pictured in Elmer Keith's *Sixguns By Keith* (1955). At today's prices I will never own one.

In 1950 S&W upgraded their .44 hand ejectors with a more modernized short action and readily available target-sighted models with highly upgraded sights. With target sights this .44 Special is known as the 4th Model Hand Ejector, or more commonly as the Model 1950 Target. Emotion says the Triple-Lock is the finest .44 Special ever made by S&W, however, reality gives the vote to the 1950 Target Model. This beautifully crafted .44 Special was offered with barrel lengths of 4 and 6-1/2 inches and rarely with a 5-inch barrel. At the same time as the Model 1950 Target, S&W also offered the version pictured by Payton in his first column, namely the .44 Hand Ejector 4th Model Military better known as the Model 1950 Military. From 1950 to 1966 more than 5,000 Target Models were produced, however the fixed sighted version, the .44 Military is much more rare with only 1,200 produced. In 1957 both of these versions lost their names to be replaced by numbers with the 1950 Target becoming the Model 24 and the Military version became the Model 21.

In the late 1960's I bought a .44 Military for $60. Then it all went downhill. I came up with a .44 Target barrel and an S&W adjustable rear sight and changed my .44 Military to a 5-inch Target Model. Although the work was performed beautifully I lost hundreds of dollars in value by doing this. Just a few years ago I found another .44 Military being offered for sale on a gun forum. The owner had asked about converting it to .45 Colt and I was all over him like (as *Gunsmoke's* Festus would say), "Ugly on an ape." I wound up buying that .44 Military for an extremely low price because of what another former owner had done. The butt had been crudely roundbutted with a very

Old Stuff still shoots! This 5-inch 1950 Military .44 Special (above) is not handicapped by its lack of finish or fixed sights. Very "Special" old stuff include both these 1926 Model and 1950 Model Military .44 Specials (below) sporting 4-inch barrels.

coarse file and the hammer had been bobbed. I was able to replace the hammer and a friend polished the roundbutt and fitted it with a pair of custom stocks. It now looks and works fine but—just as my original—hundreds upon hundreds of dollars of value have been lost.

If you should come upon one of these older Smith & Wessons, *please* leave it alone. Editor Jeff will tell you don't re-blue. I will tell you the same thing. If it needs internal parts to make it workable that is perfectly acceptable. Eddie Janis of Peacemaker Specialists absolutely will not refinish an old Colt Single Action, which has never been finished before. He believes in saving history. So do I. At least now. Too bad I did not wake up 40 years ago! GUNS

SHOOT 'EM IF YOU GOT 'EM

THE ROAD TO THE "RIGHT" .22 LR LOAD CAN HAVE TWISTS AND TURNS APLENTY.

PAYTON MILLER

M&P15-22

MAKER: SMITH & WESSON
2100 ROOSEVELT AVE.
SPRINGFIELD, MA 01104
(800) 331-0852
WWW.GUNSMAGAZINE.COM/INDEX

Action: Blowback semi-auto, **Caliber:** .22 Long Rifle, **Capacity:** 10 (detachable box magazine), **Barrel length:** 16-1/2 inches, **Overall length:** 33-3/4 inches, **Weight:** 5 pounds, **Material:** Polymer upper and lower, carbon steel barrel, **Finish:** Matte black (other options available), **Stock:** 6 position CAR-type, **Sights:** Adjustable dual aperture rear, A2 post front (Picatinny rail for optics), **Price:** $519

Finding the best-performing .22 Long Rifle load for a specific gun can be as surprising as it can be exhaustive. Back when rimfire ammo was considerably cheaper and easier to find in quantity, the best advice was pretty cut and dried. And it still holds. It goes something like this: "Get a box of every brand and type of .22 LR you can lay hands on. Group them all and go with what shoots the tightest."

And you've also got to take into consideration what you're using it for. A varmint hunter is likely to want a high or hyper-velocity HP, whereas a squirrel or rabbit hunter is probably going to be more concerned with meat damage.

Of course, with a rich array of brands, it also makes sense not only to pick what was most accurate in your particular rifle, but to remember what "runner-up" loads most closely duplicated "the winner" in actual point of impact as well as group size. This makes even more sense today, when you can't guarantee being able to find—or rat-hole—enough of your cherry-picked No. 1 stuff to put your mind at ease.

And, yes, this winnowing-out process can be surprising. Sometimes the best .22 LR load for a given rifle won't be what you think it oughta be. Case in point:

About 12 years ago, a buddy of mine's daughter got interested in 50-foot competitive smallbore rifle shooting. So he bought her a very nice Anschutz Model 1451—globe sights, serious sling, the whole nine yards. We took it out to the range, along with a GI ammo can full of—literally—every type of .22 LR we could scrounge up. It was mainly standard velocity, of course (this was not a hunting rig), but there was

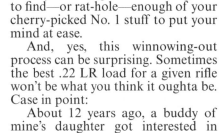

high-velocity and even hyper-velocity stuff as well.

In short, we had everything from Eley Rifle Match, Lapua Match, Winchester Supreme Match and CCI Green Tag through Winchester Power Point, Remington Mohawk, CCI Stingers, Remington Yellowjackets and a potpourri of brands and exotic names I can't even remember. At 25 yards we shot 'em all. Sandbagged, 5-shot groups. The winner? PMC Sidewinder. This relatively economical high-speed number literally put 'em all in one semi-distorted hole at 25. Now, you'd have thought this little thoroughbred of a rifle would have preferred some of the (at the time) six-buck-a box Eley or Lapua match stuff instead of a modestly-priced plinking/varmint item. *Nope.*

Turns out, of course, a lot of this was mere hairsplitting. That Anschutz shot most everything good enough for her to do well in matches with whatever ammo her coaches had on hand for the kids. But it was, to say the least, surprising. But it really shouldn't have been.

There's a whole lot of voodoo involved in why one .22 will print best with a certain load. I'm sure there's a scientific explanation somewhere. But I'm equally sure I couldn't understand it on the chance someone could come up with one. Although it's probably a safe bet your standard velocity, high-end match stuff—usually by virtue of consistent velocity and hand-inspected uniformity—is going to do better overall in any "taste test" using several rifles (and probably competition-grade ones at that).

For an adjustable sighted— or scoped—.22 the process can be fairly involved. Lots of time, lots of ammo, lots of patience required. I can remember things being simpler. Once I decided to give the treatment

With the S&W MP15-22 (below), point of impact from Winchester T-22 Match (above, left) was very close to Winchester Power-Point (above, right), an excellent small game load. Knowing this makes a quick switchover possible in the field.

to a tiny little Winchester Model 58, a Depression-era single-shot with a gumwood stock and *fixed* open sights. The challenge then was simply finding something to manage a happy union between point of aim and point of impact at 25 yards. Fortunately, the little rifle shot most everything tight enough, so it was just a matter of finding one magic brand (plus a few close-running alternates). The magic number turned out to be Winchester Power-Point, which perfectly suited the small-game role the little bolt action was designed for.

Dealing with .22 autoloaders, brings functional reliability into the mix—will the load run the gun as well as give the accuracy you want? Often it's not as simple as simply using high-speed ammo, or opting for a 40-grain bullet instead of a 29-grain "hyper-velocity" one.

I wanted to revisit the ammo selection process with a current rimfire autoloader, one as far away from what I was used to as I could find. I used Smith & Wesson's M&P15-22, a cool little blowback "AR lookalike" featuring a 16-1/2-inch barrel, polymer upper and lower, and removable aperture sights on the Picatinny rail.

Of course I could have put any

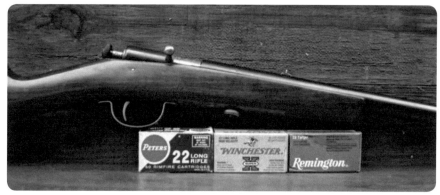

The rudimentary fixed sights on this Depression-era Winchester Model 58 simplify the search for the "right" load. Once you find something that brings point-of-aim and point-of-impact together—and delivers acceptable groups—you've found it! In this case, all three of these brands did the trick.

Standard, high or hyper-velocity. Old, new or out-of-print. To find the perfect match for your .22, there's simply no way around trying as many Long Rifle brands as you can.

WANT MORE?

Click Here:
gunsmagazine.com

MORE GUNS HERE

every month!

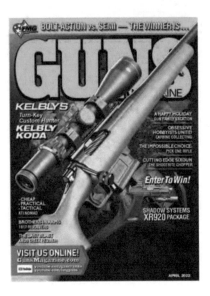

Besides being able to accept most after-market bells and whistles as a "real AR," the S&W M&P15-22 is an excellent, reliable rimfire in its own right.

.22 LONG RIFLE PERFORMANCE
S&W M&P15-22 (16-1/2-INCH BARREL)

LOAD (BRAND, TYPE, BULLET WEIGHT)	VELOCITY (FPS)	EXTREME SPREAD (FPS)	GROUP SIZE (INCHES)
Winchester T22 Match 40	1,171	122	1
Winchester Power-Point 40	1,196	110	1-1/8
Federal Gold Medal 40	1,083	45	1-1/2
CCI Stinger 32	1,493	58	1-3/4
Remington Mohawk 40	1,198	16	3/4
Eley Tenex 40	1,057	41	3/4
Remington Target 40	1,028	122	1

Velocity is the average of 5 shots measured with a Competition Electronics Pro-Chrono 10 feet from the muzzle. Groups are 5 shots fired at 25 yards.

type of optic I wanted on the rail, but since I was going to be shooting at 25 yards with a variety of ammo, I figured the aperture would be fine. And it was—easy to adjust, positive and repeatable. The 6-pound single-stage trigger broke clean as a whistle, by the way. No, not as light as that long-ago Anschutz, but the little S&W has a curb weight of 5 pounds and is not nearly as "mission specific." The only time I managed to embarrass myself was in mistaking one of the ears protecting the front

The M&P15-22 was democratic in its likes. Remington's economy Mohawk brand (left) produced results fairly close to Eley's super-pricey Tenex (right).

sight blade with the blade itself. This resulted in a "called flyer," which flew off to parts unknown.

Oh, on the question of "function with everything" reliability with an autoloader? No worries. The stuff I ran with the M&P15-22 ranged from standard velocity match grade to high velocity HP's to light-bullet (32-grain) hyper-velocity Stingers (see chart). I didn't experience anything resembling a malfunction. The winners in terms of accuracy? An unlikely tie between "pricey" Eley Tenex (*now running around 25 bucks a box*) and "price-brand" Remington Mohawk—long out of production, but probably approximated pretty closely by the company's current Cyclone or Thunderbolt brands.

I guess the lesson is the same now as it's always been. You gotta shoot 'em all and see.

Shooting Facilities provided by: Angeles Shooting Ranges, 12651 Little Tujunga Rd., Lakeview Terrace, CA 91342, (818) 899-2255 www.angeles-ranges.com.

BETTERSHOOTING

DAVE ANDERSON

J-FRAME LIGHT?

HYSKORE'S GRIPLIGHT

The CREE LED on the Griplight puts out over 100 lumens of even, bright light. It not only lights up the target, it lights up the front sight neatly.

Left: The button just behind the triggerguard activates the light. If the gun is in hand and you want the light off, just relax pressure on the button.

You can debate the value of a weapon-mounted light versus a separate light, but we'll leave that for another time. I'll just say, on a home-defense gun, I want both — a light on the gun resting on the night-stand, and a separate light next to it.

Accessory rails allow you the option. Up until now, it's an option not readily available for one of the most popular of all handguns. Since the introduction of the first Smith & Wesson J-Frame revolver in 1950, hundreds of thousands of the little wheelguns have been purchased, sometimes as the primary weapon, often as a backup, and legions of them serve as home/self-defense guns.

Among the admirers of the J-Frame is our illustrious editor, Roy. I remember a conversation with him as we were riding around in a safari truck in Africa. We were talking about the guns he used during his police career. Roy mentioned he had always carried a J-Frame as a backup and had stayed with it even during the big change to semi-autos.

Its aluminum/soft synthetic construction and high-quality light module handles the recoil of even those ultralight, scandium-framed .357 Magnums.

"I'd have given anything for the option of a light mounted on both my duty gun and the backup in those days. And before you make any wisecracks about electricity not being invented back then, I'll remind you, in Africa people have been known to disappear, and their bodies are never found."

Roy may have forgotten the conversation but he didn't forget about lights and J-Frames. It seemed no one was making what he wanted, he couldn't get anyone interested in doing it, so in the classic American spirit of innovation, he just went ahead and did it himself — with assistance from a company called Hyskore.

A GRIPLIGHT

The Griplight he designed is now in production and is made for *all* round-butt S&W J-Frames. He was hesitant to show it in our pages, but I assured him it makes sense and readers should see it. A lot of thought has been given to details. With millions of revolvers produced there's bound to be minor variations in grip size, and in the location of the pin at the bottom of the grip frame. The hole in the grip panels for the pin is just slightly oversized to allow for these minor variations. I tried the Griplight on half a dozen J-Frames (and one I-Frame) and it fit snugly and tightly on all of them.

The bottom of the grip (below the grip frame) houses a powerful lithium CR2 battery. Roy wanted lots of light and a decent run time, so the little button batteries wouldn't do. The light itself is a CREE LED putting out over 100 lumens of white light. It really lights up the room — and the front sight. Run time on a single battery is over 30 minutes.

The grips are built on an aluminum frame for strength and to act as a heat-sinc for that bright LED. It also acts as the base for the soft grip inserts. It's been tested to handle full power .357 Magnum loads, even in ultralight J-Frames. I ran 100 rounds of .38 Special +P through a current production, nickeled Model 36 and everything ran fine and still worked.

A small sliding switch on the grip bottom is the main power "on/off" switch, used to turn off the light when the revolver is being stored. With that switch *on* pressing the micro-switch on the front of the grip activates the light. By simply applying or releasing pressure with the middle finger, the light can be instantly turned on or off.

A BIT BIGGER

The longer grips are actually more comfortable than the usual small round-butt grips, and certainly make the gun easier to control and shoot accurately. On a home-defense gun kept on a nightstand the extra size is a benefit. They're a bit big for pocket carry, unless we're talking cargo/tactical pants or jacket pockets. For concealed carry I'd be thinking along the lines of an ankle or belt holster, or carried in a jacket or coat pocket. A holster with a thumb break or safety strap over the hammer likely won't work over the light. One holster I know that does work is the Mitch Rosen Workman, which just happens to be my favorite J-Frame belt holster.

The Griplight doesn't allow use of my Safariland J-Frame speedloaders. Most J-Frame owners use speed strips, loops or just loose rounds in a pocket rather than speedloaders, but I do like the option. There are no wires or switches in the left grip panel so I think it could be easily reshaped with a Dremel tool if speedloader use is really important to you.

Self-defense isn't the only role for the Griplight. Living on a fairly remote farm there isn't much chance I'll have to repel invaders. Heck, sometimes we go weeks, even months at a time without a single gun battle out here.

But, the vermin we have to deal with are *actual* vermin, such as sparrows and the occasional rat, skunk or weasel. They always seem to hang out in a dark corner of the barn or a shed. Now they'll have no place to hide. The Griplight is a handy tool, indeed. MSRP is $129.95.

THE INSIDER ™ ROY HUNTINGTON

Reunited … Roy's old Model 29 in the original box, with a 4" Bowen 29 below, added to the flock some years ago.

MAYBE HARRY WAS RIGHT

Embarrassing Photo: In the late '70s, Roy's brother needed a photo of "some guy holding a big gun" for a high school photo project. He knew Roy had a big gun, so the pose happened. Roy's not proud of this sort of pose, but the gun in his hand is the very same Model 29 which found its way home 35 years later. Were we really that young?

The set-up is surprisingly comfortable under a jacket and conceals the big sixgun handily.

Above: Roy's early Bianchi X15 holster (right) holding his original 29, and the new version with a modern S&W Classic Model 29. The new X15 had some solid design improvements.

I've had a longtime affection for S&W Model 29's of all kinds, and specifically the blued 6.5" versions. And like many of you, it was fostered by Clint Eastwood and his *Dirty Harry* movies. Not long ago I had something suddenly renew my affection for these guns, so a pause for a short story is in order.

In the middle '70s I walked into Krasne's Gun shop on upper Broadway in San Diego just as the clerk was putting a brand new 6.5" blued Model 29 into the display case. At the time they were essentially unavailable, most stores had long waiting lists and some were asking $700 to $1,000 for handguns listing for $235 at the time. The price was $235 on the tag — I said "Sold." It was just dumb luck I stumbled onto it.

Over the next several years I learned to work on S&W revolvers using that gun and a Model 19 duty gun I had. I competed in the very early days of what we called "Wildcat Combat" pistol matches in Southern California using the Model 29 — and full-power loads — hunted running jack rabbits with it, carried it off-duty at times, and shot thousands of mid-range rounds through it at targets. All loaded painfully slowly on a Lee hand loader. I also mostly carried it in one of those iconic Bianchi X15 shoulder holsters.

One day in late 1979 I decided I needed an AR-15 more and traded it off to another cop. I regretted it instantly. I had had a few good adventures with that gun — including pointing it at a Hell's Angel biker one time while off-duty. A series of newer 29's came and went, and a few stuck. But none were the same as that first-best gun.

Fate being what it is, about two years ago I found out the guy I had traded it to still had it. Gads! I found him, discovered he needed something worse than my old 29, and the trade was done. Suddenly, the old girl was back home. That's it in the picture in its original wooden case with flocked plastic cut-out pad. Even still had the original screwdriver and cleaning tools.

The original grips were gone (I had filed and sanded on them and they were ugly) so I put those nice grips from Eagle on it. More amazingly, it came home with the original X15 shoulder holster I had carried it in for countless matches, hunting trips, riding with me off-duty, traveling and hanging on the coat hook by the front door. And it all got me to thinking.

Big Guns And Big Bullets

The original holster is pretty worn, the elastic is stretched out and the leather dry. I reached out to Hope Bianchi-Sjursen, John Bianchi's daughter, who, remarkably, still works with Bianchi and Safariland, their parent company. She sent out a new version of the classic X15 and laughed when I told her the story. I found the new rig beautifully made, with some sound improvements in a few areas. I slipped it on, adjusted the straps and slid the Model 29 home. Instantly, 35-odd years slid away and a video loop of past adventures began to play in my mind.

I wondered if my memories of actually carrying that gun for hours, days, weeks at a time and thinking it was perfectly comfortable were just figments of my imagination — or was it truly so? I subjected my old gun to a couple hundred rounds of modest .44 loads (around 900 fps using Unique with a cast 240 SWC — my old favorite load) to make sure it still ran and to make sure my eyes and hands still remembered things. I had forgotten how smooth the action was and I found myself running steel plates on my rack time and time again. It was just plain fun, the holster worked great and that thump in my hand felt grand again!

For about three weeks then (being winter here in scenic Missouri as I write this) I toted that Model 29 in the new Bianchi X15 holster under a longish vest I have, a chore coat I wear a lot, or a nicer "town" coat. What'd I learn?

I'm not a big guy, 5'9" on my toes, but this new rendition of the X15 is perfectly comfortable, even with all that gun in it. I tend to let it ride on the low side, and the rear snap secures it to your belt. The off-side elastic band keeps things tidy against your side. Even that big Model 29 is an amazingly slim package once things are settled in. I could sit in the car, do chores around here, enjoy a dinner out (with a coat on, one of the pitfalls of a shoulder rig), go grocery shopping or anything else I'd normally be doing.

There were no sore shoulders, no constant adjusting of things, or prods or pokes in tender places. It was exactly as I remembered — except maybe even better. The new holster made a difference. I have great confidence in that gun and holster combo, and I'll confess I shoot it well, having spent tens of thousands of rounds with it learning to run it in about every position and situation I could think up. And that confidence is important.

A Silly Idea?

"But it only has six shots!" You're right. I carry two HKS speedloaders when I carry it, just like the old days. But those can be six extremely accurate pie-plate-at-100-yards shots, and a factory 240 SWC or Barnes HP at about

1,000 fps or so will have the final word just about anywhere.

So — is it archaic? Maybe. An antique asked to do a modern job? I think not. Am I silly to say a good man behind the trigger of a big-bore revolver isn't under-gunned? Is a seasoned shooter with plenty of practice and street sense actually well-prepared with this set-up?

I think the answer is yes — if you abide by the rules. Get to know the gun, train to use it, understand the limits and be realistic on ammo selection — then it can be a solid option for defense. As

Clint Smith is fond of saying, "It's a big gun going into the holster, and a big gun coming back out." It gets attention.

Is it the best or even a good set-up for most people? I don't think so. Is it big, heavy and can it be awkward? Absolutely. Do you need to practice with it a lot, and is it expensive to do that? Yup.

And I doubt I'd carry it in the hot summer months. But still …

As a "winter" gun, or if your spidey-sense is tingling for some reason — I think you'd have "enough gun" at-hand.

Maybe Harry had the right idea after

ADD IT UP

10 MILLION
Mossberg Model 500 shotguns manufactured to date.

100+
Design patents held by Mossberg since 1919.

14,796,872
NICS background checks in 2013.

13,090,383
NICS background checks in 2014.

88
Percentage saying CDC should not spend money studying gun violence.
(NSSF survey)

46
Percentage of adult hunters taking a child hunting with them in 2014.
(Southwick & Assoc. survey)

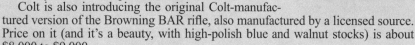

COLT 1903 RETURNS

Colt, in collaboration with Curt Wolf (who makes their Colt-branded brass Bulldog Gatling Gun!) is reintroducing the classic 1903 pocket auto (in .32 ACP). Built exactly like the originals, there are no gimmicks, modern safeties or rubber or polymer — just steel and wood. The production run will be 2,500, with 500 mirroring the General Officer's Pistol (pictured), complete with "U.S. Property" marks and Parkerizing. Initial pricing quotes hover around the $1,300 mark. But if you want one, keep your eyes open as they are likely to go fast and there is no assurance they will become production models.

Colt is also introducing the original Colt-manufactured version of the Browning BAR rifle, also manufactured by a licensed source. Price on it (and it's a beauty, with high-polish blue and walnut stocks) is about $8,000 to $9,000.

STOUT SHOP APRON

Old bud Mitch Rosen (of gun leather fame) and I are both dedicated hobby metal workers. Over the years I discovered finding the "perfect" shop apron is a bit like finding the perfect holster — you end up with a box full of rejects. Mitch had the same problem so he put his leather/sewing JuJu to work and came up with what is, in my subjective opinion, the finest shop apron ever invented. It's #8 black canvas (might stop bullets?), has black leather-finished edge binding and trim, black leather straps, pockets and even a place to hang your glasses. Mine already has a long, deep scratch in the canvas where an errant sharp bit of steel flew off a machine, attempting to make my voice an octave higher. This apron is a new level of rugged. About $140. *For more info: www.mitchrosen.com or (603) 647-2971*

EXTREME IRON

Stan Skinner, a well-known writer in our industry, is about as much of a gun-guy as any human being can be. We're old friends and between us, there ain't much Stan doesn't know about guns, from old ones to the newest plastic shooters. But like most "seasoned" gun-types, Stan appreciates the ends of the spectrum when it comes to designs. If it's big and slow, tiny and fast or just plain cool or weird, Stan knows about it and this book is your guide to it all.

From the ultra big-bore, modern, old or eclectic to just plain amazin' — Stan takes you there with good pictures and a fun read. So get 'em while you can. And they say print is dead. Ha! And at less than $20, it's a screaming deal! *For more info: www. skyhorsepublishing.com, Ph: (212) 643-6816*

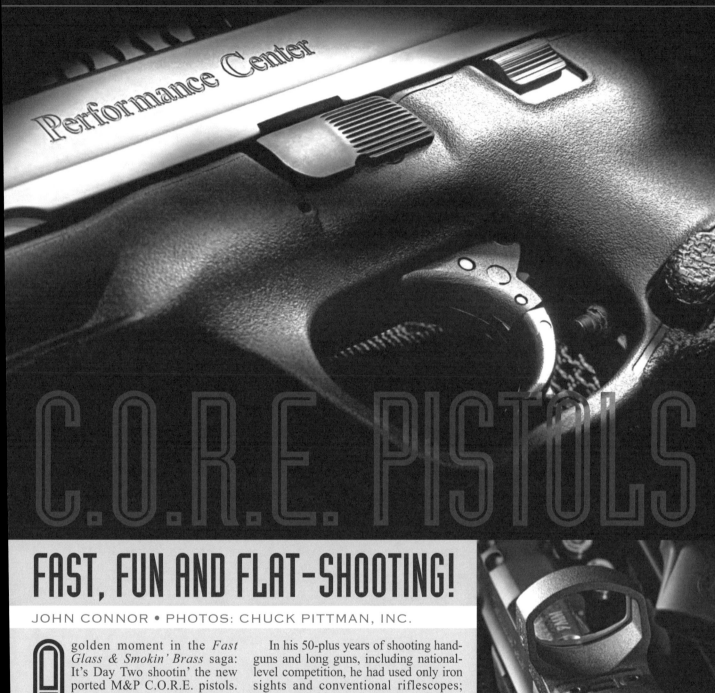

FAST, FUN AND FLAT-SHOOTING!

JOHN CONNOR • PHOTOS: CHUCK PITTMAN, INC.

A golden moment in the *Fast Glass & Smokin' Brass* saga: It's Day Two shootin' the new ported M&P C.O.R.E. pistols. I'm poppin' pills into paper with increasing speed and confidence when BH arrives. Good guy; one of the best natural shots I've known. He recently slid up hard against 60, and his formerly eagle eyes have finally gone wonky. Like us seasoned mortals he now has that vision disorder called presbyopia, or "Pick One Outta Three," meaning you've got three planes to focus on — rear sight, front sight and target — but now, you can only get a focus on one at a time, and maybe that one's kinda fuzzy too.

In his 50-plus years of shooting handguns and long guns, including national-level competition, he had used only iron sights and conventional riflescopes; never a red dot, no zero-magnification glass at all. They just hadn't interested him. He had heard scraps of scuttlebutt about reflex sights relieving that "Pick One" problem, and I invited him to try 'em out. Gave him a mini-brief on the optic, handed him the long-slide Nine, and I went back to work with the Forty.

I heard irregular, desultory shots and looked over. BH was makin' molasses look zippy; dawdling over shots, holding position way too long, seemingly intent but frustrated, blowin' steam out his ears. I asked, *Wassup, Doc?* He 'splained.

S&W

S&W'S PORTED M&P C.O.R.E. PISTOLS

C.O.R.E. PISTOLS

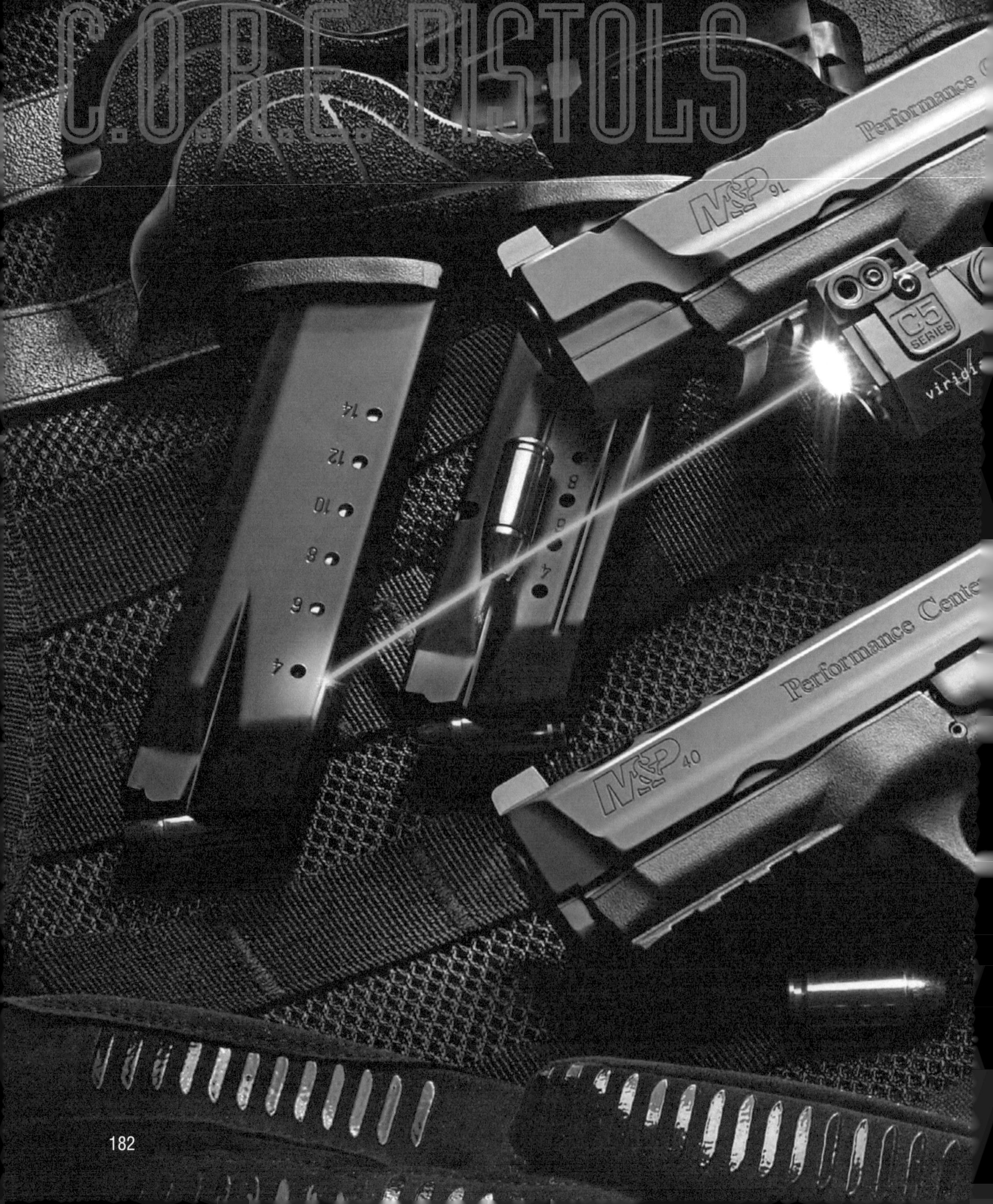

AMERICAN
HANDGUNNER

It was drivin' him nuts trying to get that triangly-thing (the Leupold DeltaPoint reticle) oriented exactly dead-center horizontally and vertically on the screen, and beyond that he was also tryin' to perch the reticle dead-bang on top of the front iron sight, and properly centered in the rear sight's U-notch. Plus, he snorted, that reticle *jittered!* He just couldn't get it dead-still. "This is stupid," he concluded. So *I* 'splained.

'Splained

"First," I says, "Don't wait for the reticle to be frozen in space. It ain't gonna happen. That delta is 7.5-MOA, but ask yourself how much it covers at handgun range, like 10, 15, 20 yards? How much does a handgun front-sight blade cover at 100 yards? Teensy reticle jitters don't mean squat." *Hmm,* he hummed.

To illustrate the rest, I put up a fresh target with a 1.25" black center, then target-taped over the iron sights and told him to ignore them. Then I had him concentrate only on layin' the screen-centered reticle on the dot and squeezin'. Next, I told him to move the reticle-overlaid dot up toward 12 o'clock on the screen and shoot. We repeated this with the reticle-covered dot at 3, 6 and 9 o'clock, then approached the target. Of course, there was a tight little 5-round group. He looked at the DeltaPoint as though it had turned into a baby dragon. His eyes goggled.

"Art thou a wizard, sir knight?" he demanded. "What sorcery is this?" (He talks like that sometimes.)

"Nay, my liege," quoth I (I go along with it). "Ain't no sorcery. It's some enchanted glass, though. Think of it as a floptical delusion, like an optical illusion but real. Once zeroed, you just lay that reticle where you want the slug to splot. Now go forth and conquer. Work that sweet reset. And on these ported jobs, you'll find the muzzle agreeably tamed."

What's this? Another stunning target? That's two 17-round groups of 9mm rapid-fired at seven yards, Hornady 125's in the clockwork, 115's in the pump. Disregard the little black arrow. Nothin' to see there. Move along.

FAST, ENCHANTED GLASS

Minutes later he was cuttin' clover-groups and chuckling. Thirty minutes after that he was hammerin' like a belt-fed 1919 Browning machinegun, tearin' out target centers and laughing. Ten minutes later he was shootin' circles around me and politely hiding a smirk. Thus ended the intro to handgun optics, and acquaintance with the pleasures of a ported C.O.R.E. pistol.

Your results may vary. *My* results varied. I recommend three days, three structured sessions, minimum: Familiarization, Skill-Building then Speed-Work. He did it in one short session, but … The guy's a wizard. Really. Now, back to our regular programming.

Evolution, Revolution, Etc.

I won't go into a lot of the mech-and-tech specs of the M&P pistols, because a ton of ink has already been spilled on 'em. Relatively light, polymer-framed, strong, tough, rock-solid reliable and commendably accurate outta the box, they're very reasonably priced for the quality. When you consider they've only been around for a bit over a decade, they've made a heck of a footprint compared to *any* competitor. With features including multiple frame sizes and calibers, ambidextrous slide locks, side-

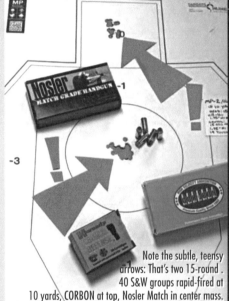

Note the subtle, teensy arrows: That's two 15-round .40 S&W groups rapid-fired at 10 yards, CORBON at top, Nosler Match in center mass.

swapping mag releases, three grip insert sizes, options in finishes, thumb safeties or slick-sides, smooth or threaded barrels, lasers and more, it's a smorgasbord of shootin' sweetness, as many of you have already discovered.

Quickly following their debut, the modern iteration of Military & Police

How do you pack a ton of quality, technology and toughness into a teensy package weighing six tenths of an ounce? I dunno, but Leupold did it in their DeltaPoint Reflex Sight. Physically, it's more rugged than it looks, with a hard-coated magnesium case, DiamondCoat protection on its wide-screen 1.02" by .75" lens, and it's completely waterproof. Functionally, it features a full 60 MOA elevation adjustment range matched by 60-MOA of windage, a distinctive 7.5-MOA delta-shaped (a triangle, like the upper-case Greek letter "delta") reticle that's easy to focus on. Many users find it far easier to track with the eye than a typical round red dot.

The techno-juju is pretty stunning. Intelligent Brightness Control (IBC) automatically adjusts the brightness of the red delta reticle, not just according to the ambient light, but "forward-looking," so it's assessing the light specifically in the direction of your target! Other magic turns it on, turns it off after five minutes without movement, then flashes it back to life instantly when put into play. Slip the rubber cover over it, and it goes to sleep at minimum power, to awaken instantly when the hood is removed. As you move from bright light into dark-ness and back again, the reticle brightness adjusts at the rate of the dilation of your pupils, so your eyes aren't lagging or playing catch-up.

There are ten different mounting bases available for a wide range of weapons, and a cross-slot base allowing mounting to any rail system. The sight can leap from handguns to carbines to shotguns to submachineguns and back again.

Otherwise, it offers the same old boring Leupold qualities, like crystal clarity, superb light transmission, easy maintenance, a full lifetime guarantee … Yawn …

The DeltaPoint Reflex Sight lists for $564 in the "all mounts" kit, and is also available with a 3.5-MOA round dot version. It's truly a case of "You get what you pay for" — in this case, quality.

pistols tore off huge chunks of the law enforcement market, with massive consumer sales following in that wide wake. It's a mark of having made your bones in the crucible when large numbers of competitive shooters adopt your service pistols.

Soon they began buggin' Smith & Wesson for more refinements. The *Pro Series* offered 5" "long slide" models in addition to 4.25" standards, and an additional kiss-an'-tickle from the Performance Center in the forms of slicked-up cycling and smoothed-out triggers. But they wanted more.

With the C.O.R.E. — Competition Optics Ready Equipment — models, M&P shooters in the action sports got pistols with slides already machined for fast glass, supplied with an array of adaptor plates to go under a contour-fitted, unobtrusive cap just forward of the rear sight. The Leupold DeltaPoint, which we tested, plus the Trijicon RMR, JPoint, Docter Red Dot, C-More STS are all accommodated.

A note: given a suggested retail price differential of only $80 between, for example, the Pro Series 5" 9mm pistol and its C.O.R.E. cousin, the optics-ready model is a sweet deal. You get about $250-$300 worth of machining and adaptor plates, and when you don't want an optic riding on it, you've got a smooth-topped "regular" Pro Series with taller, bolder iron sights, which sit higher to co-witness with most optics — and also will clear many suppressors.

Another added improvement was a new texture for the interchangeable backstraps. They're so perfectly grippy and stick-to-the-hand, owners of pre-C.O.R.E. Pro Series M&P's — like my son — have purchased the new backstraps and slapped 'em on their veteran M&P's. I wouldn't waste the words on it if they weren't *that good,* folks.

Now, for you Open Division, Wizard-Class action shooters irritated with that pesky "muzzle flip" phenomenon, ported and compensated M&P C.O.R.E. pis-tols are rollin' out of the Performance Center. On the 5" long-slides, there are four oblong ports on each side of the slide measuring about .40" long by .2", and two slots cut in the barrel at about 10 and 2 o'clock, placed .72" to the rear of the muzzle. Our test sample 4.25" barreled .40 S&W C.O.R.E. had three ports per side and two compensator slots in its barrel of similar but slightly differing dimensions — and you can bet those dimensions are no whim or accidents. The slide ports are all about lightening the slide for faster cycling.

That's not all that's different though. The ported C.O.R.E.'s also feature a new adjustable trigger over-travel stop, and a new trigger sear yielding a smoother pull, a cleaner break and faster re-set, all for about $43 more than their un-ported cousins. How's that?

Ducks In A Row

Don't ya just love it when all your ducks line right up in a neat row? Sand-wiched between vicious sleet storms, we had three days of fair skies and light winds for some great range time. Our two test pistols were a ported C.O.R.E. 4.25" barrel .40 S&W (15-1 capacity) and a ported C.O.R.E. 5" 9mm (17+1). They both checked out terrific; smooth cycling, all systems running nominal, mags locking up tight and dropping free. The 9mm's trigger gauged at a smooth 5 pounds 6 ounces and the .40's trigger pull measured 5 pounds 14 ounces. Takeup was short and sweet, the break was clean on both pistols, over-travel was virtually *zip,* and reset was very short and easy to work. The Leupold DeltaPoint optic was a breeze to install.

We had good ammo for testing. For the Nine, some Hornady Steel Match HAP in 115-gr. and 125-gr. weights, and lots of "white box" Winchester 147-gr. FMJ Target loads. Feed for the Forty was Cor-Bon 160-gr. FMJ's, Nosler Match Grade 150-gr. JHP's, and Federal Premium Personal Defense 165-gr. Hydra-Shok; great stuff. What more could we ask? This:

We managed to borrow two un-ported, non-compensated C.O.R.E. pistols to match our ported C.O.R.E.'s. Yup; a long-slide Nine, a standard-length Forty — and a twin to our sample DeltaPoint! Now we could shoot both flavors side by side to test the effects of the enhancements.

We shot the ported long Nine first. Frankly, I thought, "Nice shooter, but can I really tell any difference in muzzle behavior? Huh." Then I shot the un-ported Nine and immediately switched back to the ported C.O.R.E.; repeat-repeat-repeat. Okay, *then* I could tell. The action's got a tad more zip and muzzle flip is reduced. Cool. Then we went through the same process with the Forty — and *whoa.* The effect was such that you wanta call strangers over and say, *Dude, you gotta try this!* Then you come to your senses and hog it all to yourself.

Had to settle down and run accuracy tests; almost a waste of time. At 15 yards, 2-handed, we shot 5-round groups cadenced (about one shot per 1.0 to 1.5 seconds) with groups running 1½" to 1¾". Boring. Pushed it back to 25 yards and shot rested, two-handed. How's 1.87" to 2" grab ya? Other than learning the Nine didn't care much for the HAP 115's but loved

the 125's, there were no surprises. But inherent accuracy is the sideshow in this carnival; necessary but secondary. Fast, rapid-fire doubles, triples, speed-shifting from target to target and hammering full magazine loads is where the ported C.O.R.E.'s come to life!

I've got more words than space allows, but check this: With the Nine at 7 yards, rapid fire — like *mas rapido!* — 17 rounds, 16 of 'em within 1¾" high by 1.37", with 15 shots *touching.* With the Forty at 10 yards, rapid fire, 15 rounds into 1.75" by 1.875", with 14 touching. You get the drift. I'll take a little credit; I was having an excellent day, but ... all those other ducks, y'know?

The Wrap & The Rap

If you're a run-and-gun sport shooter or you wanta become one, a ported C.O.R.E. pistol with some fast glass on it could be your Willy Wonka Golden Ticket. If you're new to handgun optics, I recommend three longish, unrushed sessions over three days.

Day One, zeroing and familiarization; just getting the feel for it. I'd been running red dots on carbines for years, but found my brain differentiated between long guns and handguns; experience didn't help that much. I found myself trying to center the reticle and unconsciously defaulting to the iron sights, sometimes in mid-string; fought to concentrate. I put tape over 'em and that helped. Handling is subtly but significantly different. Remember, your eyes don't have to dance back and forth between three planes of focus; get a visual weld on the reticle. Forgive yourself and have fun.

Day Two is Skill-Building. Do fast doubles, start rapid engagement of multiple targets. Focus on getting the web of your hand high up under that nice beavertail; it will complement the muzzle-controlling benefit of the compensation effect. Work the hinged trigger and that fast reset.

Day Three is Speed-Work; let 'er run with the big dogs. Screw up, make up, move on and hammer. Delight yourself. It's like ice cream for the shooter's soul. It may take months to make the process intuitive, but you can nail the basics down in far less — in one day if you're a wizard, an' got some sorcery in your pocket. That helps.

Just so you know, MSRP on either one of these beauties is $812. The dot sight costs extra.

I've only got two raps on these ported C.O.R.E. pistols. Number One: I'd like some serrations up front on the slide. Number Two: Packing them up and sendin' 'em back to Smith. That *sucked.* Connor *OUT*

WINNINGEDGE

SOLID ADVICE TO KEEP YOU AHEAD OF THE COMPETITION

DAVE ANDERSON

S&W 629 .44 MAGNUM "SNUBBIE"

Being built on the S&W N-Frame, the snubbie .44 Magnum is compact in overall length but not really small or light. Recoil is manageable even with full-power Magnum loads.

With Black Hills .44 Special Cowboy Action loads the revolver is a joy to shoot.

Compact and tough, the S&W .44 Magnum model 629 snubbie puts a lot of power in a small package.

SMITH & WESSON PERFORMANCE CENTER MODEL 629
SPECS: CARTRIDGE: .44 SPECIAL, .44 MAGNUM • FRAME: N FRAME, DOUBLE ACTION/SINGLE ACTION
CAPACITY: 6 CARTRIDGES • BARREL LENGTH: 2⅝" • LENGTH OVERALL: 7 ⅝" • WEIGHT, EMPTY: 39.6 OUNCES
FRONT SIGHT: RAMP, RED INSERT • REAR SIGHT: ADJUSTABLE, WHITE OUTLINE • MSRP: $1,079

In the late 1800's the British revolver maker Webley developed a revolver small enough to be carried in a coat pocket. It had a 2½" barrel, a compact grip frame and was chambered for .44 or .45 caliber cartridges of the era. It fired heavy soft-lead bullets at relatively modest velocities of 600 – 700 fps. Webley registered the trademark "Bulldog" for the new model and it proved to be very popular. Both the concept and the name have been widely copied in other countries and by other makers.

Smith & Wesson doesn't use the term for the short-barreled model 629 from the Performance Center. Calling it a "Bulldog" doesn't quite capture the essence. Yes, it has a short barrel, round grip frame and is perfectly capable of firing heavy lead bullets at moderate velocities. But it's also capable of firing full-power .44 Magnum loads. Using the bulldog analogy, this would be a dog capable of gulping down regular bulldogs in a single bite. By any name it's an imposing and impressive revolver.

A BRUISER

The revolver is built on the S&W "N" frame, with a 2⅝" slab-sided barrel and 6-shot, unfluted cylinder. Empty weight is just under 40 ounces, about the same as a full size, steel-framed 1911. The first impression one gets on examining the revolver is the outstanding quality control. Machining of the steel components, parts fit, metal polishing, fit of grips to the frame, etc. are all beautifully done.

Excellent quality control is also evident in operation. Timing is very good, with the locking bolt dropping into the cylinder notch well before the hammer is all the way back, whether in DA or SA mode. Even after dry and live firing there was only a faint trace of a turn line on the cylinder.

The double-action pull measures between 11 and 12 pounds, smooth and even throughout the pull. Single-action pull was likewise typical S&W, breaking cleanly at about 2½ pounds with virtually imperceptible trigger movement.

The ramp front sight won't catch on clothes or holster, and the red ramp is highly visible, easy to pick up for fast shooting even though the sight radius is short. For precision shooting, from long habit, I'm at my best with a vertical, black, serrated post front sight and plain

square notch rear sight. My best 25-yard groups with the test gun were in the 3" range and though it hurts to admit it I don't think I was quite shooting up to the revolver's accuracy potential.

Even so, I can shoot the compact revolver more than accurately enough for any realistic need. The .44 Magnum chambering makes this a very versatile handgun. Of course reloaders can load to any power level desired, but between the many .44 Special and .44 Magnum loads offered, factory ammunition is available to meet most any need.

Black Hills Ammunition has a number of light recoiling, accurate and pleasant-to-shoot loads for various cartridges in its "Cowboy Action" series. I think these fun plinking loads are often overlooked by non-competitive shooters. The .44 Special load is a 210-gr. flatpoint lead bullet rated at 700 fps. Through the short barrel they averaged 640 fps, with mild recoil and excellent accuracy.

At the other end of the spectrum, full power .44 Magnum loads with 240-gr. bullets averaged around 1,100 fps from the short barrel. Recoil was quite manageable, really not much different from a 4" or 6" barreled model 29. At 40 ounces the revolver isn't a lightweight, and the lower velocity results in less recoil as well. Muzzle blast was impressive though, so doubling up with both earplugs and muffs is a good idea.

PERSONAL DEFENSE?

For concealed carry/personal defense, a couple of .44 Special Buffalo Bore loads are a nice balance of power, recoil recovery and rate of fire. The 200-gr. Barnes lead-free bullets with big hollow-point averaged 970 fps. The 200-gr. full wadcutter hard cast lead bullet in their "Anti-Personnel" loads clocked at 930 fps.

Concealed carry is going to require big pockets and/or loose floppy clothes. Despite the overall compact length and nicely shaped grip frame, the large-diameter cylinder and 40+-ounce weight loaded make it a bit tough to conceal. In practical terms it would be a good choice for someone working or playing in wilderness country. Tucked away in a corner of a backpack along with three or four assorted boxes of cartridges, it would be a useful food-provider in an emergency. The light cowboy action loads would take rabbits or grouse with minimal meat damage, and full-power Magnum loads would take deer or caribou at any range you can reliably hit a vital zone.

Besides, who says we always have to be practical? If the big bore, snubbie revolver concept appeals to you, this is probably the best example ever made.

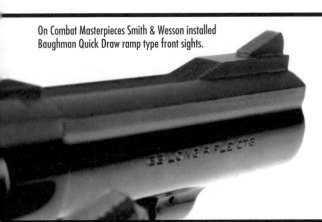

On Combat Masterpieces Smith & Wesson installed Baughman Quick Draw ramp type front sights.

S&W's MASTERPIECES

Collectively through the decades of their manufacture, S&W's Target and Combat Masterpieces were cataloged with 2", 4", 6" and 8⅜" barrel lengths.

From left these are: Combat Masterpiece Model 15, Combat Masterpiece Model 18, Target Masterpiece Model 17/K22 and Target Masterpiece Model 14/K38.

CLASSIC STYLE MEETS TOP-NOTCH ACCURACY

MIKE VENTURINO • PHOTOS: YVONNE VENTURINO

In July, 1966, shortly into my 17th year, I acquired the first handgun I actually paid for myself. It was a Smith & Wesson K-38 Masterpiece, named by the company because they felt, like their .22, .32 and .38 target revolvers, it deserved the superlative moniker.

I agree. By some manner I do not even remember, there was $65 in my pocket when I drove from my home town of Williamson, W.V., to a small village named Red Jacket where a gentleman named Robert Hendricks was

said to have a S&W K38 for sale. With my folks okay on things, Mr. Hendricks sold me the K38 for $50 plus another two dollars for a box of .38 Special 148-gr. wadcutters. Those 50 rounds were spent the same evening at the local gun club. I don't remember where the other $13 of my treasure went but likely it was for more .38 wadcutter factory loads, the price of which forced me into becoming a handloader and bullet caster a few months later.

By 1970 Mr. Hendricks and I became friends and together fired many hundreds

A special order option on Masterpieces was the .500" wide serrated trigger labeled "target trigger."

Standard trigger on most Masterpieces was a 0.265" wide serrated type. Note this Masterpiece has the screw in front of the triggerguard. It was discontinued in 1961.

of .38's on weekends, until I graduated from college and left permanently for Montana. I still remember his birthdate: March 1, 1900.

Smith & Wesson inaugurated the K-Masterpiece series just after World War II. First introduced was the K-22 in December 1946, with the K-32 and K-38 following by the summer of 1947. They were all of a type, with 6" barrels, patridge style front sights and fully adjustable rear sights. Grips were checkered walnut which the company termed Magna style. They were double actions, although some K38's were built with single action only mechanisms.

Model Numbers

In the late 1950's Smith & Wesson adopted model numbers for all their handguns and these three became the Model 17 (K-22), Model 16 (K-32) and Model 14 (K-38). By 1949, the year of my birth, Smith & Wesson had received significant requests from law enforcement agencies for variations

of the K-22 and K-38 with 4" barrels. The .22's would be for training and the .38's for police sidearms. These were given the name Combat Masterpiece. Besides barrel lengths the only significant differences between Masterpieces and Combat Masterpieces was the fact the latter had ramped front sights and a thinner rib on top of the barrel.

According to Roy Jinks' book *History of Smith & Wesson,* some small quantity of .32 Combat Masterpieces were made along with some with 3½" and 5" barrel lengths, but not as standard catalog items. What did become a standard catalog item in 1960 was a .38 Combat Masterpiece with 2" barrel. When Smith & Wesson model numbers were assigned, .22 Combat Masterpieces became Model 18's and .38's became the Model 15's.

This is where things begin to get confusing. In 1959 and 1960 the Model

14 (K-38) and Model 17 (K-22) respectively were also cataloged with 8⅜" barrels. So we have K-38's with 6" and 8⅜" barrel lengths named Model 14's. Then essentially the same revolver, except for rib and front sight, with 2" and 4" barrel lengths were Model 15's. On top of that there are K-Frame .22's with 6" and 8⅜" barrels named Model 17's but a 4" version — again identical except for rib and sight — is Model 18.

If you think that's confusing to read, consider me back as a young adult, an avid handgunner finally making a living for myself and trying to accumulate all these different models. Now factor in this following information. Due to slow sales Smith & Wesson discontinued the Model 16/K-32 in 1974 after a mere 3,630 had been made.

In 1982 and 1985 respectively they dropped the Model 14/K-38 and Model 18 .22. The Model 17/K22 lasted till 1989. Then to add to the mix in 1986 Smith & Wesson added 6"- and 8⅜"-barreled versions of the

On Target Masterpieces Smith & Wesson installed Patridge type front sights.

All Smith & Wesson Masterpieces were fitted with fully adjustable micrometer rear sights.

This screw at the top of sideplates on Smith & Wesson Masterpieces was discontinued in 1955.

Model 15. How did they differ from 6" and 8⅜" Model 14's? By the front sight I suppose — saying that because I must admit to never recognizing a target sighted K-Frame .38 with the two longer barrel lengths as a Model 15. To me they were always Model 14's.

Confused Yet?

So let's boil this down to essentials. Between 1946 and 1989, Smith & Wesson produced K-Frame, target-sighted revolvers chambered for .22 LR, .32 S&W Long and .38 S&W Special. Collectively they were offered with 2", 4", 6" and 8⅜" barrel lengths as standard, albeit some 3½" and 5" ones may show up.

Younger readers may be asking about the "reintroductions," i.e., those K-22's, K-32's and K-38's appearing circa 1990 with full underlug heavy barrels. It's simple. Those are not *my* K-22's, K-32's and K-38's. Mine were the ones around when I was growing up in the '60's. I never needed that much steel hanging on a handgun of such moderate power.

Did I ever accumulate all of the K-Masterpieces? That's a qualified yes. I never had them all together at *once*, nor have I owned all the barrel lengths simultaneously. But yes, I have owned Models 14, 15, 16, 17 and 18. Right

now in my vault are a Model 15 with 2" barrel, a Model 14 with 8⅜" barrel and a Model 18 with the only barrel length offered for it — 4".

After I moved to Montana my penchant for K-Masterpieces dissipated a bit. Riding around the mountains on horseback led me to appreciate magnums more, so .357, .41 and .44 Magnums were my carrying handguns. However, after a bit, I and a couple friends got into evening bullseye shooting matches. One had an S&W Model

Standard grips on Smith & Wesson Masterpieces were the Magna style at right but an extra cost option was target stocks as shown at left.

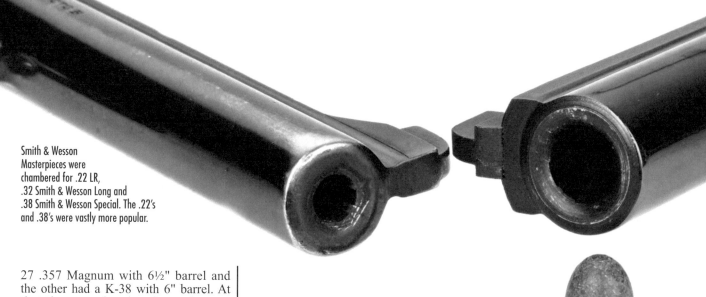

Smith & Wesson Masterpieces were chambered for .22 LR, .32 Smith & Wesson Long and .38 Smith & Wesson Special. The .22's and .38's were vastly more popular.

27 .357 Magnum with 6½" barrel and the other had a K-38 with 6" barrel. At that time my shooting focused on an S&W Model 19 with 6" barrel. None of us could dominate, so I figured to get an advantage and ordered a K-38 with 8⅜" barrel. That caused the other two guys to quit, ending our informal competitions. I don't even remember what I traded that hardly used K-38 for.

Still At It

A few years later I was happily married and minus any sort of K-Masterpiece. When my wife needed to go shopping in Bozeman she would drop me off at the Powder Horn — a very well stocked gun store on Main Street. One day in the early 1980's I was glancing in their used handgun case when I noticed a K-model with the common 6" barrel. Then I did a double take: that revolver's muzzle had too small a hole to be a .38 and too big to be a .22. Could it actually be one of those rare K-32's? It was and I got it for a ridiculously low price. Some years later an editor used his position as leverage on my good nature to talk me out of it. I hope he still enjoys it.

Along the way a friend gave me a fine Model 18 which served as my only K-Masterpiece for several years. Then three weeks ago at a gun show I spied a Model 15 with 2" barrel, which reminded me of a demonstration I saw an FBI firearms instructor do long ago. I'll tell you about it someday, but for right now I'll say that specific memory made me buy the Combat Masterpiece snubbie. In turn that fueled my nostalgia and just two days ago I picked up a like-new K-38 with 8⅜" barrel. I intend to gain the experience with it I neglected with the one back in the 1970's.

Are they really "Masterpieces?" Yes, if you can live with the power of a .22 or .38 and an ammunition capacity of six rounds, they are probably as accurate as any off-the-shelf revolvers ever made. I intend to prove that statement with test firing done in the near future.

Special order "target hammer spurs" were .500" wide and knurled. Standard hammer spur on Masterpieces was .375" wide and knurled.

A SLOWER SPIN

MIKE "DUKE" VENTURINO
PHOTOS: YVONNE VENTURINO

The S&W Model 624 in .44 Special is the type of classic keeping the revolver's mystique alive. Photo: Jeff John. Duke also doesn't care much for the modern trends in some revolvers such as full underlug barrels or brightly colored fiber optic sights (below). He can just barely accept space-age alloys.

REVOLVERS DON'T RULE THE ROOST ANYMORE. BUT THEIR DAY ISN'T DONE YET.

For 150 years the revolver was king of the handgun heap in America. It started in 1836 with Sam Colt's quickly defunct Paterson and, until the late 1980's, revolvers were still the primary duty gun of US law enforcement. The first documented instance I have found of revolvers being used in combat was in 1842. Five-shot .36 caliber Colt Patersons were used by a detachment of Texas Rangers in a battle with Comanche warriors. The tribesmen had—up to then—become used to Rangers using single-shot firearms only. This particular fracas didn't end well for the Comanches.

Revolvers are still being used in personal combat nowadays, mostly in the hands of private citizens protecting themselves or by off-duty cops (or on-duty cops using a backup snubbie). If there is any sizeable law enforcement agency still issuing revolvers as a standard duty gun, I'm not aware of it.

Personally speaking, my first revolver came in 1966—a Colt Frontier Scout .22, a birthday gift from my folks. Over the next 10 years I purchased about 50 revolvers—Colts, S&Ws, Rugers, Italian replicas of Colts, even a Charter Arms and a High Standard. Some were single action, some double action, some target models, some service models. Calibers ranged from .22 to .45. Barrel lengths ran from 2 to 8-3/8 inches. All the big three magnums—.357, .41 and .44—had been included. There were many years I never even *owned* a semi-auto.

Once Sam Colt achieved financial success with the behemoth Colt/Walker .44 of 1847, the stage was set for hundreds of different revolver models and types to appear during the next century and a half. Cap-and-ball (aka percussion) revolvers dominated until 1870. Collectors have given them names such as Dragoons, (three versions) Model 1849, Model 1851 Navy, Model 1860 Army, Model 1861 Navy, etc. Collectively, they were built in .31, .36 and .44 caliber.

These revolvers, along with Remington's excellent .36 and .44 percussion models of the 1850's and 1860's, ruled the handgun world until the advent of metallic cartridge revolvers.

Cartridge revolvers actually began in the 1850's when Smith & Wesson brought out their No. 1 chambered for .22 Short. By the Civil War a No. 2 .32 RF had come along. But the real era of metallic cartridge handguns began in 1870 with S&W's .44-caliber Model No. 3. In fact the 1870's could be considered one of the most important in regards to revolver history. In those 10 years Colt, S&W, Remington and a little-known outfit named Merwin & Hulbert manufactured hundreds of thousands of metallic cartridge revolvers.

SINGLE TO DOUBLE ACTION

Just about every gunny knows the Colt Peacemaker .45 came along in 1873. It has been the single-action revolver by which all others have been measured. Fewer people realized that S&W actually out-produced Colt with the many types of revolvers based on their top-break No. 3 large frame .44's and .45's. They were given monikers such as 1st, 2nd, and 3rd Model .44 Russians, Schofield, and New Model No. 3. The reason S&W revolvers weren't so well known in the Old West

Besides the Colt SAA, the company also developed other revolvers such as (left to right) the Colt 1860 Conversion .44, Model 1878 double action, Model 1877 double action.

Remington entered the metallic cartridge revolver market with their Model 1875 (top). It resembles the Colt SAA (bottom).

From the early days of revolvers, manufacturers have tried to come up with "pocket models, such as the Colt Baby Dragoon .31 (foreground) and the later Merwin & Hulbert double-action .38 behind it.

Duke's senior citizen brain can't accept 8-shot revolvers (right). It's stuck on six-shooters (left). Between 1907 and 1966, S&W made four basic models of N-Frame revolver chambered in .44 Specials called (below, from top) the Hand Ejector, 1st Model (Triple Lock), Hand Ejector, 2nd Model, Hand Ejector, 3rd Model, Hand Ejector, 4th Model. All these have 6-1/2-inch barrels. The top and bottom ones feature target sights.

is because a very large proportion of their top-break .44's were sold to the Russian Government.

Even fewer realize that .44-caliber revolvers outnumbered .45's by a large margin during that timeframe. No other company offered .45 Colt chambered sixguns, but S&W had .44 Henry Rimfire, .44 American and .44 Russian ones. Colt had .44 Colt and .44 WCFs (.44-40). Remington and Merwin & Hulbert also picked up the .44-40 and each offered their own proprietary .44 cartridge as well.

Another lesser-known fact is the double-action mechanism started during the cap-and-ball era and Colt picked it up during the 1870's with their small-frame Model 1877 and large-frame Model 1878. Those were actually rudimentary double actions in that they still loaded and unloaded one round at a time (via a loading gate) as with Colt SAA's. The Model 1877 fired .38 and .41 Colt cartridges, but the Model 1878 used the same big-bore rounds as the Colt SAA.

Revolvers with swing-out cylinders didn't appear until the late 1880's. The US Army to adopted a Colt .38 double action in 1892. Then in 1899 Colt brought out a big double action with swing-out cylinder. It became famous as the New Service

and was made until 1944. By the end of its production life it had been chambered for rounds as small as .357 Magnum and as large as .455 Eley.

During the same era Colt offered medium and small-frame revolvers—collectively carrying names like Police Positive, Official Police, Detective Special, Banker Special, Pocket Positive and then also tagged several of the above as "Target" when their sights were adjustable. Again speaking collectively, these smaller-frame models were chambered for rounds from .22 to .38.

S&W's first swing-out cylinder came out in 1896, and by 1899 S&W jumped on the swing-out bandwagon big time with their K-Frame Military & Police. It was the first .38 Special revolver. Prior to it S&W had some small- and medium-frame top breaks. The most famous round used in them was the .38 S&W, which is *not* interchangeable with the .38 Special.

By 1907 S&W entered the large-frame swing-out market with their New Century .44 Special, which came to be known as the "Triple Lock." Collectors came to call it the Hand Ejector, 1st Model. It was followed with 2nd, 3rd and 4th Models in a dizzying array of names and several chamberings, although .44 Special was the primary one until the .357 Magnum was invented. Some of the better-known names were Heavy Duty, Outdoorsman, 1950 Military, 1950 Army, Highway Patrolman, among others.

After the switch to model numbers (circa 1957), those built on K-Frames got numbers between 10 and 19 and N-Frames got numbers from 20 to 29. J-Frames got numbers in the 30's and 40's (with some semi-autos getting mixed in such as the 9mm Model 39).

MAGNUM ERA

The advent of magnum revolver cartridges started an entirely new era in 1935. S&W had their N-Frame named simply ".357 Magnum" and Colt quickly chambered their New Service and SAA for the new round. Late in 1955 the .44 Magnum appeared and then in 1964, so did the .41. This trio of magnums gained the most attention in gun magazines until the 1980's when the autoloader craze began. But it should be stressed that S&W was king of the magnum revolver market during that time with their Model 29 (.44 Magnum), Model 57 and 58 (.41 Magnum) and Model 19, 27 and 28 (.357 Magnum).

During the magnum timeframe Colt got "snaky." First was the Python .357, the Diamondback, then the Anaconda .44. Of course, the .357 Magnum was a caliber option throughout the SAA's several "generations." In fact, the first handgun I bought

Colt actually started the large-frame, swing-out double action in 1899 with the New Service. The one shown is the famous US Model 1917 chambered in .45 ACP.

after turning 21 was a Colt .357 Magnum SAA with a 4-3/4-inch barrel. It's still here even after being sold a couple times and bought back.

A discourse about revolvers can't be complete without talking about Rugers which began to appear in the mid-1950's. First were single-action Blackhawks and Super Blackhawks in .357 and .44 Magnum with .41 joining shortly after its introduction. The Super Blackhawk .44 Magnum with its square-back triggerguard, all-steel construction and 7-1/2-inch barrel may have been one of the most impressive and exquisite revolvers ever made. From the 1950's until 1973, Ruger single-action mechanisms were essentially of the Old Model style with safety and 1/2-cock notches on the hammers. For safety concerns they should only be carried with five rounds and the hammer down on the empty 6th chamber. In 1973 they were changed to New Models so they could safety be toted with a full six rounds thanks to a transfer-bar ignition system. Ruger eventually entered the double-action market—first with a Security-Six .357 and currently offer small- and medium-frame .357's, along with big-bore Redhawks in a wide variety of chamberings.

THE SITUATION TODAY

About 1980 two things occurred. Revolver manufacturers began to get a bit silly. S&W brought out an L-Frame but I still don't understand why since their K-Frame Model 19 and N-Frame Model 27 seemed fine to me. Furthermore, they began to put full underlugs beneath their barrels. Why put something on a handgun that serves no purpose except to make it heavier? I could always understand some revolvers not being "six-shooters." S&W's J-Frame .38's had to be five-shooters. But then there came along seven and eight shooters. I've never bothered to purchase any of these newer things except the J-Frame five-shooters.

As for Colt, they only make the SAA now as far as revolvers go and even then the company is hanging on by a slender thread. It may go the way of Winchester soon and that's sad.

Truth is in the 1980's, the supremacy of revolvers began to fade. Autoloaders seized the reins and dominate strongly today. Oh, sure, there are still some innovations such as space-age materials. I even own an S&W Model 360 with a Scandium frame. But I totally refuse to fire it in its stamp-designated caliber. Who wants to shoot a 12-ounce .357 Magnum anyway?

In my senior years I'm a dinosaur. I do own a number of semi-autos (nearly all are military collectibles). All are of steel construction. But there are many more revolvers hereabouts. I guess there always will be as long as I live.

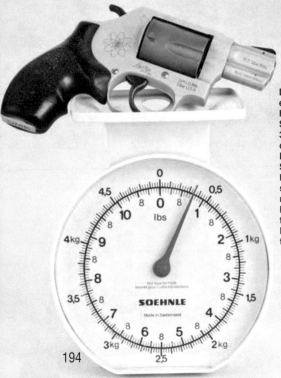

Duke's prejudices do exclude his 12-ounce S&W Model 360 which he carries often loaded with .38 Special. But he refuses to shoot .357 Magnums out of it, having learned the hard way how unpleasant they are.

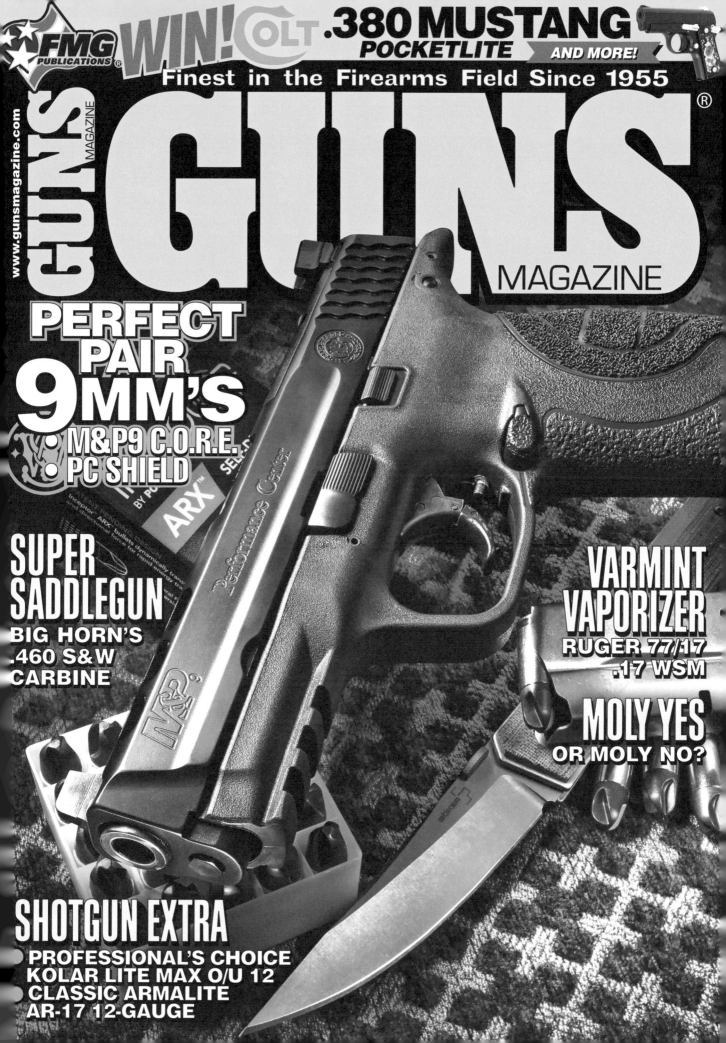

WIN! COLT .380 MUSTANG
POCKETLITE AND MORE!

Finest in the Firearms Field Since 1955

GUNS® MAGAZINE

www.gunsmagazine.com

PERFECT PAIR 9MM'S
- M&P9 C.O.R.E.
- PC SHIELD

ARX

SUPER SADDLEGUN
BIG HORN'S
.460 S&W
CARBINE

VARMINT VAPORIZER
RUGER 77/17
.17 WSM

MOLY YES
OR MOLY NO?

SHOTGUN EXTRA
- PROFESSIONAL'S CHOICE
KOLAR LITE MAX O/U 12
- CLASSIC ARMALITE
AR-17 12-GAUGE

9's on a 5

UnCommon CORE

S&W'S M&P9 PORTED

WILL DABBS, MD

The trigger on the M&P9 C.O.R.E. has an adjustable over-travel stop, allowing you to fine tune where the trigger stops. Photos: Joseph R. Novelozo

Horace Smith and Daniel Wesson joined forces in 1852 to produce the lever-action Volcanic rifle, itself designed around Walter Hunt's Rocket Ball cartridge. In 1856 Smith and Wesson allied themselves with Rollin White, the father of the bored-through cylinder, and started churning out handguns. Now after 1.5 centuries S&W's penchant for designing superb pistols has reached critical mass with the M&P9 Ported C.O.R.E. (Competition Optics Ready Equipment), arguably the world's best tool for launching 9mm rounds downrange. This pistol redefines the state of the art.

196

ROLL

S&W'S PORTED POWER PAIR

NEW CARRY KING

PERFORMANCE CENTER SHIELD

JOHN CONNOR

On December 1, 2015, shortly after I received test samples of their new Performance Center ported SHIELD pistols, Smith & Wesson issued a surprising press release: They had just shipped their 1 millionth SHIELD. Think about that for a moment. *One million SHIELDs.* Not "planned," "ordered," or "in the pipeline," but *shipped*. I know Smith & Wesson serves a global market, but let's put that in context with the United States. Our current population is about 320 million people. That would be one SHIELD for every 320 Americans. And this little pistol has only been on the market since mid-2012. Surprised now?

The SHIELD trigger is more conventional, but has been improved and is smoother in this current version. Both triggers pivot prior to start the pull to release the trigger block feature. Photos: Joseph R. Novelozo

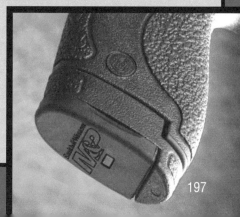

197

9's on a F

S&W'S M&P9 AND
PERFORMANCE CENTER SHIELD

ROLL

PHOTO: JOSEPH R. NOVELOZO

rnceptor
POLYCASE
SELF-DEFENSE

mance Center

MITH & WESSON
NGFIELD, MA U.S.A.

GUNS
MAGAZINE

199

The SHIELD (left) is shorter and more compact than its big brother M&P9 and does not have a rail underneath. Both share many other features such as porting, and the ported barrel is installed on the M&P9 here. Photo: Joseph R. Novelozo

The full-size M&P9 (above, left) has a much higher front sight for use with the included suppressor-ready threaded, unported barrel. The SHIELD (above, right) comes with Hi-Viz sights from the factory. The front sight has a green fiber-optic insert. The rear sight of the M&P9 is also much higher to match the front, and is of the 3-dot variety. The SHIELD has contrasting red Hi-Viz rear sight. The sights are very clear in almost any level of light. Photos: Joseph R. Novelozo

The heart of the C.O.R.E. is the S&W M&P (Military & Police) sporting a robust polymer frame, blackened stainless slide, striker-fired action, (which proved to be monotonously reliable), and a bewildering array of automatic onboard safety systems. The M&P also delivers a 1911-style grip-to-frame angle nicely suited to corn-fed American gunmen who cut their teeth on Mr. Browning's centenarian 1911.

Using the standard M&P as a foundation, the Ported C.O.R.E. incorporates a pair of dorsal slots in the barrel corresponding with vents in the slide to counteract muzzle flip. The slide is cut to accept six different miniaturized electronic sighting options. An array of mounting plates to accommodate all this variegated glass comes with the gun. As miniaturized electronics can now facilitate glowing optical sights small enough to mount on a handgun's slide without adversely affecting function or markedly increasing bulk, the C.O.R.E. embraces the concept.

The fixed steel sights are elevated to allow them to remain visible within the optical field of an electronic sight or facilitate serious use with a sound suppressor in place. The tricked-out piece I bought also includes a threaded barrel that readily interchanges with the ported version. An adjustable over-travel stop allows the shooter to fine tune the trigger's personality. The trigger incorporates a pivoting safety component in its tip that leaves the weapon inert until you are ready to fire.

The GEMTECH GM9 G-core suppressor is a monocore design wherein the heart of the can is cut from a solid bar of 7075 aluminum. The GM9 includes an onboard L.I.D. (Linear Inertial Decoupler) to ensure reliable service with the can in place. The simple threaded tube is the mystical part necessitating all the waiting, fingerprinting and transfer taxes. The GM9 is compact enough so as not to hinder tactical movement yet calms the racket down sufficiently to allow effective communication if employed indoors.

Heavy 147-grain rounds are naturally subsonic and make for friendlier suppressor food. Most everybody produces them but Winchester's Train & Defend line makes for a great combo. Train versions are relatively inexpensive FMJ ball rounds ballistically identical to the Defend hollowpoint versions.

Pack the Defend sort for social use and burn the Train versions on the range.

The M&P9 Ported C.O.R.E. is the thoroughbred of modern polymer 9mm pistols. With the ported tube in place muzzle flip is noticeably tamer and follow-on shots much faster than is the case with a comparable unvented gun. I've got long fingers so the large palm swell grip puts the end of my index finger at just the right spot on the trigger for ballistic synergy. My

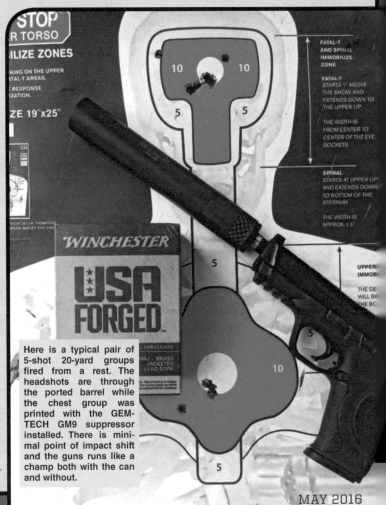

Here is a typical pair of 5-shot 20-yard groups fired from a rest. The headshots are through the ported barrel while the chest group was printed with the GEM-TECH GM9 suppressor installed. There is minimal point of impact shift and the guns runs like a champ both with the can and without.

M&P9 C.O.R.E. AND SHIELD

MAKER: Smith & Wesson, 2100 Roosevelt Avenue
Springfield, MA 01104, (800) 331-0852, www.gunsmagazine.com/index

Gun:	M&P9 Ported C.O.R.E.	M&P9 SHIELD Ported
ACTION TYPE:	Striker-fired semi-auto	Striker-fired semi-auto
CALIBER:	9mm	9mm
CAPACITY:	17+1	8+1, 7+1
BARREL LENGTH:	4.25 inches	3.1 inches
OVERALL LENGTH:	7.5 inches	6.1 inches
WEIGHT:	23.5 ounces	19 ounces
FINISH (SLIDE):	Black	Black
SIGHTS:	Fixed 3-dot	Fixed Hi-Viz fiber optic
GRIPS:	Polymer, 3 interchangeable palm swells	Polymer
PRICE:	$895,	$519

continued from page 41

The sheer numbers may be surprising but the SHIELD's popularity is not. I received one from the first wave of production and reviewed it in the March 2013 issue. In that evaluation I called it "The Goldilocks Gun," because it's not too small, not too large, but *just right*. In my XXL hands, if it were any smaller or lighter, it would likely be difficult to point and control, and recoil might be decidedly unpleasant. If any larger and heavier, it wouldn't carry so comfortably or conceal so easily.

Since then I've also found the dimensions and ergonomics provide an excellent fit for an unusually wide range of hand sizes and finger lengths. It really is an exceptionally "people-pleasing" pistol in all its size-and-shape aspects, as well as in reliability, accuracy and ease of maintenance. That doesn't happen by accident, or result from a clutch of nervous executives bleating *"We need a new subcompact pistol design! Make one! Get it to market, yesterday!"* No, it's the result of thoughtful design and execution.

A few more observations: Especially considering their numbers and relative newness, in the online forums there is a notable absence of user complaints or even casual criticism. Also, I just searched two big national gun broker sites for *used* SHIELD pistols for sale. One site had 13 listed, the other had none. What does all this tell me? Overwhelmingly, SHIELD owners are quietly, perhaps a little smugly, satisfied—and they're holding on to them. I'm one of those people.

So much has been written about the SHIELD and its mechanically similar siblings in the M&P pistol family—including, by me—I won't go into all the mech-and-tech specs. Let's talk about what's new and different.

Easily seen, the two most visible changes are the Hi-Viz fiber-optic "LitePipe" sights and the two rows of oblong slots in the slide. In any condition brighter than pitch darkness, those fiber optic sights are a fine improvement. As soon as I had paid Smith & Wesson for my original test SHIELD, I installed a set of Hi-Viz green LitePipe sights on it. Smith & Wesson opted for red pipes in the rear sight and bright green in the front—an excellent choice for both speed and precision.

The oblong slide slots number three per side, set at 2 and 10 o'clock. The forward pair of slots are functioning gas exhaust ports. Peep down through them and you'll see they align with a pair of smaller oblong slots in the barrel, also positioned at 2 and 10 o'clock about a 1/2-inch behind the muzzle. Their seemingly diminutive size and placement reflect the evolution of gas port technology.

Not so long ago gas ports were either big holes drilled in the tops of slides and barrels, or lateral trenches looking like they were cut with a fat hacksaw. Both spewed huge gouts of hot gasses and vision-killing flames in low light. Time, study and science showed smaller ports at V-angles were far more efficient at damping muzzle flip, and much kinder to the shooter's night vision.

Winchester *Defend* and Hornady *Critical Duty* ammo both performed superbly. Shown are rapid fire 9-shot groups from seven yards.

With the ported barrel installed the S&W C.O.R.E. handily tames muzzle flip. Lightweight and imminently controllable with a simply splendid striker-fired trigger, the C.O.R.E. is a fun gun to run.

stubby-mitted comrades are readily accommodated with the two included smaller grip options. The tight adjustable striker-fired trigger makes for snappy double taps. The enhanced palm swell inserts sport the perfect combination of aggressive stippling and comfortable rubber for firm purchase without undue abrasion.

Swap out the ported barrel for the threaded tube and screw on the can and I defy you not to hum the James Bond theme absentmindedly while you are busy ringing steel. I'm old and ugly, and running the tricked out C.O.R.E. made me feel young, suave, and dangerous again.

The resulting package is lightweight, fun to run, and cool looking to boot. We burned through scads of bullets both with the suppressor and without and the S&W M&P9 C.O.R.E. never hiccupped. As a suppressor host, the C.O.R.E. makes for arguably the perfect covert package. The extra weight is comfortable without becoming burdensome.

With the ported barrel in place the gun runs fast and shoots straight. The slots cut in the top of the frame accommodate the effective barrel porting system when installed and make the gun look like something out of the latest *Star Wars* movie. Magazines hold 17 rounds and drop away cleanly for delightfully smooth magazine changes.

LET US COUNT THE WAYS

How many ways could there be to throw 9mm bullets downrange? Herr Luger's eponymous pistol didn't fare too badly back in 1902 when Deutsche Waffen und Munitionsfabriken (DWM) started producing the zippy little rounds in the first place. However, in the intervening century the field of options has grown mighty broad.

John Moses Browning's P35 Hi-Power made a splash. The single action trigger is Old World awesome and the 13-round magazine offered a truly heady capacity for its day. The P35 was cut from big blocks of ordnance steel yet still managed to pull off a lithe, almost sensual vibe. The Walther P38 marked the transition between martial object d'art and industrial engine of war, offering such revolutionary features as a double action/single action trigger, a hammer-drop safety, and a loaded chamber indicator. Then a certain eccentric Austrian had the idea to build a gun out of plastic and the word GLOCK became as deeply entrenched within the English lexicon as is Microsoft or Coke.

Nowadays everybody makes guns out of polymer and the challenge is not being the first anymore. The quest is to be the best. The S&W M&P C.O.R.E. is certainly in the running to win, place or show.

GRAND SCHEME

There are indeed literally countless ways to throw 9mm rounds downrange these days. Old steel guns can be alluring and their most modern mass-produced plastic counterparts can be cheap. However, if you are looking for a versatile and effective family of guns offering models that will be all things to all shooters while still fitting into a single compact box then look no further than the S&W M&P9 C.O.R.E.

Stripped down and sporting iron sights, the C.O.R.E. runs smoother and better than your stock service pistol. A proper IWB (Inside the Waistband) holster will pack the gun effectively and covertly beneath an untucked shirt. With a nice bit of electrified glass installed the platform competes with the newest customized race guns. Hang a can on the muzzle and you are set to infiltrate behind enemy lines to rescue a lonely Swedish supermodel. If you found you wanted to distill your handgun collection down to a single versatile utility pistol, this would be it.

Smith & Wesson is a household name in the American shooting world for a reason. The build undeniably great guns and the new C.O.R.E. is the very pinnacle of their tactical offerings. Several companies now offer versions of their flagship handguns configured to take optical sights and a can. The S&W C.O.R.E. is lighter than most and utterly effective while remaining the least expensive of the lot. With two barrels and a can the gun really does offer everything the discriminating gunman might need, all in a single racy package.

GEMTECH, P.O. Box 140618, Boise, ID 83714, (208) 939-7222

Cousin MacKenzie gladly assisted with test shooting. Look close and you'll see those bright HI-VIZ fiber optic sights.

continued from page 45

Looking closely it seems the textured areas of the frame are a little more pronounced, still enhancing your grip without being so aggressive as to abrade skin or fabric. But for me, the best improvements are *inside* the ported SHIELD. The data short-sheet I first received said simply "enhanced trigger." *That* was an understatement. Both the standard trigger sear and striker plunger are replaced with Performance Center parts, plus, I suspect, complemented by some gentle kiss-and-tickle work by Smith's best gunsmiths to produce a significantly improved trigger pull and a faster, more certain re-set.

Examining my standard SHIELD and the Performance Center ported model fieldstripped side by side, the only difference I could see was in their striker plungers. The visible end of mine is rather sharp and squared, where the Performance Center part is radiused around the circumference and nicely polished. But oh, what a difference in the hand! Trigger pull weight is about 7 pounds, length of pull and re-set are consistent between the two, but the ported SHIELD's pull is significantly smoother, the break cleaner and the re-set far more crisp, tactile and even audible.

The Performance Center's goals were to reduce felt recoil while delivering improved muzzle control, speed and accuracy—and they did it. For me, the proof was on the targets and the timer.

Shooting 2-handed and rested, 5-round groups at 10 yards were roughly consistent between my standard SHIELD and the new ported model. Where they differed, the ported SHIELD's groups were only tenths of an inch smaller on average; probably the product of a cleaner trigger break. The *real* improvements appear when you simulate defensive shooting, emptying their 7+1 and 8+1 magazines rapidly cadenced about one shot per second and the ported SHIELD *really* shone when doing so 1-handed. With the ported SHIELD I also shaved a full second or more on elapsed times.

For example, 2-handed at 7 yards firing 9 shots in just under 10 seconds, one group measured 1.625 inches high by 1.875 inches wide using Hornady Critical Duty 135-grain

9MM M&P C.O.R.E. FACTORY AMMO PERFORMANCE

LOAD (BRAND, BULLET WEIGHT, TYPE)	VELOCITY* (FPS)	VELOCITY** (FPS)	GROUP SIZE* (INCHES)	GROUP SIZE** (INCHES)
Hornady Critical Defense 115 JHP	1,193	1,127	3	5.25
Sellier & Bellot 124 FMJ	1,179	1,068	3.25	3.5
Federal Hydra-Shok 147 JHP	1,050	788	3.75	2.5
Winchester White Box 115 FMJ	1,200	1,111	2.75	5.5
Winchester USA 115 FMJ	1,207	1,131	2	3.25
Winchester Train 147 FMJ	1,031	731	2.5	4.25

NOTES: *Suppressed velocity and group size. **Ported barrel velocity and group size. Chrony F-1 Chronograph set 3 feet from muzzle. Accuracy is the product of 5 shots at 20 yards. Interestingly, velocity really fell off with the ported barrel and heavy bullets while lighter rounds remained fast.

9MM SHIELD FACTORY AMMO PERFORMANCE

LOAD (BRAND, BULLET WEIGHT, TYPE)	VELOCITY (FPS)	GROUP SIZE (INCHES)
Hornady 135 Critical Duty JHP	938	1.25
Winchester 147 Defend	896	1.5

NOTES: Competition Electronics ProChrono Digital, set 10 feet from muzzle. Accuracy the product of 5 shots at 10 yards.

FlexLock. A similar drill using 147-grain Winchester Defend JHP's left 7 out of 9 rounds touching, measuring 1.625 inches high by 0.75 inch wide. Two fliers opened that group up to 2.125 inches high by 2.375 inches wide. Overall, 1-handed rapid-fire groups with the ported SHIELD were about 25 to 30 percent smaller than groups shot with my standard SHIELD—and a shade faster. Is that pudding proof enough?

Reliability can be summed up thusly: I had one failure to feed fully into battery from the first magazine load—period. In all-angles all-holds testing I fired 200 rounds of 147-grain Winchester Train (a perfect match for their Defend loads). Those and the Hornady Critical Duty ammo shot straight and functioned flawlessly.

It wasn't long after the first ported full-size M&P pistols appeared that users began demanding ported SHIELDs too. Smith & Wesson has delivered them and more. There are now 16 variants of the SHIELD to choose from, and this Performance Center Ported SHIELD certainly earns a top slot in that lineup. All that's left is for you to try one! Connor *OUT*

ICONS ALL

DUKE PICKS THE MOST RESPECTED GUNS OF THE 20TH CENTURY.

MIKE "DUKE" VENTURINO
PHOTOS: YVONNE VENTURINO

What were the most respected American guns of the 20th century? Guns introduced after 1900 and gained fame because the American populace bought them, used them and *still* uses them.

Let's start back near the beginning of the 20th century, specifically the year 1908. My vote for one of the most respected revolvers is Smith & Wesson's Hand Ejector 1st Model, often nicknamed the "Triplelock." It's not only that Triplelocks deserve respect due to their superb quality and the fact they were the introductory vehicle for the great .44 Special, but descended from them are all the subsequent S&W N-Frames. Collectively, N-Frames ranged in calibers from .38 Special to .455 Webley.

Without N-Frames, there may have not been a magnum era. S&W introduced the world to magnum handgun cartridges in 1935 with the N-Frame .357 Magnum and followed with the .44 Magnum in 1956 and .41 Magnum in 1964. I believe I have owned a sample of every basic version of N-Frame revolvers in calibers .38 Special, .357 Magnum, .41 Magnum, .44 Special, .44 Magnum, .45 Auto/.45 Auto Rim and .455 Webley.

When S&W began numbering models, the 10 N-Frames were 20 to 29 included (left row top down) the M20 .38 Special, M21 .44 Special, M22 .45 Auto/.45 Auto-Rim, M23 .38 Special, (middle row top down) M24 .44 Special, M25 .45 Auto/Auto-Rim, M26 .45 Auto/Auto-Rim, (right row top down) M27 .357 Magnum, M28 .357 Magnum, M29 .44 Magnum.

Duke's pick for most respected sporting rifle is the Model 70 Winchester. His standard one at top is a Featherweight .30-06. At bottom is his .308 Featherweight with aftermarket stock.

BROWNING'S 1911

A mere three years after the Triplelock came an autoloading pistol that remains to this day the most respected one of all time. It was the Model 1911, designed at the behest of Colt by John M. Browning. It was adopted by the US Army in the year of its introduction and remained the service sidearm until replaced by the 9mm Beretta M9 in 1985.

The respect the basic 1911 design has earned is evident by the countries who adopted it. Besides the United States I instantly think of Argentina and Norway, both of whom manufactured the 1911 for their militaries. The design has also been made in Spain and China and even now, in the Philippines for the civilian market. However, the greatest factor in judging the respect in which it is held is by how many American gunmakers copy it. Colt introduced it and still makes the 1911, as do large and small handgun manufacturers. Big name outfits like Ruger and S&W have 1911's, and newer companies such as Kimber, Springfield Armory, Les Baer, Wilson Combat, STI, Dan Wesson, SIG SAUER and too many others to list.

Also in the running for most respected sporting rifle is the Remington M700. This .222 Remington Magnum specimen of Duke's is his coyote rifle. Its accuracy (inset) is why Duke has hung on to it.

Duke's pick for most respected pistol of the 20th century is the Colt Model 1911 .45 Auto.

Duke has great respect for Ruger Blackhawks as fine utility handguns, with special regard for those chambered in .30 Carbine.

The original 1911 caliber was, of course, .45 ACP, but since then it has been chambered in .22 LR, .38 Super, 9mm Luger, 10mm and others I'm forgetting. I have 1911's in practically all those calibers at this writing.

GARAND'S M1

Now let's turn our attention to long guns. Without a shred of doubt I think the most respected military rifle ever produced in American factories is the M1, often nicknamed the Garand after its designer John C. Garand. Its length of service was not the longest for American battle rifles. The basic AR has been issued for a much longer period. However, in terms of sheer number of rounds fired in combat, I'd have to vote for the M1. It was the United States Army's official rifle starting in 1936 and the standard Marine Corps rifle starting in 1941. It served through the world's greatest conflagration—World War II—and was still standard for both services during the three years of the Korean War.

Being semi-auto, fed by 8-round "en-bloc loaders" commonly called clips, and equipped with perhaps the best battle sights ever put on a service rifle. The Garand is so widely respected—a full seven decades after World War II—that competitions centered on M1s are still being fired nationwide. And, of course, its .30-06 caliber has garnered the full respect of American hunters for over 100 years.

"By now I'm sure someone is asking, 'What about shotguns?' I know as much about shotguns as I do about snowshoes. That's saying I've tried them, but didn't like it much."

Although considered heavy by many of today's hunters, Duke's friend Kirk Stovall (above) shot this cow elk with his M1. Garands are still so popular (below), there are competitions for them all over the country.

Just a year after the Garand's official adoption by the US Army, Winchester introduced what is—in my humble opinion—the most respected sporting rifle ever. The Model 70 is still in production and always an excellent choice for the American hunter.

The Model 70 has been produced in dozens of calibers from .223 Remington to .458 Winchester Magnum. I have owned them chambered for .220 Swift, .257 Roberts, .270 Winchester, .308 Winchester .30-06 and .300 H&H Magnum. The .300 H&H was sold to raise funds for my wedding and all the others—except the .308—went for one reason or another. My .308 was expertly fitted prior to my ownership with a Mannlicher-style stock. I've hunted with it in Montana, California, Texas and Africa.

Personally, I feel the best version of the Model 70 was the Featherweight. Standard versions—as introduced in 1937—are relatively heavy rifles, weighing up to 10 pounds, scoped. The Featherweight weighs about 2 pounds less. Winchester dropped the Featherweight during the great 1964 shakeup but reintroduced it in a fancier stocked edition in about 1980. Nowadays Model 70's are being made in South Carolina in too many styles to list here.

REMINGTON'S MODEL 700

Right on the heels of the Model 70 in regards to public respect has to be the Remington Model 700. It has also made in a huge variety of calibers from .17 Remington to .458 Winchester Magnum, plus a large variety of styles. I've owned them in .222 Remington, .222 Remington Magnum, .223 Remington, .243 Winchester, .270 Winchester, .280 Remington .308 Winchester, .30-06 and .300 Winchester Magnum. The only one still with me is the .222 Remington Magnum; kept not because of its beauty, but for its very respectable ability to place bullets close to one another. Although it has a standard-weight barrel, it is a sub-MOA grouper with a variety of loads. I keep it ready for coyotes prowling too close to our home.

RUGER'S BLACKHAWK

Sturm, Ruger & Company is one of the most respected firearms manufacturers today, so picking their "most respected gun" is tough. But I'm going with the single-action Blackhawk simply because the options are near amazing and I've owned a mess of them. The standard blued steel Blackhawk (aluminum alloy grip frame) comes in .357 Magnum, .41 Magnum, .45 Colt and .30 Carbine. There is a stainless version (all steel) .357 Magnum. And then there are "convertibles." Those are .357 Magnum Blackhawks with an auxiliary 9mm cylinder and .45 Colt ones with auxiliary .45 ACP cylinder. My personal favorite? Their .30 Carbine version, I admit, is *loud,* but it is also one of the most accurate revolvers I've ever machine-rest tested. And that's a quality always worthy of respect.

By now I'm sure someone is asking, "What about shotguns?" I know as much about shotguns as I do about I do about snowshoes. That's saying I've tried them, but didn't like it much. So I'm judging "shotgun respect" as a bystander. And I come up with the Remington Model 870 pump-action 12 gauge. I've heard people far more knowledgeable than me on shotguns recommend them for everything from home defense to duck hunting.

Argue with me on this if you wish. I won't argue back. 🔫

THE MOST "SPECIAL"

SMITH & WESSON'S MARVELOUS MIDDLEWEIGHT IS THE UNDISPUTED CHAMP OF DA REVOLVERS.

MIKE "DUKE" VENTURINO
PHOTOS: YVONNE VENTURINO

To me, the greatest single development in double-action revolvers for the 20th century is Smith & Wesson's introduction of the K-Frame in 1899. Its introductory caliber was .38 Special, although K-Frames have also been chambered for .22 LR, .32 S&W Long, .32-20, .38 S&W and .357 Magnum.

Right now some big bore fanatics are bellering, "Hold up, Duke. The N-Frames are holy. The Smith & Wesson .44 Special is without sin and N-Frame magnums have been movie stars."

OK. That's probably true. No movies were ever made about K-Frames I know of. But consider this: Roy Jinks, S&W historian and author of *History of Smith & Wesson* (13th Printing from 2003), claimed more revolvers built on the K-Frame had been made up to 2003 than all other S&W handguns *combined*.

S&W used names for their revolvers until 1957. Some K-Frame examples? How about Victory Model, Masterpiece, Combat Masterpiece, Combat Magnum and Military & Police (M&P). After 1957, K-Frames received model numbers such as Model 10 (M&P), Models 14, 16 and 17 (Masterpieces in .38, .32 and .22 sizes respectively) Model 15 Combat Masterpiece and Model 19 Combat Magnum. And there were others.

S&W K-Frames were made in an amazing variety of barrel lengths: 2, 2-1/2, 3, 4, 5, 6, 6-1/2 and 8-3/8 inches. Perhaps I've missed one, but most are there. The K-Frame's intended purposes have been small game hunting (.22), combat (.32, .38 and .357) and bull's-eye target competition (.22, .32, and .38).

A FRAME FOR MEMORIES

The very first handgun I bought for myself was a K-38 Masterpiece (aka Model 14). I purchased it from a Mr. Robert Hendricks of Red Jacket, W. Va., for the sum of $50. Mr. Hendricks and I later became shooting buddies.

Another shooting buddy at the time was Mike Bucci (nicknamed "Butch"). We were seniors in high school together. His father was chief of police of our small town in the West Virginia coalfields. Mr. Bucci gave his son a K-Frame M&P .38 with a 6-1/2-inch barrel so we didn't have to share my K-38.

The K-Frame (center) preceded the J-Frame (left) and the N-Frame (right).

As young fellows more interested in shooting than sitting in classrooms, Butch and I figured out a scam. The easiest class for seniors was journalism. It was the last period of the day and the class's job was to put out the school newspaper. With neither of us having much interest in writing, Butch was assigned as ad salesman, and I was advertising manager. Butch would tell the teacher, Mrs. Jessie, that he was having trouble selling ads about town and could I help him? (Actually, he'd already filled his quota.) She would give me a pass and Butch and I would hightail it to the gun club 3 miles out of town. We already had our revolvers in the trunks of our cars. Then we'd spend some very pleasant afternoons shooting our K-Frames.

Because we had an "in" with the police department, we'd often pester them to show us what they carried. Almost all were S&W Model 10 M&P .38 Specials, which varied in condition from pristine to rusted shut. One officer had a Model 15 (which we had never seen before). It was—in essence—the same thing as my K-38 except it had a 4-inch barrel. (Later I found out they also made the Model 15 with a 2-inch barrel.)

Another time I was exposed to law enforcement people was in 1974. Then I was working in Yellowstone National Park and was acquainted with a Ranger named Jack Ford. It wasn't until a passel of Secret Service agents arrived to guard Jack that I realized he was the new President's son! The agents on this assignment were mostly younger guys, so naturally I engaged them in gun talk. Along with Uzi submachine guns, they had Remington Model 700's in .308 and some sort of shotgun, I don't remember. Their handguns were S&W Model 19 .357 Combat Magnums with 2-1/2-inch barrels. One of the agents invited me to come along on their next range day, but the head agent nixed it.

FIRST PICKS

Back in West Virginia—being in college and low on funds—Mr. Hendricks made me a deal. He would buy brand-new S&W revolvers, and I could do a set amount of work for them. When I'd worked my way to the purchase prices, I got the guns. They included a 4- and 6-inch Model 19, a 4-inch Model 18 in .22 LR and a Model 12 Airweight .38 Special (a 2-inch snubbie with an aluminum alloy frame.)

By then I was making my summer forays to Montana between college semesters and those K-Frames went with me. My absolute favorite became the 6-inch Model 19. I won a lot of turkeys in cow-pasture competitions with it.

I've always been known for having a good memory, but I simply can't recall where any of those K-Frames went. Regardless, by the late 1970's, they'd all been sold or traded—even my favorite Model 19. Except for a late 1940's vintage Military & Police .38 I picked up for $65 in 1978, I was "K-Frameless" for about 25 years.

During that span I was dimly aware Smith & Wesson revolvers were undergoing many changes. There were many types of stainless K-Frames introduced. Then came an L-Frame to fill the gap between the K and N sizes. Also full-length lugs

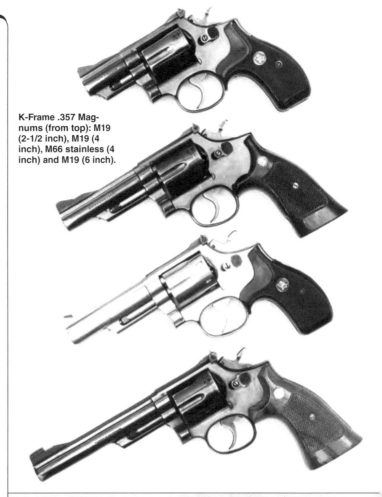

K-Frame .357 Magnums (from top): M19 (2-1/2 inch), M19 (4 inch), M66 stainless (4 inch) and M19 (6 inch).

K-Frames with target sights (from the bottom up) include the M15 .38 Combat Masterpiece (2 inch), M18 .22 LR Combat Masterpiece (4 inch), M17 K-22 (6 inch) and M14 K-38 (8-3/8 inch).

A S&W M12 with aluminum alloy frame (left) and a S&W M15 with square butt represent the virtually defunct K-Frame snubbie contingent.

209

beneath barrels began to appear. This seemed a waste of steel and merely made K-Frames heavier for no reason I could discern.

Then after so many years of non-interest on my part, S&W K-Frames and I were reunited. During the early part of this century, I began building my World War II collection. To add to it, I bought an S&W Victory Model with a 5-inch barrel. It was different from standard M&P .38's in that it had military Parkerizing and was chambered for .38 S&W (aka .38/200 in British nomenclature). It was one of those Lend-Lease guns sent to Britain during WWII.

America also bought a considerable quantity of Victory Models during the war, but of course chambered for our own .38 Special. Interestingly, most of the wartime K-Frames went to our Navy or Marine Corps aviators and were worn in shoulder holsters. Barrel lengths included 4 and 5 inches. In my cardiac rehab exercise class there is an elderly gent who flew as a rear gunner in a TBF Avenger off the aircraft carrier *San Jacinto.* He said he carried one of those Smith & Wesson's until his crew had to ditch in the ocean beside their carrier, and

This M19 .357 was special ordered with target stocks, target hammer and target trigger.

it was lost as he exited the plane. I imagine it joined a passel of other Victory Models at the bottom of the Pacific.

A little known fact is the US Air Force issued K-Frame .38 Combat Masterpieces to guards, MPs and various personnel, and it was mainly at their behest that S&W developed the Airweight versions. In fact, the earliest Air Force K-Frame Airweights also had aluminum cylinders, but this was a

failed experiment because they cracked.

Perhaps in an effort to relive my youth, I've been buying some K-Frames. However, I'm looking mostly for types I've never owned before. In the past few years, I've acquired a Model 17-5 .22 LR, a 2-inch Model 15, .38 and a couple of 8-3/8-inch Model 14's—and even an 8-3/8-inch Model 48 .22 Mag. Some I've kept and some I've passed on after a bit of shooting. Most recently, I added an M&P 2-inch .38 Special. It's worn cosmetically but mechanically perfect. Since it was made in the year of my birth, I think it's a keeper and a good mate to the 5-inch one I bought in 1978.

To close, I will relate one reason I've respected K-Frames so much. Once I mounted that 5-inch M&P in my Ransom Rest and from each chamber I fired 10 rounds of Remington 148-grain wadcutters. Then I fired 10 rounds using all six chambers randomly. The average group size of those 70 rounds was a mere 1.1 inches. That wasn't a fluke. I've never had a K-Frame that was a poor shooter.

I guess that's why I've always liked them so much.

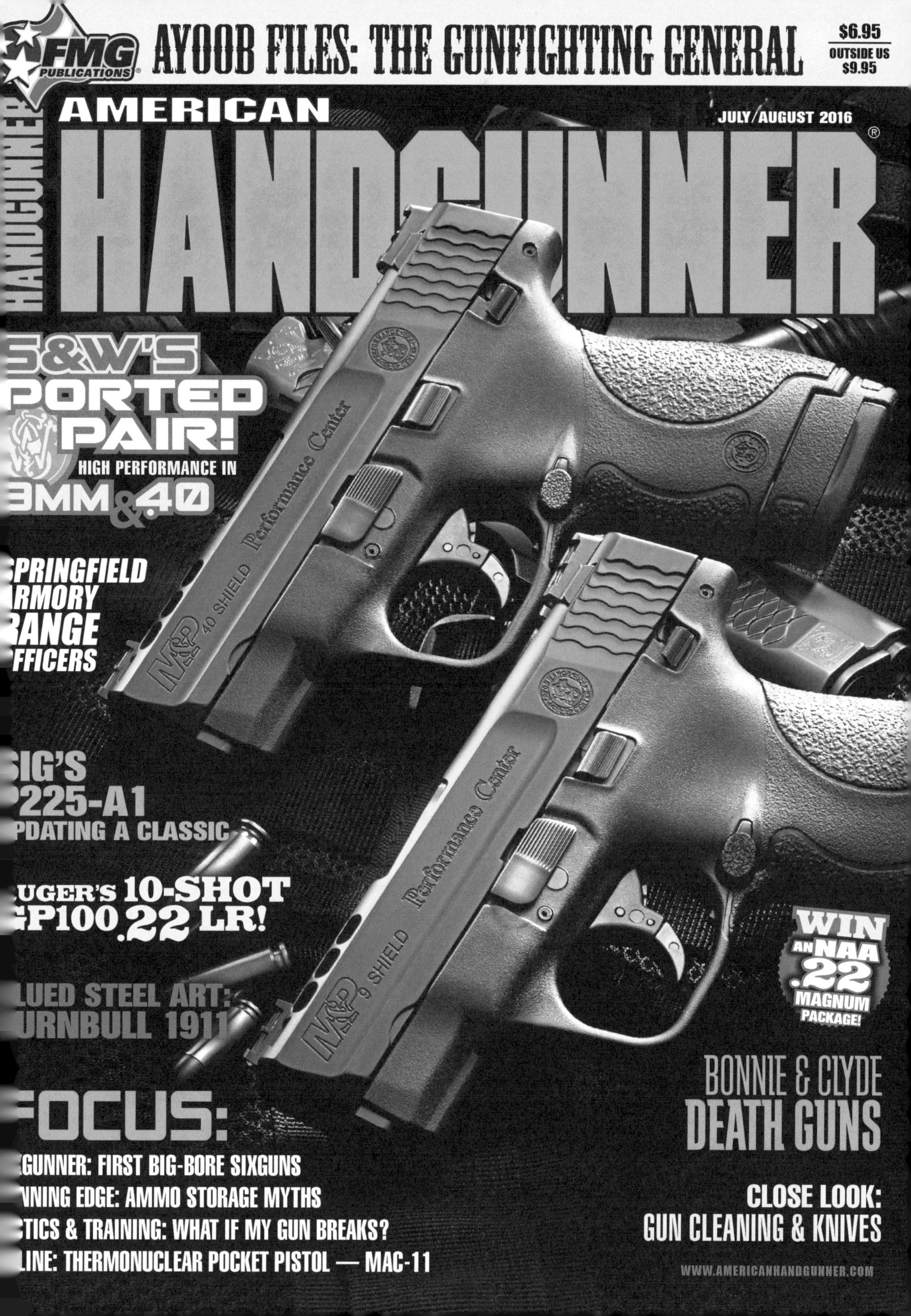

AYOOB FILES: THE GUNFIGHTING GENERAL

$6.95
OUTSIDE US
$9.95

AMERICAN
HANDGUNNER

JULY/AUGUST 2016

S&W'S PORTED PAIR!
HIGH PERFORMANCE IN
3MM & .40

SPRINGFIELD ARMORY RANGE OFFICERS

SIG'S P225-A1
UPDATING A CLASSIC

RUGER'S 10-SHOT GP100 .22 LR!

BLUED STEEL ART: TURNBULL 1911

WIN AN NAA .22 MAGNUM PACKAGE!

BONNIE & CLYDE DEATH GUNS

FOCUS:

SIXGUNNER: FIRST BIG-BORE SIXGUNS
WINNING EDGE: AMMO STORAGE MYTHS
TACTICS & TRAINING: WHAT IF MY GUN BREAKS?
BOTTOM LINE: THERMONUCLEAR POCKET PISTOL — MAC-11

**CLOSE LOOK:
GUN CLEANING & KNIVES**

WWW.AMERICANHANDGUNNER.COM

A nice balance here, of modern ported technology and old-school 1911-tech. Note the machine engraving on this SW1911 Engraved model. Who says you need to live with black plastic only? A trio giving you a weekend Barbecue gun to round out the package! Old school meets new school.

PORTS, SIGHTS AND TRIGGERS DONE RIGHT!

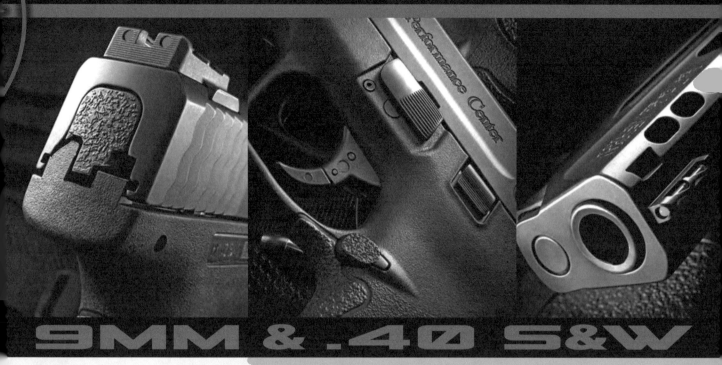

9MM & .40 S&W

JOHN CONNOR

S&W'S NEW PERFORMANCE CENTER PORTED M&P SHIELDS

ow popular are the M&P *SHIELD* pistols? Test samples of the new Performance Center SHIELDs arrived just before December 1st, 2015, when I received a stunning press release: Smith & Wesson had just shipped their *one millionth* SHIELD; not "planned," not "ordered," not "in production," but one million *shipped!* Thinkle onnit, okay? The SHIELD had only been available since mid-2012; about three and a half years.

PHOTOS: CHUCK PITTMAN, INC.

S&W PERFORMANCE CENTER
9MM & .40
PORTED M&P SHIELDS

Ports and HIVIZ "LitePipe" fiber optic sights are featured on the new SHIELDs.

S&W M&P SHIELDS 9MM & .40

Smith & Wesson serves a global market, but I'll bet the overwhelming majority were sold in America, so let's look at it in US context: That's about one SHIELD pistol for every 320 Americans — almost 24,000 SHIELDs per month since production kicked off. And all of that has been driven not by the marketing department's dreams, but by *demand.*

The numbers are staggering, but the SHIELD's popularity is no surprise. I received one of the first SHIELD 9mm's out of the pipeline and reviewed it for the March 2013 issue of *GUNS* Magazine. I called it "The Goldilocks Gun" because I quickly found it's not too small and not too large, but *just right,* not only for my XL-plus hands, but for smaller and even larger hands too. For me, if it were smaller or lighter, it would likely be difficult to point and

control, and recoil might be decidedly unpleasant. If it was any larger and heavier, it wouldn't carry and conceal so comfortably and easily.

Sure, besides being light, slim, flat and agile, it also enjoys the M&P family attributes of reliability, practical accuracy and ease of use. But in my opinion, what has contributed most to the SHIELD's broad people-pleasing power has been a superb combination of dimensions, geometry and subtleties of shape, curvature and touch, creating great ergonomics. That's no accident; just smart design and engineering.

A few other notes. I checked some online forums for complaints about the SHIELD. They were notably absent, and most complaints were ridiculously stretched apples-to-oranges comparisons; more like apples to squid and oranges to Ferraris, plus the usual "I just don't like plastic guns" carping. Then I checked two of the largest online firearm broker sites, searching for used SHIELDs for sale. I found 13 on one and none on the other. *Thirteen?* With a million SHIELDs out there? This tells me virtually all SHIELD owners are quietly pleased with their SHIELDs — and hanging on to them. I'm one of those guys.

Miles of text have been written on the mech-and-tech details of the SHIELD and its mechanically similar siblings in the M&P family — including, by me — so I won't re-hash it all here. Let's talk about what's new and different about these Performance Center puppies.

Upgrade & Enhance

The two most visible changes are the two rows of oblong slots in the slide and the *HIVIZ* "LitePipe" fiber-optic sights. For any light conditions other than pitch black, the fiber optic sights are a real improvement. In fact, shortly after paying to keep my original "standard" T&E SHIELD, I installed a set of green HIVIZ LitePipe sights on it. Smith & Wesson selected red pipes for the rear sights and bright green for the fronts. Having now shot both, I think Smith made the better choice — they're excellent; bold and fast.

The oblong slide slots number three per side, set at two and ten o'clock. The forward pair are functioning gas exhaust ports. Peer down through them and you'll see they align with a pair of smaller oblong slots in the barrel, also positioned at two and 10 o'clock about one-half inch behind the muzzle. Their seemingly diminutive size and placement reflect the evolution of gas port technology.

For years I shied away from ported pistols. Early attempts at gas ports were either big holes drilled in the tops of slides and barrels, or lateral trenches looking like they were cut with a fat

This SW1911 is presented just for fun, to balance the ports. Comes with a wooden presentation box too!

buzz saw. Both spewed massive gouts of hot gasses and vision-killing flames right up into your line of sight in low light. Time, study and science showed smaller ports at V-angles were actually more efficient at damping muzzle flip, and much kinder to the shooter's night vision. There was definitely a point of diminishing returns, and those early gas ports went way over it. Some still do, but not those on these SHIELDs.

> "THE VISIBLE IMPROVEMENTS ARE CERTAINLY VALUABLE, BUT FOR ME, THE BEST IMPROVEMENTS ARE INSIDE THE PORTED SHIELDS."

The visible improvements are certainly valuable, but for me, the best improvements are *inside* the ported SHIELDs. The data sheets I first received on 'em read simply "enhanced trigger." That was a real understatement. The standard trigger sear and striker plunger have been replaced with Performance Center parts, and obviously there has been some serious kiss-and-tickle work by the Center's best gunsmiths to produce a significantly improved trigger pull and a faster, more certain reset.

Examining my early-production standard SHIELD and the Performance Center ported models field-stripped side by side, the only apparent physical difference I could see was in their striker plungers. The visible end of mine is rather sharp and squared, where the Performance Center part is radiused around

S&W'S NEW M&P'S

the top circumference and nicely polished. But oh, what a difference in the hand! Trigger pull weights — 6.5 to 7 pounds — length of pull and reset are fairly consistent between the two, but the Performance Center SHIELD's pull is significantly smoother, the break much cleaner and the re-set far more crisp, tactile and even audible.

> **Obviously there has been some serious kiss-and-tickle work by the Center's best gunsmiths to produce a significantly improved trigger pull and a faster, more certain reset.**

The Performance Center's goals were to reduce felt recoil while delivering improved muzzle control, speed and accuracy — and they did it. For me, clear proof was on the targets and the timer.

Data Doesn't Lie

To better evaluate performance of the ported SHIELDs, I had my "standard" 9mm SHIELD, but lacking an un-ported .40 SHIELD, I used SOMP — "Some Other Maker's Pistol" — in .40 S&W; two ounces heavier, with a 4" barrel versus the 3.1" of the SHIELD.

Ammo used was, in 9mm, Hornady *Critical Duty* 135-gr. FlexLock and Winchester *Defend* 147-gr. JHP's. In .40 S&W, Cor-Bon *DPX* 140-gr. HP and Hornady *Critical Defense* 165-gr. FTX — all excellent choices for serious social work. In that order, average velocities clocked 938, 896, 1,094 and 1,042 feet per second. Yeah; both those .40's were pretty hot — and stout, for a light subcompact pistol.

Almost purely *pro forma,* because the SHIELD's practical accuracy is well established, I shot some 5-round groups at 10 yards from a rested position, 2-handed. Results were good — no surprise there — with little difference between the ammo flavors or between the pistols, ported and un-ported. In 9mm, groups ran 1.25" to 2.5" with Hornady (HDY) and 1.5" to 2.5" with the heavier WIN DEF.

In .40 S&W, groups measured from 1.87" to 2.87" using DPX and 1.37" to 3.06" with HDY. In 9mm, the

ported SHIELD's groups were barely, fractionally tighter, I think, due to its smoother trigger. In .40 S&W, groups were virtually identical between the ported SHIELD and un-ported SOMP, and I'll give the credit for that to SOMP's longer barrel. But rested, two-handed slow-fire groups are not what SHIELD pistols were bred for. They strain at the bit for speed and violence.

The SHIELD is a defensive pistol, designed primarily to be pulled from concealment, pointed or quickly sighted and rapidly engaged in confrontations which are overwhelmingly fast, close and violent. There are countless drills which can both prepare you for the role of defender in those encounters, and also develop, test and polish both your skills and your handgun's capabilities. To best evaluate the value of the sights, porting and trigger upgrades of the Performance Center SHIELDs, I used what I call the "Onrushing Ogre Drill."

The Drill

This presumes you're being aggressively attacked by a fast, powerful, determined — and probably drugged-to-the-gills — psycho; one who may not be, let's say, "sufficiently disappointed" by a single round or a brisk double-tap followed by a "pause to assess," as is taught by lots of trainers. It presumes you're gonna need five, six or more rounds of sustained, accurate fire; not a "mag-dump," where you're just jerking the trigger at max speed and hoping some rounds find his OFF buttons, but steady controlled "lead input" at about one round per second.

I shot them on full size IDPA silhouettes, which feature a 6" square kill zone in the gourd and an 8" circle in center mass. Imagine your goblin moving quickly toward you — and remembering most scumbags aren't disciplined shooters, but the closer they can get the more likely they are to kill you. Using that one-second per shot time as a guide, your goal is to deliver neutralizing shots as fast as you can keep them accurate. Too fast and you'll drop shots; too slow and he's on top of you, with fatal consequences. You've got to find the Magic Meridian. As I found out, lessened muzzle movement, a smoother trigger with a cleaner break, and especially, working a crisp reset can give you a significant edge.

Now, you've *got* to work that reset to get best results; pulling cleanly and completely through the trigger stroke, and disciplining your finger to allow the trigger to return *only,* but positively, to the reset point. From reset, you've got virtually zero travel to the break, which makes for far better accuracy. It takes lots of practice and every design is different. *Put in the work — it pays!*

A simple summary: At 10 yards I shot Ogre drills standing, 2-handed. At

slower timing, the Performance Center SHIELDs barely edged out my standard 9mm SHIELD, and the SOMP .40 drew almost even. My take on that was, given a little distance and a solidly locked two-hand hold at a relaxed rate of fire, the Performance Center effects were less evident. Putting on some speed, the advantage of the ported SHIELDs grew greater in both accuracy and faster elapsed times.

But from the moment I began shooting the Ogre one-handed standing at seven yards, the combined effect of the Performance Center's porting, sights and triggers drew away like Seabiscuit racing a parked car, delivering tighter groups while shaving seconds — especially with the .40! I'm not a big fan of the .40, but I concluded, for whatever reason, I could actually work the re-set more efficiently on the .40 than on the 9mm. File that under "Huh. Hooda thunkitt? Not me."

One-handed, my standard 9mm SHIELD was somewhat embarrassed. The .40 SOMP was blown in the weeds. I put them away and kept shooting the new guys, getting tight 5- and 6-shot groups well centered in the sweet spots and running consistently under a second per round. When greater accuracy makes the difference between hitting the OFF switches or not, and a second can save your life, well … Yeah; I was impressed.

Rap & The Wrap

I had one failure to feed completely into battery with 9mm and two with the .40; all within the first 20 rounds through each pistol. I'd call that normal for any new auto. From there on it was smooth running. The mag springs are fairly stiff, so save your fingers and use a mag-loader. Both SHIELDs came with one flush-fit magazine and one "+1" extended-baseplate mag. Size XL gloves are tight on me, so if your hands are that size or larger, be aware you can control these pistols *much better* using the +1 mags — especially with the .40. Deal with the extra half-inch of butt length; it's worth it. That's it for raps.

Despite the embarrassment to my original SHIELD, these are clearly better guns, and I shoot 'em better. The suggested retail price of a Performance Center SHIELD is only $70 more than a "standard" SHIELD (around the $520 mark or so). HIVIZ LitePipe sights alone run about $106, and the cost of porting, trigger work and a Performance Center sear and striker plunger? You see where I'm going with this, right? Here's a tip: HOT DEAL!

Now I have to go pet my old SHIELD, and assure her she's still loved; just maybe not quite as much. *Connor OUT*

SNUB-NOSED S&W'S / BEFORE J-FRAMES

Duke found these two Smith & Wesson M&P .38 snub noses at a recent gun show.

When someone says snub-nosed Smith & Wessons to us ancient sorts, my mental image is of a 5-shot, .38 Special J-Frame with a 2" barrel. Prime examples are the Model 36 *Chief's Special*, Model 38 *Bodyguard*, Model 43 *Centennial Airweight* or even the Model 60 *Chief's Special* Stainless.

For nearly 45 years before the J-Frames' debut, Smith & Wesson had other revolvers with 2" barrels. They were 6-shooters, built on the K-Frame; again mostly .38 Specials but some .32's and also some chambered for the ancient .38 S&W. These were the famed Military & Police, a moniker which stuck even after Model 10 was applied to them in 1957.

The K-Frame appeared in 1899 as an introductory vehicle for the new .38 S&W Special but was also chambered as .32-20. It was not until 1905 a 2" barrel was offered. Butt shape could be round or square and finish could be blue or nickel-plated. Both versions had color case hardened triggers and hammers. Perhaps the visual dead giveaway of earlier M&P's/Model 10's of any barrel length was its half-moon shaped front sight. Somewhere in the late 1960's or early 1970's that was changed to a serrated ramp.

On the last afternoon of a recent gun show I finally had a chance to peruse dealer tables. I was about to make the pronouncement — to myself — "Well my money is safe today." That's when I looked into a glass display case and saw two "snub-nosed" M&P .38's. Perhaps it was their contrast setting side by side which caught my attention. One was old, blue-worn and with the half-moon front sight. The other was nickel-plated, pristine and with the serrated ramp front sight. Both were square butt and wore S&W's Magna-style checkered walnut grips with, of course, the older one showing a bit of wear. Both were .38 Specials.

A TWO-FER

Being a willful sort I blurted out to the gent behind the table, "What will you take for both?" His answer was satisfying and now I own them. As close as I can determine the old one was made about the year I was born, 1949, and the newer one circa 1981. It's doubtful anyone knows how many M&P Smith & Wesson revolvers were made with 2" barrels. The percent of total with that length has to be small, which still doesn't compute to rare. The total number of M&P revolvers made to date must be around five or six million at least. Roy Jinks' book *History of Smith & Wesson* says 3,000,000 were made by 1967. They are still listed on Smith & Wesson's website but only with 4" barrels.

Two other variations of K-Frame snub noses are the Airweight version (left) and the Combat Masterpiece (right). Both are .38's.

AIRWEIGHTS AND ACCURACY

Even after the 5-shooter J-Frames made their debut in 1950, Smith & Wesson brought out new 6-shot snubbies. One was the Model 12, which was simply a Military & Police with a 2" barrel but with an aluminum alloy frame instead of steel. Another from the 1950's was the Model 15 Combat Masterpiece, which was short barreled with fully adjustable target sights. Then in 1970 the stainless steel Model 64 was also offered as a snubbie. It was the M&P just made of a different metal.

Practical shooting distance for snub-nosed revolvers is say zero feet to 10 yards or so. I must say, though, in the past I've witnessed some superlative shooting with them out to 60 yards on the old police training course. But I can't do it. Still, my M&P snub noses hit point of aim or just a tad bit high with loads pushing 150/160-gr. bullets at about 750 to 800 fps. And they recoil a lot less than the little J-Frames, even though they wouldn't be so unobtrusive for concealed carry.

Duke's M&P snub nosed .38 fits perfectly with his long-owned M&P .38 with 5" barrel.

BIG GUN

The superb accuracy, fine trigger and ergonomics making the S&W Model 41 a first-rate target pistol also make it an excellent choice for small game. The knife is a UK Bushcraft from Spyderco.

S&W MOD. 41 VS.

It happens every year: Fall comes and it's time for the squirrels to change color and start falling off the trees. The squirrel is challenging due to its size, rapid movement and unwillingness to stand still. It can be particularly irritating due to its supremely destructive nature — and tendency to mock you when you miss a shot. Seldom one to do things the easy way, I've typically hunted squirrels with a pistol as a matter of choice. In a situation where circumstances limit your options, though, a handgun may be the only gun available. For those who choose to plan for this eventuality, it makes sense to consider pistols capable of performing more than one role: target, hunting or even defense.

From this framework, the .22 often comes up due to its versatility and both the relative availability of ammo — compared to, say, a .480 Ruger — and the ability to carry a fairly large quantity of ammo with minimal weight

Using some of the same design elements as the 41, the Marvel precision .22 conversion is capable of equal accuracy while allowing you to use the familiar frame of your defensive pistol. The .45 is a Nighthawk Falcon, capable of outstanding performance in its own right.

The scoped Performance Center 41 after checking the zero at 100 yards. Yes, four of the five shots are in about an inch. The Model 41 is capable of one minute of accuracy at 100 yards with the right ammo!

Now readily available from Century Arms, the .22 LR Beretta 71 is justly famous both for its superb reliability and its use by Israeli security forces. While in the same size range as a PPK, it's still capable of sub-2" accuracy at 25 yards. The knife is an Ox Forge Special Forces bowie.

BERETTA MOD. 71 JEREMY D. CLOUGH

TRIPLE DUTY RIMFIRES!

To take the 41 down, the barrel comes easily upward and out, and the slide can be drawn back, lifted up, and run forward off the frame.

Marvel Precision Unit 1 .22 conversions in Commander (top) and Government Model (bottom) configurations. Also available with a traditional full slide, both models can be had with extended, threaded barrels for use with suppressors such as this Gemtech Outback.

and bulk. While it's nobody's idea of a good stopper, the traits making one .22 pistol better than another as a defensive pistol are the same traits making it a good small game gun. Low recoil, which makes it easy to shoot (especially in rapid fire), and exceptional accuracy are both attractive features. With this in mind, let's look at three rimfire semi-autos which can pull triple duty.

S&W Model 41

Probably the premier American .22 target pistol (with all due respect to the fine Ruger MK III and its forebears), the history of the 41 begins strangely enough in Belgium with the Clément pistol S&W copied for its first semi-auto pistol, a .35 caliber released in 1913. Both it and a refined successor in .32 ACP performed dismally and disappeared from the market in 1936. Smith applied its efforts to the revolvers for which they are justly famed, and about 20 years passed before they ventured into the auto-pistol field again.

When they did, they cautiously took their time. Tool room prototypes of what would become the 41 were debuted in 1947 (some less-reliable sources say as early as 1941) at the National Matches at Camp Perry, where S&W gathered feedback on the design from their intended audience. After 10 years of refinement, the finished gun was released in 1957. Perhaps the most obvious sign of its development in a military context is its grip angle.

While most .22 pistols feature the raked-back angle better suited to feeding the rimmed .22 LR cartridges, shooters required to shoot an M1911 in competition preferred a rimfire with a grip angle closer to that of the .45. Incidentally, this preference is also what led to the creation of the High Standard "Military" model, which differs from their earlier pistols primarily in its more-vertical grip angle and was supposedly created to overcome the Army's preference for the M41.

What survived of S&W's early Clément-based pistol are two of the distinctive features of the 41. The fact the sights are mounted directly to the barrel, eliminating the play from having one or both on the slide, and the use of a trigger guard takedown system, a feature perhaps best known on the Walther PP/PPK series pistols, can be traced back. In all fairness, Smith's 9mm M39, the first American DA auto, was released about the same time and was clearly influenced by Walther's P38, so it's probably appropriate to give credit to both European makers.

Lineage aside, the 41 was well-received, and for good reason. Its solid heft, crisp single-action trigger and superb accuracy are the perfect recipe for a target pistol. In 1958, when the military tested the 41 for use as a possible match pistol, they found it shot an average group of .87" at 50 yards. Its performance was later used to develop their formal standards for .22 target pistols, which did not exist at the time it was tested.

A slightly simplified version called the 46 was developed at the request of the Air Force, as well as a .22 Short version for Olympic competition (conversions were available for the .22 LR pistols), neither of which were particularly long-lived. Fortunately, the 41 remained, and is still in Smith's catalog today.

Modern 41

All of which brings us to our test gun. The 41 sent for testing weighed in at a hefty 2 pounds 15 ounces, nearly a half-pound more than my Smith Performance Center M1911 .45. No doubt, part of this is due to the slab-sided 5½ " barrel. While the 7⅜ " barrel of the original 41 is beveled on the top and has an M1911-like stirrup cut on the bottom, the current production 41 retains the full profile of the barrel, adding stabilizing weight towards the muzzle (a 7" version is also available).

Sights consist of a square Patridge front sight and an adjustable rear with a broad, flat serrated face. The trigger's finely-serrated face is almost fully as wide as the trigger guard. While it's advertised at 2¾ to 3¼ pounds, our well-traveled gun broke crisply at 1 pound, 10.9 ounces as measured on a Lyman digital trigger scale sourced from Brownells. The sculpted checkered wood target grips, with their prominent thumb rest and '50's style flair at the bottom, fit comfortably in the hand.

Think of it as a responsive implement of your will seemingly able to intuitively hit wherever you mean for it to. After a decade and a half of testing pistol accuracy in the Ransom Rest (which we did not do with the 41), it's been my experience there's a noticeable cutoff when pistols average 1½ " or better at 25 yards. They simply seem to have a "can't miss" quality making them far easier to shoot accurately. This characteristic is even greater with the 41, which can shoot groups that size at *four* times the distance.

In addition to our iron-sighted 5½ " test gun, Smith also offers an optics-ready version from the Performance Center having an integral 1913/Picatinny rail on top of the barrel and a removable front sight. In addition to time on the square range, I had the chance to shoot both models of the 41 on an S&W-sponsored varmint hunt at the Silver Spur Ranch outside of Encampment, Wyoming and those results were even more impressive.

Surrounded by the Rockies and the Sierra Madres, the 43,000+ acre Silver Spur offers lots of opportunity — and even more if you can make long shots. Compared to hunting grey squirrels in the forests of the Southeast, the long, open vistas of the West require much finer accuracy and the 41 did not disappoint. When I checked the zero on the PC pistol, it shot a little more than an inch at 100 yards. That's right: one minute of angle, with a .22 pistol. That'll do.

While I didn't do a formal accuracy test with the iron-sighted gun, it performed beautifully over the course of two days shooting prairie dogs and ground squirrels and I found I shot it better than the scoped PC pistol. The only problem I ran into the 41 (which occurred much later in the test) is it developed a habit of failing to extract as it got progressively dirtier. This is not surprising: the way you get accuracy is to reduce tolerances, which means less room for dirt and grime. To fix the problem, clean the chamber regularly. I have it on good authority every 500 rounds is a good benchmark, but I tend to shoot things until they don't work anymore before cleaning.

The only drawbacks to the 41 are its price (it has three zeroes ...) and the bulk, which makes the gun easy to shoot well but may be a drawback for some. But like anything excellent, the enjoyment of ownership remains long after the price is forgotten. Apologies to Rolls Royce for that bit.

Smaller Scales

On a different side of the scale is the Beretta 71, which has a substantially lower price (often in the mid-$300 range) and is both smaller and lighter. A smaller-caliber, evolutionary step between Beretta's 1934 pocket pistol — its Walther-influenced 951 9mm (of which the commonly-found Helwan Brigadier is a copy) and the 92F adopted by the US military — the 71 is perhaps best known for its use by the Israeli Mossad, purportedly as an assassin's tool.

While 70-series Berettas (there's also a Model 70 as well as 72-75) originally came in .380 ACP, .32 ACP and .22 LR, the .22 is the one with the notoriety, and which also hasn't always been easy to find. This changed when Century Arms began importing 71's in quantity a couple years ago, reportedly from Israel. The Century Berettas are now readily available and come with a fake suppressor installed to gain the points required for the gun to be imported. While the fake suppressor installation is a permanent one, it can legally be removed by the end user and most enterprising gunsmiths will have no trouble getting it off the barrel. In addition to cutting a pound of weight off the gun, removing the fake can reveals 1/2 x 20 threads on the muzzle, to which we quickly added a Silencerco 1/2 x 28 adaptor. This let us run a suppressor on the 71, and we shot it both with and without the can.

Reputed to be the most reliable rimfire semi-auto in the world, the alloy-framed, single-action 71 weighs barely over a pound and is also quite accurate. I shot groups as small as 1.5" at 25 yards with it, hampered only by the smallish sights. With its open-top slide and sleek, contoured trigger guard, the 71 has a distinctively raked-back look. While it feels quite different in the hand from most centerfire defensive pistols, it's quite comfortable. The original 8-round magazines are difficult to find, however aftermarket ones are readily available.

Other than the grips, which tend to be a bit bulky, it's in the same general size range as the Walther PPK. While not in the same accuracy class as the 41, it's an easily concealable .22 which can be suppressed for quiet practice and is still capable of accuracy well beyond what you'd expect from a pistol of its size.

.22 Change-Out Magic

The third gun isn't a pistol at all: it's a conversion. .22 conversions can be had for virtually all the major defensive pistols, from SIG SAUER to the Browning Hi-Power and guns from Beretta, CZ, GLOCK and of course the M1911. Conversions give you the option of being able to use the heavier, centerfire cartridge for defensive work while still being able to practice and hunt with .22 ammo.

Rimfire conversions have been made for the M1911 for almost as long as it has been around and there are many fine options on the market. The best known for accuracy, though, is the Marvel Precision conversion, which is routinely found on the firing line at Camp Perry and rivals the Smith 41 for ability to put it shots close together. How close? The first two Marvels I had in the Ransom Rest averaged 1" at 50 yards, with some loads averaging .5" — again, one MOA. Clay pigeons on the 100-yard berm are fair game and it's your fault if you miss.

In all fairness to the 41, some of the Marvel's accuracy results from design features borrowed from it (and which also appeared on the Kart and Day .22 conversions which came before the Marvel). Unlike most conversions using a full size slide, the Marvel uses the 41's split slide design with the sights fixed to the barrel, which locks down on the receiver with a clever screw serving double-duty as a recoil spring guide rod. Not only does this eliminate movement of the sights relative to the barrel, the reduced mass of the lower-profile slide is easier for the anemic recoil of the .22 LR to cycle.

For those who prefer the aesthetics of a full size slide, Marvel offers a "Unit 2" version with a full slide, but the original (known now as the "Unit 1") can handle a broader range of ammunition reliably and is the more accurate of the two. Both are available with an extended, threaded barrel for those who legally possess suppressors. For those attached to the power of their .45 ACP, it's hard to think of a better way to make the same gun useful for so many things.

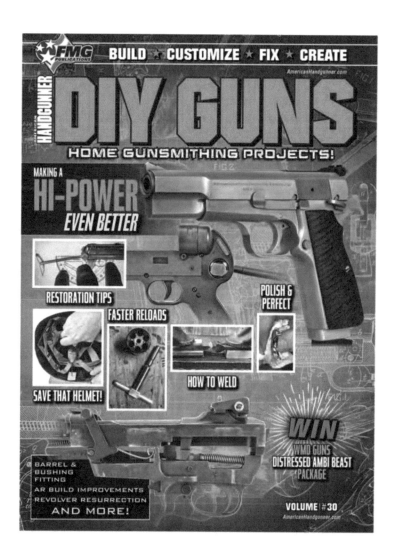

GOLDEN-AGE ARTIFACTS

Two of Duke's old Smith M&P .38's serve as a Wayback Machine to the days when crafting revolvers was an art as well as a science.

Never let it be said I hesitate when buying good used guns. Finish wear (short of major pits) bothers me not a bit as long as mechanical function is still perfect. Two of my revolvers are prime examples of this. They are among the finest of my handguns. But at the same time they're two of the rattiest looking.

Duke's two Smith & Wesson M&P .38 Specials. One is a 2-inch, one is a 5-inch. They may look a bit beat, but both are gems from America's Golden Age of Revolvers.

They are Smith & Wesson Military & Police .38 Specials—the same revolvers gaining the Model 10 moniker circa 1957. Mine predate the name change, having been made in the late 1940's. Postwar M&P's had 2-, 4-, 5- and 6-inch barrel lengths. Mine wear 2- and 5- inch barrels. The blue finish on one has turned mostly a dull black interspersed with areas of brown patina. The other one has most of its original blue but mixed in with what's left are some lighter areas of holster wear. Also something hard has impacted this second M&P along the way, leaving a couple of small divots on the barrel and topstrap.

According to various sources, the barrel lengths of my two are the rarest. The 5-inch I bought at a small Montana gun show in 1978 for the grand sum of $65. Somewhere along the way during the past 38 years the original grips have disappeared, but I'm sure they were on it in the beginning. Today it wears a nice set of Bear Hugs made for me by Deacon Deason shortly before his untimely passing.

This gun happens to also be one of the most inherently accurate revolvers I've ever mounted in a machine rest. Once I fired five 5-shot groups from each chamber and then five more groups loading five of the six chambers at random. The ammunition I used was Remington 148-grain .38 Special wadcutters. Range was 25 yards and the average of all the groups was only 1.25 inches.

The second M&P is much newer to me. I bought it early in 2016 at another Montana gun show. The price was considerably higher than the first one, but what attracted me to it was its least-common 2-inch barrel length. It still wears its original S&W Magna checkered walnut grips.

Although made just a few years apart, there are some interesting differences in these two M&Ps. The 5-inch has an "S" prefix before its serial number 822XXX, indicating it was made soon after World War II. According to the *Standard Catalog of Smith & Wesson* by Jim Supica and Richard Nahas, the S prefix started in September 1945 at serial number 811XXX. In1948, at the end of the second million M&P run,

the prefix was changed to C and the serial numbers started all over again. My 2-inch M&P has C before SN 108XXX. The catalog says that "C1" guns were made beginning in 1948 and C223XXX was made in 1952, so mine is somewhere between those two years. I'd like to think it was made in 1949—the year I was born.

Also in 1948, the M&P's basic action was changed from a long hammer throw to a short hammer throw. The general consensus of serious revolver shooters of the era being the long version gave a smoother double-action trigger pull. Considering my two samples I believe this to be correct.

What is also correct is the general quality of Smith & Wesson revolvers from that era was superb. I have no reason to think either of my M&P's has been worked over, so I think their fine, crisp single-action triggers are representative of the species. With a Lyman gauge my 5-inch M&P averages 3 pounds, 6 ounces. My 2-inch averages exactly one pound more.

Designed as a fighting handgun from its inception in 1899, sights on M&P's are fixed. (There were some target sighted ones offered early on in the 20th century.) "Fixed" means a groove down the topstrap for a rear sight and, until 1952, a half-moon shaped front sight forged integrally with the barrel.

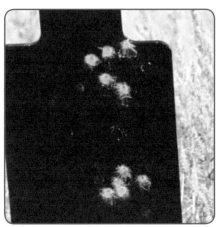

Two 10-yard groups fi ed with the older 5-inch M&P as fast as Duke could aim and squeeze the trigger. The lower group was shot single action. The upper was double action.

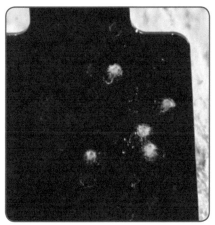

The best Duke could do at 10 yards with the 2-inch M&P with its stiffer DA trigger was this. Maybe there is something to the old-timer's preference for the earlier "long hammer throw"—although the longer sighting radius of the 5-inch gun might have had something to do with it.

These sights are among the hardest to change for zeroing. About the only thing possible for less than an expert gunsmith is filing down the front to raise the point of impact. As the photos show, both of mine print slightly right at 10 yards. The 2-inch prints about 4 inches above point of aim while the 5-inch hits dead on for elevation.

The C-prefix M&P's were the same ones given the Model 10 designation in 1957. By 1967 when the D prefix was applied, 3 million M&P/Model 10's had been produced. The Model 10 is still in Smith & Wesson's catalog, but only with a 4-inch barrel. Surely, the total made in 117 years is at least 5 million. I don't know the current figures.

For a while during that great span of years, nearly every cop in America carried an M&P S&W revolver in his holster. I doubt if any are still there.

S&W MODEL 629 .44 MAGNUM HUNTER

This Performance Center tweaking of the company's signature N-Frame makes for a no-nonsense big-game tool.

As I wandered about the last SHOT Show, my path crossed the Smith & Wesson booth several times. Of course I had to stop and check out all the offerings. But a particular revolver kept catching my eye– almost as if it were calling my name. I asked Tony Miele, S&W Performance Center head, about this unique looking Model 629. Tony took the time to elaborate on its numerous attributes. Many PC offerings evolve from original designs, then receive additional embellishments such as a custom-tuning and fitting. This was such a revolver. When Tony finished, I knew the enhanced Model 629 was coming home with me.

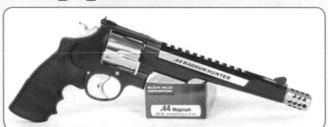

Without an optic, the Model 629 Magnum Hunter (above) is considerably sleeker. And those sights are quick to acquire and fully adjustable. The gun (below) obviously likes Black Hills 240-grain JHPs, as this 6-shot 25-yard group shows.

A spring bear hunt in Idaho would be a good excuse to give this model a workout. After all, it was slated to be the ultimate hunting handgun. The last time I hunted Idaho was way back in 1981. I'd taken a mountain lion in the Middle Fork of the Salmon River with a .44 Mag. This time my friend Wade Derby of Cross Hair Consulting organized the hunt with an outfitter who specializes in running black bear with hounds but also offers hunting over bait as well. Either way, a .44 Magnum will handle any black bear encounter.

Over the years I've taken several black bears but a lot of water has made its way under the bridge since. I was long overdue for another bear hunt. And spring was more than enough justification to get out in Idaho's backcountry—and see what this M629 Magnum Hunter is all about.

N-FRAME DELUXE

When the revolver arrived it came inside a nice black padded case with the S&W Performance Center logo embroidered in gold. Also included with the .44 Magnum Hunter was a UTG Tactical red/green dot sight. It features a 4-MOA dot. The 38mm optic weighed a touch over 9 ounces. This big N-Frame itself tipped the scales at 57.5 ounces, not counting the optic.

This handgun supports a 7.5-inch barrel (1:20 twist) plus an internally threaded muzzlebrake. Frame, cylinder and brake are made of stainless steel. The gun sports a very distinguished black tone on the frame and much of the barrel. The brake, hammer, trigger, cylinder, cylinder latch and the barrel's slab sides are polished stainless. The 2-tone effect is eye-pleasing, providing a subtle contrast.

A matte engraved "Performance Center" on the right barrel flat and ".44 Magnum Hunter" on the left lend an air of distinction without being gaudy. The dovetailed front sight features a bright red vertical overlay to work with the black adjustable rear sight. For those wanting to use iron sights exclusively, the contrast makes the irons quick to align. One feature I appreciated was the integral Picatinny rail—a little over 4 inches long, allowing ample room for mounting various optics.

The UTG Tactical optic was painless to mount and could be situated on the rail at different places for individual preferences. The user-friendly red/green dot sight has nearly unlimited eye relief. Windage and elevation adjustment knobs along with the illumination adjustment are located on the sight's housing. Flip-open lens caps and a battery are included.

The smooth, chrome trigger comes with an overtravel stop consisting of a pin located in the back of the trigger—another nice feature from the Performance Center. Deep checkering on the chrome hammer spur provides positive, non-slip single-action cocking. With pronounced fingergrooves, the Hogue grip provides a very comfortable feel and will be welcome when heavy loads are

The 38mm UTG Tactical red/green dot (above) mounts painlessly on the Model 629 Magnum Hunter's integral rail (below).

The cylinder chambers are not counter-bored, but are chamfered.

on the menu. The serrated stainless cylinder latch is easy to open.

The fluted, stainless cylinder is not counter-bored but with closer inspection, a keen eye will detect a slight chamfer at the top of each chamber. The model (629-7) and serial number are engraved on the frame under the yoke.

Thanks to Lyman's electronic digital trigger pull gauge (which eliminates a lot of guesswork), I found the Magnum Hunter's single-action trigger broke at an average 5.45 pounds. The break was clean and crisp, but to be honest I was a little disappointed and expected a lighter single-action pull. The double-action pull was smooth and broke at 11.8 pounds. You definitely could tell this revolver had undergone action tuning.

Overall the fit and finish was exactly what you'd expect from the Performance Center. The cylinder locked up tight with no wobble. This is a premium revolver which has been enhanced with noticeable refinements and detailed finishing—just what you'd want in an "ultimate hunting handgun."

The .44 Magnum is my favorite revolver cartridge for big game. For the non-handloader, an array of factory ammunition is at your disposal. For this black bear hunt I tested a variety of 240-grain loads from Winchester, Federal, Fusion, Hornady, CorBon, HPR, DoubleTap, Buffalo Bore and Black Hills. Also tested were handloads consisting of Hornady's 240-grain XTP, Sierra's 240-grain JHC and Nosler's 240-grain JHP—all propelled by H110 in Starline brass with CCI primers. Handloading the .44 Mag provides a ton of flexibility from casual plinking to high-octane performance. With the help of Redding's T-7 Turret Reloading Press and Redding's carbide die set, a lot of enjoyment can be had from assembling your own favorite loads. Quickly, too.

By the time I finished shooting all the ammo at hand, several things had become apparent. One, the Magnum Hunter is accurate. Most of my initial testing was conducted from 25 yards and it was pretty common to find 6-shot groups inside 1.5 inches. Considering the optic has a 4-MOA dot covering an inch at this distance (plus a single-action trigger pull over 5 pounds), I was pleased. But I sure wouldn't want the dot any larger for hunting purposes and would prefer something in the neighborhood of 2- or 2.5-MOA. Aesthetically speaking, the UTG optic with its 38mm tube diameter works well but stands out like the proverbial sore thumb.

Secondly, the custom muzzlebrake is effective. After a lengthy range session, I was not fatigued in the least. This brake helps dissipate muzzle rise and felt recoil to the point factory rounds were comfortable to shoot for extended periods. Sighting-in was effortless with only minor adjustments required. The green dot stood out well for my eyes but I'm sure the red one would be useful under certain lighting and background conditions. There are five levels of dot intensity to accommodate varying situations.

The Magnum Hunter kept producing consistently tight groups with Black Hills' 240-grain JHP so I took a box and ran them out to 50 yards. While I didn't really anticipate shooting a bear any further, I was more than pleased with the groups—well inside minute-of-bear. At this point I had run an ample amount of lead through the revolver and felt ready to look for a bruin. The accuracy from this revolver gave me all the confidence necessary.

MODEL 629 MAGNUM HUNTER

MAKER: Smith & Wesson, 2100 Roosevelt Ave., Springfield, MA 01104, (800) 331-0852, www.gunsmagazine.com/index

ACTION TYPE: Single/Double Action, **CALIBER:** .44 Magnum, **CAPACITY:** 6 rounds, **BARREL LENGTH:** 7.5 inches, **OVERALL LENGTH:** 14 inches, **WEIGHT:** 57.5 ounces, **FINISH:** 2-tone, **SIGHTS:** Adjustable sights with Red/Green dot sight, **STOCK:** Synthetic, **PRICE:** $1,369

There are some misguided individuals—generally from the anti-hunting segment—who argue hunting over bait or with hounds is unsportsmanlike. Neither method gives the quarry a fair chance. In reality, this uneducated opinion is largely a result of emotionalism and a far cry from the truth.

I was hunting in an area with a healthy bear population—I saw trail camera pictures for 5 days with many different bear photos. We hunted 5 mornings with the hounds and even though a couple of good races ensued, no bear was treed. And keeping up with the hounds is quite a workout! Then we spent 5 nights hunting over bait and never saw a bear—so much for either method being a slam-dunk. So I came home empty-handed and enjoyed dinning on some delicious "tag soup."

Spending four hours every evening in a blind gives you plenty of time to look through optics. I am convinced if a bear *would* have appeared, the green/red dot sight would have worked well. But we do have other options and before deer season rolls around, I plan on mounting a 4X Leupold handgun scope on the Model 629 Magnum Hunter.

There's no doubt this revolver will handle whitetail encounters out to 100 yards or so—and the accuracy potential will be enhanced with the scope. Surely the deer won't be as lucky as those Idaho bears. When my luck takes a turn for the better, I'm betting the Model 629 Magnum Hunter will shine in many hunting situations.

It's a keeper.

BLACK HILL AMMUNITION, P.O. Box 3090, Rapid City, SD 57709, (605) 348-5150, www.black-hills.com, **CROSSHAIR CONSULTING,** Wade Derby, P.O. Box 864, Oakley, CA 94561, (925) 679-9232, www.crosshairconsulting.com, **KORELL OUTFITTERS,** P.O. Box 653, Emmett, ID 83617, (208) 584-3884, www.korelloutfitters.com

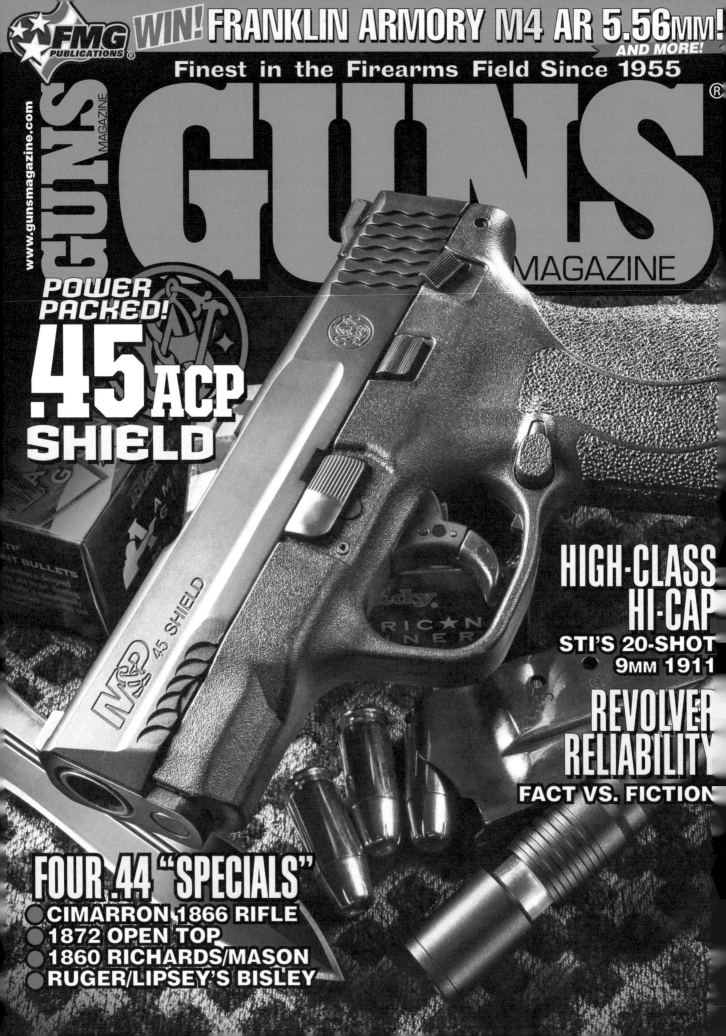

Load more content anytime.

GOING FULL

The stainless steel slide and frame (right, top) is nicely sculpted for concealed carry and the slide is coated in black Melonite. Mas advises against using the forward under-slide serrations to manipulate the slide. The triggerguard (right, middle) is rounded and the trigger itself pivots to start the release. Mas found the trigger smooth and light. Although some testers found the stippling too aggressive (right, bottom), Mas found it glued the pistol to his hand and caused no discomfort in shooting. This version features a safety just under the rear slide serrations, and to the left is the slide release. Below is the mag release, which is positive in use yet secure from accidental dropping of the mag in carry.

The S&W Shield proved utterly reliable in our test. Mas handed it around to a large group of disparate people in his classes and it ran 100 percent. The knife is a Kruder Bliss Black.

BORE

MASSAD AYOOB • PHOTOS: JOSEPH R. NOVELOZO

S&W'S SUPER-POPULAR SUBCOMPACT IS NOW AVAILABLE IN THE ALL-AMERICAN .45 ACP.

In only about 4 years after its introduction, Smith & Wesson's Shield variation of their polymer-framed, striker-fired Military & Police series had already sold a million units. The pistol fit the hand well, with great trigger reach, yet was slim and flat as well as compact in all dimensions, and hit the bull's-eye of its target, the concealed carry market. Originally offered in 9mm Parabellum and .40 S&W (with the former by far the most popular), it was introduced in .45 ACP in 2016.

The .45 Shield met with instant welcome. Two claims stood out from early adopters: "awesome trigger" and "great ergonomics." When my test sample Shield .45 arrived, serial number HNS6552, one of my test crew got to shoot it before I did. Steve Denney, a retired police supervisor, told me it had come out of the box shooting left, but he corrected it with a universal sight pusher. Thanks, Steve!

Steve was the first on the test team to shoot this gun. He was the first to like it, but not the last.

FIRING LINE

In the month of August 2016 I had the chance to pass this gun around to fellow instructors while teaching in Delaware, Pennsylvania, New Hampshire, and Connecticut. We could all tell we were shooting a .45 Shield and not the 9mm or the .40 (duh!), but this group of experienced handgunners were pretty much agreed the recoil was less than we would have expected from a full-power .45 ACP out of a petite polymer pistol weighing only about 21 ounces unloaded.

The right-hand-only thumb safety was easier for me to off-safe than the ones on my other Shields, though there seems to be no visible difference in dimension. (If you'll forgive a pun, my thumb just tells me so, even if I can't put my finger on it.) However, to on-safe, I had to turn the pistol a bit and break my hold for the shooting hand's thumb to reach it, or use my support hand thumb. I find the same true with my 9mm and .40 Shields. For those who don't care for a thumb

safety at all on this type of pistol, S&W offers the .45 Shield in a no-thumb-safety configuration.

CAPACITY

Each Shield in each chambering comes with one short magazine for maximum concealment of the loaded pistol, and one extended magazine creating room for the pinky finger on the grip. In the 9mm, round count is 7 and 8 respectively, while in both .40 and .45, it's 6 and 7. In each caliber, add one more for the chambered round; these pistols are engineered to be "drop-safe."

Recoil is subjective. Firing the 9mm, .40, and .45 Shields side by side on my range, the 9mm naturally kicked the least. To my own subjective senses, the .40 (with 180-grain subsonic FMJ) and the .45 (with 230-grain FMJ) were about equal, and neither objectionably more than the 9mm. For perspective, recoil is a lot more comfortable in the .45 Shield than .38 Special + P in the 5-shot, all-steel J-Frames once S&W's bread-and-butter concealed handguns. Only one shooter felt the Shield .45's greater recoil wasn't worth the bigger hole. Several other testers said, "I'm getting one of these." And one already had. He goes by the Internet *nom de plume* of "Justin Opinion" and his review of the .45 Shield can be found on the GunsAmerica website.

ERGONOMICS

Reach to the trigger is short. This is one reason it has become very popular for folks with smaller hands. My fingers

The S&W Shield is shown atop Hornady American Gunner ammunition, a Kruder Bliss Black knife (727-753-8455, www.krudoknives.com) and a Streamlight Stylus Pro USB UV, (610-631-0600, www.streamlight.com).

BORE

S&W M&P
.45 ACP SHIELD

GUNS

.45 ACP FACTORY AMMO PERFORMANCE

LOAD (BRAND, BULLET WEIGHT, TYPE)	GROUP SIZE (5 SHOTS, INCHES)	GROUP SIZE (BEST 3, INCHES)
Federal 230 RTP	2.3	0.55
Remington 185 JHP	1.45	0.30
SIG SAUER 200 JHP	3.8	1.9

Notes: Group size the product of 5 shots at 25 yards.

"Justin Opinion" demonstrates why he likes the .45 Shield. The arrows show brass in the air from two rapid shots and the pistol is already coming back on target.

are about average length for an adult male, and this lets me get my distal joint instead of the pad of the index finger on the trigger, affording more leverage.

The .45 Shield has a new, more aggressive stippling pattern. It's one of the first things a shooter notices picking it up. Shooters with .45 Shield experience seem split on this. I really like it, and so did most folks on the test team. On the Internet however, I see a few owners who feel the stippling is too aggressive, and feel it stings their hand upon recoil. Using my usual hard grasp I did feel the stippling each time the .45 Shield discharged, but it was closer to a "tingle" than a "sting." If I had been shooting a thousand rounds a day, I might have changed my opinion partway through. The aforementioned Justin Opinion loves the rubbery Talon grip treatment for the Shield .45, and with this or a grip sleeve available, any downside to the .45 Shield's aggressive stippling pretty much goes away.

TRIGGER

A few years ago when Jim Unger of Smith & Wesson showed me the first Shields at a trade show, I exclaimed, "My God, Jim, the trigger is better than on your regular M&P's!" Déjà vu! Almost everyone who tried our test sample said something like, "That's the best pull I've ever felt on a factory Shield!" There's a light, grit-free take-up… then a smooth, short "roll," and finally, a clean release.

CARRYING THE SHIELD

As the .45 Automatic Colt Pistol version joins the 9mm and .40 S&W Shield in your gunshop's showcase, we are reminded why this pistol has become so popular for concealed carry permit holders, off duty cops and uniformed officers who carry backup guns. The .45 is 1.05-inch thick at its widest point, and the 9mm and .40 only 1/10-inch narrower. The Shield's dimensions widen the number of its concealed carry options.

In a belly band, it conceals and carries quite comfortably under a tucked-in shirt in crossdraw, appendix, or behind on the strong-side hip. In the former two positions it's short enough it probably won't dig into your groin or thigh when sitting.

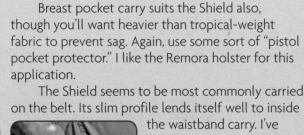

With loose-fitting pants and a pocket holster (above, left), trouser pocket carry is possible with the Shield. Most carry the Shield in a hip holster. This CrossBreed IWB (above, right) proved extremely comfortable.

I found the Shield a little big for pocket carry, but many have found it more adaptable for this purpose than I. Its flat profile conceals well in "Dockers"-style dress slacks, or in cargo pants. Use a pocket holster!

Breast pocket carry suits the Shield also, though you'll want heavier than tropical-weight fabric to prevent sag. Again, use some sort of "pistol pocket protector." I like the Remora holster for this application.

The Shield seems to be most commonly carried on the belt. Its slim profile lends itself well to inside the waistband carry. I've found the CrossBreed with its wide, soft leather backing to be exquisitely comfortable with both .45 and smaller Shields. For the many who prefer outside the waistband holsters, the thinness of the Shield combined with its short dimension from butt to top of slide allows the best possible concealment while still affording swift access.

Don't carry a pistol of this type loose in a pocket, or with anything else in the same pocket that's holding it and its holster! For those who disregard this advice, the option of a right-hand-only thumb safety on the Shield allows at least one safety net.

M&P 45 SHIELD

MAKER: S&W, 2100 Roosevelt Avenue, Springfield, MA 01104, (800) 331-0852, www.gunsmagazine.com/index

ACTION TYPE: Striker fired semi-auto, **CALIBER:** .45 ACP, **CAPACITY:** 6+1, 7+1, **BARREL LENGTH:** 3.3 inches, **OVERALL LENGTH:** 6.5 inches, **WEIGHT:** 20.5 ounces (unloaded), **FINISH:** Armornite over stainless steel, **SIGHTS:** 3-dot, fixed, **GRIPS:** Integral polymer frame, **PRICE:** $479

There's not a lot of size difference between Shields. Here are the .45 (top), .40 (center, with mini Viridian light attached), and (bottom) the 9mm.

Testing the Shield .45's trigger pull on the Lyman digital gauge, average pull weight from the toe of trigger ran 6 pounds. Average from the center of trigger turned out to be 6.63 pounds, which is less than the usual difference between these two measuring points on a pivoting trigger like the Shield's.

At 25 yards from a Caldwell Matrix rest on a concrete bench, S&W's .45 Shield was tested with factory loads in the three most popular bullet weights for the caliber. Group size was determined between the farthest shots being measured, center-to-center of the bullet holes, to the nearest 0.05-inch. Overall group size came first, a good determinant of what the gun could do in stabilized, experienced human hands with stress factored out, followed by measurement of the best three hits, which is a reliable predictor of what the whole 5-shot group would have been with the same gun and ammo from a machine rest.

Remington's 185-grain JHP put all five shots in 1.45 inches, and the best three 0.30 center to center. This amazing "sub-group" consisted of one raggedy hole, the third bullet hole all but disappearing at the bottom between the other two in the cluster. This was the best group of the test.

SIG V-crown 200-grain JHP delivered five hits in 3.80 inches, the best three in 1.90. The 230-grain full metal jacket is the classic training load for a .45 ACP, and was represented here with Federal's RTP, which stands for "Range, Target, Practice." This load put all five 230-grain FMJ's into 2.30 inches (talk about coincidence!) and 0.55 for the best three. Needless to say, I was happy with the accuracy.

RELIABILITY

I lost count of how many rounds got put through the gun by the many hands offered a chance to shoot it, but several hundred including ball, assorted JHP, and even the occasional lead bullet reload went downrange. There were zero malfunctions of any kind. The only Shields I've seen malfunction in classes turned out to be bone dry, and once lubed perked 100 percent again. I expect similar performance long-term with the .45 version.

Worn in a Galco belt slide after 3 months plus carrying a full-size, all-steel 1911, the feathery Shield almost felt as if it wasn't there; I kept touching it with my forearm or elbow to make sure the holster wasn't empty. Concealment under an un-tucked, open-front shirt was fine. Switching a Kydex IWB from Green Force Tactical, the Shield .45 disappeared under a T-shirt... for a bit less than an hour. Remember our discussion of the aggressive stippling? The skin on my side was not as forgiving as that on my palm. I tucked in the T-shirt between gun and flesh, donned a vest, and all was fine again.

Dislikes? There were a few. I've mentioned the downside of the stippling issue, and the difficulty in putting it on-safe 1-handed. I am still trying to figure out the purpose of the ugly, vestigial little scallops on the lower front of the slide. They're too small to give traction to a support hand performing a chamber check from the front, and to my mind, are close enough to the muzzle on this very short pistol for me to worry about using. Several users on the Internet and a couple of my test team complained about getting the last round or two in the magazine by hand, though even my old arthritic fingers could do it. I did notice inserting a full magazine with the slide forward on a tactical reload took a good, solid smack to guarantee seating, and this is a downside point for me.

The perks clearly outweigh the quirks,

SPIN CLASS FOR BOOMERS

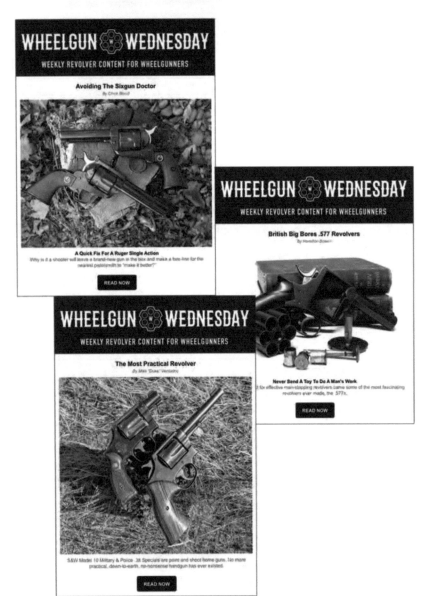

Steve Denny's sight adjustment was spot on. Remington 185-grain gave Mas the tightest group from the 25-yard bench right where he aimed them.

The SIG 200-grain V-Crown JHP fired at 25 yards delivered fine accuracy from the small pistol.

Even practice ammo delivers fine accuracy. Here Federal RTP 230-grain FMJ fired at 25 yards from the S&W Shield .45 put three together.

though. The accuracy was much better than I had dared to hope for, the recoil controllable, and the size almost unnoticeably greater than the smaller Shields that preceded the .45. It's an excellent value at a manufacturer's suggested retail of $479 comparing favorably with the price of subcompact .45's of similar design, weight, size and capacity.

CROSSBREED HOLSTERS, 224 N Main, Republic, MO 65738, (888) 732-5011, www.crossbreedholsters.com, GALCO, 2019 West Quail Ave., Phoenix, AZ 85027, (800) 874-2526, www.usgalco.com, GREEN FORCE TACTICAL, P.O. Box 42, Florahome, FL 32140, www.greenforce-tactical.com, REMORA CONCEALMENT, P.O. Box 990340, Naples, Florida 34113, (239) 434-7200, www.remoraholsters.com, TALON GRIPS, 2522 Copper Ridge Drive B5, Steamboat Springs, CO 80487, (970) 879-9600, www.talongrips.com

SMITH & WESSON SIXGUNS
Part III of an occasional series on gun books.

In 1869, Smith & Wesson brought out the first big-bore, cartridge-firing revolver with the break-top Model 3 chambered in .44 S&W American. Not only did this revolver fire a serious cartridge, it was very easy to unload and reload. When a latch in front of a hammer is unlocked, the entire barrel and cylinder assembly rotates 90 degrees downward and the ejector assembly automatically ejects the fired cartridges. It took a couple of seconds to refill the cylinder, rotate the barrel and cylinder assembly back into place, and the gun was ready to fire.

The American went through numerous changes culminating in the .44 Russian New Model Number Three. It would be four years after the first big bore S&W, the .44 American, before the Colt Single Action Army, the fabled Peacemaker, would be offered. Even with S&W's head start, there is a most important reason why the Colt "Won the West" and just about every "B Western" movie hero carried a Colt Single Action Army .45. The S&W .44's were mostly sold overseas. Of 60,000 plus S&W Third Model Russian .44's produced from 1874 to 1878, only 13,500 went to the commercial market. The rest went to Russia, Japan, and Turkey.

DOUBLE ACTION ARRIVES

Three years after Colt introduced the Model 1878, S&W came forth with their first double action revolver. In 1881, S&W introduced the .44 Double Action 1st Model. They did exactly as Colt, that is, they basically simply added a double-action trigger to their single action Model 3. They did not, however, have to change the grip frame as the Model 3 already had a rounded butt and a slight hump at the top of the back strap. S&W's Double Action .44 Russian would be manufactured until 1913, however, all frames were made prior to 1899. Approximately 54,000 were manufactured.

In the 1890s Colt led the way with a series of modernized double-action revolvers with swing out cylinders. Before the turn of the century they were offering their large-framed, double-action, 6-shot New Service while S&W concentrated on the medium-framed .38 of 1899 which would come to be known as the Military & Police. Then in late 1907 S&W took the lead as far as double-action sixguns go with the first N-Frame, the New Century. They would never relinquish this lead throughout the rest of the century. This first modern big-bore, swing-out-cylindered S&W was also known as the .44 Military, Model of 1908, First Model Hand Ejector, however it is most commonly and affectionately known as the Triple-Lock.

There are many excellent books available covering the history of S&W sixguns. Two books which cover much of the history of S&W are connected with the longtime historian of S&W, namely Roy Jinks. In 1966 Jinks collaborated with Robert Neal to produce *Smith & Wesson 1857-1945* which just as it says covers the story of S&W from the first tip-up .22 through the era of WWII. Then in 1977, Jinks published *History of Smith & Wesson* which covers everything in the previous book as well as the Chiefs Special .38, the .357 Combat Magnum, and the .44 and .41 Magnums. These books are must haves for anyone interested

Taffin's reference library of Smith & Wesson sixguns covers the company pretty thoroughly.

in S&W sixguns.

While Roy Jinks tells us all about the history of S&W, Jerry Kuhnhausen's *The S&W Revolver A Shop Manual* tells us how the classic Smiths actually work. Jerry covers disassembly, tools, servicing and cleaning, parts, adjustments, basic repairs and troubleshooting. Exploded drawings of 44 of the S&W revolvers are provided and, just as in his other books exceptionally clear photographs are provided to aid us in basic care and repairs. Again, I am no gunsmith, however by following Kuhnhausen's text and helpful photos even I can do some of the basic operations. History of sixguns is important to me and so is this textbook of mechanics.

As mentioned earlier one of the most important historical sixguns is the first cartridge-firing, big-bore revolver in the S&W No. 3 American. I am fortunate (thanks to Diamond Dot surprising me) to have an original S&W American No. 3 complete with ivory stocks. This particular .44 was re-finished by S&W in 1952 and I still shoot it using cartridge cases made from .41 Magnum brass and hollowbase lead bullets. Black powder only, of course. Charles W. Pate has written a book dedicated totally to the first .44, *Smith & Wesson American Model In US and Foreign Service*. This history in detail is a most valuable asset to anyone who values the contribution S&W made by introducing this first big-bore cartridge revolver.

Pate starts at the beginning with the firearms leading up to the development of the Model No. 1 .22, carries over to the Model No. 2 and its use in the Civil War, and the subsequent advent of the Model No. 3 American. Both Civilian and Military Models are covered as well as the Russian involvement with the No. 3 American. This resulted in the development of the .44 Russian cartridge which was not only important in itself but would be lengthened to become the .44 Special and then lengthened to become the .44 Magnum. This is a large book with over 400 pages and profusely illustrated.

While Pate's book basically covers the Model 3 American, gunsmith and author David Chicoine's *Smith & Wesson Sixguns of the Old West* covers all of the single- and double-action S&W top-break sixguns. In

addition to the American, S&W produced a long list of top-break revolvers during the frontier era including the Model 3 Russian, New Model No. 3, and the .45 Schofield as well as double-action top-breaks in .44 Russian, .44-40, and .38-40. Chicoine begins with the history of these classic S&W sixguns and provides an in-depth look at all the Model 3's. All of these are black powder revolvers and instructions for their basic care and maintenance along

This booklet on the Model 29 .44 Magnum was issued by the Smith & Wesson Collectors Association in 2003. It is rare, so if you see one, snap it up.

with shooting, disassembly, and cleaning are provided.

Information is also included on the modern replicas, the Schofield and No. 3 Russian. This is a large book with nearly 500 pages covering all aspects of use and care of single action S&W's. He finishes up with reloading information, and most importantly cautions against the use of smokeless powder. A section is provided on all the cartridges available in the Top-Break S&W's as well as contemporary cartridges.

I recently purchased a S&W New Model 3 Target Model with a well-worn finish but excellent mechanically chambered in the very strange .38-44 S&W Target cartridge. This cartridge case was nearly 1-1/2 inches long and used a bullet of 0.358-inch in diameter completely enclosed in the case. Chicoine provides the information I need to come up with cartridges to enable me to shoot this long obsolete cartridge.

Friend Tim Mullin has produced a Smith & Wesson Trilogy quite valuable to anyone who appreciates S&W sixguns.

The page numbers of the three volumes are sequential meaning the second volume starts numbering pages where the first leaves off and the third volume picks up after the second.

First comes *Magnum: The S&W .357 Magnum Phenomenon.* As the title implies this book is basically about the S&W .357 Magnum and the following versions, the Highway Patrolman and the Combat Magnum. Mullin starts with the big-bore cartridges available in the first third of the 20th century, moves into the .38 Super and the .38/44 Heavy Duty, and then the .357 Magnum. The latter is covered in total including publicity, famous shooters of the time who took up the .357 Magnum, barrel lengths, sights, finishes and just about anything else one could want to know.

Then comes *The K-Frame Revolver: The S&W Phenomenon, Volume II* covering all the medium-frame Military & Police-sized sixguns in all aspects.

This is followed up by *Serious Smith & Wesson's The N-And X-Frame Revolvers: The S&W Phenomenon, Volume III.* Here we have all the really big S&W's, the Triple-Lock .44 Special and all the subsequent models, the .44 Magnum with an in-depth look at all of them plus the relatively new .500 and .460 S&W Magnums. Virtually everything ever built on an N-Frame or larger is featured in this book with none other than Elmer Keith pictured on the dust jacket.

An absolutely must-have text for anyone purchasing or looking to purchase a classic S&W or any other later models is *Standard Catalog of Smith & Wesson 3rd Edition* by Jim Supica and Richard Nahas. Nearly 800 models of S&Ws are covered from the first .22 right up to the latest available when this book was published. Each model is covered in depth with production numbers, serial number ranges, values at the time of publication, and on and on. This is the first source I go to when I want to know anything about S&W's.

In 2003 the Smith & Wesson Collectors Association published a booklet by Bill Cross and Bob Radaker entitled *Smith & Wesson's .44 Magnum, The Model 29.* For anyone who is a user and admirer of the original .44 Magnum, this booklet, if it can be found, is a most valuable resource. ◥

www.gunsmagazine.com

Finest in the Firearms Field Since 1955

GUNS MAGAZINE

®

MAGAZINE

BEAR ESSENTIAL

.500 S&W SUPER SNUBBIE

20 CARTRIDGES

500 S&W MAGNUM

CUSTOM

500 S&W MAG
500 gr FP XTP

LEUPOLD

POWER + PEDIGREE
BENELLI 12-GAUGE SUPER BLACK EAGLE 3

AUTO-INNOVATION
BERETTA APX 9MM
COONAN MOT .45 ACP

CLASS ACT!
CZ's BREN 805 S1 5.56MM

MARK HAMPTON
PHOTOS:
JOSEPH R. NOVELOZO

The stubby 3.5-inch barrel (above) is covered with a shroud and locked firmly in place. The arrangement provides better accuracy—if you can stand behind it! A green fiber optic HI VIZ front sight (below) is mated to a square notch full adjustable S&W factory rear sight.

Hogue grips are standard. Even with all their cushioning, shooting full-power .500 S&W ammo from such a small gun is punishing.

BIG BAD BELLY GUN

SMITH & WESSON REDEFINES CCW WITH THE X-FRAME .500 S&W FOR DEFENSE AGAINST, WELL ... *ANYTHING.*

A few short years ago one of my best friends and I were enjoying some incredible fishing on the Naknek River in Alaska. Those big king salmon could burn off line and give anglers some heart-pounding action. Steve, my fishing and deer hunting buddy and I were in the middle of some of the best fishing you could possibly find. There were only two annoying factors bothering us—black flies and brown bears.

We could deter the black flies with our cigars most of the time. The bears on the other hand were a different matter. Frequently bears would roam around camp so you had to constantly be on the lookout when cleaning fish or attending to other chores. We were continually looking over our shoulder when wading along a tributary dumping into the river. Tracks were everywhere and we weren't the only ones fishing the area. We are headed back to Alaska this year, fishing the same waters as before, only this time I will be carrying a peace-of-mind insurance policy—the S&W 500.

At first glance, the .500 S&W Magnum appears to be a huge revolver cartridge—and it is compared to the popular .44 Mag and lesser rounds. The S&W 500 revolver based on the company's massive X-Frame model is an impressive looking beast. At the

The smoothed tuned trigger (above) has no external sharp corners either, thank heavens. The heavy, unfluted cylinder (below) holds 5 rounds of .500 S&W ammo.

241

BIG BAD BELLY GUN

X-FRAME
.500 S&W

PERFORMANCE CENTER

1942 · 2017
75 YEARS

BUCK USA

242

OCTOBER 2017

GUNS MAGAZINE®

MODEL S&W 500

CALIBER: .500 S&W Magnum
MAKER: Smith & Wesson, 2100 Roosevelt Ave., Springfield, MA 01104, (800) 331-0852, www.gunsmagazine.com/index

TYPE: Double-action revolver, **CAPACITY:** 5, **BARREL LENGTH:** 3.5 inches, **OVERALL LENGTH:** 9.9 inches, **FRONT SIGHT:** HIVIZ fiber optic, **REAR SIGHT:** White outline adjustable, **GRIP:** Hogue synthetic, **WEIGHT:** 56.8 ounces, **MATERIAL:** Stainless steel, **PRICE:** $1,609

shooting range, both revolver and cartridge are often perceived as mammoth big bores. But when you are close to a brown bear—especially a *big* brown bear—the cartridge doesn't seem a bit too big at the moment! The one and only brown bear I've taken with a handgun squared an honest 9 feet, 10 inches with a skull measurement over 27. From 80-some yards I can honestly say he looked like a Volkswagen with a head—impressive and intimidating! The sheer size of some of these big bears will provide some perspective in relation to the cartridge. There is *no* such thing as being over-gunned.

With a barrel length of 3.5 inches, I immediately thought about recoil, and who in their right mind wouldn't? I have some experience with the cartridge dating back to when it was first introduced by S&W back in 2003. After obtaining a license to hunt with the revolver in Zimbabwe, I took a dandy Cape buffalo using CorBon's 440-grain hardcast offering. This was the only buffalo I have taken with one shot. The cartridge delivers a serious payload for any big or dangerous game. I hope a brown bear never gets me in a situation where I have to shoot, but I have confidence the .500 S&W Magnum would save the day if I hold up my end of the deal.

As it comes out of S&W's production/custom shop, the Performance Center Model S&W 500 is a serious carry gun for circumstances mentioned above. This colossal X-Frame is all stainless steel with a brushed satin finish. My test gun came with HIVIZ green fiber optic front sight. The rear sight is solid black, adjustable and features a square notch.

The slab-sided 3.5-inch barrel has Performance Center inscribed on one side, .500 S&W Magnum on the other. A full-length underlug houses the cylinder ejector rod. The front of the trigger is smooth with an over-travel stop incorporated. My trigger broke smoothly at just less than 4 pounds in single-action mode and just shy of 9 pounds in double action. The tuned action is just what you would expect from the Performance Center. The large, wraparound Hogue rubber grip features finger grooves and provides a secure, comfortable hold.

An unfluted cylinder is home for 5 rounds of powerful .500 S&W Magnum. The cylinder is not counterbored. The revolver is easily cocked thanks to the large, serrated hammer spur. The revolver tips the scales a shade over 56 ounces when empty and the weight comes in handy when shooting high-octane loads. This Performance Center revolver is shipped with an attractive gun rug featuring gold embroidery.

AMMO CHOICES

Looking around the ammo bin I found some factory offerings from CorBon, DoubleTap, Buffalo Bore and Hornady in bullet weights ranging from 300 to 440 grainers. CorBon originally produced ammo when the big .50 caliber handgun hit the market and today offers several options including a 275-grain DPX, 325-grain Hunter A-Frame and a 440-grain hardcast. Hornady offers a 300-grain FTX and their 500-grain XTP. Both Buffalo Bore and DoubleTap provide some serious medicine capable of solving any problem.

I contacted my friend Chris Hodgdon and ask him for recommendations regarding a milder load for practice. I wanted a load to shoot at the range for practice without creating a ground tremor. Chris informed me, "On the .500 S&W we do show Trail

BUCK 119
PAT COVERT

Buck Knives is an icon of American cutlery lore dating all the way back to 1902 when Hoyt Buck made his first knife out of a simple file blade. The first production knives for the company were fixed-blade hunting knives, the forbearers of the Buck 119 model gracing these photos. Although much of Buck Knives' fame has centered around the 110 Folding Hunter—and rightfully so—the 119 is a worthy legend in its own right.

During WWII Hoyt Buck donated many of his "hunting knives" (which very much resembled the 119 we know today) to US troops in battle around the world. After the war he and son Al moved from Idaho to San Diego, California, and formed H.H. Buck & Son. Soon after, the Bucks were producing a nice selection of fixed-blade knives including their flagship 119 and it has endured to this day—not only serving many a hunter but troops as well, particularly during the Vietnam War.

The Buck 119 here is the 75th Anniversary 119 Special which sports the classic 6-inch upswept clip-point blade of the original done up in 420HC stainless steel—a longtime Buck standard. Like the original, the blade has a Fuller groove for

A big gun deserves a honkin' big knife, and the classic Buck 119 has been in such a role in sport and war since WWII.

added strength (these are often referred to as "blood grooves" but serve no such purpose). The 119 Special is available in two models. The one shown here features an aluminum guard/buttcap with a black phenolic handle. A more upscale model with brass furnishings and Cocobolo wood handle is also offered. A 75th Anniversary medallion graces the handle of each. Retail for the 119 Special is $96 (aluminum) and $136 (brass). The Buck 119 is not only the effective workhorse it has always been—it's a chance to hold 75 years of history in your hand!

BUCK KNIVES, 660 S. Lochsa Street, Post Falls, ID 83854, (800) 326-2825, WWW.GUNSMAGAZINE. COM/INDEX

LEUPOLD LTO TRACKER

MARK HAMPTON

LTO TRACKER

MAKER: Leupold & Stevens, 14400 Northwest Greenbriar Parkway, Beaverton, OR 97006, (503) 646-9171, www. gunsmagazine.com/index

THERMAL SENSOR: 206 x 156, Operating TEMP: -4F to 140F, TEMPERATURE DETECTION RANGE: -40F to 572F, Fixed Focus 6X Digital Zoom, DISPLAY RESOLUTION: 240 x 204 pixels, STARTUP TIME: < 3 seconds, DETECTION DISTANCE: 600 yards, BATTERY: CR123, RUN TIME: 10 hours continuous, PRICE: $909

I'm the polar opposite of a gadget guy but occasionally something techy comes along and really catches my eye. Take the new Leupold LTO-Tracker for example, a really neat, practical device to make life easier for hunters.

This thermal optic tracker is very compact weighing less than 10 ounces and just 5.8 inches long. You can clearly see the heat signature of game up to 600 yards, day or night. This is not a night vision unit but senses heat so it works both night and day. The LTO-Tracker has 6 optional thermal palettes so you can adjust to whatever works best for your eyes—and the situation. You can cycle through the color palettes, red, green, white hot, black hot, black highlight and white highlight until you find what best fits. It can detect and display temperatures as low as -40 degrees Fahrenheit. This

The Leupold LTO Thermal Imager can help hunters find game day or night.

unit features a beneficial 21-degree field of view. The control reticle allows for quick on-target acquisition. If extreme conditions are encountered, no worries, the LTO-Tracker performs in temperatures from -4 to 140 degrees F.

The unit itself is built like a tank, rugged and waterproof. I was impressed at the crisp image quality thanks to the 30HZ refresh rate while viewing horses and cows behind my house. It was pitch black and you could see the thermal images clearly. With a continuous 6X zoom, I could determine the heat signature from well over 300 yards. This unit will not only help hunters recover downed game, but it will detect blood as well. Now it makes finding a blood trail easier and increases the odds of recovering game. I like it!

I've been using Leupold scopes most of my life. They offer superb optical quality. Now I'll add the LTO-Tracker in my backpack. It will never be noticed—until I need it.

Boss as a nice alternative for pleasant subsonic trigger time. Since this powder is extremely fast burning, we show only lead bullets as jacketed bullets would drive up pressures substantially. Trail Boss can't be double charged because of its unique bulk density."

After procuring some Trail Boss I got on the phone with Robin Sharpless of Redding Reloading. Robin suggested their Titanium Carbide set. With the help of quality Starline brass and Winchester LRM primers,

I was ready to load some mild rounds for the mighty .50-caliber magnum. Chris Hodgdon also shared some data taken from a 10-inch barrel. With a 375-grain lead bullet, a starting load of 8 grains of Trail Boss yielded 764 fps and a maximum of 12 grains showed 926 fps. Moving up to a larger 440-grain lead bullet, a starting load of 7 grains revealed 643 fps and a maximum 10 grains showed 799 fps. With a shorter barrel obviously we would see decreased velocity in a pleasant shooting round. My

friend Glenn Swaggart was kind enough to send me some cast bullets he received from Bryan Reece—a great guy who knows his stuff. I was now able to test Trail Boss with 400-grain cast bullets.

Sierra offers two cannelured bullets for the .500 S&W and I wanted to experiment with both. My good friend Carroll Pilant from Sierra provided their 350-grain JHP which was designed for expansion. He also sent some of Sierra's 400-grain JSP bullets. These larger ones were made for deep penetration. I used Sierra loading data for their bullets which suggests Lil Gun to be a top choice for accuracy and hunting loads in both bullet weights. I didn't have any Lil Gun on hand so I loaded the Sierra bullets with Accurate 9 and Alliant 2400.

At the range my friend John and I set up the Oehler 35P chronograph, then flipped a coin to see who would shoot first. John won the coin flip, so in reality, I won. I could detect John wasn't looking forward to the unenviable task. To say factory loads were robust could be interpreted as an understatement. It was a handful to say the least. Our groups were not outstanding and I'll freely admit we should have been able to do better. But this revolver was designed to keep you from being mauled, clawed, chewed-up and eaten—not to produce tiny bug-hole groups in paper. The big .500

This 25-yard target was made shooting 400- and 410-grain cast bullets over Trail Boss powder. Trail Boss tamed recoil substantially and provided pleasant shooting of the big .500 powerhouse. Photo: Mark Hampton.

S&W has a nice trigger with a smooth cycling action. The green fiber optic front sight made target acquisition quick and easy. And those rubber Hogue grips were an asset as well. The handloads with Sierra bullets were mild, comparatively speaking.

The 400-grain cast bullets from Bryan Reece with Trail Boss gave the gun a complete change in personality. This was a very mild, pleasant load as Chris Hodgdon said it would be. When shooting the big S&W .500 Mag, Trail Boss is my new friend. These loads provide enjoyable range time and groups tightened up significantly—imagivne that! Now we're having fun!

.500 S&W MAG HANDLOADED AMMO PERFORMANCE

BULLET (BRAND, BULLET WEIGHT, TYPE)	POWDER (BRAND)	CHARGE (GRAINS WEIGHT)	VELOCITY (FPS)	GROUP SIZE (INCHES)
Sierra 350 JHP	2400	30.5	1,121	2.22
Sierra 400 JSP	AA9	31.9	1,285	2.10
Cast 400 SWC	Trail Boss	8.2	686	1.03
Cast 410 HP	Trail Boss	8.0	626	1.10

NOTES: All handloads were developed with Starline brass and WLRM primers.

.500 S&W MAG FACTORY AMMO PERFORMANCE

LOAD (BRAND, BULLET WEIGHT, TYPE)	VELOCITY (FPS)	GROUP SIZE (INCHES)
Hornady 300 FTX	1,627	2.40
Hornady 500 XTP	1,164	2.95
Buffalo Bore 375 Barnes XPB	1,541	3.18
DoubleTap 400 WFNGC	1,360	2.88
CorBon 275 DPX	1,532	2.80

NOTES: Groups the product of 3 shots at 25 yards. Chronograph screens set at 12 feet from the muzzle.

When fishing in Alaska, carrying the large revolver will be important. Thanks to Diamond D Custom Leather and their Guide's Choice Chest Holster, toting the large S&W will not be an issue. This well-designed chest rig allows the revolver to ride next to your chest with easy accessibility. The handmade leather was designed, tested and produced in Alaska by a company with first-hand experience fishing in streams shared with big bears. This simple, comfortable, easy-to-adjust holster adapts well whether you're wearing a shirt, jacket, or fishing vest. The company offers other fine leather goods including their "Alaska Tough" leather belt. I had to get one of these double-lined belts (which are available in different widths and colors).

When we start fishing in Alaska this year, I'll be eager to get my line stretched by those big king salmon. My buddy and I both will be armed with cigars for those annoying black flies and mosquitoes. But if and when we run into brown bear problems, the S&W 500 will be resting in the Guide's Choice Chest Holster with 5 rounds of insurance. It's a revolver ideally suited for this very purpose. Truthfully, I hope we don't see any bears. But I'll be prepared if we do.

DIAMOND D LEATHER, 504 W. Hjellen Dr., Wasilla, AK 99654, (907) 631-4212, www.diamond-dcustomleather.com, REDDING RELOADING, 1089 Starr Rd., Cortland, NY 13045, (607) 753-3331, redding-reloading.com, REECE CUSTOM CASTING, 6477 S. County Rd. 875 E, Cambridge City, IN 47327, (765) 541-8584, SIERRA BULLETS, 1400 West Henry St., Sedalia, MO 65301, (888) 223-3006, www.sierrabullets.com

FMG PUBLICATIONS

$6.95 US

CANADA $7.95

AYOOB FILES: HI-POWER SHOOTINGS!

AMERICAN HANDGUNNER

SEPTEMBER/OCTOBER 2017

S&W's DEPENDABLE DEFENSE:
M&P M2.0/M637 & 586 K-COMP

UGER: SR1911 TARGET/ MERICAN COMPACT

AN WESSON OMM OAR LASTER

RNBULL'S UGER MK IV LASS-GUN

C ENCORE .223/.44 MAG

WIN
A COONAN INC.
.357 MAG. CLASSIC PACKAGE!
TOTAL VALUE: $1,788.94

FOCUS:
NING EDGE: LOCKED BREECH?
NDLOADING: .38 SUPER HEAVY BULLETS
RRY OPTIONS: SIMPLY RUGGED HOLSTERS
TICS & TRAINING: FADS, FANTASY OR FIGHT?

BEHIND THE SCENES: BLACK HILLS AMMO

ONLINE: TRIGGER TIME WITH THE TERMINATOR

WWW.AMERICANHANDGUNNER.COM

SMITH & WESSON
.38 S&W SPL + P

RUGER
ARX
.38 SPECIAL
SELF-DEFENSE
AMMUNITION

A FULL-SERVICE SIDEARM

PHOTOS: CHUCK PITTMAN, INC.

COULD S&W MAKE THE M2.0 M&P PLATFORM ANY BETTER?

PAYTON MILLER, EXECUTIVE EDITOR, GUNS MAGAZINE

BEATS THE HECK OUT OF US HOW ...

Within every legendary handgun company there are individual product lines, generally centered around a specific application, or in modern Tacti-Speak, a "mission" (although in many cases it's more of a marketing ID). Ruger's Blackhawk brand encompasses heavy-duty single-action revolvers. Colt's "Snake Guns" encompassed their premium double-action revolvers (Python, Diamondback, Cobra, etc.).

With Smith & Wesson, the evocative buzzword is "Military & Police"— a term easily pre-dating them all,

having first appeared in 1899. M&P offerings initially covered no-frills service revolvers in K- and N-Frame sizes. But the M&P label sort of faded away when Smith began hanging specific model numbers on everything — which considering the scope of their product line — was inevitable.

However, in 2005 the M&P stamp returned with a vengeance. The platform wasn't a fixed-sight "classic reissue" service revolver from a nostalgia series this time. It was a polymer-framed, striker-fired duty pistol initially offered as a full-sized 9mm or .40 S&W. It was obviously a major

M&P M2.0
MODEL 637
586 L-COMP
S&W

company effort to recapture the American LE market from several, shall we say, *competitive* products of Austrian, German, Italian and Swiss parentage.

Nobody could, of course, compete with Smith when it came to wheelguns. Problem was, the only revolvers cops appeared interested in anymore seemed to be backup snubbies. In short, S&W had been getting their lunch eaten in the domestic "auto-centric" marketplace and they decided to do something about it. It only seems natural they resurrected the M&P brand, which — then as now — seems a natural for duty sidearms.

The rollout included a Big Splash media push that has yet to be equaled. It worked out splendidly, the pistol was an unqualified hit, and S&W wasted little time in expanding the resurrected M&P line to include mid-size and compact versions, eventually including the Shield and Bodyguard as well as some specialty LE-oriented revolver models and their entire AR lineup.

A Work in Progress

Shooting the latest version of the M&P — the M2.0 — is an eye-opener. The success and popularity of the original version certainly speaks for itself, but the M2.0 still manages to embody the shopworn "New and Improved" marketing cliché. No, it's not another Performance Center-tweaked version (there have been several), but it might pass for one, although it's straight from the Big House.

Not content with launching one SKU of a new model, Smith has eight — two .45 ACP's (one with a thumb safety), three in .40 S&W and two in 9mm. "SKU," for those of you too embarrassed to ask, stands for Stock Keeping Unit. Not very sexy, but there you are. I used to keep my mouth shut and pretend I knew what it meant until, ashamed, I finally asked. The SKU on mine was 11537 (remember that, you'll be tested on it later). What it translates to is the following.

The "big" one has a 5" barrel in 9mm with an OAL of 8.3" and a 17+1 capacity. Cosmetically, we're looking at a Sandbox-inspired Flat Dark Earth color scheme (on our test gun), Armornite corrosion-resistant finish on stainless steel and what the company calls an "aggressive" grip texture (it is indeed!). Sightwise, we're looking at a drift-adjustable 3-dot setup. And there are four interchangeable palm-swell grip inserts so you can tailor the fit to your own mitt. And the MSRP on this one is $599 — a number which in terms of real-world prices will most likely not stand for long. Still, reasonable even at that price.

So, you're probably asking yourself what all the hoo-hah is about. How is this M&P substantially different than the one they rolled out a dozen or so years ago? Well the trigger is consider-

WHEELGUNS ROCK

I carried a beloved 6" hard-chromed S&W Model 19 as a reserve on the Chula Vista PD in the middle 1970's. I learned to shoot accurately with that gun in DA-only competing in PPC matches. My trustworthy Smith came with me when I got hired full-time on the San Diego PD beginning in 1978. At the time we weren't allowed to carry a "custom" gun but the range master knew I was a gun-guy (was top gun in my academy) so he signed off on it as a "test" gun. Bless him. Those early years found me relying on revolvers for front-line work daily and I never felt under-gunned — ever. When we transitioned to autos in the late 1980's I still kept a J-Frame tucked away in an ankle rig. And off-duty — more often then not — found me armed with a revolver.

These two admirable guns from S&W represent some of the best stock revolver engineering I've seen, period. Both functioned perfectly out of the box, both are as accurate as I can hold and both offer power, reliability and amazing value. You couldn't build a custom revolver from a basic gun for the money you'd spend on either one of these. And, being engineered from the beginning as a unit, most stock guns tend to be reliable and well-sorted right off the bat.

The M637 has a delightfully smooth action which is indeed noticeably lighter than a stock gun's. The grips are a departure too, a bit like the old-school "Fuzzy Farrant" stocks that were smaller at the bottom, and fit your hand well. Pretend to grip a gun, now look at your hand. You have more room at the top of your grip than at the bottom. Yet most revolver grips are big at the bottom. Fuzzy's grips looked funny, but they worked. I think the fact they looked different than traditional stocks eventually killed them. Fortunately, S&W doesn't think the idea is a bad one. I'm pleased to see this, and they are especially comfortable in my medium-sized hands. I also like the fact the gun has a hammer. Watching it helps new shooters better learn to stage a trigger, and, it simply looks right to have a hammer there to my eye!

It's rated for .38 Special +P with no bullet weight limits. While snappy with high performance ammo, I think it really shined with some 148-gr. wadcutters. At 15 yards, shots to the head-zone were a snap, but about 3" low and a bit to the left — not unusual with fixed-sighted guns of any sort. I ran about 150 rounds of assorted ammo through it and it ran fine. This is a classic "grab it and go" J-Frame, light, smooth and very shootable. Do I need another J-Frame? No, but this one is so delightful, it's not going back.

The 586 L-Comp showed the fit and finish the Performance Center is known for. Grips are Spegle-like in design and feel comfy but a bit square at the back. The gun is hefty (over two pounds) but digests full-power .357 Magnum loads easily because of that. Hearing protection is a must as that comp blasts like hell-fire. Sights are classic S&W with a Tritium insert in the front. The chambers (seven) are all chamfered and there's a trigger stop nodule on the rear of the trigger appearing to be hand-fitted as there are delicate file marks on it.

If you loved the 3" round-butt K-Frames you'll love this. Adding a bit of beef to the mix offers a certain stability as you move from target to target. At 15 yards this seems to be easily a 2" gun with everything put through it. I'm thinking it will outshoot me with wadcutters "out there" but it rained cats and dogs here when I was going to do that. If you're a weekend gamer/shooter, need a solid home defense gun, or are focused and dedicated enough to haul around a hunk of iron, you've found a new friend here. The term "personal firearm" comes to mind when I see it on my desk. "Oh that? It's my personal firearm," you might say to someone. It sends out self-confidence vibes all on its own. "I'm here, I can help protect you." I believe it.

What would I do? I'd round off those grips some and possibly add a bit of skateboard tape to the back-strap. Then I'd be 100-percent happy. But — I'm pretty happy now. Wheelguns still rock. No fooling.

---

ably better — crisper and lighter than most will remember from the original. The trigger reset is both tactile and audible — which is a fancy way of saying you can feel and hear it reset. In addition the interior steel "chassis" is longer than on the original, all the way along the polymer frame as a matter of fact. Rigidity is increased, yet recoil seems less. In addition, the slide itself has been slightly slimmed and "re-contoured," although not blatantly so.

Now, the original one I experienced at the long-ago media unveiling in Springfield, Mass., was in .40 S&W and wouldn't shoot 180-gr. ammo worth a whoop — although things did improve when I switched to 165's. (It seems 180-gr. .40 S&W was initially "coin of the realm" in the early days of the "Ten Lite.") But I never could manage the trigger properly. It was okay in 7-yard speed drills, but drove me a little crazy in deliberate 25-yard shooting, let alone my attempts at 50 yards.

If this improved trigger was all they did on the new M2.0, I'd have been sold. But "on paper" 25-yard results from a rest with the M2.0 was far better — say 3" to well under 2" with an assortment of 115- and 124-gr. FMJ

ammo. Am I simply — then as now — a better shooter with the lower-recoiling 9mm? Twelve or 15 years ago a younger and dumber me would have denied that vehemently. But that was then and this is now. So, my uselessly qualified answer is *probably*. I left my Ransom Rest at home so I can't swear this new version is more accurate than the old, but it is easier to *shoot* more accurately.

Jeff Cooper used to refer to this as the difference between "intrinsic" and "inherent" accuracy. The former being what the combined human element and gun are capable of, the latter being simply what the gun is capable of with no human involved.

Revolving Items

To bookend the M2.0 unveiling, we also saw a pretty pair of reminders

Smith can "still dance with what brung them." Of course we're talking revolvers and the proof here is a pair of pretty cool ones — a J-Frame snubbie and an L-Frame. Both, incidentally, are Performance Center products.

Being an old-time copper, His Editorship Roy has a soft spot for Smith revolvers of any frame size in the .38/.357 range, so he simply had to take both back to the Royal Compound in Missouri, where he gave each a thorough

FULL-SERVICE

blasting (see sidebar for His Most Subjective Insights).

The first is the Enhanced Action Model 637. What it is, is a stainless steel/aluminum-alloy, PC-tuned J-Frame 2" snubbie chambered for .38 Special Plus-P. Actually, S&W lists the barrel length as 1.875", but I wouldn't lose any sleep fretting over any velocity loss penalty for the fractional difference. The M637 features sculpted custom wood stocks too. I, for one, am grateful the Smith Performance Center saw fit *not* to instead offer something .357-capable. After all, why pay extra for a beautifully tuned J-Frame only to subject it — and you — to magnum-type abuse? By the way, the stock is great. They tout the action as being 20 percent lighter and smoother than a stock one and I won't argue the point. It's excellent.

If you're really interested in a short-barreled, unmanageable blowtorch, why not pick something heavier (see next paragraph)? Obviously intended for the concealed carry market, the Model 637 weighs 15 oz. and sports a shockingly low MSRP sticker for a Performance Center gun — $525. Oh, and the official SKU number? It's 170349.

Bigger Brother

The Model 586 L-Comp, is another Performance Center offering. Smith & Wesson, if you'll recall, introduced the L-Frame 586 back in 1980 as a sort of size compromise for shooters who simply insisted on a heavy diet of .357 Magnum ammo, yet didn't want to step up to an N-Frame. The L had the same grip size as the smaller K, but its beefier construction made it a better choice for magnums, both from the standpoint of gun wear *and* shooter fatigue.

My first serious revolver was a Model 586 and it stood up to a .357 regimen I wouldn't have wanted to subject my K-Frame Model 19 to. This 586 L-Comp is a blued, 3" barreled number with a 7-shot cylinder and adjustable sights. Which, for me at least, would be mandatory on anything you're going to subject to the point of impact shifts inherent in the 700–1,600 fps velocity range of a .38/.357 chambering.

At any rate, the 7-shot 586 L-Comp's barrel is a ported, full-lug tube, which ought to tame some of the muzzle up-flip. It features a PC-tuned action and a Tritium front night sight. The stocks are checkered rosewood. At 37.5 oz. with an 8" OAL, this may not be the optimum size/weight for a CCW gun, but if you want to pack a whole lot of power in a reasonably compact package, this one's worth looking at. And compared to a traditional 6-shot revolver, the 586 L-Comp may just classify as "high cap." The $1,208 MSRP is more in keeping with the Performance Center menu than that of the M637, but it's a lot of gun for the money. The SKU? 170170.

The upshot of all these new goodies from Smith? The company apparently has no intention of staying off the cutting edge of product development. It's tough to think of what else they could do to the M&P pistol, but don't bet against them coming up with something.

SMITH & WESSON
.44 COMBAT MAGNUM

BIG-BORE PUNCH FROM A SHORT-BARRELED L-FRAME.

I n November 1955, Smith & Wesson presented Bill Jordan with the first .357 Combat Magnum. This 6-shot medium-frame revolver weighed 1/2 pound less than the original .357. This was a very significant development, however, one month later it was overshadowed by the introduction of the first .44 Magnum. Both of these classics are now gone, however, they have been blended together in the 5-shot L-Frame Combat Magnum chambered in .44 Magnum.

**MODEL 69
COMBAT MAGNUM**

MAKER: Smith & Wesson, 2100 Roosevelt Ave. Springfield MA 01104, (800) 331-0852, www.smith-wesson.com

TYPE: Double-action revolver, **CALIBER:** .44 Magnum, **CAPACITY:** 5, **BARREL LENGTH:** 2-3/4 inches, **OVERALL LENGTH:** 7.8 inches, **WEIGHT:** 34.4 ounces, **FINISH:** Stainless steel, **SIGHTS:** White outline adjustable rear, red ramp front, **GRIPS:** Fingergroove, pebbled rubber, **PRICE:** $859

The first L-Frames were the Model 586 and 686 chambered in .357 Magnum. There were some who complained about the original .357 Combat Magnum not being able to digest a significant amount of full-house .357 loads, so the L-Frame was beefed up in the forcing cone area and fitted with a full under-lug barrel while keeping the Combat Magnum K-size grip frame. S&W also offered other L-Frames, most notably 5-shot .44 Specials including the Model 696 and the Mountain Light Model 396. Then in 2014 the company expanded on the 5-shot .44 Special theme with their first 5-shot .44 Magnum—the Model 69.

Now S&W has taken the .44 Magnum Combat Magnum a step further by introducing the same model with a 2-3/4-inch barrel. Everything else is virtually the same as found on the longer-barreled version. Weight is now at 34.4 ounces resulting in a sixgun which is closer to being a Perfect Packin' Pocket Pistol. This makes it somewhat easier to carry and conceal, however, the shorter barrel and slightly lighter weight—at least in my hands—accentuates the felt recoil quite a bit.

Admittedly, the vast majority of my sixgunnin' heart belongs to the old classics—notably those beautifully bright

blue-finished magnums from the mid-20th Century. However, I have to admit this newest iteration of the L-Frame is exceptionally attractive. It's a glass-beaded stainless 5-shot DA sixgun with an overall length of 4.2 inches. Sights are typical S&W adjustables—white outline rear matched up with a red ramp front. To add a touch of distinction, the frame screws, hammer, trigger and cylinder release—as well as the sights—are matte black, contrasting nicely

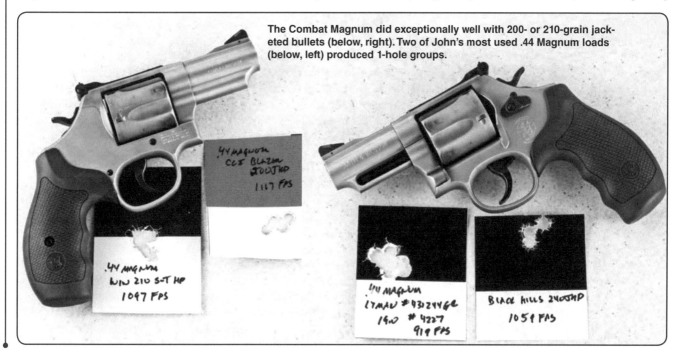

The Combat Magnum did exceptionally well with 200- or 210-grain jacketed bullets (below, right). Two of John's most used .44 Magnum loads (below, left) produced 1-hole groups.

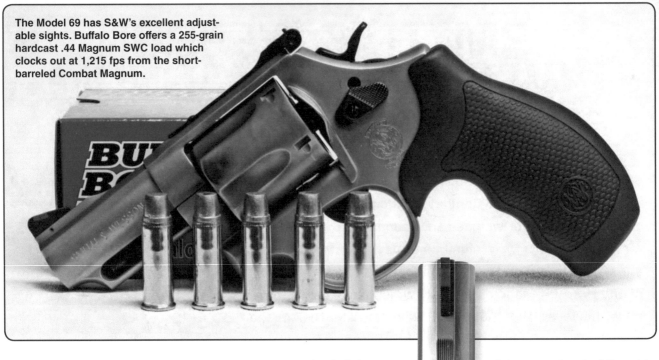

The Model 69 has S&W's excellent adjustable sights. Buffalo Bore offers a 255-grain hardcast .44 Magnum SWC load which clocks out at 1,215 fps from the short-barreled Combat Magnum.

with the matte stainless steel of the rest of this excellent big-bore revolver.

The front of the cylinder is chamfered for easy holstering and the muzzle has a deep concave crown that protects the rifling. The right side of the barrel is marked in two lines with "44 Magnum" and "Combat Magnum." The pebble-grained rubber grips are the wraparound finger-groove style. The single-action trigger pull on my test gun was 4-1/4 pounds, while the DA pull measured 14.

The cylinder locks at the front of the frame with a modernized version of the old Triple-Lock setup instead of locking at the front of the ejector rod. This is

The Model 69 is the first to bear the barrel marking of "Combat Magnum." The barrel is a 2-piece affair consisting of the barrel proper and a shroud.

accomplished with a ball-detent at the juncture of the frame and yoke. Since this is a 5-shot .44 Magnum, the locking bolt notches on the cylinder are in between chambers so there's no weak spot under each one.

Thus far I have test-fired the short-barreled Combat Magnum with both .44 Special and .44 Magnum factory loads and handloads, including both jacketed and cast bullets. Since this is mainly a self-defense revolver, all of my testing to this point has been at a normally accepted self-defense distance of 7 yards or 21 feet. It shoots so accurately with every load tested I have no doubt it will certainly perform well at longer distances.

I used nine .44 Special loads (5 factory, 4 handloads) and eleven .44 Magnum loads (7 factory, 4 handloads), for a total of 20 different loads. The "worst" .44 Special load grouped in 1-1/8 inches while the tightest shooting Specials measured 3/4 inch.

With the .44 Magnums the results were even better. This surprised me—especially considering how much concentration it now takes for me to shoot full-house .44 Magnum loads in such a relatively lightweight sixgun. This time the worst load measured an inch, while the best put 4

shots into 1/2 inch, followed by three loads measuring 5/8 inch and three other loads measuring 3/4. This is astounding, again, at least in my hands, from such a short-barreled, heavy recoiling pistol.

It was especially gratifying to find two of my favorite .44 Magnum loads both grouped into 5/8. These were the Black Hills 240-grain JHP (which has been a favorite hunting load for several decades now) and the other my everyday load of the Lyman 431244 Thompson gas-checked hardcast bullet over 19.0 grains of 4227 right at 920 fps. I appreciate having the option of more powerful loads if needed, however, this relatively easy-shooting number will handle most of my sixgun chores these days.

I still miss the old classics with their hand-fitted, forged steel parts, pinned barrels, and cylinders recessed for case heads. The amazing thing to me is any time I've tested any one of the 21st century sixguns against the old classics, the new version always wins both in durability and accuracy. This latest Combat Magnum is certainly no exception. It's a fine revolver and I like it.

A SLICKER SNUBBIE
PART 1: TURN YOUR S&W J-FRAME INTO A "J-PLUS."

After a lifetime of shooting medium and large-frame revolvers, developing a crush on S&W J-Frames late in life brings with it a steep learning curve. A J-Frame is a beautiful thing, but is less forgiving of shooter error than, say, a 6-inch Model 14 K-Frame. Tons of practice can overcome it, but some alterations and/or additions to the revered Snubbie Platform can help. So without further adieu, let's examine a few.

A 3-inch J-Frame like this M49 has undeniable dimensional disadvantages over a 2-inch gun, but the added sight radius can pay off, as this slow-fired 50-foot DA group shows. The ammo? Black Hills .38 Sp. 125-grain +P JHP.

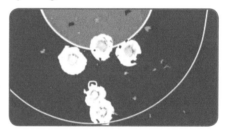

SPRINGS AND SIGHT RADIUS

The sight radius on a 2-inch J-Frame means you really should do everything you can to "cheat." Replacing the trigger return spring can really improve the double-action pull, but if you go too low on the poundage it can cause trigger return issues. As far as mainspring replacement, well, as Elmer Fudd might say, "be *vewy, vewy* careful" about going too light there as well. Your CCW snubbie is *not* the gun you want to have primer poppin' issues with.

We got a set of trigger return springs from Brownells as well as some replacement mainsprings from Wolff. On one M49 we left things alone, but for another we lapped the trigger return spring block and swapped out the stock 15-pound spring for a 13 pounder. It made the trigger a lot smoother and ignition was still 100 percent. Another "customy" touch? We replaced the original narrow, grooved trigger with a slightly broader smooth-faced one, which my shooting buddy Thomas Mackie just happened to have floating around in a spare parts bag. This made things even sweeter.

AN EXTRA INCH

Another way to cut down the difficulty of shooting a 2-inch gun is to simply find a model variant with a 3-inch barrel. That extra inch of sight radius helps a lot, not to mention the velocity enhancement (with select loads) a 3-inch has over a 2. Want an example? We found Black Hills 125-grain +P JHP to average 867 fps from a 2-inch Model 60 and 953 fps from a 3-inch Model 36. But be that as it may, most serious J-Frame packers go for the 2 inch.

One thing we learned: Learning to shoot a 2-inch well requires practice. It's kinda funny how guys will shoot the living hell out of their nice adjustable-sighted, 4- or 6-inch K- or L-Frames when those will likely not be the Smith they'll have on them in an emergency. And that may be one reason I finally decided to start seriously fooling with J-Frames.

Unless you're contemplating using a snubbie in Slowfire Bull's-eye Competition, any J-Frame is—for all practical purposes—"double-action-only" despite the mechanical specifics of action type. Of course, lacking the courage of my convictions I simply can't jettison the single-action option totally with one of the Centennial-type "hammerless" variants, which may explain my fondness for Smith's hump-backed Bodyguard style with its shrouded—but still thumb-able—hammer.

But recently I've had the opportunity to shoot S&W's Scandium 340PD, a very cool Centennial-type variant which—even though billed as a .357—does not mean you're required by law to use the darn things in it. Unless of course that's all you can find

Thomas Mackie's mini-workshop for swapping out trigger return springs from Brownells, mainsprings from Wolff, a stone for lapping the trigger return block and assorted tools, lubes and potions. But don't go too light on the trigger return spring, let alone the mainspring!

IT'S ALL IN THE BREAK

In the course of tormenting myself with an all J-Frame diet, I asked our resident snubbie guru Roy Huntington for some real-world practice tips. He's packed, cursed, loved, and shot them for many years as a copper. Here's what he had to say:

"Sight picture ain't as important as trigger control—which is paramount. I like to stage those J-Frame triggers. Like any Smith, they have that subtle "two clicks" as you press.

Press to that first click, then at the second one—as the bolt clicks home into the cylinder—press it like a single-action trigger. Eventually, the two clicks will become one smooth press. But you "feel" them to know when the final let-off is due. What works for me is to shoot a 6-inch DA revolver first. Then move to a 4-inch, then a 3-inch J- or K-Frame if you have one. Then—and only then—go to that finicky 2-incher. Practice this regimen—in the same order—in one session. And keep the trigger press the same for each gun."

You've heard the word. Let us all grab a bucketful of wadcutters and hit the 15-yard-and-under range.

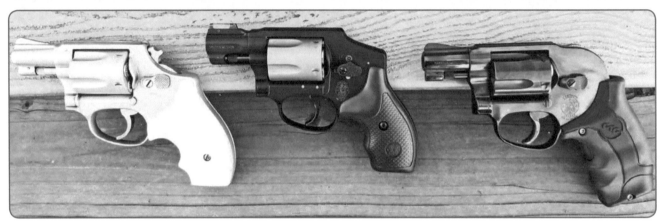

S&W's J-Frame model numbers and options come and go, but the 3 main types are typified by (left to right) the: M60 exposed hammer (although the spur has been bobbed here), M340PD "hammerless" Centennial-style, and the M49 Bodyguard with a shrouded-but-thumb-cockable hammer. The 340PD sports factory synthetic stocks. The M49 has Crimson Trace LaserGrips. The M60? Eagle Grip's Secret Service-pattern polymer "mother-of-pearl."

(or you're as tough as a 2 dollar steak). But the 340PD is feathery light at 11 ounces unloaded. One other thing, the trigger pull on the one we shot was just about 9 pounds, smooth, and shorter than the one on our doctored M49. So maybe I came to this "hammerless" concept a bit late as well.

Editor Jeff, a fan of the Centennial style, put it this way: "The whole geometry of the trigger stroke just *feels* different." Using Buffalo Bore's Tactical Low-Flash, Low Recoil 158-grain .357 load, the 340PD proved plenty accurate at 50 feet. Still slammed me a bit, but Thomas didn't seem to mind at all. It clocked at 1,070 fps and might be the top choice if you simply gotta take advantage of the .357 option (we'll cover this snubbie in-depth in an issue or two).

Since you're dealing with fixed sights, it's best to find a serious "carry load" hitting at point of aim at snubbie yardages. With my 3-inch M49 this turned out to be Black Hills 125-grain +P JHP. It groups very well, but more importantly hits POA. Since this is

stout stuff from a J-Frame, I searched for a relatively inexpensive practice load which shoots to the same (or reasonably close) POA and is a bit kinder and gentler on me *and* the gun. I still feel (based on some long-ago advice) if you're going to shoot a J a whole lot, you want a non-alloy item. But although I do love pinned barrels and carbon steel, the 340PD is awful nice…

But back to my semi-cheapo practice load, which turned out to be Winchester USA 130-grain FMJ, a very easy to shoot number generally available in bulk pack format at Walmart. In lieu of that, Aguila's near-identical item worked just as well. Standard Black Hills 148-grain Match wadcutters shoot amazingly tight, but too much "low right" for my M49 at 50 feet. But from our 2-inch M60 they were money in the

bank. Handloaders, of course, have more load-tailoring latitude.

With most of our 2-inch guns, Federal Premium's 130-grain HST JHP +P load shot pretty much to POA, and from Thomas's 2-inch M49 delivered spot-on 3-inch 50-foot groups. Which leads me to believe the guys at Federal—who concocted this stuff specifically for snubbies—knew what they were doing. *(To be continued next issue).*

Payton Miller

A SLICKER SNUBBIE
PART 2: GRAB AND GO ESSENTIALS.

In this wrap-up of the J-Frame snubbie column we started last issue, let's deal with a couple of critical items. And since they're the first thing you grab, let's start off with grips. OK, *stocks* for you nomenclature purists.

First, the obvious. Use whatever you shoot best with. Whatever orients your gun properly at first grab, whatever is most comfortable with heavier loads (including those nasty magnums) and—if concealability is an issue—whatever leaves the smallest "footprint."

Today's S&W J-Frame lineup offers a lot more options than the skimpy, old-school walnut panels I recall from early *Shooter's Bibles*. Today, you can get sculpted, hand-filling "comfort enhancement" in walnut or synthetic persuasion. If comfort is paramount, the extended "3-finger" style is likely to appeal to you. If maximum concealment's your goal, a shorter "2-finger" style is probably going to do it. We're not talking pocket autos here, so an extended magazine "pinky perch" isn't an option. It's either 2 or 3 fingers, although the very comfortable Crimson Trace LG-350 LaserGrip kind of splits the difference, besides offering "low- and no-light" utility.

This is by no means a knock on those old-style minimalist service grips. A lot of guys still prefer them (although some add Tyler-T grip adapters) because they are unquestionably "speedloader friendly," which is not always the case with beefier stocks.

SPEEDLOADERS

Speaking of speedier reloads, a lot of snubbie users like Bianchi Speed Strips. I'm more comfortable with the bulkier HKS speedloader (the model stamped "36" with the telltale 5 holes instead of 6). There

These S&W Model 49s sport two excellent aftermarket grip options. At top is Eagle Grip's Secret Service pattern in rosewood. Built for concealability, it's one of the best abbreviated options out there. At bottom is Altamont's longer Altai Silverblack. It combines good looks with the kind of comfort you'll appreciate with +P ammo—or (shudder!) magnums.

NUCLEAR NINE

A new 9mm load from NovX Ammunition combines the ARX copper/polymer projectile concept with a stainless steel casing. In other words, no brass, no lead. Their Engagement Extreme load features a fluted 65-grain projectile with a claimed muzzle velocity of 1,575 fps and a rotational speed of 116,000 rpm. We tried some out at 20 yards using a 3.4-inch barreled Kahr K9 over sandbags. Evidently that ARX bullet works nicely with the K9's polygonal rifling. Our 4- out of 5-shot groups were at 2 inches and, more importantly, were only 1-1/2 inches under our point-of-aim, which surprised us.

Frankly, we had no idea where the speedy little 65-grainer was going to impact. The K9 in question, incidentally, puts Black Hills 115-grain JHPs only about 2 inches higher at that yardage. Our chrono results were 1,513 fps—very impressive considering barrel length. Recoil was negligible from our all stainless steel Kahr. The extreme spread was a mere 20 fps. This stuff retails for about $27.99 per box of 26 (that's a little over a buck a round for the math-challenged). They also offer a +P version of this same load that should bump the fps factor up even further. But this stuff is *plenty* fast as is. For further info, contact NovX Ammo, (912) 988-3019.

are a couple J-Frame models available cut for 5-shot moon clips, such as the Performance Center Pro Series M442. Or there are conversion outfits such as TK Custom or Pinnacle High Performance who do it. Personally, I've only used moon clips in N-Frames before, but this sounds like a good idea. Those .38 conversions will work with or without the moon clips.

Of the J-Frame holster styles we tried, the majority were inside-the-pocket ones, which are about perfect for guys wearing pants (short or long) with roomy pockets, or vests with pockets. The three we tried—Blackhawk's Tecgrip, the DeSantis Nemesis

SPIN CLASS FOR BOOMERS

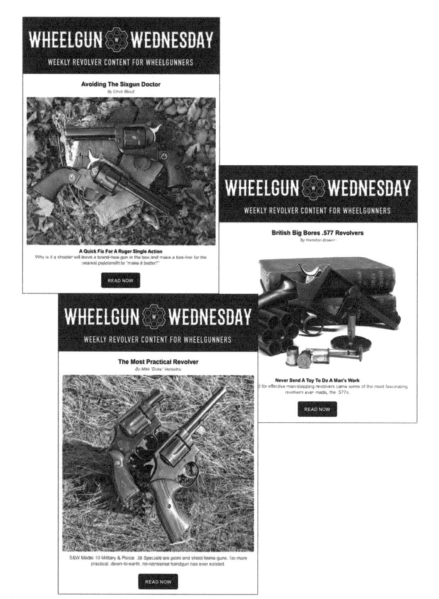

Eagle Grips' Secret Service pattern grips are as comfortable to shoot with as an abbreviated concealable set is going to get. And (below) they don't interfere with an HKS speedloader.

and Galco's Pocket Protector were relatively "synthetically inexpensive," ranging in price from $18.75 to $25.99. All featured a grippy outer surface to keep the holster in your pocket as you draw your gun. All of them worked well for us, however, the Blackhawk Tecgrip can be had for 3-inch snubbies. The other two, of course, can house a 3-inch gun, but some barrel is going to be sticking out the open end.

3 RULES

At this point we should probably hit on the obligatory cautionary notes as regards pocket holsters. (1) Always use them. Never carry a snubbie loose in your pocket. I've heard horror stories regarding dimes working their way into places on pocketed snubbies you *really* don't want them to be. (2) Keep your "carry pocket" reserved for your holstered snubbie only—nothing else. No car keys, penknife or loose change. (3) Never reholster with the holster in your pocket. Take out the holster, insert the gun, and *then* return the whole enchilada to your pocket. Oh, and the business about keeping your finger out of the triggerguard during a draw goes double here.

www.GunsMagazine.com/index, Altamont, (217) 643-8145, BLACKHAWK, (800) 379-1732, Crimson Trace, (800) 442-2406, DeSantis Holsters, (800) 424-1236, Eagle Grips, (800) 323-6144, Galco Gunleather, (800) 874-2526

2ND CHANCE Smith

RE-LIVING YOUR YOUTH? IT CAN HAPPEN.

J.B. WOOD

Those who have followed my writings over the years will know I'm an auto-pistol person. So, they may be startled to learn my first handgun was an old revolver! It was a classic top-break .32 Smith & Wesson. The time was 1948, and I was 14 years old. With my father's OK, it was purchased from an elderly antique dealer named Bell Smoot in Elizabethtown, Ky.

J.B.'s first gun was a S&W named (simply) the Double Action .32 S&W.

He replaced it recently with this 4th Model. After replacing the broken grips, J.B.'s otherwise very nice Double Action .32 is up and running.

The price was $15 and I had saved up enough from small gunsmithing jobs to pay for it. It was carried on several camping trips in the Colesburg hills, and was once fired to discourage a bobcat from entering the food-tent. A few years later, it was, alas, traded off for my first auto-pistol. Hey, in those days, the only way to get another gun was to trade what I had.

Now, let's fast-forward about 65 years to late in 2016. A local guy wanted to dispose of an inherited handgun. When I saw what it was, I had to have it. A .32 S&W top-break, in excellent condition except for the original hard-rubber grip panels which were chipped and broken. This time, I paid a lot more than $15 for it.

I knew where to get replacement grips: Vintage. Founded by David Byron, the company was later sold to a nice lady in Florida. Subsequently, she passed it on to Triple K, a firm already noted for replacement magazines and fine leather-goods.

Triple K has maintained the extremely high quality of Vintage grips. Once, many years ago, I obtained a set of SAUER 38H grips from Vintage, and noticed on the inside, they had German military acceptance markings. I called to tell them that mistakenly, they had sent me their pattern originals. But no, the copy pair was just that good.

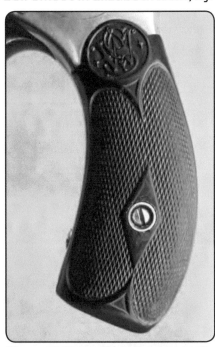

The superb Vintage/Triple K replacements for the broken original grips fit very well.

On my "new keepsake" Smith & Wesson, the grip edges were a perfect fit. I had to alter slightly the depth of the recess for the stabilizer cross pin at the bottom. Old S&Ws have some variation there. Well, it's good to sort of have my first handgun again, and think about those camping trips. This time, I'll keep it.

www.GunsMagazine.com/index,
Triple K, (619) 232-2066

Payton Miller

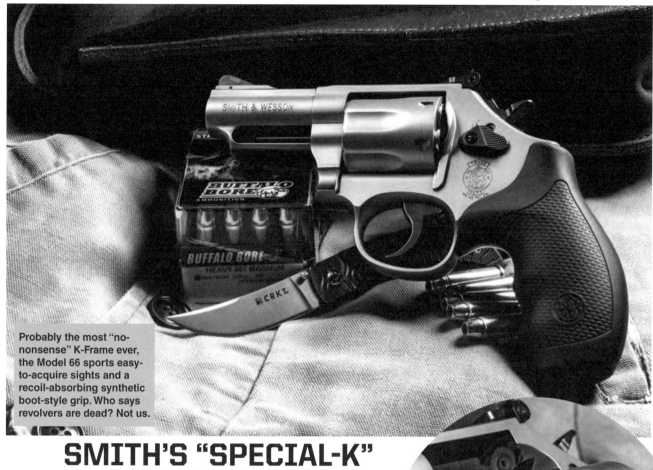

Probably the most "no-nonsense" K-Frame ever, the Model 66 sports easy-to-acquire sights and a recoil-absorbing synthetic boot-style grip. Who says revolvers are dead? Not us.

SMITH'S "SPECIAL-K" MODEL 66 .357
RESURRECTING A "SUPER SNUBBIE."

In 1971 S&W introduced a stainless-steel version of their Model 19 .357 Magnum. Without rehashing the history of Bill Jordan's K-Frame M19 dream gun, the M66 — as it was listed — became a go-to tool for cops and we mere citizens, much as the original blued version (introduced in 1957) had been.

The Model 66's superiority to the previous models of fixed-sight, skimpy stocked service revolvers was — like the groundbreaking M19 — readily apparent. Excellent adjustable sights and the ramped front blade allowed proper zeroing throughout the considerable velocity and bullet weight/style range of .38/.357 loads.

If there was a gripe with the M19/M66, it generally concerned the perceived inability of the K-Frame to withstand large doses of .357 Magum pounding. I've heard arguments to the effect this is an exaggeration. It may be or it may not be, but whatever it is probably has a lot to do with your definition

Two enhancements to the new Model 66 Combat Magnum include a sleeved barrel (left) and a ball-detent lockup point (above) shown here after an obvious range session!

of what "large doses" of .357s constitute. I've shot my share of M19s and M66s and all I can say is this: I got tired of the magnums well before the guns did!

The fact of the matter is, with a couple

of exceptions (notably Remington's 125-gr. Golden Saber and a couple of Buffalo Bore "Low Flash, Low Recoil" offerings), the .357 is probably pretty abusive to medium-frame guns over the long haul. Anyone seriously contemplating shooting a ton of mags had better get a bigger, heavier gun. Smith did compromise, however, with the larger, heavier L-Frame M586 introduced in 1981.

Perhaps because of the popularity of autos in the LE market, or the success of the L-Frame, the Model 66 was discontinued in 2006. But there's a lot of K-Frame addicts out there, and the Model 66 was reintroduced two years ago in 4.25" trim. Now the company has introduced the "snubbie" version which — to many — is still the ultimate carry gun. And I'm tending to agree.

OLD AND NEW

Next to my Model 15, my original 2.5" M66 (a 66-1 actually) is probably my all-time favorite K-Frame. So naturally the first thing I did was a comparison between it and the new Model 66 Combat Magnum. The three main points of departure for my old model are its pinned barrel, recessed charge holes and a hammer-mounted firing pin. The new gun's barrel is 2-piece (shrouded) and is 1/4-inch longer, having a commensurately longer ejector rod/housing too. Then there's the ball-detent lockup most likely intended to pacify those who might fret about magnum wear. I don't fret about it because I don't shoot mags that much. Oh, the new M66 is just about three ounces heavier than the original.

The matte stainless construction on the newer model appears duller than my old gun, plus the new one has a black trigger, hammer and cylinder release latch. I left the skimpy walnut service stocks on my old gun. My only concession toward enhancing things was the addition of a Tyler-T grip adapter, which forever solved any problems of speedloader clearance. The new gun has a synthetic Hogue-style boot grip, which is very comfortable and presents no obstacle to an HKS speedloader.

Both the double- and single-action trigger pulls on my "new model" M66 were excellent. A very smooth 11 lbs. for the DA and a crisp 3.5 lbs. for the SA.

RANGEWORK

The gun shot well as we worked our way through five commercial .357 loads and four .38 Special ones. The sights are excellent, featuring a fully adjustable rear

"I'VE SHOT MY SHARE OF M19s AND M66s AND ALL I CAN SAY IS THIS: I GOT TIRED OF THE MAGNUMS WELL BEFORE THE GUNS DID!"

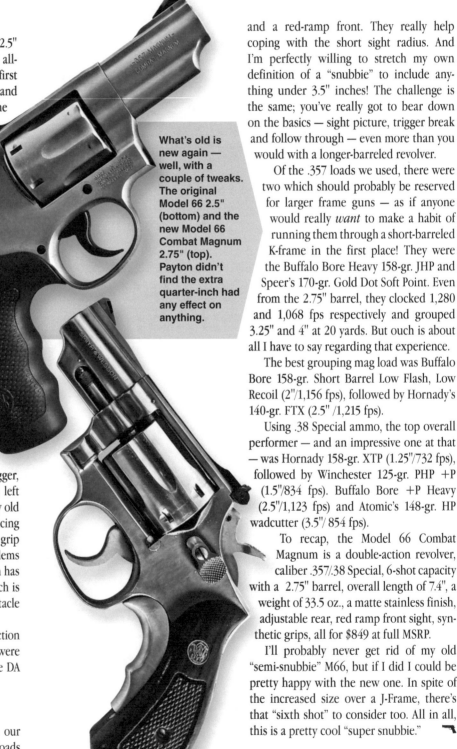

What's old is new again — well, with a couple of tweaks. The original Model 66 2.5" (bottom) and the new Model 66 Combat Magnum 2.75" (top). Payton didn't find the extra quarter-inch had any effect on anything.

and a red-ramp front. They really help coping with the short sight radius. And I'm perfectly willing to stretch my own definition of a "snubbie" to include anything under 3.5" inches! The challenge is the same; you've really got to bear down on the basics — sight picture, trigger break and follow through — even more than you would with a longer-barreled revolver.

Of the .357 loads we used, there were two which should probably be reserved for larger frame guns — as if anyone would really *want* to make a habit of running them through a short-barreled K-frame in the first place! They were the Buffalo Bore Heavy 158-gr. JHP and Speer's 170-gr. Gold Dot Soft Point. Even from the 2.75" barrel, they clocked 1,280 and 1,068 fps respectively and grouped 3.25" and 4" at 20 yards. But ouch is about all I have to say regarding that experience.

The best grouping mag load was Buffalo Bore 158-gr. Short Barrel Low Flash, Low Recoil (2"/1,156 fps), followed by Hornady's 140-gr. FTX (2.5" /1,215 fps).

Using .38 Special ammo, the top overall performer — and an impressive one at that — was Hornady 158-gr. XTP (1.25"/732 fps), followed by Winchester 125-gr. PHP +P (1.5"/834 fps). Buffalo Bore +P Heavy (2.5"/1,123 fps) and Atomic's 148-gr. HP wadcutter (3.5"/ 854 fps).

To recap, the Model 66 Combat Magnum is a double-action revolver, caliber .357/.38 Special, 6-shot capacity with a 2.75" barrel, overall length of 7.4", a weight of 33.5 oz., a matte stainless finish, adjustable rear, red ramp front sight, synthetic grips, all for $849 at full MSRP.

I'll probably never get rid of my old "semi-snubbie" M66, but if I did I could be pretty happy with the new one. In spite of the increased size over a J-Frame, there's that "sixth shot" to consider too. All in all, this is a pretty cool "super snubbie."

www.GunsMagazine.com;
Smith & Wesson, (800) 331-0852

DRIFTING BACK TO IRON

HEAVY LEVERAGE

AN ULTIMATE FIGHT STOPPER

WANT MORE?

THE NIGHTHAWK CUSTOM AGENT 2

RUGER 10/22 CUSTOM COMPETITION

THE ESSENTIAL OPTIC

IL-BOSSIN' TRAPPERS

URUS .357 MAGNUM RAGING HUNTER

OUT OF THE BOX

S&W'S MODEL 340 PD
A MAGNUMIZED WORKHORSE

Payton Miller

"Well," said my shooting buddy Thomas Mackie, massaging his right hand with only a slight grimace, "now I can say I've done it…."

The "it" in question involved lighting off five reasonably quick rounds of .357 Magnum from a J-Frame S&W snubbie with a minimal curb weight — specifically, the lightweight 340 PD.

"A .357 Magnum option is okay, I guess," he said, once circulation had returned to his hand. "But I sure wouldn't wanna make a *career* out of it."

"You remember the way old-timers used to describe these kinda guns?" I asked. "Carry a lot, shoot a little." A cute punch line for sure, but a too-flip description of an excellent carry snubbie — a cool heir to a long line of Smith J-Frames.

There's also a flip-side to the "Plus-P's Plenty for Me"

argument and I've heard it from very knowledgeable CCW types. Basically, it's "give me all the power I can get!" With the 340 PD, you're free to explore all ammo possibilities, but very few are going to want .357s for regular practice.

NON-SNAG, LOW DRAG

The original S&W Safety Hammerless ceased production in 1940 but the concept was resurrected in 1952 as the Centennial. Today there's a J-Frame subset of these "hammerless" models exhibiting the same simplicity of operation making their predecessors so highly regarded.

This "simplicity" of course, involves the tacit acceptance you're going to be shooting a snubbie double-action anyway. So why even deal with the option of

Power in a compact package is the key to the 340 PD's appeal. And those factory synthetic grips give clearance to an HKS speedloader.

May the force be with you: S&W's ultralight 340 PD. The unconventional bit of cutlery used for window-dressing? Spyderco's Squarehead. Photo: Joe Novelozo

At 50 feet the best .357 results were with Buffalo Bore's 158-gr. Low Flash, Low Recoil JHPs. The top .38 Special performer, shown here, turned out to be Speer 135-gr. Gold Dot +P at 1.75".

"hammered" single action? After all, it could provide just one more level of distraction should it ever come time to use the gun in the type of emergency it was designed for.

The 340 PD — at $1,019 MSRP — is obviously a premium offering, featuring a 2-piece sleeved barrel, scandium frame and a titanium cylinder. There's a small stainless steel insert in the topstrap right above the forcing cone, appearing to act as insurance against "flame-cutting" from the high pressures of magnum loads. From the left side it looks like a little silver horizontal "J" against the dark anodized scandium.

There's also the admonition *No Less Than 120-Gr. Bullet* etched on the bottom of the barrel sleeve. I'd surmise this is to caution anyone from using short, lightweight screamers that could be more likely to jump the crimp. It's a perfectly sensible caveat. Having a tied-up CCW gun would be the nightmare of nightmares — one from which you might not awaken.

The bright green HIVIZ fiber optic front sight is very quick to acquire. Blessedly, the flat-top bracket for it provides a whisper of "square post" sight picture to make grouping the gun easier. On top of this, the scandium/titanium combo makes for a distinctive 2-tone silver/black effect.

LET'S GET SHOOTIN'

The dimensional rundown is cut-and-dried Smith snubbie: A 2" barrel, 6.3" overall length, 5-shot cylinder and synthetic grips. The kicker, naturally, is the 11.2-oz. weight and magnum potential. We only took advantage of the .357 chambering

Concessions to "magnum force" included a stainless steel J-shaped insert to combat flame-cutting in the scandium topstrap. The green fiber-optic front speeds up sight acquisition.

enough to try a pair of magnum loads. The first was Buffalo Bore's Low Flash, Low Recoil 158-gr. JHP. The other was SIG's 125-gr. Elite V-Crown JHP. From the 340 PD the 158 was stout. And (not to whine too much) the 125 — at 1,128 fps — was *brutal*.

Once we passed the Manly Magnum Test, we thankfully returned to the .38 Specials. At 50 feet we grouped the following .38 Special loads: Black Hills 148-gr. Wadcutter (610 fps), Black Hills 135-gr. +P JHP (843 fps), Federal Premium 130-gr. HST JHP +P (770 fps), Speer 135-gr. GDHP +P (780 fps) and Aguila 130-gr. FMJ (648 fps).

Five-shot groups from sandbags ranged from an outstanding 1.75" (Speer 135s) to 2.25" (Black Hills 148s) to 3-3.5" for the remaining .38s. With the full-pop SIG 125-gr. .357 JHPs we managed to put four out of the five in 4". With the more manageable Buffalo Bore 158-gr. Low Recoil mags we managed to stick three out of the five in 1" even, although the remaining pair were about 3" left of that.

For grouping purposes from a rest, carefully staging the DAO trigger is what we did. It was smooth and consistent — with a slight hitch tipping us off at the pause point. However, it should be noted everything from this test gun shot a bit left — probably inconsequential at close range. But if this gun were mine, I'd do something about it after first settling on a carry load and a practice load that hit reasonably close to one another.

www.GunsMagazine.com/index;
S&W Ph: (800) 331-082

More Here:
americanhandgunner.com

S&W'S M&P .380 SHIELD EZ

AN EASY-TO-MANIPULATE DELIGHT

JEFF JOHN

If you have trouble working today's semi autos, look no further than the S&W M&P P380 Shield EZ 2.0. The key thing to look at is the "EZ" — because that's exactly what it is. By building a bigger, locked-breech .380, S&W made manipulation easier for those with hand-strength issues. Even with the hammer down, cocking effort is only 12 lbs., and about a half-pound less if the pistol is cocked. And a semi-auto action is easier on hands and wrists because it extends the felt recoil duration.

The new Shield EZ is lightweight at 21.5 ozs. with a full 8+1 payload of 95-gr. ammo. It's got an ambidextrous thumb safety (you can order it without one), a grip safety, internal firing-pin block, full-length grip — all my fingers fit, and mag changes don't pinch my pinky — easy-to-see 3-dot sights and an accessory rail.

The frame is polymer, and the slide and 3-5/8" barrel are of stainless steel with an Armornite finish. Overall length is 6.7", providing a longer sight radius than most of its contemporaries, and it comes with two magazines, all for a budget-friendly $399 MSRP.

EZ ERGONOMICS

Along with stylish serrations at the back of the slide are two small "wings" at the end of the slide. They don't rise so high they become snag points as they're "melted" into the slide some, but really give your fingers the extra leverage.

The trigger is smooth and light and has only a hint of take-up before breaking at 4-3/4 lbs. If you like single-action autos, you'll adapt to this one fast. The triggerguard's inside mold-line is light, and didn't raise the usual blister other polymer-frame guns give me. There's also no "in-the-middle-of-the-trigger-face" safety lever either.

The extractor rises above the ejection port to provide a tactile loaded-chamber indicator and the fixed 3-dot sights are windage-adjustable only. They give a great sight picture, but as my eyes age I prefer a bit more daylight between the front blade and rear notch. I'm sure there will be after-market sights for the EX soon if you want a change.

The gun will fire with the magazine removed, which I think is a good thing. The mag catch is reversible and easy to reach and the mag well is generously sized for fumble-free changes. The mags drop free easily too. The slide stop — directly above the mag catch — is unobtrusive, and due to its rounded shape, it's easy to manipulate.

HAMMER-FIRED

You don't have to squeeze the trigger to fieldstrip this gun. The takedown latch is on the left side under the ejection port, so you just clear the gun, lock the slide back and depress the lever.

Not a tiny "pocket" gun like most .380s, the EZ is specifically made to be fumble-resistant, with controls and surfaces scaled to be manipulated easily even by people with limited strength and mobility. Photo: Roy Huntington

S&W's Shield EZ has excellent nightstand manners, especially when equipped with the Crimson Trace Rail Master Green Laser. The A.G. Russell Ti FIST is a "one-finger flick" folder as easy to deploy as the pistol.

Then ease the slide forward, and push it forward off the frame with your thumb. The recoil spring is captured, and won't fly loose. The head of the guide is diamond-shaped and the spring must be oriented correctly upon reassembly. But all in all, the EZ *is* easy.

I shot 2-handed offhand groups at 15 yards from a rifle rest mounted to a camera tripod. Before grouping the gun, I shot it for fun at clay targets to break it in and get a feel for it. During the first couple hundred rounds there were a couple of minor fumbles where the slide didn't go into battery once and a stove pipe with a loaded cartridge surprised me. But once I hit the 200-round mark, things sailed along. That's not uncommon when breaking in a new semi-auto so keep that in mind when you buy one! Things need to "settle in" some and it's perfectly normal. One maker even recommends at least 500 rounds to break-in!

THE "SHORT 9" SHINES

Modern bullet technology has enabled the current crop of .380 loads to punch far above their weight. All I used shot to about the same point-of-aim vertically at 15 yards, with some veering a little more left than others. The average for all the groups was just over 3" with a few groups going well under. Three loads tested — Black Hills JHP (935 fps), Fiocchi JHP (904 fps) and Hornady American Gunner (945 fps) feature Hornady's proven 90-gr. XTP. All three were 100 percent reliable and the most controllable.

The hotter Hornady Critical Defense — topped with the 90-gr. FTX — stepped out at 968 fps and features low-flash propellants. It has a plastic tip filling the hollowpoint to aid expansion and keep the cavity from filling with material that might restrict expansion.

One other specialty load I tried was Black Hills Honey-Badger, featuring a Lehigh Defense 60-gr. bullet at an impressive 1,137 fps. This load shot to the same vertical point of aim as the heavier ones but to the left a bit. A non-expanding load, the HoneyBadger bullet is nonetheless highly effective and its light weight still assures up to 18" of penetration. Being solid, it also performs well against barriers in self-defense situations.

The point of the Shield EZ is a gun large enough to manipulate without strain, in a caliber still adequate for defense. It is both things, indeed. Magazines are also very easy to load. I did not find them any harder to fill

Hornady's Critical Defense 90-gr. FTX bullet and their more-affordable American Gunner have bumped up the performance of the .380 ACP.

with eight rounds at the end of the day than at the beginning. There's a small button on the side you can use to depress the follower to make loading even simpler, like you see on many .22 auto magazines. I found it was just as easy to depress the top round with my left thumb and insert the next one as you would normally load a magazine.

A BIT OF A DRILL

As a "graduation exercise" I shot a 9-shot group with each at 15 yards. The Fiocchi put six shots into 1-1/2" and the overall nine into 3-1/2". The Honey Badger put six shots into 2-1/2" with three errant shots pulling out the group to 5". The vertical stringing with the HoneyBadger load is likely due to my constant fight with 3-dot sights. I prefer to level the front blade with the top of the rear blade, but when the dots are aligned, the front post dips a little. Operator error there, but keep this in mind if you're having the same issue.

In shooting long strings (like nine shots in a row), little lapses in concentration quickly become evident. I'm sure aligning the dots instead of the blade caused the vertical, but wind ended the day, and successive storm fronts precluded me from going out again to prove it. Putting six of nine tightly gives me confidence the gun will deliver — if I can tighten the loose nut behind the trigger.

GREEN LIGHT THIS IDEA!

A laser sight is a natural for the Shield EZ and Crimson Trace has been a go-to source for them for decades. Their new Rail Master green laser is much easier to see during daylight in a red vs. green comparison. It tucks neatly out of the way on the rail below the Shield EZ without the use of the

The slide ends in "wings" on both sides to aid grasping. They're melted, hardly noticeable, but really improve the leverage needed to rack the slide. If you have trouble running a slide, the EZ is for you.

The day's accuracy winner was Fiocchi's JHP and Black Hills' HoneyBadger. These 9-shot groups were shot at 15 yards. Jeff's POA was dead center of the Pro Shot Splatter targets.

All controls are easy to reach on the Shield EZ. The action can also be cycled with the safety "on" which is significant.

The sights are of the 3-dot variety. The loaded chamber indicator looks like it's high enough to interfere with sighting, but it doesn't.

Nine to Five ain't just a movie title: The S&W Shield EZ isn't much larger than a J-Frame .38. But it's flatter and holds those nine rounds!

extra plates supplied. I generally prefer the laser dot to show just above the front sight rather than where the bullet strikes, which is usually under the front sight.

In practice, I took too much time looking for the dot when zeroed for the bullet's impact, since the dot was under the sights and I couldn't see it! I found hit speed and accuracy was better in dim light practice if I used the laser as a guide to acquire the iron sights, which I've long trained to do.

Regardless of the sights used, the Shield EZ is an easy-racking, easy-loading .380. It's an excellent beginner's self-defense gun and the "manual of arms" to run it is simple and easy to learn. It's a tool those lacking physical strength can use with confidence. The EZ may change the concept of using autos for limited mobility users!

Editor's note: Some very early production Shield EZs (including our test sample) have a minor issue with the safety moving to the "on" position when using ammunition producing a high level of felt recoil. S&W will upgrade the safety of any EZ produced prior to April 4th, within a certain serial number range. Call (800) 331-0852 or email MP380EZAdvisory@smith-wesson.com to see if your pistol qualifies. You will be instructed on how to proceed if it does.

www.GunsMagazine.com/index; S&W Ph: (800) 331-0852; Crimson Trace Ph: (800) 442-2406; Proshot Products Ph: (217) 824-9133

S&W .22 VICTORY TARGET MODEL
PRECISE AND NICELY PRICED!

John Taffin

Every new shooter, whether using rifle, sixgun, or semi-auto pistol should start with a .22. The reasons are obvious and all of them promote practice — little recoil, low noise level and relatively inexpensive ammo.

One of the finest .22 target pistols ever offered is the Smith & Wesson Model 41. It's for serious target shooters and — due to its price — won't appeal to everyone. But several years ago S&W offered a very reasonably priced Victory Model and now we have the Victory Target Model priced at only $429 and probably available at local gun shops for under $400.

The Victory Target features target sights consisting of a fully adjustable black rear matched up with a ramped, black post front. The target trigger has an adjustable trigger stop. The Victory also features a match-grade, 5.5" stainless bull barrel, stainless steel slide and frame, a polished feed ramp and beveled magazine well. It comes with two 10-round magazines with a button on the side to depress the magazine spring for easy loading. Weight unloaded is 36 oz. I find the Victory Target balances perfectly in my hands.

A Picatinny-style rail is included for scope mounting. To install it, remove the front screw on the rear sight assembly to allow the entire assembly to slide off and be replaced with the rail, rings and scope.

The cocking piece at the rear of the slide has serrations to help manipulate the slide, which does *not* stay open on the last shot. I prefer all semi-auto pistols of any caliber to have the lock-open feature on the last shot. This lack is the only negative thing I can find with the Victory Target Model.

The pistol comes with two sets of polymer grips — one set with a thumb-rest on the left panel, one set with a thumb-rest on the right. This allows you several options. Mine was to use both panels without any thumb-rest whatsoever. Grips are highly subjective and the two plain panels feel best to me. I also like the overall texture of the grips — and the somewhat round-bottomed backstrap. Both the front and rear backstrap

John ultimately put a 4X scope on his Victory Target Model. Installation is easy with the supplied Picatinny rail.

are checkered and match up with the grip panels giving a very secure feeling while shooting.

AN EXTENSIVE AMMO MENU

Shooters often buy a new .22 along with one box of ammunition — or at least just one brand — of ammunition and are then disappointed to find their new acquisition doesn't perform as well as expected.

I've always figured it takes at *least* 10 different types of .22LR ammo to find out exactly what a gun prefers. With the Victory Target I enlisted 20 different types of ammo from six different manufacturers. The only malfunctions that occurred can be traced to ammunition — CCI's Quiet .22 didn't have enough energy to work the slide.

But the more I shot, the better the Victory Target performed. In fact my shooting partner Denis claimed the more we shot, the closer the Victory Target got to the performance level of his cherished Model 41!

One of the first loads we tried was the Federal Champion HP, which clocked out at 1,065 fps. When the gun had less than 50 rounds through it, this particular load grouped just under 2" for nine shots at 15 yards. But after I'd run 200 more rounds through

Variety is the spice: The Victory Target was tested with a variety of standard and high-velocity loads.

the barrel, the same load grouped in 1". Some pistols just need some break-in time.

The two most accurate loads I found were the Remington Thunderbolt and Winchester's T22 Target with both giving 3/4" groups. Other loads in the 1" neighborhood included CCI Standard Velocity (925 fps), Winchester 333 HP bulk pack, (1,030 fps), Winchester Power Point HP (1,085 fps), Winchester Wildcat HP (1,120 fps) and Remington Golden Bullet (1,085 fps).

Formal bull's-eye target shooting is no longer anywhere near as popular as it was when I was a kid, however, plinking,

varmint and small game shooting, and rimfire silhouette are all extremely popular. And for these purposes, the Victory Target would be as good a choice as it would be for punching paper.

The Victory Target Model is a welcome addition to my accumulation of .22 semi-auto pistols from at least a half-dozen manufacturers. The stainless steel construction and polymer grips make it suitable for outdoor carry in a proper holster and it is also accurate enough with the right loads to handle anything we might expect a .22 pistol to do.

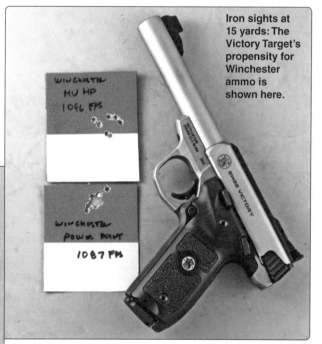

Iron sights at 15 yards: The Victory Target's propensity for Winchester ammo is shown here.

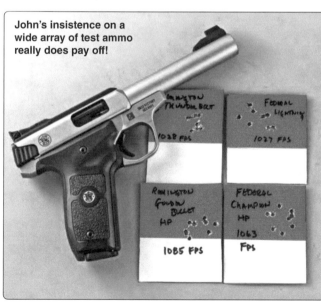

John's insistence on a wide array of test ammo really does pay off!

The next step for me is to do some concentrated shooting with a 4X scope in place that helps to remove some of the human error. Since the scope base comes with an integral rear sight, I went with quick-release mounts that allow me to use the scope, then remove it when iron sights are called for or when I want to carry it in a holster.

This kind of versatility I like.

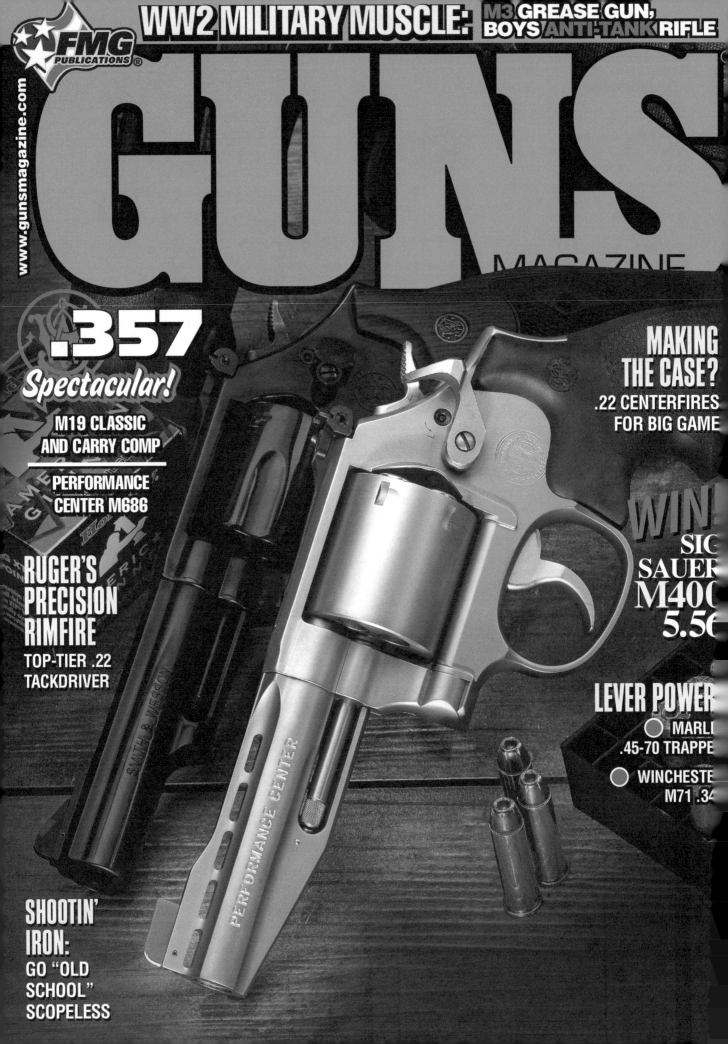

FMG PUBLICATIONS®

www.gunsmagazine.com

WW2 MILITARY MUSCLE:
M3 GREASE GUN, BOYS ANTI-TANK RIFLE

GUNS
MAGAZINE

.357
Spectacular!

M19 CLASSIC AND CARRY COMP

PERFORMANCE CENTER M686

RUGER'S PRECISION RIMFIRE
TOP-TIER .22 TACKDRIVER

MAKING THE CASE?
.22 CENTERFIRES FOR BIG GAME

WIN!
SIG SAUER M400 5.56

LEVER POWER
- MARLI .45-70 TRAPPE
- WINCHESTE M71 .34

SHOOTIN' IRON:
GO "OLD SCHOOL" SCOPELESS

Looking for more?

S&W's 686 PC is a competition-class thoroughbred for discerning wheelgun addicts. And it's an L-Frame as opposed to the blued K-Frame M19. Roy's is the 4" six-shot version.

BIG GUN
LITTLE GUN

JOHN TAFFIN

PHOTOS: **ROBERT JONES/
THE IMAGESMITH, LLC**

S&W'S M19 CLASSIC,
CARRY COMP &
PERFORMANCE CENTER 686

In 1955, Smith & Wesson introduced the .357 Combat Magnum which would become the Model 19 two years later when the company went to a model-numbering system. It was offered on the .38 Special M&P K-Frame instead of the standard .357 Magnum N-Frame. This resulted in a weight reduction of approximately 1/2 lb. This, coupled with the smaller cylinder, made the Combat Magnum very desirable to those who carried a sixgun all day.

This medium-framed magnum concept came about at the prompting of double-action legend Bill Jordan, who envisioned it as a sixgun to be shot mostly with .38 Specials and loaded with .357 Magnums while "on duty." But over the years .357 ammo changed, with more and more shooters going to 110- and 125-grain fast steppin' loads which soon took their toll on the thin forcing cone of the M19. Because of this, the M19 was replaced with the L-Frame Model 586 with a larger cylinder and forcing cone diameter while still maintaining the M19 grip frame (see sidebar for Roy's adventures with the L-Frame).

THE CLASSIC

My original M19 has been in use for well over 50 years with nary a problem, however most of my loads have been with cast bullets. In 1967 S&W made two significant changes to the M19/Combat Magnum. They round butted the grip frame and cut the barrel lengths to 2-1/2" making it much easier to conceal. The first report I saw of this sixgun was by

The reintroduced M19 classic sports a slightly longer barrel than the 4" original but sports the original "Combat Magnum" stamp. Photo: Roy Huntington

Cop-carry classic: The M19 — Bill Jordan's dream gun — is a manageable, medium-frame .357. Photo: Roy Huntington

BIG GUN
LITTLE GUN

GUNS®
MAGAZINE

DECEMBER 2018

M19 CLASSIC, CARRY COMP & PERFORMANCE CENTER 686

Perfectly framing the .357 Magnum — the blued M19 Classic "K" and the stainless, non-fluted "L" PC 686.

LET'S UP THE ANTE TO L

A fully adjustable rear completes the sight picture. Note the "teardrop" hammer.

S&W's Performance Center 686

Roy Huntington

Like most of you, I'm a die-hard revolver-guy. At an S&W unveiling late last year, they showed off the 4" 6-shot model of their new Performance Center 686 (along with the 7-shot "Plus" Model with a 5" barrel — cut for moon clips). Being a semi-old guy with a big gray mustache, I sorta' stood out from most of the fit, muscled young writers and bloggers in attendance. During test firing, I noticed the revolvers were gathering dust as the string of fancy-new autos got worked out *hard*.

So I spent some quality wheelgun time and soon found a few of the younger fellows watching. They eventually asked me questions like "How do you shoot a revolver like that?" — since I was actually *hitting* the targets. I explained to a couple of them about staging triggers and shooting only DA and stuff like that. They nodded. Then they went back to autos.

After the dust settled from an informal shoot-off they had among us, I found I was first, and Mike Humphries, Executive Editor at *American Handgunner*, was second. Suddenly we got stared at. But I know why we did well. We cleaned the plate racks with the revolvers, while most of the younger guys had to slow way down, still leaving lots of plates standing. All of which shows wheelguns are still fighting tools, as well as great fun in competition — even rock-solid for home defense too. And these new Performance Center L-Frames are at the top of all those categories.

THE CUSTOM TOUCH

Not long ago it used to be that in order to get the sorts of features on this 686 duo you had to spend big bucks on custom mods to an already pricy base gun. Our test gun had the Performance Center over-sized cylinder release, orange front sight (you can swap it

Skeeter Skelton. He said "I *like* it."

The original M19 was dropped in 1999 with a special run, the M19-8 chambered in .38 Special in 2000. This is a very rare M19 with just over 200 being manufactured. The stainless version — the M66, arrived in 1975 and lasted until 2004. Now both are back with the M66 Combat Magnum arriving last year and now the M19-9.

It took 20 years but our patience has finally paid off; the M19 Combat Magnum is back. The original was available in Bright Blue or nickel. Although the original guns from 1955 to 1957 were cataloged as Combat Magnums they were not marked as such. This resurrected version is the M19 Classic and has a Bright Blue finish representative of the original, but it differs in that it is marked on the left side of the barrel "Combat Magnum" and the barrel length is 4.25" instead of 4" as on the original. The official model number is 19-9 — meaning there have been nine changes since the M19 arrived nearly 65 years ago.

For added strength for those magnums, it features a ball-detent locking point.

Except for the relatively unnoticed increase in barrel length and the 21st Century internal changes common to all S&W sixguns, this latest version looks much like the original. One difference not immediately noticeable is the fact the grip frame is round butted and the grips themselves are of the round-butt to square-butt configuration.

Sights are excellent consisting of a fully adjustable black rear sight mated up with a red ramp front sight. Cylinder and frame are both carbon steel while the barrel is stainless steel. Weight is just over 37 oz.

I shot it with a variety of .38 Special and .357 Magnum loads from Buffalo Bore, Hornady and Black Hills with all loads performing well. With Black Hills .38 Specials, both the 125-gr. JHP and the 100-gr. Honey Badger ATX put five rounds in 1-1/4" at 20 yards with muzzle velocities of 900 fps and

out), tuned action, unfluted cylinder, vent-rib barrel, hard chrome trigger with stop and a custom teardrop-shaped hammer spur on the hard chrome hammer. I found through use, the teardrop shape is there, I

A sleeved, vent-ribbed barrel is capped off with an easy-to-acquire orange blade that can be swapped out.

think, to offer clearance for the over-sized release.

The smooth trigger is somewhere between a standard and a classic target trigger in width. "Just right" comes to mind. Grips are Hogue-style (might even be made by them, I'm not sure). The cylinder has a conventional lock-up, with a detent for the front of the ejector rod and the standard rear-locking pin protruding from the ejector star into the recoil shield. Timing was spot-on, and the action smoother than most standard production revolvers of the brand. I'm a picky guy and I think a touch of the hands of an S&W action master could turn this into a spectacular action easily and without much work at all. For most shooters, I think it would be fine and would shoot-in soon.

COMPETITION, COMBAT, CRITTERS

At an affordable $966 MSRP for either model, you essentially get competition-ready guns right out of the box. The bright

front sight, all-steel construction, fast cylinder release, slight muzzle-heaviness and great actions make these contenders for the weekend competition warrior. And — as skills progress — lend themselves to more custom touches like enhanced actions, different sights, grips and more. There's also a wide-range of holsters in both leather and synthetics fitting the L-Frame models.

Shooting the test 4" Model, I found it to be typical S&W. What I mean is, it *loved* .38 target wadcutters. At my backyard range shooting off the porch, it was pretty easy to hold 1.75" groups. Everything worked fine and there were no misfires, showing the action was light, but still reliable. The over-travel stop was set perfectly.

These are both burly, stout guns easily able to handle full-power .357 Magnum loads and I fired a few for fun. No issues at all, and the weight and good grips made it actually enjoyable. Either of these guns could double as a hunting revolver. The oversized cylinder release is easy to find and sure under your thumb, the ejector works perfectly allowing full-length case ejection and that bright

Speed solution: The extended cylinder latch is a typically innovative Performance Center touch.

orange front sight jumps right out. You could also mount a dot sight or scope on one using various after-market mounting systems and have a good field gun.

The new Performance Center 686 models are handsome, well-conceived, solidly made and work as-advertised. What's not to like there?

1,050 respectively.

My most used .357 Magnum load is the Black Hills 125-gr. JHP. It's my turkey hunting load, and with an accurate sixgun it's no problem to take the head off a turkey with it. In the newest M19 it clocks 1,350 fps and groups 1-3/8". A most interesting alternative is the Buffalo Bore .38 Special 150-gr. Hard Cast Wadcutter. At 935 fps (plus excellent accuracy) it makes a very good "anti-personnel" load.

I've been shooting M19s since the early 1960s. This latest version does not have as smooth an action as my original, however, it's stronger and shoots better and is most assuredly more comfortable — so much so in fact I don't have to mostly shoot .38 Specials — .357s will get the nod most of the time. I don't question the sixgun standing up to heavy doses of them.

THE CARRY COMP

Another new model is the Performance Center M19-9 with a 3" barrel. The Carry Comp is designed for CCW. Now snub-nosed .357s are notoriously hard kickin' when it comes to felt recoil. Because of this I started my test-firing with a lot of .38 Special loads and found it felt more like shooting a .22. When I switched to .357s I expected to pay the price, however, I found the felt recoil was more like a .38 Special. There are always trade-offs in life and the trade-off here is the reduction in recoil goes along with an increase in noise. Shooting .357s with jacketed bullets is always a noisy proposition, but in this case is even more so because of the PowerPort vented barrel. This consists of one large port in front of the front sight and it really does its job recoil-wise. I'll happily accept the increased noise for the decreased upflip.

The sights on the Carry Comp consist of a fully adjustable rear sight matched up with a tritium front night sight. Two sets of grips are included — one is custom wood with checkering and finger grooves designed for concealed carry with an open back strap and fitted flush with the bottom of the butt.

The second set — which I used for extended sessions — is a synthetic rubber boot grip with finger grooves. It covers the back strap and also extends below the butt. These also help keep felt recoil at a minimum.

The cylinder, frame and barrel shroud are carbon steel while the barrel itself is stainless. Weight is just over 34 oz. and the MSRP is $1,092.

"THIS IS SOME LITTLE SNUBBIE. ACCURATE AND EASIER TO SHOOT THAN A J-FRAME AND DARN NEAR AS EASY TO PACK!"

John even tried some Black Hills .357 158-gr. stuff in the Carry Comp and found the results to be impressive. The port cut in the top of the barrel right in front of the Trijicon Night Sight may have helped some! Photo: John Taffin

John isn't crazy about .357 Magnum recoil these days, but he found the M19 Classic remarkably accurate with Black Hills .38 Special 125-gr. JHP +P. Photo: John Taffin

Sensible solution: The Carry Comp comes with two sets of grips — a finger-grooved walnut set for concealed carry and a longer rubber boot grip for lengthy shooting sessions. Photo: John Taffin

Since this is a sixgun designed for concealed carry, all test-firing was at 7 yards. Sixteen different .38 Special loads were used with the average for five shots at 7 yards being right at 1" or less. Black Hills 125-gr. JHPs clocked out at 770 fps with a 1-1/8" group. Others included Black Hills 100-gr. Honey Badger (935 fps and 1"), Speer Gold Dot 125-gr. JHP (855 and 3/4"), Buffalo Bore 150-gr. Hard Cast WC (890 and 7/8"), and Hornady 140-gr. XTP-JHP (715 and 7/8"). Most accurate? Hornady 158-gr. XTP-JHP (635 and 1/2").

Switching to the more serious .357 loads, I continued to have the same accurate results with the Black Hills 125-gr. JHP at 1,275 fps and a five shot group of 1". Then came Black Hills 158-gr. JHP (1,055 fps and 7/8"), SIG 125-gr. FMJ (1,250 and 7/8"), HPR 125-gr. JHP (1,120 and 1-1/8"), and the Cor-Bon DPX 125-gr. JHP (1,135 and 1").

This is some little snubbie. Accurate and easier to shoot than a J-Frame and darn near as easy to pack!

S&W'S PERFORMANCE CENTER
MODEL 986 9MM

PROOF EVEN MARK CAN LEARN SOMETHING NEW

MARK HAMPTON

The 7-shot titanium cylinder uses moonclips for fast reloads and reliable operation.

When His Editorship suggested I do some work with a Smith & Wesson Performance Center gun I was eager to jump on the ship. This was until I found out the gun was a 2.5" 9mm revolver. While I didn't say anything with my "outside" voice, I was certainly thinking, "What am I going to do with this?" After all, don't we have enough semi autos of every conceivable configuration available in 9mm? Why does anyone need a 9mm revolver? It was challenging, but I tried my best to go into this project with an open mind.

Right off, and against my better judgment, I liked the looks of this little revolver. It came with a nice hard case and two moonclips included. The gun itself is attractive, with a glass-bead finish and nice-looking wood grips. Fit and finish were exactly what you would expect from the Performance Center — excellent. The titanium alloy unfluted cylinder was cut for moonclips and has a capacity of seven rounds. The slab-sided 2.5" custom barrel wears a

Above, left: At seven yards with American Eagle Syntech ammo the 9mm 986 shot like a laser. Mark feels it'd make a great defensive gun as well as a tidy field gun for potting small game or general back-up work. It's plenty accurate for 25-yard rabbits!

S&W's Performance Center Model 986 in 9mm with 2.5" barrel is a lot of gun in a small package.

recessed precision crown with *Performance Center* etched on the right side, *9mm* on the left. The reddish orange ramped front sight is dovetailed into the barrel. The rear sight is fully adjustable with an all-black square notch.

Those good-looking custom grips are lightly textured and contrast well with the stainless frame. The front of the trigger is wide and smooth with a trigger overtravel stop featured behind the trigger. The rear portion of the hammer spur is serrated and made for reliable cocking in single-action mode. My test gun's trigger broke at 4.3 pounds in single action, minus any gritty feel. The double-action pull was a tad heavy for my likes, but it was crisp and smooth. Overall the revolver tips the scales around two pounds when empty.

Attitude Adjustment

It didn't take long to appreciate the Performance Center tuned action. After all, this is a hand-fitted, hand-tuned revolver and the action is smooth and slick. I'm thinking if you wanted to lighten the DA a bit, you could have the work done, but in all honesty, once I got shooting, I didn't notice any issues at all. I loaded a truck full of 9mm ammo and headed for the range to see how this finely tuned revolver performed.

During the testing phase, with my shooting buddy John, we launched a variety of bullet weights from Winchester, Federal, Black Hills, HPR, Hornady's Critical Defense and DoubleTap. From previous 9mm evaluations I've been fond of American Eagle Syntech ammo — the stuff looking like red lipstick. Their 115-gr. load is clean burning and developed specifically for range work. It's designed to reduce fouling, using a high-tech polymer bullet coating — giving it the lipstick appearance. Most of the range work found 115-gr. FMJ bullets from all manufacturers to work well, but those 77-gr. lead-free hollow point bullets in the DoubleTap line are serious contenders for personal safety.

We engaged targets from 7 to 15 yards with all brands of ammunition. The supplied moonclips made loading

The Model 986 (lower) in comparison to an older Model 37, Airweight .38 Special. The 986 gives you two more shots, modern design and construction, full-moonclip loading and adjustable sights!

easy and quick. Most of our shooting was undertaken in single-action mode, off-hand, since we're essentially handgun hunters forced into this new arena getting to know about defensive revolvers! The gun points well and we could align the sights on target quickly. We never encountered any mishaps during a lengthy shooting session. Wife Karen joined in the fun and I could detect she was enjoying herself — maybe a little too much. I wasn't planning on purchasing this gun but Karen quickly gained confidence in the revolver. After shooting several rounds she said, "This would make a good gun for home protection." And she's right. Low recoil, lightweight, sure reloads and reliable action all translates into confidence, which is what you need in a defensive handgun, right? I'll be writing this check.

New Ideas?

After shooting the PC Model 986, I have experienced a bit of attitude adjustment. I can see where this revolver deserves a respectful position in our shooting gallery. First, it goes along nicely with other semi-auto 9mm guns I have in the arsenal. The same ammo for both types of guns plus you can find cheap 9mm ammo almost anywhere makes perfect sense. Karen enjoyed shooting the S&W as much as we did and she feels more comfortable with the revolver over the semi-auto.

My wife is probably not the only person concerned with personal safety to appreciate the reliability

of a revolver. Karen also enjoys knowing she can shoot this revolver in single- or double-action mode. This 7-shot PC gun makes an ideal bedside piece for home defense. It also serves well as a vehicle gun on road trips since it's compact and handy. It also makes a great little field pocket-pistol when you're away from home. The adjustable sights and good single-action trigger means small game up to 25 yards is a piece of cake.

Semi autos may be trendy today but don't ever think the revolver is dead. For home or personal defense — and especially for revolver aficionados — this S&W Performance Center Model 986 in the classic 9mm makes a good choice for a variety of reasons. Karen wants to keep this one — and this is good enough reason for me. Even old guys like me can indeed learn new things, it seems.

Federal's Syntech ammo uses a polymer coating on the bullets to help keep range pollution down. It does look a bit like red lipstick though!

Unlike many autos, one of the charms of a revolver is it will run any type of semi-auto ammo it's chambered for! Mark had exactly zero glitches during his test.

THE RETURN OF THE

Barrel markings on the current Combat Magnums.

From left to right, .357 Mag. K-Frames: 2½" Model 66, 2¾" Model 66, and 4" Model 66.

COMBAT MAGNUM

Targets fired with the S&W .357 Combat Magnum.

The latest .357 Magnum Combat Magnum is a six-shot K-Frame.

I n 1935 Smith & Wesson lengthened the .38 Spl. and introduced the original .357 Mag. revolver, which is now known as the Model 27. Built on the N-Frame, the new and powerful .357 Mag. became immediately popular with shooters. There was, however, one major drawback — it was a very heavy wheelgun. Some, most notably Border Patrolman Bill Jordan, started calling for a lighter-weight duty handgun. The result in 1955 was the first Combat Magnum, a .357 Magnum built on the smaller K-Frame. In the closing days of 1955 Smith & Wesson also introduced the first .44 Mag., which is now known as the Model 29. Now shooters had a choice of a relatively lightweight .357 Mag. or the larger N-Frame .44 Mag.

However, the .357 Combat Magnum, which became known as the Model 19 and its stainless steel counterpart, the Model 66 which arrived in 1971, experienced problems in the forcing cone area. So, 30+ years ago Smith & Wesson came up with the L-Frame. The Model 586 and its stainless counterpart the Model 686 featured the same grip frame as the original Model 19 while increasing the size of the frame in the forcing cone area and also using a larger cylinder. The barrel also featured a full under lug. This newest Smith & Wesson was not as light and easy to pack as the Model 19/66, however it was much stronger and the problem in the forcing cone area was solved.

RETURN OF THE KINGS

S&W has brought back the classic Combat Magnum in the Model 66 .357 Mag.

K-Frame (top) and the Model 69 .44 Mag. L-Frame (below).

B y the time the 21st century rolled around the Combat Magnum was gone. However, Smith & Wesson has now recently resurrected it as fraternal twins. Featuring "Combat Magnum" markings on their barrels, the two sixguns arrived in 2014 — one as a six-shot K-Frame Model 66 in .357 Mag. and the other a five-shot L-Frame Model 69 Combat Magnum in .44 Mag.

Smith & Wesson reached for the epitome of a "perfect packin' pistol" with the Model 69 Combat Magnum in .44 Mag. This is a stainless steel, five-shot, double-action sixgun. Sights are typical Smith & Wesson adjustable sights with a white outline rear sight matched with a red ramp front sight. The frame screws, hammer, trigger and cylinder release as well as the front and rear sight are matte black finish and contrast nicely with the matte stainless steel of the

SIXGUNNER

rest of this excellent big-bore revolver. The front of the cylinder is chamfered for easy entrance into a holster and the muzzle has a deep concave crown which protects the rifling.

The grips are wrap-around finger-grooved style of pebble-grained rubber. The single-action trigger pull is 4¼ lbs. while the double action measures 14 lbs. The cylinder locks at the front of the frame with a modernized version of the Triple-Lock set up instead of locking at the front of the ejector rod. Since this is a five-shot .44 Mag., the locking bolt notches on the cylinder are in between chambers so there is no weak spot under each one.

The Model 66 Combat Magnum .357 Mag. is not identical to the Model 69, but I think we can call it a fraternal twin with the basic difference being the chambering and it having 6 shots instead of 5. Call this another perfect packin' pistol.

Long & Short of It

So what was left to do with these two sixguns? The answer of course was to turn them into perfect packin' pocket pistols — for large pockets, of course. This

is exactly what Smith & Wesson has done with both of these Combat Magnums, now offering them with 2¾" barrels.

> ## Smith & Wesson reached for the epitome of a 'perfect packin' pistol' with the Model 69 Combat Magnum in .44 Mag.

Test-firing began with the Model 66 and I was soon surprised by the accuracy exhibited at a self-defense distance of 7 yards. I was also surprised at the relative mildness of the felt recoil as well as the very respectable velocities obtained with this relatively short barrel length. The Black Hills 158-gr. JHP clocked out at just under 1,100 fps with 5 shots in an astounding, for me, 1/2" group at 7 yards followed by the Buffalo Bore 158-gr. JHP that grouped in 5/8" with a sizzling reading on the LabRadar of 1,375 fps. Lighter bullet weight factory loads applicable for self-defense also performed exceptionally well. Hornady's 140-gr.

XTP-JHP registered 1,225 fps with a 1¼" group; Speer's 125-gr. Gold Dot JHP, 1,220 fps and 7/8"; and the Winchester 145-gr. SilverTip HP produced a 3/4" group of 5 shots at 1,215 fps.

I was also quite pleased with the results with two of my handloads using Rim Rock cast bullets. The 158-gr. SWC JHP over 15.5 grains of #4227 is just under 1,100 fps with a 1⅛" group while the 180-gr. LBT WFN heavy-weight gas checked bullet with 14.0 grains of the same powder is just over 1,100 fps and a 1" group.

Heavy-Hitter

Earlier I mentioned how I was surprised at the accuracy possible from the Model 66 Combat Magnum. I was even more surprised by what I was able to accomplish with the Model 69 .44 Mag. Combat Magnum. It proved to be even more accurate, and the most surprising thing to me was I was able to keep my concentration during recoil as the Model 69 is just 1 oz. heavier than the Model 66 at 34.5 ozs.

Whether test-firing with factory or handloads, .44 Spl. or .44 Mag. loads, this latest .44 Mag. from Smith & Wesson routinely grouped its shots well under 1" at 7 yards. Buffalo Bore offers several .44 Spl. Options, all of which perform exceptionally well. The 255-gr. Keith load clocked out at 880 fps with a

SHOOTING FOR THE MOON

MIKE "DUKE" VENTURINO
PHOTOS: YVONNE VENTURINO

Smith & Wesson produced this Model 22 .45 ACP as the Thunder Ranch Special circa 2005. Note half-moon clips, full-moon clips and .45 Auto-Rims in speed loader.

THE INS AND OUTS OF WHEELGUN CLIPS AND RIMS

During World War I, the US Army issued .45 ACP cartridges already loaded in half-moon clips designed specifically for Model 1917 revolvers.

24 REVOLVER BALL CARTRIDGES CAL .45 MODEL OF 1911 IN CLIPS
FOR DOUBLE ACTION REVOLVER CAL. .45 MODEL OF 1917
SMOKELESS POWDER   MUZZLE VELOCITY 800±25 FT. PER SEC.
Cartridge Lot No.
Class 47, Div. 1, Drwg. 5   Manufactured by The Remington Arms Union Metallic Cartridge Company, Inc., Bridgeport, Conn.

50 CARTRIDGES
BALL
CALIBER .45 M1911
LOT TW
18086
TWIN CITIES ARSENAL

Whoever at Smith & Wesson was responsible for inventing the little pieces of spring steel commonly called "half-moon clips" should have received recognition. This was prior to the United States' entry into World War I in 1917. Those simple devices made it possible for rimless .45 Automatic Colt Pistol (ACP) cartridges to serve in revolvers. In turn both Smith & Wesson and Colt converted their large-frame sixguns to supplement the US Army's handgun supply during the war's armament emergency.

In a move nigh on unique in American military firearms history, both companies' .45 ACP revolvers were designated US Model 1917, notwithstanding the fact no two parts were interchangeable between them. Colt's version was based on their New Service handgun introduced in 1899. Smith & Wesson's was their large N-Frame, Hand Ejector, 2nd Model revised from the 1st Model only two years prior. Between 1917 and 1919 when the government cancelled orders, the two entities collectively produced over 300,000 Model 1917's.

Back To The Future

As additional proof the idea of a .45 ACP revolver was a good one,

Duke fired this 10-shot group from a machine rest with lead alloy bullets from this S&W Model 25 .45 ACP.

Duke loading S&W Model 22 .45 ACP with .45 Auto-Rim loads using speed loader.

S&W
TRR
M-22
.45

230 hard
AR-R-P
1⅝ Factory

Duke fired this group from his S&W Model 22 .45 ACP revolver using Remington .45 Auto-Rim factory loads with very soft bullets.

note the fact Colt kept the caliber as an option until New Service production ceased in 1944. Smith & Wesson sold Model 1917's commercially until it was revised as the Model 1950 Military. At the same time a target-sighted Model 1950 was also added and five years later a heavier barreled version named Model 1955 Target was introduced. These 1950s-vintage .45 ACP Smith & Wessons became the Models 22, 26 and 25, in the same order. Except for Model 25's which lasted until 1991, the others were dropped in the 1960s.

There is more. Early in this century Smith & Wesson returned to the .45 ACP revolver concept with a variety of Model 22's, among them a 4" Thunder Ranch Special and a 5½"-barreled copy of the Model 1917. At this point I'm stopping because I can say here every one of the above mentioned .45 Auto revolvers have passed through my hands at one time or the other. Several are still here.

Fly In The Ointment

Now allow me to reverse myself. Although I applaud the idea of "half-moon" clips they are seldom used in my .45 Auto revolvers. This is because the little buggers are darn hard to load and unload with my arthritic senior-citizen hands. This isn't a big criticism of the original idea. After all the military wasn't worried about saving brass; only about getting revolvers to function with rimless ammunition. The clips were there to serve as a pseudo rim.

Therefore, I also applaud some unrecognized geniuses who were part of the Peters Cartridge Company circa 1921. American gun buyers evidently thought highly of .45 Auto revolvers but complained about half-moon clips being a nuisance. Bright thinking at Peters

resulted in putting a thick rim on .45 ACP cases. They named it .45 Auto-Rim and it was and is a hum-dinger!

In my considered opinion, the .45 Auto-Rim is the best non-magnum big-bore revolver cartridge. Its ballistics can easily duplicate standard .45 Colt factory loads. If you already handload .45 ACP's all that's required for the .45 Auto-Rim is the proper shell holder. Also, it has been written much in the past that .45 ACP revolver barrels were cut with shallow rifling, therefore they perform best with jacketed bullets instead of lead alloy types. Not so. Take note my sample groups shown with this article.

And now it's time to return to clips. Brass for .45 Auto-Rim isn't uncommon; Starline sells it in bulk. But it's certainly not as common as .45 ACP brass. So naturally this makes many shooters favor cheaper .45 ACP cases. This brings us to full-moon clips as sold by Ranch Products. Instead of 3 rounds, full-moon clips hold 6, in effect becoming speed loaders. Upon first trying full-moon clips I again complained about my fingers having trouble pulling empty cases out. Then I became aware of a small, wrench-like, Ranch Products tool that snaps those empties out with little effort.

Hold Those Horses

It has often been written clips or rimmed cases aren't needed for .45 ACP revolvers. Rimless cases can work fine because headspacing is done by the case mouth on the chamber edge. Then you just use a rod to punch out empties. Most revolvers will work this

way most of the time. The problem is this: A revolver's hammer blow can be cushioned by driving the case deeper into the chamber. With clips and rims, all .45 ACP revolvers will fire all of the time.

Revolvers for .45 ACP were a great idea. They still are. Evidence of their popularity is the fact they have been made to the tune of several hundred thousand over a 100-year period. So, if you want to get on the bandwagon, just make sure you understand their strengths, their weaknesses, and how best to use them. Oh, and be sure to have fun as well!

The only thing needed to handload the .45 Auto-Rim with .45 ACP dies is the proper shell-holder.

GET YOUR HANDS DIRTY

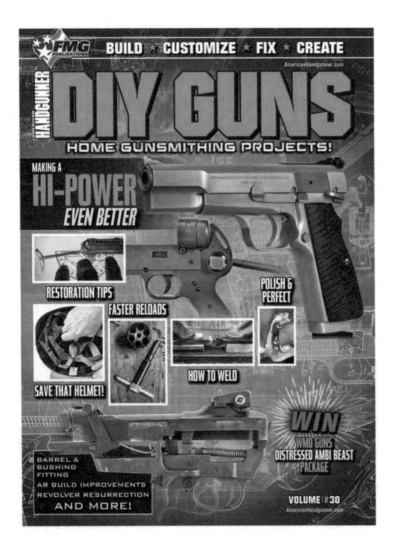

4-shot group at 7 yards of 7/8"; the 190-gr. cast hollowpoint, 1,015 fps and 3/4"; the 200-gr. Wadcutter Anti-Personnel load, 925 fps and 1"; and the Lead-Free Barnes 200-gr. TAC-XP registered 950 fps and a 3/4" group. This is very consistent performance.

Switching to my handloads, the most pleasant shooting Oregon Trail 240 RNFP over 5.3 grains of Trail Boss registered 700 fps and grouped in 3/4" and is definitely a load which can be shot all day long. Switching to a little more powerful load consisting of the Lyman #429421 Keith bullet over my standard 17.5 grains of #4227 was just under 900 fps and also resulted in a 3/4" group. Okay, I had waited long enough; now was the time to switch to .44 Mag. loads. My all-time favorite hunting load in .44 Mag. is the Black Hills 240-gr. JHP. Over the years it has racked up an impressive record of nothing but one-shot kills on Whitetail deer, exotic sheep and a cougar. In my long-barreled .44's this load is 1,300 fps+, however it drops down to 1,060 fps in the 2¾" barrel of the .44 Mag. Combat Magnum. It did shoot incredibly well with 4 shots in 5/8" at 7 yards.

Buffalo Bore also has a variety of .44 Mag. loads which are consistently accurate. The 255-gr. SWC load clocks out at just over 1,200 fps with a 7/8" group and the two Anti-Personnel loads, both of which grouped in 3/4", are the 200-gr. full wadcutter at 1,170 fps and the 180-gr. JHP which tops out at over 1,325 fps from the short-barreled sixgun. Winchester's 210-gr. Silver-Tip hollowpoint is a relatively easy shooting 1,100 fps and puts all of its bullets in a one-hole 1/2" group just barely larger than the diameter of the bullet.

These days I rarely need full power loads and it was gratifying to see my "Easy Old Man Shooting" .44 Mag. load of the Lyman #431244 Thompson Gas Check over 19 grains of #4227 clock out at 920 fps with all the shots in 5/8". This is definitely an everyday carrying load in the short-barreled .44 Mag.

The New Classics

Anyone who is a regular reader knows my heart belongs to the old classics and especially the classic double-action S&W sixguns produced before the 1960s. Long gone are the recessed cylinder case heads, pinned barrels and forged parts. These older guns may stir my soul more than the newer ones; however, we cannot take away the performance these newer guns provide. Any time they are stacked up against my favorite classics, they always win no matter whether the criteria be strength or accuracy. These two new Combat Magnums are no exception.

THE INSIDER™
ROY HUNTINGTON

"Those Damn J-Frames Can't Shoot Worth Beans!"
FACT OR FICTION?

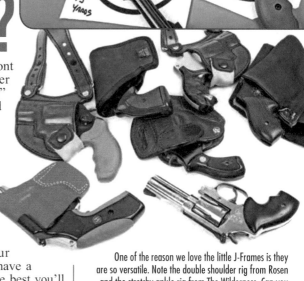

All groups shot at 15 yards from a wrist rest and I didn't really take my time at all. I messed one shot up with the J-Frame but otherwise, you can see the groups are essentially the same.

When I was a cop I used to carry a couple of $100 bills in my wallet when I had range duty. When the various detective units would qualify, some of the dicks simply couldn't hit anything with their various 2" snubbies and would rant and rave about how those guns were "pieces of garbage!" I'd sometimes sidle up next to them — sighing in commiseration at their frustration. Their 7-yard targets often looked like 50-yard buckshot targets. "Yup, (sigh, harrumph) those damn things sure can't shoot," I'd say, looking with disgust at their snubbie. "Hey, I know, use my 4" Model 19 (handing them my holster gun) and have a go at it again. Oh, if you don't want that piece of crap snubbie, I'll give you a hunnert bucks for it right now (flashing the $100 in my hand)." I had pretty good luck sometimes, and scored some cool old guns. If I had a guy who really wanted to learn, though, I'd show them what was needed to hit well and could usually get them up to speed. "Hey, these work pretty good after all!" they'd say. Yup.

I used to shoot the hell out of the little guns using "free" range ammo and learned a thing or three about how to run them. So, what's the secret?

First off, it's not a secret. Everybody knows what to do, but not everybody does it all the time. Let's do a little demystifying of some things.

Start Big

If *all* you own is a 2" revolver, this might be a little harder, but not impossible. If you have other wheelguns, grab a 6" barrel .38 or .357 if you have one. A 4" will do, but a longer barrel to start would be best.

Now for some science. You can shoot a rifle more accurately for several reasons, but the long barrel really isn't one of them — other than it allows a longer *sight radius*. A scope helps too, but that's something different. A long sight radius means you can better see differences in the relationship between the front and rear sights. The longer the sight radius the "finer" you can hold. It's why old school bullseye shooters used to make extensions moving the front sight out farther on a 1911 pistol.

Now translate that to a snubbie vs. a 6" barrel. The longer barrel is easier to "sight" with, the heavier gun helps too — but the real challenge is controlling your trigger press. You'll never have a perfect sight picture, and the best you'll get is "pretty darn good" — so don't mess up what you do have by a cruddy trigger press. The drill is this: Use your longer barreled revolver and practice good sight pictures — and *perfect* trigger presses. Do some dry-firing, then shoot real groups (say, five rounds) at about 15 yards using a good wrist rest. Use light target loads if you're shooting a centerfire. Any decent revolver should be capable of shooting 1" to 1.5" (at most) at 15 yards so "aim" for that.

After it seems you've settled down and are shooting consistent groups, move to a 4" gun if you have one. Do the drills all over again. Don't get spooked by the shorter barrel, both guns will shoot essentially the same size groups. Keep your mind focused entirely on the trigger press. If you're willing to try, shoot it all double action, "staging" your trigger so the very final let-off is almost like a single action even though you pulled the trigger though the DA mode. Get it?

The Acid Test

Okay, now it gets serious. What you've been doing is simply developing your trigger talent. You might be surprised to note the vast majority of "casual" shooters — people who have not had any formal training, which is generally most shooters — usually have terrible trigger skills. That single skill can turn a 15" group at ten yards

One of the reason we love the little J-Frames is they are so versatile. Note the double shoulder rig from Rosen and the stretchy ankle rig from The Wilderness. Can you spot the odd-gun out in the picture? They work great too!

into a 1" group. It's *that* important.

Now it's time to break out your snubbie. Practice dry-firing (it won't hurt the gun at all). Then once you've settled down and think you're working the trigger smoothly, it's time to apply what you've learned. Get your rest sorted out, put up a clean target, wipe your mind clear and don't fixate on "Oh my god, this is the gun I can't hit anything with!" Because, actually, the gun can shoot similar groups. Honest.

Shoot a few rounds. *Think* about what you're doing, what you *did* and how the shots are hitting. If you're pressing smoothly, with no jerks, twitches or hurry, you should begin to see groups which might have shocked you before. If you're not, go back to a longer barrel to get your confidence back. Then back to the snubbie. When I shot PPC matches, they had a "Snubbie" match where shooters used 2" guns out to 50 yards with absolutely amazing results. Often, the top shooters' scores mirrored what most shooters got using heavy-barreled 6" target guns.

Those little guns *can* shoot. You just have to apply a bit of talent — and don't let 'em spook you! Reminds me of that old saying about it being "The jerk behind the trigger, not the jerk of the trigger." Don't be that jerk in either case.

J-FRAME GOODIES

Since we're talking about them, here's a cool way to gussie-up your favorite snubbies and improve their handling. The white grips are Eagle Grips polymer "Synthetic Mother Of Pearl" Secret Service style on a Model 49 Bodyguard. Look for their amazing Kirinite synthetic grips if you'd like a splash of color and pizzazz. Eagle's Rosewood Secret Service grips are on the top gun in the other pic. Below it lurks another Bodyguard wearing Altamont's Silverblack Laminates. Pics are courtesy of Payton Miller, Exec. Editor of *GUNS*. Seems we're surrounded by guys who love these little guns, and are happy to see accessory makers haven't forgotten about us! *For more info: www.americanhandgunner.com/index; Eagle: (800) 323-6144; Altamont: (800) 626-5774.*

MILT SPARKS QUALITY

The Summer Special, originally designed by that icon of holster-making, Bruce Nelson, is the benchmark for IWB designs. With permission from Bruce, Milt Sparks marketed the Summer Special from the early days, and the model has been a mainstay for Milt Sparks Holsters ever since. This is the Summer Special 2, with a few changes from the original. The metal stiffener in the top band (allowing one-handed holstering) and sight rails are there, but the two belt loops are interchangeable in the SS2 to fit different belt sizes. There are also elements of the Executives Companion model, all of which make the SS2 very versatile. This rig shows absolute top-notch craftsmanship, quality of materials and sheer excellence in design. At $110 it's a tremendous value for anyone wanting a no-compromise carry holster for their personal protection handgun. I can't say too much about how impressed I am with this holster — and the company. *For more info: www.americanhandgunner.com/index; Milt Sparks: (208) 377-5577.*

ADD IT UP

250
Exhibitors at first SHOT Show in St. Louis in 1979.

57
Number of exhibitors who have attended every show since — including FMG!

1.8 MILLION
Women hunters in 2001.

3.67 MILLION
Women hunters in 2016 (and growing).

696,449
Chevy car sales in 1948.

$1,381-$1,750
Cost of Chevy Fleetline and Fleetmaster in 1948.

20
Percentage increase in knife crimes in Britain over 2016.

WEBLEY MARK VI MINI

I just love sharing the latest one of these with you. Adding to the growing collection of classic revolvers and autos comes this 1/4 scale hard cast zinc model. They are also Silver electroplated then oxidized to bring out the details. Our own Mike Venturino supplied pics of his original gun to assure this one came out just right! Get your own (and add your name to the list so you're notified when the next one is out) by touching base with them. The price is only $19.95 plus a small shipping charge. I'm having fun watching my own collection grow and you should too! *For more info: www. firearmsassurefreedom.com, email: hamptonweaver@bellsouth.net.*

THE SAINT PISTOL

Our own Mike Humphries attended the release event of some cool new Springfield Armory products lately. According to Mike, "Springfield Armory may have made its name with traditional firearms such as the M1A series of rifles and its line of 1911 pistols, but it has also pushed the envelope with cutting-edge new products. From its voluminous XD line of handguns to the introduction of the SAINT 5.56mm AR-15 rifle series last year, Springfield is staying ahead of the curve. Continuing that pattern is its introduction of the SAINT AR-15 pistol, a shorty variant of the SAINT AR rifle. It's 26.5" in overall length and weighs 5.5 lbs. The pistol is based off of the traditional direct gas impingement system operation of the AR and features a 416R stainless steel 7.5" barrel with a 1:7" twist rate. It's chambered for 5.56 NATO." There's lots more about this new pistol and we'll be covering it soonest. *For more info: www.americanhandgunner. com/index; Springfield: (800) 680-6866.*

BEHIND ENEMY LINES

DAVE ELLIOT

S&W parachutes behind the lines: Sterling Hayden's .357 registered Magnum sported a 6.5" barrel as well as a Call gold bead front sight, squared notch rear sight and checkered "Magna" grips. According to S&W records, it was ordered factory sighted at 25 yards with a six o'clock hold.
Photo: David Elliott

In this promotional photo, Hayden, sporting a Hawley pith helmet and shouldering his M1903 Springfield, demonstrates the correct marksmanship techniques for which the USMC is famed — and feared.
Photo: St. Charles History Museum, St. Charles, Illinois

In this still for the 1952 movie, *Denver and Rio Grande*, Sterling Hayden actually uses his handgun sights in an action sequence, a concept that demonstrably leaves many current tinsel town heroes clueless.

STERLING HAYDEN'S REGISTERED MAGNUM

It might be surprising to some in more recent generations there was a time when many of our celebrities and entertainers were more than just carnival barkers and snowflakes agitating for the latest peculiar social or political cause. People like Jimmy Stewart, Clark Gable, Lee Marvin, and of course, Audie Murphy, to name just a few, were big screen American heroes — for real. Many had real-life bona fides matching or even exceeding the impressive characters they played in the movies. Ideals such as patriotism, courage and sacrifice often shone brightly in the art of their time.

Many of the stars of the day "walked the walk," and those who didn't at least respected those who did. To be sure, Americans living in the time of Hollywood's Golden Age commonly held an expectation the men and women who portrayed their heroes would actually be the real-deal and not merely loud-mouth actors.

One such real-deal was Sterling Hayden — AKA Lt. John Hamilton — was a leading-man who made over 50 movies in the course of his storied career. There were highly memorable roles in such films as *The Killing*, *Dr. Strangelove* and *The Godfather*. He was indeed an American original who led a life as colorful and daring as any.

Silver Star

When WWII broke out, the upcoming star abandoned his lucrative Hollywood contract to fight the Axis. He enlisted in the Marines, was eventually commissioned as an officer and assigned to the OSS. He served in the Mediterranean Theater supporting resistance fighters throughout the Balkans. Hayden's assignments chiefly included coastal reconnaissance and running supplies through the German blockades across the Adriatic Sea. On these missions he drew heavily on his considerable civilian experience as a yachtsman and seafarer.

His exploits were ultimately recognized with the presentation of the Silver Star for gallantry in action as well as a personal commendation from no less than Yugoslavia's Marshal Tito. The *Washington Post* reported the following quote from one of Hayden's 1944 rating records: "He is essentially a seaman and has demonstrated great skill in handling small vessels on clandestine missions along the Dalmatian coast. He has great courage and has shown an almost reckless disregard of his own life where duty is involved."

A Registered Magnum

Hayden's personal sidearm of choice was the relatively new Smith & Wesson .357 registered Magnum, a gift from his uncle before his deployment. According to Hayden, that uncle was also a part-time firearms instructor for the New York State Police.

In his critically acclaimed and introspective 1963 autobiography, *Wanderer*, Hayden describes himself as a new Marine officer reporting for duty in Italy: "He stood six foot five in his leather jumping boots and weighed close to 230 lbs. A British parachute emblem and a small American flag were neatly stitched to the sleeves of his combat jacket. There was also the conventional military insignia, and a .357 Magnum revolver strapped to his thigh." No other clue or rationale is given as to why Hayden chose to carry the big S&W over the M1911. Perhaps fans of wheel guns and high-velocity handgun cartridges need none.

At any rate, Hayden, like many of us, found it easier to acquire a great gun than to hold onto it. He reluctantly sold the pistol to a fellow OSS officer in his unit so he could visit his wife, the legendary British actress and model Madeleine Carroll, who was then a volunteer nurse at an American Army Air Force Hospital in Foggia. The officer, an Army lieutenant at the time, also carried the pistol during combat jumps and brought it home after the war. He had it restored at the S&W factory in 1954 at the suggestion of S&W representative Arch Dubia, whom he met at the National Matches that year.

Memorable Pair

Almost needless to say, the revolver and Sterling Hayden proved a perfect match. Both figuratively, in the audacity

of their character, and, literally, as a custom-crafted gun made to the user's specifications, they were a matched set. Because of the rarity and exquisite workmanship of the Registered Magnum, as well as the then comparatively high-performance characteristics of the cartridge, it takes little imagination to believe the towering Hayden and his long-barreled S&W made quite an impression on the Yugoslav partisans with whom he fought.

It's also a safe bet Hayden's .357 — incidentally along with Patton's famed ivory-gripped version — was one of probably only a few registered Magnums actually carried on the front lines. And most likely the only one carried *behind* them! Truly, it was a unique weapon, for a unique man, in an extraordinary place and time.

Hayden's revolver was ordered with the Call gold bead front sight option, one of at least 10 available on the registered Magnum.

Hayden shoulders a mean looking shotgun while standing with perennial bad guy character actor Timothy Carey on the set of Stanley Kubrick's 1956 film noir, *The Killing*.

Hayden poses for a publicity photo for the 1955 Western *Shotgun*. Hayden's ability to properly and realistically handle weapons required no coaching.

The registered Magnums exhibited stellar workmanship and attention to detail in unusual ways. Concentric circles were closely scored in the sides of the hammer as a means to lessen any potential friction against the internal frame.
Photo: David Elliott

SMITH & WESSON MEETS

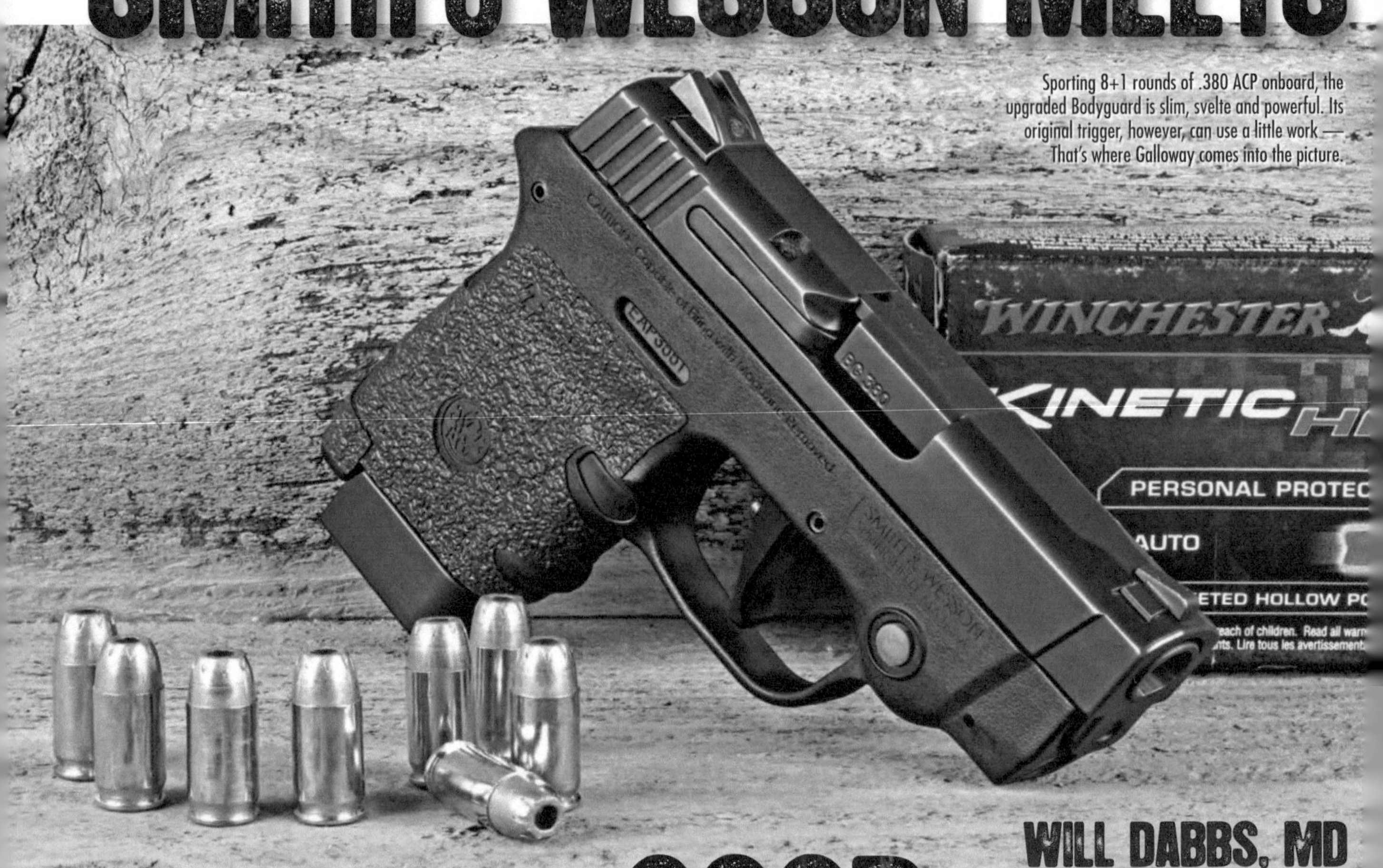

Sporting 8+1 rounds of .380 ACP onboard, the upgraded Bodyguard is slim, svelte and powerful. Its original trigger, however, can use a little work — That's where Galloway comes into the picture.

WILL DABBS, MD

MAKING A GOOD GUN GREAT

The Smith & Wesson Bodyguard .380 ACP pocket pistol is almost — but not quite — awesome. Running on a miniaturized version of John Moses Browning's inimitable linkless recoil driven action, the Bodyguard packs as much power as possible into a truly tiny package. Unlike many .380 pocket guns, the S&W Bodyguard has the same sorts of features and controls you might find on a proper full-sized combat handgun. This aspect alone sets the little gun apart from its peers.

The Bodyguard is legitimately tiny. Weighing a paltry 12 oz. empty and sporting an overall length of only 5.3", the Bodyguard will ride comfortably in the palm of your hand or the front pocket of a pair of jeans. Both front and rear sights are drift-adjustable and cut from stainless steel. The 2.75" barrel is stainless steel and the frame is lightweight polymer. The gun is also available with the niftiest integral laser sight.

What most appeals to me about the Bodyguard are the controls. The gun has a push-

Your standard daily loadout should include a flashlight, a proper blade, a watch and a compact carry gun. Since Galloway Precision's resurrection of my Bodyguard, it's become an EDC gun again.

GALLOWAY PRECISION

Right: The forward latch is for takedown, the middle catch is the slide release and the rear device is the manual safety. Sights are cut from steel and drift adjustable and the mag release is right where it belongs.

The S&W Bodyguard .380 is indeed tiny. By applying some innovative design and materials science the S&W engineers built a pocket gun actually fitting into a pocket.

Here's all the stuff the artisans at Galloway removed and replaced from my Bodyguard.

button magazine catch in the same spot as a 1911, as well as a slide release comparably oriented. There's also a nice crisp manual safety activated with the thumb of the strong hand when firing right handed. If you want it you can use it. If you don't, then just leave it switched off. Everything is easy to access and intuitive to use.

The trigger, however, is an altogether different beastie.

The Bodyguard sports a long, thick, heavy DA trigger. This design offers an added measure of safety for a pocket pistol and provides a second strike capability should your day end up extra-sucky. However, it's really long and heavy. The weight itself is not particularly onerous but the length of pull is, conservatively, about 12 feet. You pull and pull and pull and eventually the trigger breaks, but you have to work for it. Enter Galloway Precision.

Galloway Particulars

Galloway Precision markets themselves as your polymer carry pistol specialists. They upgrade guns from Ruger, Kel-Tec, Smith & Wesson, GLOCK, and SIG offering trigger jobs, magazine extensions, polished feed ramps, and improved guide rods. Galloway takes all these good guns and makes them markedly better. Naturally all of their parts are made in America by Americans.

Galloway offers several different upgrades for the Bodyguard. The first order of business is that atrocious trigger. The Galloway Short Stroke kit replaces the trigger bar with a hardened billet steel component and a new flat-faced Santiago trigger. The Santiago

trigger has a pre-travel stop built into the trigger itself as well as an adjustable setscrew determining post travel. The kit also includes an increased rate hammer spring, a decreased rate blocker spring, and a decreased rate firing pin return spring along with a hammer spring spacer. This kit is the end result of years of experience with the Bodyguard platform, and the trigger is available in three colors.

The next step is to replace the original factory guide rod with a new one formed from billet steel, along with a corresponding 13-pound recoil spring. The Galloway artists then polish the pistol's feed ramp and give the little gun a general once-over, smoothing and deburring the chassis. Lastly, they added a +1 magazine extension to my existing magazine along with a 10 percent increased rate magazine spring. This brings the little gun's capacity up to 7+1 without any significant geometric penalty.

And?

The Galloway transformation is intriguing. The overall treatment does not lighten the trigger pull at all. The pull is simply shortened and made much more crisp. Where previously the trigger just kept going and going, now it reaches a distinct breaking point about 35 percent shorter than the original. This abbreviated trigger travel retains the same safety attributes of the original long double-action design while making the gun much more pleasant on the range.

The 13-pound recoil spring mitigates felt recoil and ameliorates muzzle rise. The .050" hammer spacer increases the hammer spring rate to spunk up the

impact of the firing pin. This makes the gun more reliable with stiffer primers.

On the range the overall effect simply makes the tiny little gun more pleasant to run. Where previously the gun's geometric envelope made it appealing enough to overlook the questionable trigger dynamics, now the gun is actually kind of fun despite its diminutive stature. While a pocket pistol need not be particularly enjoyable to remain effective, a positive shooting impression means better, more frequent training and subsequently more familiarity and positive muscle memory.

Ruminations

The full treatment from Galloway Precision on your S&W Bodyguard .380 will set you back about $200. So long as you don't enjoy some draconian local laws you can legally ship your pistol directly to Galloway for the upgrade and receive the gun back without involving an FFL. Considering this is a piece of equipment upon which I will entrust the lives of my family, the upgrade seems a reasonable investment. Parts and workmanship are all top flight throughout, and they even offer applique grip material to enhance your hold on the gun if desired. As I had already applied a set of thermosetting Talon grips to my gun,

GALLOWAY

such stuff was superfluous. The Talon grips are precision cut and stick in place with industrial adhesive. You then set the cement with a hairdryer, and it stays there for the rest of time.

I bought my S&W Bodyguard .380 years ago because I was enamored with the integral laser and combat style controls. The tiny platform and bantam weight made it easy to tote, while S&W quality meant the gun fit me well and ran reliably. However, the long mushy trigger had relegated the gun to the wall of the gunroom rather than my pocket, years ago. The factory trigger was just so long and stiff I didn't like shooting the gun. If I can't get behind practicing with a handgun it becomes a showpiece rather than a working tool.

The Galloway Precision treatment dropped my S&W Bodyguard .380 back into my pocket. The gun is still the best combination of portability, modest weight, and superb ergonomics of any defensive .380 pistol in my collection. However, now with the Galloway Short Stroke kit installed, the S&W Bodyguard .380 trigger makes the pistol a working gun once again.

Optimized

The 5.5-lb. striker fired trigger on your GLOCK 42 will always be more pleasant on the range than that of any DA-only pistol. However, the S&W guys built the Bodyguard .380 around a double-action trigger for a reason. This gun is not designed to ring steel a football field away. It's intended to ride inconspicuously and comfortably on your person until being called upon to save your life in the midst of the direst of life's emergencies. You want the gun to shoot accurately and reliably every time you pull the trigger, but you must also trust it to be safe when you carry it concealed. The combination of S&W design and Galloway optimization does just that.

If you own an S&W Bodyguard .380 and you plan to use it for real as your daily carry gun you might want to let the artisans at Galloway Precision work a little magic on it. They retain all that is wholesome and righteous about the original firearm and polish out the bad stuff that made it a suboptimal defensive tool. The end result is reliable, capable and more human friendly. My Bodyguard .380 now shoots about as well as it carries. I tote mine regularly and feel ready to face anything unpleasant life might throw at me.

CLASSIC S&W N-FRAMES
THE 1950 TARGET .45 AUTO RIM

This custom 1950 Target .45 Colt was built by gunsmith John Gallagher using a Highway Patrolman and a 1950 Target barrel.

The 1950 Target is rarely found chambered in .45 Colt.

One of our local gunshops, Boise Gun Company, had two 1950 Targets in the case one day. They came from the same collection, both had 6½" barrels and S&W Diamond Magna stocks, however they were not both .44 Specials. One was marked "45 CAL. MODEL 1950." When S&W introduced the 1950 Models with the new short action and improved rear sight they not only made them in .44 Special but also chambered them for .45 ACP/.45 Auto Rim. These are even rarer than those found in .44 Special. I ended up with both after digging up some trading stock!

The roots of the 1950 Target .45 go way back, all the way to 1917. As we prepared to enter WWI we were lacking in firearms and it was immediately found the 1911 .45 could not be manufactured fast enough (See Duke's *Shooting Iron* column in this issue). An engineer at S&W came up with a brilliant idea — the half moon clip. The standard 2nd Model Hand Ejector was chambered in .45 ACP and by loading three rounds in these new clips, reloading and ejection was made easy and reliable.

Some of John's favorite bullets for the .45 AR include the Lyman/Thompson #452490GC and the RCBS #45-270SWC.

THE BIG IDEA

Once you sort out bullet sizing, the .45 AR can be a tack-driver.

In the early 1920s Remington came up with a second excellent idea concerning the 1917. Instead of loading .45 ACPs into half moon clips, Remington decided to simply add a rim to the .45 ACP case. The result was the .45 Auto Rim (AR). It was basically loaded with the same bullets and specifications as the .45 ACP, however over the years we've learned the .45 Auto Rim is perfectly capable of handling the same bullets used in the .45 Colt and can match it in performance with some loads.

My friend the late Jimmy Clark was one of the top pistol marksmen of all time and he was also a superb gunsmith. He won many pistol matches and also developed many of the techniques and upgrades used by pistolsmiths today. In the late 1940s/early 1950s bullseye shooting was king. The standard match called for a .22, a Centerfire and a .45 to compete. Jimmy customized a Model 1917 to shoot the .45 phase. This was before so many pistolsmiths, including Clark, turned their talents to turning the 1911 Government Model into a target pistol.

Here's a typical target shot with the 4" 1950 Target Model .45 AR. Don't you just love those 4" N-Frame Smiths!

When S&W brought out the 1950 Target in .45 Jimmy bought two of them and was disappointed to find they wouldn't shoot his cast bullet loads.

He complained loudly to S&W and as a result the 1955 Target arrived. The latter had several improvements, including a heavier bull barrel, target hammer and trigger, and a barrel cut to better handle cast bullets. The resulting 1955 Target is almost a dead ringer for the .44 Magnum, arriving in late 1955 with the same target hammer, trigger and heavy bull barrel.

I've always heard the story of the 1950 Target .45 not being able to handle cast bullet loads and someday I wanted one just to see for myself. You know how some days seem to take forever to get here, however

Lyman .45 bullets for the .45 AR include #454424, #452424 & #452490GC. John said some .45 AR loads can chase .45 Colt power!

SIXGUNNER

mine finally arrived with the spotting of those two 1950 Target Models at Boise Gun. In 1950 Jimmy Clark was using the same cast bullets used in 1911s and these bullets are normally sized to 0.451". When I put pin gauges through the cylinder throats of the 1950 Target I had, I found every one of them measured 0.455". Perhaps that's the reason they wouldn't shoot cast bullets very well! I sized my bullets to 0.454" and the problem was basically solved.

Versions And Loads

The Model 1950 Target .45 is one of three target version S&W sixguns of 1950. One of the others was, of course, the .44 Special, however the .38/44 Outdoorsman also received the improvements of 1950, so all three are basically the same gun in different chamberings.

The .45 version came standard with checkered hammer, serrated trigger, Patridge front sight and diamond Magna stocks. My example is not totally standard as it has a target trigger and hammer plus a square red bead in the face of the Patridge post front sight blade. I don't know if this is factory or was added later. Although for normal use I prefer the slim barrel of the 1950 Target whether chambered in .44, .45 or .38, I can see why target shooters would prefer the heavier barrel of the 1955 Model. The extra weight just seems to help the sights to hang right on-target.

I have two favorite bullets for use in the .45 Auto Rim. One is from RCBS and was designed for use in the Colt Single Action. It's a semi-wadcutter patterned after the Keith bullet and when using my wheelweight alloy they cast out at 281 grains. Even loaded over 6.0 grains of Universal at 865 fps this is still an awesome load from the old Auto Rim.

My second favorite bullet is from Lyman, designed specifically for the .45 AR although it's also a superb hunting bullet in the .45 Colt. Lyman catalogs it as #452490GC, the GC standing for gas check. This one weighs 255 grains and I also load it over 6.0 grains of Universal for over 880 fps. This one is also quite accurate, with groups running right at 1".

1955 Target

The 1955 Target was put forth as an improvement over the 1950 Target and it was in many ways. However, my example has the same .455" throats found in the 1950 Target, meaning neither one will perform very well with hardball. However even hard cast Oregon Trail bullets sized to .452" work quite well.

The 1950 Target is rarely found in .45 Colt, however the 1955 Target, which became the Model 25, also had a spin off Model 25-5 chambered in .45 Colt. When my friend Paco Kelly gave me a 6½" barrel from a 1950 Target years ago I put it away hoping to someday use it as the basis for a custom sixgun. I finally sent it off with a Highway Patrolman to gunsmith John Gallagher to have it made into a .45 Colt.

There are two problems that can hamper such a conversion. Some of the .357 Magnum cylinders have bolt notches too deep to safely allow conversion to .45 Colt, and secondly the 1950 Target barrels, at least as reported over the decades, would not necessarily handle cast bullets. If it was possible, I asked Gallagher to build a 5" Perfect Packin' Pistol in .45 Colt.

> **Instead of loading .45 ACPs into half moon clips, Remington decided to simply add a rim to the .45 ACP case. The result was the .45 Auto Rim (AR).**

He re-chambered the cylinder, cut the barrel to 5" and re-set the front sight while doing a beautiful job of tapering the rib on top of the barrel to match up with the narrower ramp of the front sight. He tuned the action, set the trigger pull at a beautiful creep-free three pounds, and re-finished the barrel to match the matte blue finish of the original Highway Patrolman. I added an old pair of Skeeter Skelton Bearhug stocks.

Everything worked out perfectly! Using hard-cast bullets or even soft-swaged lead bullets makes no difference to this .45 — it simply puts them all in one hole. Not only do my carefully tailored homebrewed loads do this, Buffalo Bore's factory load with a 255-gr. commercial cast SWC Keith-style bullet cuts one ragged hole, with a muzzle velocity right at 1,000 fps. It's not an original .45 Colt 1950 Target by any means however that makes no difference to me, as a collectible to me is a sixgun that shoots well.

Some of you may wonder why I choose the .44 Special when there are so many .44 Magnums around. Others won't understand why anyone would even bother with the .45 Auto Rim or even the .45 Colt in a custom 1950 Target. The reason is simple. These are all great cartridges, and actually decisions like this don't have to be explained to those who understand. If you have a real sixgunner's heart — you understand perfectly.

WHICH GUN
is right for you?

TURN HERE
for help

americanhandgunner.com

Looking for more?

Try here:

gunsmagazine.com

S&W M&P
.380 SHIELD EZ

A CARRY QUANDARY – QUASHED!

ROY HUNTINGTON
PHOTOS: ROB JONES/THE IMAGESMITH, LLC

The call went something like this: "Hey Roy, can you break free for a quick two-dayer to S&W for a new gun launch?" — it was Matt Spafford, their media liaison guru. "We're announcing something very cool and want to make sure *Handgunner's* there to cover it!"

"Um ... uh ...," I said, doing my best editor impression. "Promise me it's not a polymer frame 9mm and I'll come."

"Ha! I've got you on that, so now you *have* to come. Looking forward to seeing you soon, bye."

For some reason I kept thinking I'd just been had by a professional. I also leaned on Mike Humphries, the executive editor here, figuring if I had to suffer through it, so would he. And just so we're clear — I don't mind polymer

A rail on a .380? You bet — just the ticket for home defense.

CAUTION: Capable of firing with Magazine Removed

M&P

S&W M&P
SHIELD EZ .380

80 AUTO

SMITH & WESSON
SPRINGFIELD, MA U.S.A.

NBZ5086

CE

TLR-8®
STREAMLIGHT.
Patented

autos, and I even own some. I'm just always wishing and hoping gun companies would do something *new* with the concept. We'd see, wouldn't we?

The Big Day

I normally don't talk about the whole "visit the factory" thing as it's just the vehicle to get info to us. But this time was different. Oh, the arrangements were standard, the "Harrumph-Harrumph" handshakes normal, even the meeting room had a PowerPoint waiting breathlessly to get our attention. But it's what happened over the next couple of hours that stands out.

Oh, and here's the part where I say what an idiot I am, by the way.

After the smiles and a few new products were shown, there was a sort of hush, then Jan Mladek, general manager of Smith & Wesson and M&P brands, held the PowerPoint remote button up, pointed it at the computer — there was a collective bit of breath-holding — and he mashed the button.

A black polymer-framed semi-auto appeared magically on the screen.

The breaths were held for a microsecond longer, then a long, sad-sounding sigh escaped about 15 writers and editors.

But we were all wrong. And some, like me, were more-wronger than others.

Jan expected this I think. He smiled broadly and announced, "The new M&P .380 SHIELD EZ."

A .380? But it was big. This wasn't like the Bodyguard at all, or the two dozen pocket .380s currently offered "out there." It was like a regular SHIELD, sorta' (but it had a funny bump on the back of the grip) and might have even been a bit longer. But it was in .380 — begging the question hanging in the air in the room:

"But why?"

There were mutterings, muffled coughs as throats were cleared — and no small amount of shoulder shrugging going on. Including me.

"Mike," I said, speaking behind my hand, "am I being stupid or is this a silly idea for a new gun?"

"I sure don't get it," whispered Mike. But he may have just been being kind to me since I'm technically his boss. Or he honestly didn't get it. Which turned out to be the case. Just like me.

The Gun

The hosts passed out a .380 EZ to each and every one of us as we sat at the tables. There were mini-flurries of motion as guns came out, were cleared and then closely examined. I immediately noticed how easy the slide ran.

"You see," said Jan, "many of our customers are getting older or are infirm or otherwise find it difficult to operate a full-power slide, like one on a 9mm or even a small, pocket .380."

Heads nodded.

"So we thought," he continued, "let's do something different here and make a gun easier to operate and easier to control, taking advantage of the lower recoil of the .380. Hence the SHIELD .380 EZ name."

My brain was still muddled. So we have a "big .380" essentially. But who would carry it? Who would buy it? Why not just get a 9mm SHIELD and learn to run the slide? I'd taught older people to do that very thing. But as I thought about it, I also recalled how they often struggled doing it. And this gun's name is, after all — EZ. Get it?

Outside during a break, S&W's Jim Unger sidled up to me saying, "Well, what do you think?" He seemed proud of what they'd done.

I confessed to him I wasn't "getting" it and just saw a big .380 with a polymer frame.

"Wait until you shoot it and get to know it better," he said, smiling. It was what I'd call a "knowing" smile. I began to doubt my initial thoughts.

Changing Minds

We moved to the range area at the S&W Academy and, while we shot our way through a good-natured mini-competition with a cross-section of new guns, we got to know the EZ. The more I shot it, the more I liked it — and the more I understood what was going on. After about 200 rounds I understood *exactly* why this was, dare I say it — a brilliant idea. On the range, Mike eased up next to me, lifting his muffs, saying, "I get it now. Do you?"

Ta-da. We all were getting it.

The EZ can be had without external thumb safeties — but the grip safety stays.

Re-insert the line about me being an idiot here. But that was before — now I was an advocate.

Ask any gun store sales guy what does he do when a "Uh, we'd like to look at a home defense gun but we don't know anything about guns" customer comes in. He points them at everything from .22 Autos and 4" .38 revolvers to standard sized 9mm polymer guns. Some even show them small-framed revolvers and tiny .380s — shame on them, by the way. Factor in older people — even experienced older shooters — the infirm, many women, younger shooters, etc. and you realize exactly *none* of those guns are "just right" for them.

If you'd ask me before what I'd recommend I'd have gone down that same list. The thought, the very "idea" of what

S&W introduced, had never entered into my sieve-like brain. Why *not* a bigger .380 with an easy to run slide, modest recoil and adequate stopping power? There were a rare few in years passed, but ammo at the time wasn't up to snuff, so we basically ignored them. And they lacked some modern features. Add a light rail, external safety and even a grip safety and you have a defensive auto any beginner could manage.

I realized I was holding an answer to all those challenges.

The Specifics

I've been living with this particular SHIELD .380 EZ for about four months at the time of writing. I've put around 550 to 600 rounds of all sorts of ammo through it. I almost hesitate to say this fearing you won't believe me, but it's

SHIELD but would conceal as easily.

The grip safety pivots on the bottom (like an old 1903 Colt pocket auto) and regardless of how I gripped the gun — including riding the external safety with my thumb — the web of my hand always depressed the grip safety just fine. There's a bit of a beavertail built into the frame and it really promotes a high grip, which is good. There's also small ledges built right into the very rear of the slide to help you get a grip when you run the slide. A marvelously clever touch, especially for older, weaker or arthritic fingers.

The magazine has little nubs on either side of the follower allowing you to pull the follower down as you load. Again, it makes the chore much easier. Honestly, why don't all autos have those?

The gun is actually hammer-fired and not a striker gun, so it's technically single action. You can get it without the external thumb safeties but you do need the grip safety so don't think about pinning it down. The grip safety on the EZ won't allow the gun to fire unless it's depressed and the trigger is pulled fully to the rear. The designers know best on this one.

The sights are white, 3-dot and the rear is adjustable for windage using a supplied tool. Interestingly, you get to it under the sight, in the roof of the slide. A small hex screw is loosened, sight adjusted, then tightened again. The EZ

honestly never bobbled, even once. And in retrospect, I don't recall any of the sample guns at S&W glitching either.

That's essentially unheard of in the world of the .380 and I'm thinking it has to do with the longer slide and "bigger" format. Feeding any auto is all about timing, and being able to run a long slide likely means a slightly slower slide velocity translating to an easier trip into the chamber. Ditto for extraction and ejection. It's why most 5" 1911s run more reliably than the shorty ones.

The mechanics are simple and contribute to the success of the concept. It's got an 18-degree grip angle, like a 1911, and the trigger on my gun measures around the 5-lb. range and isn't bad for a polymer gun. It even has an over-travel stop built into the trigger guard. It also has a top-pivot trigger and no center "safety" flipper thingy. It's a nice, wide, solid trigger. At 6.6" long, the EZ's a bit longer than a standard

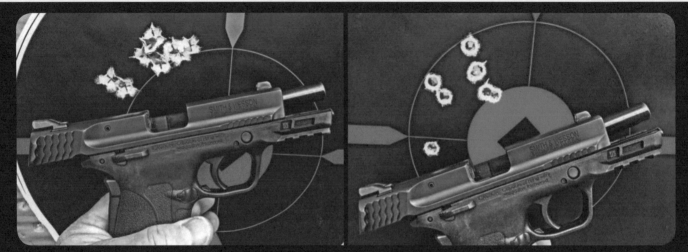

Left: Roy got this group with Black Hills HoneyBadger .380 ACP, a 60-gr. solid copper fluted bullet. Take away the two "bad" ones and that's a 1.25" 8-round group at 25 yards. Not too bad for any auto, much less a polymer .380. Right: SIG's 90-gr. V-Crown .380 smacked this 1.5" 8-round group at 25 if you ignore Roy's oops shot. The EZ delivered consistent, excellent accuracy with most loads.

comes with two, 8-round magazines and both actually hold eight rounds. They're well-constructed, have bright orange followers and are clearly marked for round count. All of this goes toward the "keep it simple" concept.

But Wait, There's More

That slide really is easy to run and it surprises me every time. There's also a loaded chamber indicator you can feel as well as see. The grip texture is like a SHIELD's but seems more modest in texture. I really like it, and it felt like very fine, slightly worn sandpaper.

The magazine release is reversible, but not ambi, so you can put it on the side you favor. Disassembly is easy too, and you don't need to pull the trigger to get it started. Lock the slide back, rotate the take-down lever and the slide/barrel comes right off forward. Easy. Or is that EZ?

There's the normal light rail, and I found mine fits all sorts of lights I had on-hand, so it won't be an issue finding one fitting your budget easily. I actually recommended S&W offer a sort of "Home Defense Kit" to include a simple light. We'll see.

The stainless slide and 3.67" barrel are coated with something S&W calls Armornite — a "keep it from getting rusty" coating. Between that and the polymer frame, there's no need to worry about the daily grind of concealed carry here. Toward this end, my sample gun weighs 18.2 oz. on my postal scale, with an empty magazine inserted. It's light but not so feathery you can't feel it in your hand. It'd be very easy to carry every day, and is a great nightstand gun for home defense for we "average" mortals with some time under our belts.

Shooting Surprises

Just before I wrote this I sat down to do some serious targeting. In previous months I'd kept the EZ on my desk and now and again I'd take it outside and bang away at a couple of plates I keep handy just to get rounds through it. I had fired it off-hand at targets and found it always seemed to hit a bit high and to the left, although it always ran fine regardless of the load. Careful targeting at 25 yards showed it does indeed shoot a bit high and to the left, but close enough "for government work" as my dad used to say. It'll be easy to tweak the rear for windage once I settle on a load I like best.

The thing surprising me was how accurate the EZ actually is. It particularly liked Black Hills 60-gr. HoneyBadger (a solid copper, fluted load) and the SIG 90-gr. V-Crown load. The HoneyBadger averaged about 1,210 fps over my

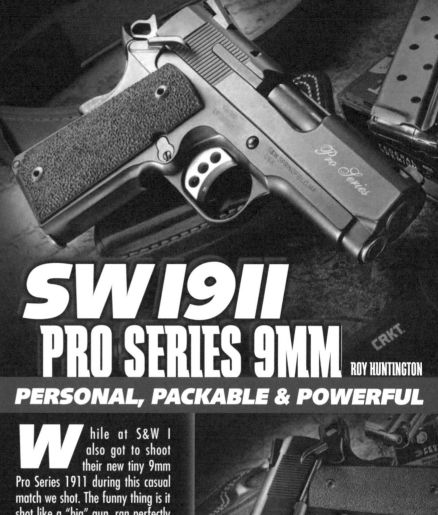

SW 1911
PRO SERIES 9MM
CRKT.
ROY HUNTINGTON

PERSONAL, PACKABLE & POWERFUL

While at S&W I also got to shoot their new tiny 9mm Pro Series 1911 during this casual match we shot. The funny thing is it shot like a "big" gun, ran perfectly (unusual for a short-slide 1911) and had a slide surprisingly easy to run. Not quite in the same easy league as the .380 EZ, it might still open the door to someone who enjoys smaller 1911s but wrestles with this pesky slide on a .45. This blend of Performance Center know-how, engineering and parts, coupled with production on the factory floor means you get a gun sort of "in-between" a stock production pistol and a full-house Performance Center gun.

This translates to affordability and performance at the same time. I liked this gun so much I just had to show it to you here. The combination of "Officers"-sized round-butt grip holding eight rounds of your favorite 9mm, and the short overall length (6.9" with 3" barrel) means it's easy to carry. The Scandium frame makes it light, and that easy-to-run slide is just a delight to work. I put about 450 effortless rounds through my sample gun and it ran just fine. It showed tight sub-2" vicinity groups at 20 yards with a bunch of different ammo types, and being a 9mm, recoil was easy to manage.

This is a pleasant, appealing little gun, weighing only 26 oz. in spite of its stainless slide and barrel. Think: CCW use, home defense, weekend IDPA type competition for fun and also allows you to be in compliance if you have one of those draconian 10-round mag bans haunting you. It begs to be put into a simple IWB holster or belt slide and made your everyday-gun. It's what a personal pistol should be. At a full MSRP of $1,330 it's essentially a custom, chopped, 9mm — for a production gun price.

For more info: www.americanhandgunner.com/index; S&W Ph: (800) 331-0852

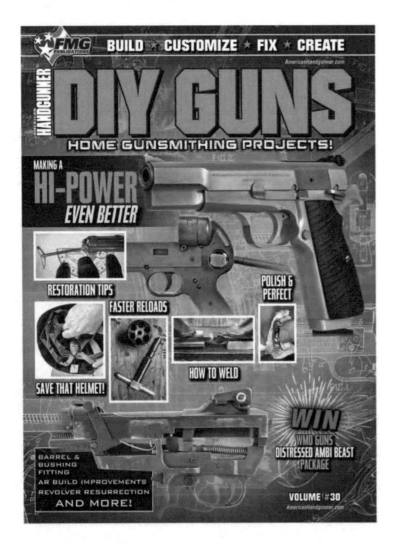
S&W .380 SHIELD

chrono while the SIG delivered around the 935 fps mark. The HoneyBadger's best group (eight rounds) was about 2.25" but if you take out the worse two, that group becomes 1.25" which is likely what it'd do in a mechanical rest. The SIG load delivered about 3" but included one I pulled. Take that out and we suddenly get a more realistic 1.5".

This is stunning accuracy for a .380, and frankly top-tier accuracy for any production semi-auto in any form. And I did notice it was sheer pleasure to shoot the EZ and not be beat-up by recoil. It allows the shooter to really concentrate on trigger press. I think I've found my new "teaching" gun.

An interesting side note is the fact virtually all of the brass from my last shoot landed about six feet to my right, just forward of the gun, in a pattern about four feet wide. It looked like I had swept the brass into a loose pile. Amazingly consistent ejection, from both loads.

Final Thoughts?

Easy, actually. Holsters fitting the SHIELD series mostly fit the EZ if they're open-bottomed, but there are also dedicated rigs for the EZ too. It's light, highly functional, has adequate stopping power with modern ammo (no +P though, please), can handle a rail light and fits a wide section of hand sizes, including my own smallish hand. Since the parent M&P design has been around since 2006, the basics are proven in the field. No doubt companies like Apex Tactical will be introducing fancy triggers and such for the EZ in no time.

What would I change? Not a darn thing. I honestly couldn't think of a single "bad" thing. At an MSRP of $399, this is a "buy it and put it to work right now" gun. Since it's so accurate, I truthfully wish I had an adjustable sight on mine so I could dial it right in if I wanted to. Squirrel hunting with a .380 might be fun.

If I described *you* here, then you're also looking at what just might be an answer to your dilemma. And — this is the *best* answer I've seen.

Note: A few of the very earliest pistols shipped had an issue with the safety bouncing-on with certain heavy loads. Pistols shipped prior to April 4, 2018 may need an upgrade. To see if your pistol is subject to this, call S&W (or go online) at (800) 331-0852 or email them at MP380EZAdvisory@Smith-Wesson.com.

TAFFINTESTS

THE SIXGUNNER HIMSELF: GUNS, GEAR & MORE JOHN TAFFIN

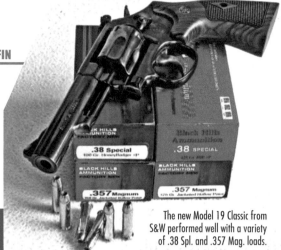

RETURN OF THE COMBAT MAGNUM
S&W'S CLASSIC MODEL 19, REBORN!

The new Model 19 Classic from S&W performed well with a variety of .38 Spl. and .357 Mag. loads.

The Model 19 Carry Comp shot this group at 7 yards for John.

Bill Jordan, Marine combat veteran and Border Patrol Chief Inspector when he retired in 1965, was directly responsible for the Smith & Wesson .357 Combat Magnum. In 1986 Bill spoke of how the Combat Magnum came about: "In 1950, Smith & Wesson introduced the Model 15, a 4"-barreled version of its K-Frame Masterpiece series acclaimed by law enforcement officers. The only thing wrong with it was it was a bit too light for defensive use, especially the barrel and it was chambered for the .38 Spl. cartridge.

Bill decided he wanted a lighter and much easier to carry .357 Mag. than the original larger-framed Smith & Wesson .357 Mag. which arrived in 1935. What he wanted was a .357 Mag. sixgun on the smaller K-Frame with a heavy 4" barrel with an extractor shroud similar to those used on the larger frame .357 Mag. revolvers, target grips and target sights. On November 15, 1955, the first production medium-frame .357 Mag. was completed and dubbed the Combat Magnum. Jordan called it the answer to a peace officer's dream.

Jordan envisioned the Combat Magnum being carried with .357 Mag. loads while using .38 Special loads for practice. Some complained of the smaller Magnum not holding up to continuous use of .357 loads. Personally, I've never experienced any problems resulting from using .357 loads in several Model 19s in all three barrel lengths as well as both blue and nickel models.

Most of my .357 Mag. loads over the past half-century plus have been assembled with #2400 and my own cast bullets, either the Lyman-Keith #358429 173-gr. plain-based or Lyman-Thompson #358156 gas-checked bullets. Curiously, I have a K-Frame 4" Model 19 which will handle heavier loads without complaining than an N-Frame 5" Model 27. Fired cases literally fall out of the 19 while they stick in the 27, proving once again every sixgun is a law unto itself.

MORE THAN A NUMBER

In 1957 all Smith & Wesson sixguns lost their personal name and became a number. The Combat Magnum became the Model 19 and when it appeared in stainless steel form in 1975 it was known as the Model 66. The original Model 19 was dropped in 1999 while the stainless steel Model 66 lasted a few years into this century. Recently, the stainless steel Model 66 Combat Magnum was resurrected and now this year the Model 19 is back.

While the original Combat Magnum

The Resurrected Model 19 (left) compared to an original blued Combat Magnum and stainless steel Model 66.

and the resurrected 21st-century version look like twins at first glance, there are differences. Internally they're quite different as the modern version, which is known as the Model 19 Classic, has all of what Smith & Wesson calls "enhanced with modern internal components" while still maintaining the look and feel of the original models.

Both of these sixguns have bright blue finishes and came with the diamond in the center target stocks. However, the new Model 19 has a round butt frame concealed under the grip. My hands have certainly changed since the mid-1950s, first becoming tougher and stronger and then beginning their downhill slide. This, of course, means the stocks are not as comfortable to me

as they were 60 years ago.

My favorite .357 Mag. load for carry today is the same load I use on turkeys in areas where I'm not required to use a shotgun. It's the Black Hills 125-gr. JHP. In a long-barreled, scoped .357 Mag. it works fine for head shooting turkeys. Loaded in a carry gun, it's rated as one of the most dependable stopping loads. In the Model 19 Classic it clocks out at

The Carry Comp comes with two sets of stocks ...

... one fancy wood set and another rubber set for everyday carry.

MORE HANDGUNS HERE

americanhandgunner.com

With lines sure to have a positive impact on your heart rate, Roy's Bowen conversion of a classic 38/44 Heavy Duty to .45 Colt is notable for its singularity — and ability to whisper to whoever sees it.

This 15-yard off-hand group with the war-weary Victory shows what they could do — and still can! Without the flyer, that's a solid 1" group using Black Hills 148-grain target wadcutter ammo. Roy didn't have enough original military ammo to shoot any groups.

TAFFIN TESTS

1,350 fps and will put 5 shots in just over 1" at 20 yards. This sixgun also works very well with .38 Spl. rounds such as the Black Hills 125-gr. JHP (900 fps) and their 100-gr. HoneyBadger (1,050 fps) with the same accuracy as the .357 load.

Sights on both consist of a fully adjustable rear sight and a ramp front sight. The modern version has a red insert instead of the plain black front sight of the original. Barrel length was 4" and is now 4¼". The original was known as the Combat Magnum but was not marked on the barrel; the new Model 19 Classic has "COMBAT MAGNUM" on the left side of the barrel. In 1955 the Combat Magnum was all blued steel; now frame and cylinder are carbon steel while the barrel is stainless steel.

Today's Take

A second version of the new Model 19 comes from the S&W Performance Center and is known as the Model 19 Carry Comp. This serious little packing pistol comes with a 3" barrel and, as the official name suggests, is compensated. The front sight, which is a Trijicon unit, is set back from the front edge of the barrel enough to allow room for the port. This port makes a huge difference in felt recoil, making .38 Spl. loads feel like shooting .22s and full-house magnums seem more like .38 Spl. shots.

Just as with the Model 19 Classic, this version has a rounded butt. It comes with custom wood grips that do not fill in the backstrap or under the butt and have one finger groove on the front strap. In addition to this grip Smith & Wesson also provides a very comfortable, more hand-filling wrap-around rubber grip that also fills in at the bottom of the butt.

This grip combined with the porting makes this the most comfortable short-barreled .357 Mag. gun I've ever fired. In fact, I enjoyed shooting this one so much I gathered up all the ammunition I could find and went through 16 different .38 Spl. loads and seven .357 Mag. loads. All loads were fired at a self-defense distance of 7 yards with groups averaging 1" or less. My favorite Black Hills 125-gr. JHP clocked out at 1,275 fps and placed 5 shots in 1". The Black Hills 158-gr. JHP at 1,055 fps and the SIG SAUER 125-gr. FMJ (1,250 fps) are also excellent shooting and delivered groups less than 1".

The Performance Center Model 19-9 Carry Comp has an MSRP of $1,092 while the 19-9 Classic Combat Magnum's MSRP is $826.

More Here:
americanhandgunner.com

Massad Ayoob
Photos: Gail Pepin

VIABLE IN A SQUARE WORLD?
S&W'S 3" K-FRAME 'ROUND-GUN'

Old school but still cool. This 3" round-butt M66 sits in a period Bianchi No. 3 holster next to a DeSantis 2x2x2 cartridge pouch.

Amidst a tsunami of polymer-framed autoloading pistols we're seeing a groundswell of renewed interest in double-action revolvers. Some of the most popular are the 3" barreled K-Frame Smith & Wesson wheel guns in round-butt configuration.

Why this particular variation? The fact they're relatively uncommon is the least of it. The "3KRB" has a lot going for it. Let's examine *why*.

APPEALING FEATURES

The 3" barrel — with the correct outside-the-waistband holster — protrudes less from beneath the hem of the concealing garment than a full-length service revolver.

The extra bit of barrel gives it a smidgen more velocity than a 2" or 2.5" specimen. Perhaps the greatest tactical advantage over the more common shorter barrels is the full-length ejector rod, making an emergency reload much more positive.

The K-Frame is still medium in size, reasonably concealable but with much better handling in actual shooting than the smaller J-Frame. Its cylinder holds a full six rounds instead of five, its trigger reach is optimal for the average adult male hand and it has just enough heft to keep recoil manageable without making the wearer list to one side. And, of course, there's the famously-smooth trigger pull.

The round butt seems to conceal distinctly better than the square one and the round butt was the configuration of the very first Smith & Wesson .38 Hand Ejector Model of 1899. Some of us feel it fits our hand better than the more common square-butt S&W as well.

Taken all together — and we're being subjective again here — lots of us think this

Old and new 3KRB: From top left the M13 .357, the M547 9mm and M66 .357. At right the new .357 M19 K-Comp from S&W's Performance Center.

Retired cop Steve Denney still loves to hammer things with sweet-shooting 3KRB revolvers.

particular S&W configuration simply has exquisite balance, not only in the tactile sense, but in looks too. There are also elements of habituation and tradition. My friend Vant Abercrombie recently retired from a distinguished career as a police investigator. The day after his retirement he put away his issue 16-shot .40 caliber polymer pistol and strapped on his favorite 3" S&W Model 65. "It's comforting to have a classic .357 at my side," he says.

WHAT'S OUT THERE?

Smith 3KRB's are most commonly encountered with fixed sights. In .38 Special, this includes the chrome-molybdenum steel Model 10 series (blue or nickel) and the Model 64 stainless. In .357 Magnum, it's the Model 13 in chrome-moly, and the Model 65 in stainless. The 3" Model 13 was the last service revolver the FBI issued before changing to autos. The least common variant is the Model 547 in 9mm

> "The day after his retirement he put away his issue 16-shot .40 caliber polymer pistol and strapped on his favorite 3" S&W Model 65."

Luger, said to have been made originally for the French government.

All these have naked ejector rods except for another rare variant, the Model 65 Ladysmith, which has fixed sights but also the shrouded ejector rod more commonly seen on the adjustable-sighted .357 Combat Magnum.

Adjustable sight versions are much less

common. Round butt 2.5" .357 Combat Magnums were hugely popular but the 3" option was never cataloged and always was a special order for a distributor or (usually) law enforcement. The stainless 3" Model 66 is thin on the ground, and while I've heard of 3" Model 19's, I've never actually seen one. The Model 66 is my personal favorite among the 3KRB guns simply because its adjustable sights (changed to MeproLight versions on mine) allow me to dial in precisely with any of the wide range of .38 Special to top-end .357 Magnum loads.

Good news: You no longer have to haunt gun shows and GunBroker.com to find one. S&W has reintroduced the adjustable-sight Model 66 with a 2.75" barrel — close enough! — and I recently had a chance to shoot the K-Comp 3" Model 19 with a ported barrel and Trijicon front sight from the Smith & Wesson Performance Center. ⌐

French rarebit: This long-out-of-print Smith M547 9mm showcases the distinctive 3KRB look to a "T."

THE .357 MAGNUM:

JOHN TAFFIN

Since the .357 Magnum arrived in 1935 — heralded as the most powerful sixgun in the world — it has been followed by plenty of other hard-hitting cartridges. If you're looking to put a serious hurt on something or someone, the choices are many: .44 Magnum, .41 Magnum, .454 Casull, .475 and .500 Linebaugh, not to mention heavy-loaded .45 Colt rounds and longer-than-standard cartridges such as the .460 and .500 S&W Magnums.

Today it's pretty easy to look at the .357 Magnum as a shadow of its former self whenever matched against these more powerful rounds. However, the .357 is no less a great cartridge than it was in the beginning and, in fact, still is. Thanks to better bullets, more types of powder available, and stronger, better-built wheelguns, it's even

better than it was 85 years ago.

Let's take a look at where the round came from, some early uses, the men who popularized it and some of the best .357 Magnum revolvers past and present.

MOTOR BANDITS AND BIG GAME

During the 1920s the bad guys were winning the war against the good guys simply because gangsters were much better armed. The V8 Ford had arrived and was used to great success by bank robbers of the time. Confrontations often saw good guys armed with .38 Specials going against gangsters in fast-moving vehicles and armed with Thompson SMGs and Browning Automatic Rifles.

In the late 1920s both Colt and Smith & Wesson addressed the problem. From Colt

came the .38 Super or Super .38 (depending upon who was speaking) chambered in their 1911 while Smith & Wesson used their .44 frame revolver chambered in .38 Special to handle what we now often refer to as .38/44 rounds. The special revolvers arrived in April 1930 as the .38/44 Heavy Duty using a pre- Plus P loading of a 158-gr. bullet at 1,175 fps. It was a good start but for the boys at S&W it was only the beginning.

Phil Sharpe is the main figure responsible for the .357 Magnum and to come up with the case for the ammo, he simply lengthened the standard .38 Special from 1.155" to 1.290" to prevent the more powerful round from being dropped in a .38 Special cylinder. Such mistakes could result in a disaster for the shooter or any one standing close by.

The original S&W .357 Magnums were known as Registered Magnums. This quartet features 8-3/4, 6-1/2, 5, and 4" barrels.

Golden Age treasures: A trio of 5" .357s from the 1950s.

The Original High-Pressure Wheelgun!

PART 1

ACCORDING TO SHARPE:

"The .357 Magnum cartridge was born in my mind several years ago. On a hunting trip with Col. D.B. Wesson, Vice-President of Smith & Wesson, a pair of heavy frame Outdoorsman model revolvers were used with a large assortment of handloads developed and previously tested by myself. In the field they proved entirely practical, but Col. Wesson was not content to attempt the development of a Magnum .38 Special cartridge for ordinary revolvers and set to work on a new gun planned in the field. For more than a year before the release of this gun, Col. Wesson manufactured a few pilot models, building and rebuilding each one, redesigning this and that until he found a suitable combination. I did not design the gun or the cartridge, however a number of my ideas were incorporated in the design of this gun, tested through an understanding of handloading problems, and a number of weak points in ordinary revolvers were quickly corrected."

THE IDAHO CONNECTION

Meanwhile back at the ranch — literally — in North Fork Idaho, Elmer Keith was seeing how much he could get out the .38 Special using the S&W .38/44 Heavy Duty. His load, using his long-nosed #358429 170-gr. bullet clocks out at 1,400 fps when duplicated and fired through my 8-3/8" Smith today. The

"… Col. Wesson used the new combination to take antelope, elk, moose and even grizzly bear. Only the antelope required two shots!"

first .357 Magnum loads from Winchester used large primers and clocked over 1,500 fps using the Sharpe bullet that's based on the Keith bullet. It's somewhat lighter and different in dimension from the Keith form, having been engineered to fit the S&W .357 Magnum. It has approximately 5/6 the bearing surface of the Keith bullet.

Keith used his .38/44 loads in the new sixgun and reported excellent accuracy. The 600-yard targets in Ed McGivern's *Fast and Fancy Revolver Shooting* were shot using the Keith .38/44 loads in an 8-3/4" .357 Magnum.

To promote the new sixgun — simply called the .357 Magnum — and cartridge, Col. Wesson used the new combination to take antelope, elk, moose and even grizzly bear. Only the antelope required two shots! One of the first complaints we hear today is

the .357 Magnum isn't powerful enough for big game hunting but Col. Wesson obviously wouldn't agree. I would not hesitate to use the .357 on deer-sized critters including antelope and feral pigs though I wouldn't use it on elk, moose and grizzly bear *unless* it was all I had.

Most of us fire very few rounds at game. I fire approximately 300 rounds per week but in the last four years I have fired five rounds at game animals using the .454 to take an elk and a bison, the .44 Magnum for another elk and two deer-sized critters were also taken with the .44 Magnum. The latter pair could easily have been taken with the .357.

REGISTERED MAGNUMS

In 1935 the first .357 Magnums from Smith & Wesson were known as Registered Magnums as they not only had a

serial number but also a special registered number signifying they were literally hand built. Wesson not only promoted the cartridge by hunting but special Registered Magnums went to the right people.

The very first 8-3/4" barreled one went to the FBI's J. Edgar Hoover while Phil Sharpe received the second. Originally the company believed all .357 Magnums would have 8-3/4" barrels as they would only be used for hunting. Dedicated sixgunners, however, had other ideas.

In 1935, Col. George Patton purchased his 3-1/2"-barreled .357 in Hawaii. These shorter-barreled guns became very popular with peace officers, especially FBI agents. Delf "Jelly" Bryce retired his .44 Special Smith & Wesson for a .357 Magnum and was arguably the fastest and most accurate sixgunner of all time in serious situations.

Pre-Model 27s
with 8-3/8, 6-1/2
and 5" barrels.

I was privileged to know Col. Walter Walsh who used the .357 Magnum as an FBI agent prior to WWII. Another FBI agent to receive an early .357 Magnum was Frank Baughman (who developed the Baughman Ramp Front Sight). Gun No. 8 went to Ed McGivern while actor Jimmy Stewart had No. 100. Roy Rogers took a short-barreled .357 Magnum to Africa but I don't know if it was a Registered Magnum — probably not.

When I was in high school I read of Sasha Siemel, the noted jaguar hunter in South America who also had one of the early short-barreled .357s. Elmer Keith's early prototype 6-1/2" specimen (he didn't care for the longer barrel length) recently sold — along with all of his guns at auction — for just under $29,000.

The Registered Magnums were all specially ordered with a number of options as to barrel length, sights and grips. Each was hand built. Barrels were pinned into the frame and cylinders had recessed case heads. Smith & Wesson soon found all this was an exceptionally expensive proposition to manufacture and within a few years dropped the idea of registering these beautiful sixguns. However, by the time World War II erupted, fewer non-Registered Magnums had been made than Registered Magnums.

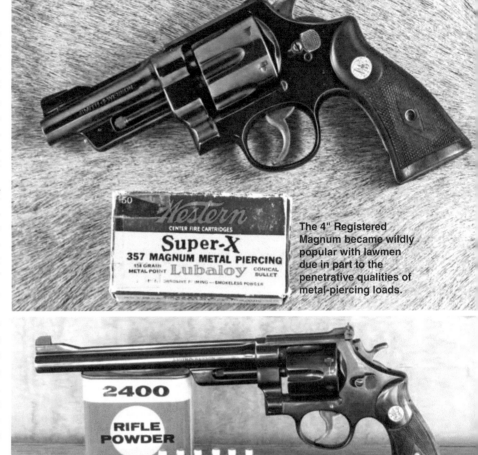

The 4" Registered Magnum became wildly popular with lawmen due in part to the penetrative qualities of metal-piercing loads.

One of the best powders for the .357 Magnum? Still good old 2400.

PRE-MODEL 27

After the war Smith & Wesson resumed production of the .357 Magnum but by 1949 had only completed 142 guns. Beginning in 1950 the .357 Magnum, as well as the rest of the N-Frames were changed from the pre-war long action to the shorter action we know today. From 1950 until 1957, when all Smith & Wessons received model numbers,

barrel lengths were standardized at 3-1/2, 5, 6, 6-1/2 and 8-3/8". Today all of these are known as Pre-Model 27s. The Model 27 went through various changes and can be found with model numbers from 27, 27-1 up to 27-6 before the standard model was removed from production in 1994.

All of the Registered Magnums, Pre-27s, and most of the rest of the Model 27s with their various numbers are exceptional revolvers. However, don't think an early numbered 27 or Pre-27 shoot better than the later guns. My nickel-plated 8-3/8" Model 27-3 outshoots my Pre-27 with the same barrel length. I have a pair of 5" 27-5s which are some of the last production model .357 Magnums made and they routinely out-shoot my Pre-27 and early Model 27. For many years I tried to find a 6-1/2" .357 Model 27 of any "dash" variation and never could. Then I not only found one, but two, and both proved to be Pre-27s. They are excellent shooters.

I'll always have a passion for the .44 and .45 sixguns but I can no longer handle a steady diet of heavy loads in the big-bore revolvers. At least — as this is written — the N-Frame .357 Magnum and I are still on very close speaking terms.

(To be continued)

Skeeter Skelton was very fond of the 5" .357 Magnum.

THE .357 MAGNUM

JOHN TAFFIN

Still powering some of our finest revolvers

PART II

In the 1950s when the sixgun was still supreme among peace officers, there were many who asked for a less expensive .357 Magnum. The 1954 result was the Highway Patrolman. It was offered only in 4 and 6" versions and without the beautiful Bright Blue finish found on the original model, nor checkered top strap and barrel rib. These matte-blue sixguns were designed for heavy-duty use without worrying about the finish. The first brand-new DA sixgun I ever purchased was a 4" Highway Patrolman. In 1957 this workhorse became known as the M28.

Both the M27 and M28 are relatively heavy and by the mid-1950s, peace officers were looking for an easier-to-carry .357. Border Patrol Inspector Bill Jordan discussed the idea of a K-Frame .357 with S&W. The result? The .38 Special Combat Masterpiece was given a longer cylinder, a heavier barrel complete with an enclosed ejector rod, plus different heat treating to come up with the 4" Combat Magnum. Jordan called it "The Answer to a Peace Officer's Dream."

Smith soon offered a 6" version for field use and a round-butted 2-1/2" for easier concealability. In 1957 the Combat Magnum became the M19. It was discontinued in 1999. However,

John is set for all possibilities in the field with this duo of scoped and iron sighted M97 .357s from Freedom Arms.

the stainless variant — the M66 — has come back and is available in 4-1/4" trim and as a Performance Center round-butt 3" with an efficient porting system (see the *GUNS* December 2018 issue).

To my eye, the most serious looking sixgun ever produced was the 3-1/2" N-Frame .357 Magnum followed very closely by the 2-1/2" M19/M66. Today the semi-auto may be king among law enforcement and other shooters but the .357 is just as good as it ever was — possibly better. The 125-gr. JHP has a reputation for stopping power and I also use it for hunting turkeys. Six shots have gotten me six of the big birds.

From time to time S&W brings back "Classic Models" such as the original .357 Magnum/ M27, the Highway Patrolman/M28 and the Combat Magnum/M19. If I had to choose the best Smith .357 with my heart, my No. 1 choice is the original N-Frame. But if I'm to be guided by my head, my choice would definitely be what is probably the best .357 ever to come from the company — the M686.

John rediscovers his love of the .357 with the new stainless edition of the Combat Magnum.

L-FRAME COMPROMISE

In the 1980s there was concern the K-Frame M19 Combat Magnums were not holding up well to newer .357 Magnum loadings, especially the 110- and 125-gr. JHPs. The problem seemed to be in the relatively small forcing cone area. Remember, the M19 Combat Magnums were the same size as the .38 Special Combat Masterpiece. Bill Jordan said he envisioned the K-Frame .357 as a gun to be used mainly with .38s for practice and .357s for duty. I don't know if I agree with this philosophy as we tend to perform the way we practice — which means just practicing with .38s may not lead to efficiency with .357s on duty. For most of us this wouldn't make any difference but it could for law enforcement personnel.

My Combat Magnum/M19s have never been a problem because I've mainly used them with cast bullets which are much kinder on forcing cones. But S&W looked for a better answer and this better answer was the L-Frame series packing more steel in the forcing cone area and cylinder while keeping the grip frame the same size as the M19.

Striking gold! John recently found this King pre-war custom Colt SAA .357 with all the King touches including cockeyed hammer, wide checkered trigger, short action and full-length rib with adjustable rear sight.

These guns also had full underlug barrels basically giving a Colt Python-style sixgun at about half the price. These were offered in both blued and stainless steel with the fixed sighted versions known as the M581 and M681 respectively. The adjustable sighted L-Frames were the M586 and M686. A long list of L-Frame .357s have been offered over the past 40 years or so in 2-1/2, 4, 6 and 8-3/8" barrel lengths. Some had a seven-shot cylinder. These are now the flagship .357 Smith & Wessons. If you want an S&W .357 for the toughest possible duty, this is it.

But there are many .357s available from other makers as well. Let's take a look at some.

The Python (above) is often acclaimed as the finest revolver Colt ever made. This 6" specimen — tuned by Fred Sadowski — was given to John by a late friend. Bill Jordan was directly responsible for S&W's .357 Combat Magnum — an easier-packing medium-frame option (below).

COLT DA AND SA OFFERINGS

After the .357 Magnum arrived Colt chambered it in both their DA New Service and the Single Action Army. Production of both models was suspended prior to WWII and after the war, both had disappeared. However, in the 1950s the .357 made a comeback at Colt. First came their .357 Magnum in the early 1950s — basically a .38 Special Officers Model Match turned .357. Then in 1955, the Python arrived. Many consider it the finest revolver ever offered by Colt!

Originally this was a very heavy sixgun chambered in .38

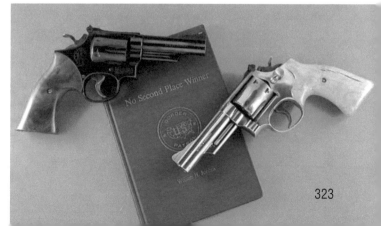

The full underlug Ruger GP100 is probably the most rugged .357 available.

This .357 Magnum Ruger Blackhawk (above) has given John excellent service for more than 60 years. A hot item during the early days of Metallic Silhouette shooting was Dan Wesson's "purpose built" .357 Magnum (below).

Special for target shooting. To cut down some of the weight, the barrel rib was ventilated and the engineers realized they had something capable of handling much more than the .38 Special — the .357 Python was born! Originally with a 6" barrel, it was offered over the years in additional barrel lengths of 2-1/2, 4 and 8". I lusted after a 4" Python in the 1960s so much it hurt.

The Python is long gone from production and my shooting examples today are a 6" tuned by Fred Sadowski and a Cylinder & Slide-sweetened 8" tackdriver. Originally offered in Colt Royal Blue, a few stainless steel versions were also produced. The Python is long out of production and probably won't be seen again.

In late 1955 Colt resurrected the Single Action Army with the first two chamberings being .357 Magnum and .45 Colt. Three of my favorite .357 single actions are Colts. These include a 1921-vintage SAA converted to .357 Magnum prior to WWII and totally customized by King Gun Sight Company. King added a full-length rib with adjustable rear sight to the 5-1/2" barrel, shortened the action and installed the wide checkered trigger and cockeyed hammer.

The second is a New Frontier from the 1960s with a 7-1/2" barrel. The third is an SAA fitted with a 5-1/2" New Frontier barrel and an S&W adjustable rear sight.

THE BLACKHAWK ROLLOUT

When Ruger decided to introduce their first centerfire they chose the most powerful cartridge available at the time, namely the .357 Magnum. The original Blackhawk — now known as the Flat-Top — was the same basic size as the Colt SAA except it had a virtually unbreakable coil spring operated action along with a heavy top strap and an adjustable rear sight. The first barrel

324

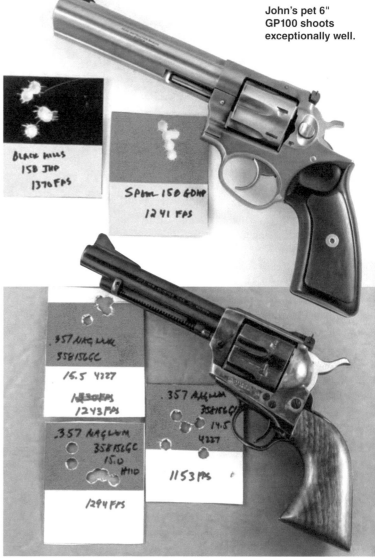

John considers S&W's L-Frame series — the M586/M686 — the ideal tool if you intend to do a lot of ":357 Magnum-ized" shooting. This 6" model puts John's handloads where he wants them.

John's pet 6" GP100 shoots exceptionally well.

John had this Colt SAA .357 Magnum fitted with an S&W adjustable rear sight and a New Frontier barrel. The results speak for themselves.

length offered was 4-5/8" and this was later joined by a 6-1/2" version, along with a rare 10".

I acquired my first Ruger .357 in 1956. It was difficult in those days to find magnum brass so I fired thousands of rounds of the Keith .38 Special load through it, alongside my S&W Highway Patrolman. Keith's .38 load used his 170-gr. grain bullet and enough #2400 powder to make it hotter than many of today's .357 offerings. In 2005 Ruger resurrected the original .357 Blackhawk with the New Model Flat-Top. When Ruger went to the New Model action in the early 1970s, the .357 was chambered in the full .44 Magnum-sized frame. I never did care for it as much as the original size.

Ruger went "double action" .357 with the Security-Six which was replaced by the improved GP100, offered in both blue and stainless. The stainless version is about the toughest sixgun you could find for carrying in all kinds of weather. Until recently all GP100s had full-length underlug barrels but they are now offered as the Match Champion model with the standard barrel — my choice for everyday packin'!

AN '80s SUPERSTAR

In the 1980s Dan Wesson literally owned silhouette shooting. The reason? They listened to the long-range shooters and gave them what they wanted — a heavy-barreled .357 with excellent adjustable rear sights and interchangeable front ones. Many of us shot the revolver category using the 8" model.

Because of the relatively short cylinder we used .38 Special brass loaded with 180- to 200-gr. cast bullets. These were slow-moving loads — under 1,000 fps — but they always got the job done. Dan Wesson recently resurrected their .357 Magnum revolver.

SINGLE-ACTION SUPREME

Freedom Arms originally chambered their almost-custom revolvers in .454 Casull but they decided to eventually reach out to shooters who wanted the best single-action revolver possible chambered in other calibers. One of these was the .357 Magnum and silhouette shooters soon discovered it was the best sixgun available for their long-range chores.

Those first .357s from Freedom Arms were chambered in the full-sized, five-shot M83. In 1997 they brought forth the six-shot .357 M97, which is slightly smaller than the Colt SAA. The M97 — whether you choose fixed or adjustable sights — is an excellent .357 for everyday carry. Both the M83 and M97 provide superb accuracy.

FAVORITE HANDLOADS

Over the years (make that *decades*) I've shot a lot of different loads in a long list of .357 Magnum sixguns and leverguns. I've settled on two current most-used ones. These are the 158-gr. Lyman/Thompson #358156 gas-checked cast bullet over 14.0 grains of 2400 and the NEI #200.358 gas-checked 200-gr. bullet over 12.5 grains of IMR4227.

My current most-used .357 Ruger is the New Model Flat-Top Stainless 5-1/2". This is an excellent everyday carry piece and with the above loads clocks out at 1,335 and 1,075 fps respectively. The 200-gr. load is superbly accurate.

I must admit there was a time in my life — when I got bitten by the "big bore bug" — I looked down on the .357 Magnum. Today I've grown older and smarter, and now give this great cartridge its well-earned due.

A "SPECIAL" LOVE
THE GREAT .38 STILL MAKES SENSE!

Like so many shooters my age, I began handloading with the .38 Special in 1966. Throughout life I've been a "lister" — my made-up word for someone who keeps lists. By 1980 I'd loaded over 50,000 .38 Special rounds but by then I was handloading enough different cartridges the act of trying to keep a list of them was too involved.

In my early adult years, by now living in Montana, .38 Specials didn't greatly appeal to me. Going out into grizzly bear habitat north of Yellowstone National Park, I always packed a magnum revolver of some sort — a .357 or .44. Although my .38 Special handguns got shoved to the backburner in those days, I've seldom been without one.

Also during this time period I still fired quite a few .38 Specials through various .357 Magnums.

MANAGEABILITY, ACCURACY

In 1966 my very first .38 Special was a Smith & Wesson K38 (aka the Model 14) with a 6" barrel. My most recent — purchased in 2018 — is a Colt SAA 2nd Generation with a 5-1/2" barrel. In between have been virtually every all-steel Smith & Wesson .38 Special and many of their "lightweights" with alloy frames. A single Colt Detective Special graced the line-up.

In my experience .38 Special revolvers are — in general — capable of near phenomenal precision (as in 1" groups at 25 yards). Once I did an experiment with a late '50s or early '60s Colt SAA .38 Special with 7½" barrel. Using a Ransom Pistol Machine Rest, each chamber was fired for five 5-shot groups at 25 yards.

I then fired all the chambers for the same number of groups. Count 'em — 30 groups fired in one afternoon. No cleaning was done between strings of shots and the ammo was Remington 148-gr. Match Wadcutters. As I remember the total average for 30 groups was about 1.10".

One reason I've always liked the .38 Special because it's a pussycat in the recoil and noise department, at least in full-size revolvers. In small-frame 5-shooters it can be a bit much for extended shooting. With medium-frame guns it's easy to train people to shoot to a minimum of proficiency, which, I assume, was one reason it became the standard of most American law

K-Frame extremes: bottom is a 2" Model 15. Top is an 8-3/8" Model 14.

The .38-44 was a higher-pressure load intended only for large-frame .38 Special revolvers.

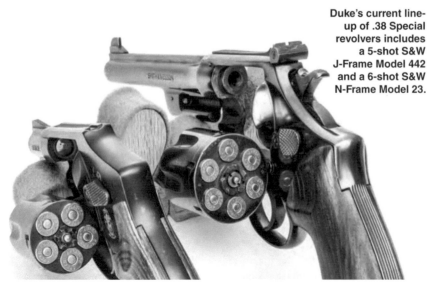

Duke's current line-up of .38 Special revolvers includes a 5-shot S&W J-Frame Model 442 and a 6-shot S&W N-Frame Model 23.

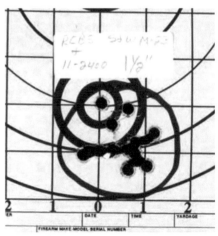

Accuracy plus: This 25-yard 12-shot group was fired from machine rest with an S&W Model 23.

enforcement outfits for many decades. I remember my hometown, which had about a dozen officers — they were allowed to carry .357 Magnums but loaded with .38 Specials.

POWER BOOST!

My only real shooting buddy was named Mike Bucci (nicknamed "Butch"). His dad was chief of police for our little town. So Butch could have his own .38, his father passed onto him a fine Smith & Wesson Model 20 Heavy Duty, built on the large N-Frame. Those first appeared in 1930 so cops could have a more powerful sixgun. The cartridge introduced especially for it was the .38-44. In all dimensional aspects the .38-44 rounds were identical to ordinary .38 Specials except for their headstamp and a velocity increase from about 850 to 1,150 fps.

At first Butch felt slighted because my K38 had adjustable sights but his Heavy Duty wore fixed ones. To show him the truth of the matter I made some .38-44 equivalent handloads. I wasn't guessing how

A smorgasbord of factory loads have been offered for .38 Special (from left): 158-gr. RN, 148-gr. WC, 200-gr. RN, 130-gr. FMJ, 158-gr. SWC, 158-gr. JHP and 158-gr. RN/FP (Cowboy Action).

— in those days Lyman's reloading books listed .38 Special loads with higher velocities than seen in manuals today. Then, at our shooting spot, I sat two bricks side by side about 50 feet away. The first one I shot with my K38 with a 150-gr. cast bullet and 3.0 grains of Bullseye. The brick just fell over. Next, I shot one with Butch's revolver and the heavy .38 Special load. The brick shattered. Butch never felt inferior afterwards although I doubt he ever fired another hot handload through his .38. (Butch was a

good friend and lots of fun. Sadly he died of cancer at age 21.)

Quite often over the years people have asked me what handgun I would recommend for home defense. To one and all I recommend a quality double-action .38 Special. Mostly they balk, saying they thought I would have recommended a specific 9mm semi-auto. Some go as far as to ask "Sure, but what do *you* keep by the bed?" In all honesty I reply, "A 12-gauge pump shotgun ... and a .38 Special revolver!"

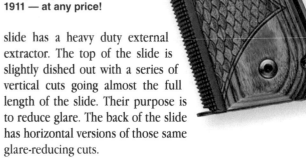

S&W SW1911SC E-SERIES

COMMANDING ROUND-BUTT, SCANDIUM FRAME 1911

David Freeman

The handsome round-butt Scandium Commander has everything David wants in a 1911 — at any price!

S ome of us were carrying slim pistols before slim was cool. Before the S&W Shield, Springfield XD-S, G43 and SIG P365, there was the … dare I say it? The 1911. And, for easier concealment, 1911s with 4-1/4, 4 and even 3" barrels. It's true Smith & Wesson came late to the 1911 party (actually, a year shy of 100 years late, since the first S&W 1911s rolled out in 2010) and they got rave reviews.

But — I already had my 1911 bases covered, or so I thought. It's funny how a gun can endear itself to you when it wasn't even on your radar. It was like that for me and the S&W SW1911SC E-Series Round Butt Commander (*Okay, it's a mouthful*). After I got mine, I quickly realized if I put in an order for a custom 1911 from any one of America's greatest (and priciest) gunsmiths, I couldn't think of anything I'd ask for this production Smith didn't have.

GOOD LOOKS PLUS …

How a gun looks is always important and this one is a cool combination of black and stainless steel S&W calls "Duo-Tone," although you can also get them in solid black if you like. The slide has unusual serrations on each side — they're like fish scales. I found them easy on the hands while providing an excellent purchase for racking the slide or a press check, although on this gun the press check is unnecessary because there's a view port on top of the slide at the back end of the chamber through which you can see if there's a round in the chamber.

The ejection port is cut low and beveled. S&W calls it a "Combat Ejection Port." The right side of the

The S&W SCE Commander (left) is barely wider than a Springfield XD-S .45 (right).

slide has a heavy duty external extractor. The top of the slide is slightly dished out with a series of vertical cuts going almost the full length of the slide. Their purpose is to reduce glare. The back of the slide has horizontal versions of those same glare-reducing cuts.

Trijicon night sights are mounted front and rear — exactly what I'd order on a custom gun. An ambidextrous safety? Yes, and it's not tiny like a stock 1911 safety but it's not one of those honking big ones either. To me the size and width is just right and it snaps solidly into place, on or off. The gun comes with beautiful rosewood grips with the same fish scale pattern as on the slide, plus a nice little diamond with the letter "E" to remind us this is an "Enhanced" 1911.

The trigger and hammer are the skeletonized lightweight jobs we all love. The hammer settles nicely into the beavertail when it's cocked, and the trigger pull is an easy 4.9 lbs. with 0.0125 take-up and a crisp, clean break. The muzzle is recessed and the firing pin is titanium. The trigger must be pulled for the gun to fire — dropping the gun will not make the firing pin go forward to strike a primer.

OTHER ENHANCEMENTS

S&W opted for an oversized extractor. There's a memory bump on the grip safety and just below the grip curves into what we typically call a round butt which really *does* equate to easier carry in IWB mode. I really like checkered front and back straps to help my grip and this model comes with 17 LPI on both. Coupled with those attractive fish scale rosewood panels, the security of my grip on the gun is superb.

The "SC" in the model name stands for Scandium, a very lightweight but extremely strong alloy combined with aluminum in the frame to lighten the load while maintaining durability. Unloaded, the gun weighs 28.8 oz. It comes with one 7-round magazine and one slightly extended eight rounder. I elected to replace them both with Colt 8-round magazines so I always have nine rounds on board, with nothing extending from the butt of the gun.

NO WIDEBODIES HERE

Since slim is in, I decided to compare the S&W SCE Commander to one of my favorite carry guns, the Springfield XD-S

This 15-yard offhand group with Black Hills ammo is typical. David takes full responsibility for the flyer!

.45 ACP. Would you believe the body width of both guns is the same at 0.91"? At their widest point there is a 0.30" difference. The total width — including the ambidextrous safeties on the Smith is 1.35, whereas the width of the XD-S at its widest point is 1.05. This makes no noticeable difference inside the holster.

I can't afford one of those $3,000 to $6,000 (or more) custom guns but I feel like I got one with the S&W 1911SCE Commander. One trip to the range was all it took for me to put it into my "carry rotation." At the range I compared it to other 1911 Commanders from Colt, Ruger, SIG and Springfield, and it held its own. Several times since I've used the S&W to test various types of ammo, including the newer, lightweight fluted rounds from Inceptor and Lehigh. It's as accurate as any of the other guns and more accurate than most and I've never had any kind of failure to feed or extract. It's a delight to shoot.

Smith and Wesson catalogs them at an MSRP of around $1,500, which should probably make the street price somewhere around $1,250.

PERFORMANCE CENTER SHIELD 2.0
S&W'S CCW "PHENOM" GETS A HOTROD MAKEOVER

David Freeman

The Smith & Wesson Shield has now become the 2.0 version and the Performance Center mod shop has added enhancements with a ported model. The gunsmiths at the Performance Center conceptualize, engineer and handcraft their products from the ground up and comprise the "Best of the Best" — each with an average length of service at S&W of over 23 years. What they've done for the Shield, in addition to porting the barrel and slide, is to polish the feed ramp and hood, tune the action, install a PC sear and test fire each gun for function.

The PC touch: Alongside the S&W Shield Model 2.0 comes a Performance Center model with tuned action and ported barrel and slide.

A PLATFORM EVOLVES

Introduced in 2012, the Shield is a continuation of the polymer-framed, short-recoil, locked-breech Military and Police (M&P) line introduced in the summer of 2005. The intention was to go head-to-head with GLOCK in the law enforcement market. Since its introduction, the M&P has captured a large percentage of this market. But while targeted at LE agencies, the M&P is extremely popular in the commercial market.

For the Shield, S&W took the power and features of their full-sized M&P and put them into a slim, lightweight pistol the size of your hand. The M&P Shield is easy to conceal, offering professional grade features with simple operation and reliable performance. It was one of the first of what we've come to call "single-stack nines," attractive to the concealed carry crowd. Although the 9mm was the first one introduced, it was quickly followed by a .40 S&W version, and by early 2017, a .45 ACP version. S&W announced in November 2015 they had sold over one million Shields, and they've continued to sell well.

The Performance Center added two ports in the Shield's barrel and six ports in the frame to dissipate redirected gasses. The ports reduce muzzle flip and felt recoil.

The 2.0 version was first announced with the full-size M&P in January 2018 with the Shield 2.0 version following later the same year. It's a bit of a facelift based on feedback from Shield users over the preceding five years. The 2.0 has a refined trigger for a smoother pull, crisper break and a more audible, tactile reset. The frame stippling has been changed to give the shooter a better grip on the pistol — it's a bit rougher, almost like sandpaper, but it does give you better purchase. The machining of the slide is a bit different, with a softer bevel and some fish scale serrations toward the front of the slide that aren't on the original model.

The Performance Center added porting to help reduce muzzle flip and to provide some reduction in felt recoil. PC 2.0 Ported Shields are available in six flavors: two 9mms, two .40 S&Ws and two .45 ACPs. The difference in the two models for each caliber is the sights. You can opt for Tritium night sights or HIVIZ fiber optic sights. The two 9mm models have thumb safeties. None of the .40 S&W or .45 ACP models have them, though all Shields have internal safeties and trigger safeties.

LESS FLIP, BETTER BREAK

To find out how the porting works and to determine if there was any negatives — such as blinding muzzle flash or potential burns on the hands — I spent an afternoon shooting five different types of ammo through both the PC 2.0 Ported Shield and a non-ported original. I also enlisted the aid of some additional shooters to get their overall opinion of the new model.

The first thing we all noticed about the PC 2.0 Shield is the trigger. It's definitely smoother. I checked it later with my Lyman Trigger Pull Scale and determined only a slight difference in the pull weight — 5.5-lb. average for the PC 2.0 Shield compared to a little over 6 lbs. for the original Shield. The real difference was in how it *felt* — the smoother pull, the tactile break and the reset. None of us even noticed any muzzle flash. The PC engineers apparently took care of this problem by how they placed the ports on the barrel and slide. The barrel ports are at 10 and 2, well forward on the barrel. The slide has three corresponding holes on each side moving rearward from the barrel holes. The arrangement seems to be very efficient.

Shooting at 7 yards from a standing two-handed position, all shooters were able to put all their rounds within a pie plate-sized target. The ported Shield wasn't more, nor less, accurate than the older one, but it was easier on the hands and more pleasant to shoot. With an MSRP of only $539, it's definitely worth the money to have a Performance Center gun to brag about!

S&W'S MODEL 610
THIS CLASSIC COMEBACK IS A PERFECT "10"

Mark Hampton

Using an UltraDot L/T mounted with Weigand's new mini mount, the big N-Frame performed flawlessly and wasn't picky about ammo.

The reissued S&W M610 10mm will be welcomed by shooters and hunters alike.

After searching for a good used S&W Model 610 for quite some time, I discovered a couple of things. First, they are not hiding behind every bush — they've become somewhat difficult to locate. Second, when you do find one, the cost may involve seriously diminishing the kid's college fund. Therefore, when I heard the announcement of S&W reintroducing the M610, I immediately ordered one.

Over the past few years, the 10mm Auto cartridge has become much more popular. I'm not really sure if it's personal defense, recreational shooting, or hunting — or perhaps a combination of all three — driving the market but one thing's certain, the 10mm comeback is for real. Jan Mladek, General Manager of S&W and M&P brands said, "We felt it was important to offer a 10mm revolver for personal protection and handgun hunting. The N-Frame has long been a staple in big-bore revolvers and the 10mm is a natural caliber addition to the line." Well, I'm thrilled S&W reintroduced the 10mm to their revolver offerings.

Built on the large S&W N-Frame, the gun is ideal for launching the 10mm Auto while it is also capable of handling the .40 S&W. This is a good-looking revolver as the stainless steel frame, cylinder and barrel match up well aesthetically to the black synthetic grips.

The round-butt grips have slight finger grooves and are most comfortable. I appreciate the full under-lug and, if I could wave my magic wand, I'd really like an unfluted cylinder. The trigger face is smooth and wide while the revolver is easy to cock in single-action mode, thanks to the wide, checkered target hammer.

The new M610 is offered in two barrel lengths — 4 and 6.5". The 10mm provides plenty of horsepower for home defense and personal protection. It is also a good option for close-range whitetail or wild hogs. Since I'll be using this gun for hunting, the longer barrel was chosen. My test gun tipped the scales a tad bit over 50 oz. and balances extremely well with the longer tube.

The gun arrived in a nice blue hard case with three moon clips provided. The moon clips make loading and unloading painless. There are quite a number high-cap semi-autos chambered in 10mm, but moon clips narrow the "reloading speed gap" on the revolver side.

If you're target shooting at the range in ideal lighting conditions, iron sights will suffice. The factory front sight features an interchangeable black blade while the rear sight is fully adjustable and includes a white notch outline. However, with aging eyes I am not going to try fooling myself — I need optics, especially for those early morning or late evening opportunities. I don't see open sights well enough to place a bullet where it belongs 100 percent of the time.

For many years I've enjoyed the dependability of UltraDot, so it was an easy choice to mount their L/T reflex sight on the M610. The four MOA dot size will show up nicely on a big hog's shoulder and the unit has 10 brightness settings, allowing you to adjust the dot according to light conditions. This is a great asset!

Mounting the UltraDot L/T on the S&W was easy, thanks to Weigand Machine and Design's sleek and clean-looking mini Weig-A-Tinny mount. (Weigand has a mount for all K-, N- and X-Frame S&W revolvers.)

Loaded with a truckload of ammo, I was ready for a trip to the range to see what the M610 could do. After a few quick adjustments on the UltraDot, the gun was sighted-in at 25 yards from a sandbag rest. The trigger broke crisp and clean, as I've experienced with other S&W models. It didn't take long before five- and six-shot groups were in a cluster. DoubleTap, HSM, SIG, Hornady and a few other brands of ammo were tested and the M610 proved very manageable with recoil a non-issue. HSM 180-gr. JHP put four rounds in the same hole and the other two were almost touching. The M610 flat-out *shoots*!

I see close-range deer and hog hunting in my M610's future. There are some excellent hunting loads from a variety of manufacturers including Hornady, DoubleTap, Federal, Underwood and HSM. For plinking, I'll stick with the 180-gr. FMJs.

I'm probably not the only shooter glad to see S&W reintroduce their M610. It's already found a secure spot in my handgun battery.

www.smithandwesson.com
www.jackweigand.com

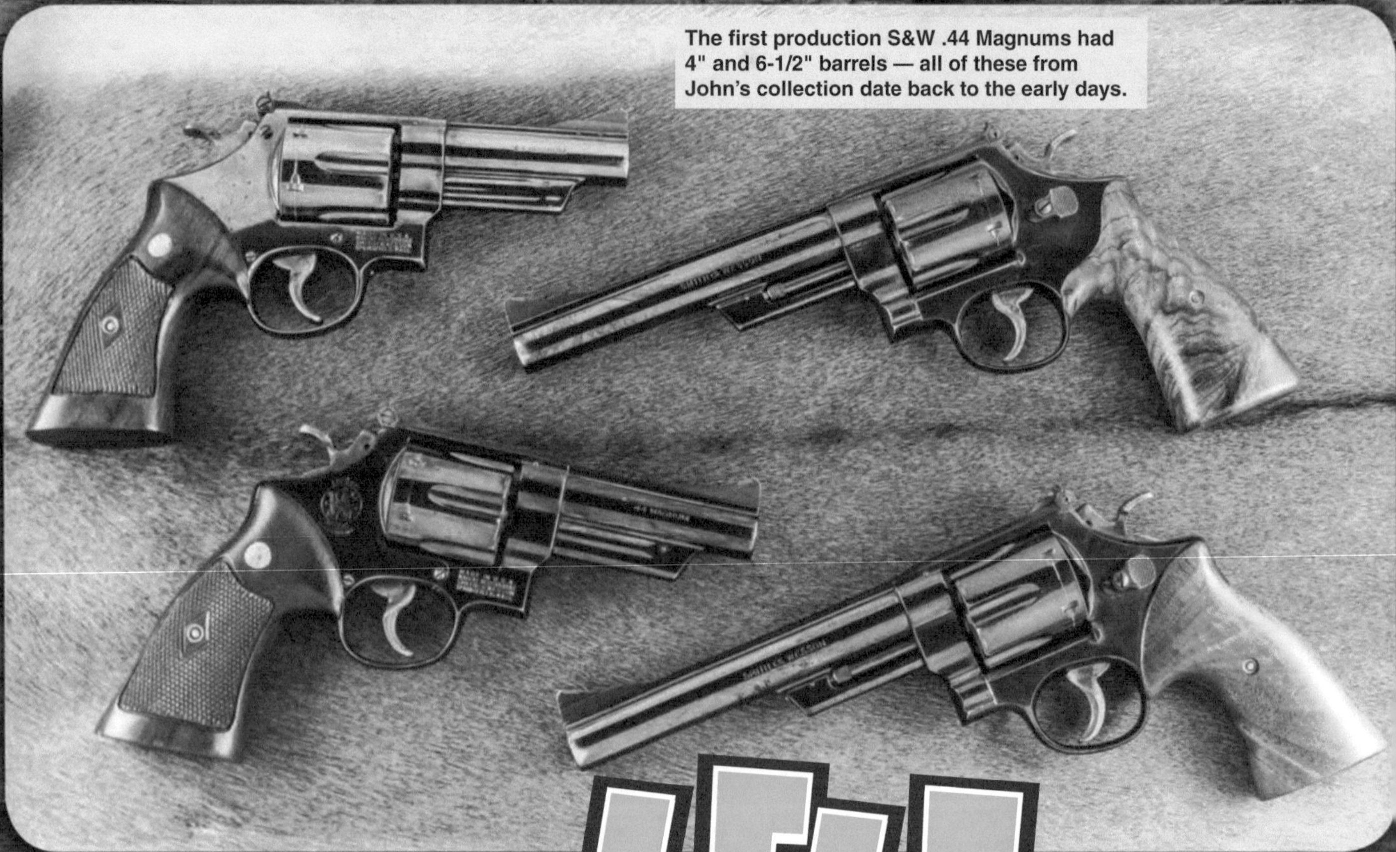

The first production S&W .44 Magnums had 4" and 6-1/2" barrels — all of these from John's collection date back to the early days.

THE .44 MA

Ruger's .44 Magnums include (top-bottom) the Super Redhawk, Super Blackhawk and Redhawk. John shooting his first Smith & Wesson .44 Magnum (right) acquired in 1962.

In addition to 4", 6-1/2" and 8-3/8" standard production .44 Magnums in the mid-to late 1950s, Smith & Wesson also produced a special run of 5" sixguns (lower right).

GNUM OPUS

These are two of John's early .44 Magnum hunting sixguns — a 10" Flat-Top Blackhawk Ruger (top) and an 8-3/8" Smith & Wesson.

John Taffin

The .44 Magnum has now been around for well over 60 years and it seems like a good time to look back at this excellent — perhaps even *all around* — sixgun load and the fine revolvers which have been made for it.

IN THE BEGINNING

The .44 Magnum basically begins with Elmer Keith. If you are not a reader of Keith, now would be a good time to start. Although he has been gone now for over 35 years and some of his writing is definitely dated, for much of his life Elmer was way ahead of his time. His books *Sixgun Cartridges & Loads* (1936) as well as *Sixguns* (1955) and his many articles in *American Rifleman* from the 1920s and 1930s make fascinating reading and are filled with real sixgun knowledge. In the closing pages of his

HISTORY REVEALED –
FROM SOMEBODY WHO WAS THERE!

Elmer Keith had one of the first 6-1/2" .44 Magnums cut to 4-1/2" and engraved and ivory-gripped by the Gun ReBlu Co.

Keith experimented with his heavy .44 Special loads in the Pre-WWI S&W Triple-Locks.

Bisley Model Grip Frames (L-R) — Colt Single Action, Texas Longhorn Arms Improved Number Five and the Ruger Bisley Model.

Ruger produced less than 1,000 each of the original Flat-top Blackhawk .44 Magnums with 10" and 7-1/2" barrel lengths.

"My friends and I all fired it and lied, claiming the recoil wasn't too bad."

1955 book, Keith wrote: "We desperately need a modern, up-to-date, full powered factory loaded .44 Special — The King of all handgun cartridges."

For 30 years, Keith had been writing about his heavy handloads in .44 Special sixguns — the Smith & Wesson Triple-Lock and 1926 Target Model along with the Colt Single Action. His standard load was 18.5 grains of #2400 under his hard cast, 250-gr. #429421 bullet loaded in the old-fashioned folded, or *balloon head*, cases. With the coming of modern solid head brass, he dropped his load back to 17.0 grains of #2400. Both loads yielded around 1,200 fps from 6-1/2" and 7-1/2" barreled sixguns.

For those same 30 years, to no avail, he had been trying to convince ammunition manufacturers to bring out his .44 Special load. Product liability is nothing new and they were afraid someone would blow an

old .44 Special apart. Keith claimed there would be no problem with any Colt or Smith & Wesson heavy-frame sixgun, as he had been shooting his loads in pre-World War I Triple-Locks for years.

SOMEBODY HEARD

One person who did listen was Carl Hellstrom, president of S & W in the early 1950s. He showed interest in Elmer's pet load and discussed the prospect of a new .44 sixgun with Keith. Hellstrom asked Remington to produce the ammo and they agreed if Smith & Wesson would produce the sixgun.

The new .44 Remington Magnum was 1/8" longer than the .44 Special. This was done so it would not chamber in .44 Special sixguns and in 1954 Smith & Wesson re-chambered four 1950-manufactured Target .44 Specials to the new round. Remington

received one of the new revolvers for testing and it was soon obvious the 39-oz. weight of the .44 Target Model was too light for the recoil of the new .44 "Special-Magnum." For all those years Elmer Keith had asked for 1,200 fps and the new round achieved 1,500+ fps, or 25 percent faster than Keith had asked for!

To provide a needed increase in weight, S&W produced a revolver with a barrel 0.15" greater in diameter and a cylinder 0.18" longer. This brought the weight of the 6-1/2" sixgun up to 48 oz. or 3 lbs. By early 1955, tests were completed and S&W began tooling up to produce what at the time was simply known as the .44 Magnum. The first factory revolver was completed on December 29, 1955 and shipped to Remington. In January, the next two were completed and these went to the NRA for testing by Maj. Julian Hatcher while the other was shipped to Salmon, Idaho to Elmer Keith. By the end of 1956, more than 3,000 S&W .44 Magnums were produced in both the original 6-1/2" length and an easier-to-pack 4" version. The longer barreled 8-3/8" did not arrive until 1958.

As a kid fresh out of high school, I fired one of the first of the 4" .44 Magnums a local gun dealer had. Rather than sell it, he rented it out at six shots for 50 cents and it was a real attention getter for his range. My friends and I all fired it and lied, claiming the recoil wasn't too bad.

Reporting in *American Rifleman* for March 1956, Maj. Hatcher said: "In shooting the .44 Magnum, we found it advisable to use gloves, as the recoil can only be described as severe.… I fired quite a few shots with this gun, but I must honestly confess it is not an unmixed pleasure."

Elmer Keith, writing in the *Gun Digest,* looked upon the .44 Magnum quite differently than Maj. Hatcher. "The big gun is, I would say, pleasant to shoot, and does not jar the hand as much as do my .44 Special loads from the much lighter 4" barreled .44 Special S&W sixguns … the recoil has not bothered me in the slightest nor have

several old sixgun men complained."

At the time, reading both of these reports I felt the truth was somewhere in between and I leaned towards Maj. Hatcher's conclusion. In Elmer Keith's report in the *Gun Digest* entitled "The .44 Magnum One Year Later," he said he had fired the new gun 600 rounds the first year. This averages 12 rounds per week. There may be a lesson in there!

THEN THERE WERE THREE

By 1958, .44 Magnums were available from Ruger, Smith & Wesson and Great Western as well. The Great Westerns did not last long after the factory closed in the early '60s, leaving the only U.S.-made .44s available from Ruger and Smith & Wesson. These were the Super Blackhawk and what we know as the Smith & Wesson Model 29.

Dirty Harry changed all this. Clint Eastwood's unrealistic portrayal of the San Francisco cop who packed a .44 Magnum created such a demand for .44s the Smith & Wessons were selling close to double their retail price.

This false demand turned out to be a good thing as other manufacturers decided

to get in on the .44-craze and soon .44s were available from, by my count, 13 different manufacturers. Besides the defunct Great Western, .44 Magnum sixguns were available from Smith & Wesson, Ruger, Dan Wesson, Interarms, Mossberg (Abilene), U.S. Arms (Seville and El Dorado), High Standard (Very rare Crusaders), plus foreign .44s from Europe. Uberti contributed the Cattlemen and Dakota, along with others from Arminius, Llama, Astra, R.G., F.I.E., and Sauer & Sohn.

By now, the stage was set for .44 Magnums to become even more popular. Both Ruger and Dan Wesson took advantage of the fact they were able to build a larger and stronger double-action sixgun around the .44 Magnum cartridge. Ruger soon brought out their second double-action .44 Magnum, the Super Redhawk, which is even stronger than the almost indestructible Redhawk.

The Ruger Bisley arrived in the mid-1980s. Some of my friends in the industry said it "was an answer to a question nobody asked." I had to disagree — at least in my hand it was a great improvement over what Elmer Keith called the Ruger Dragoon,

In 2006 Ruger issued the 50th Anniversary Model (top) of the original .44 Magnum Blackhawk.

or Super Blackhawk. At the time, I had a pair of .44 Special Colt Bisley Models I liked very much and found the Ruger Bisley grip to be an improvement over the Colt Bisley grip.

ACCURACY

What kind of accuracy can one reasonably expect from a .44 Magnum sixgun? There are three major factors involved, namely the particular sixgun, the load, and the shooter. I am not personally satisfied with any sixgun or load combination shooting less than 1" groups at 25 yards off sandbags. Some .44s will gobble up anything and spit 'em out accurately — well, *almost*. Others are very picky about which load combination they will accept.

As a general rule, with some exceptions of course, I have found the harder you push 'em, the tighter they shoot. Also, generally speaking, 300-gr. bullets will normally have greater accuracy than 250-gr. or lighter bullets. I have experienced sixguns that couldn't shoot less than 3" groups with 250-gr. bullets but become one-holers when loaded to the max with 300-gr. bullets. The fun is in the search for the best loads.

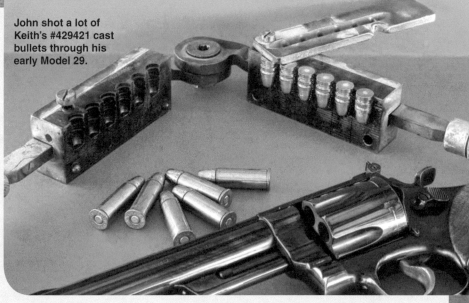

John shot a lot of Keith's #429421 cast bullets through his early Model 29.

A good .44 Magnum will shoot right alongside any other sixgun target revolver. Elmer Keith always said the true test of any sixgun is shooting long range. The .44 Magnum can be loaded accurately enough to keep 10 out of 10 shots on a silhouette ram's body at 225 yards. Loaded with 300-gr. bullets at 1,300 to 1,400 fps, it becomes a premier hunting handgun when used with common sense and reason.

Chopped and channeled to become a 3" "belly gun" and again properly loaded, it is a highly effective defensive weapon. There are so many excellent jacketed bullets and cast bullets available it would take more than a lifetime of shooting to cover all the possibilities.

Col. Charles Askins once stated the .44 Magnum should have been still-born. I'm certainly glad it wasn't.

S&W'S PERFORMANCE CENTER

Performance Center Victory Target with fiber optic sights shot well. A "dot" sight might do even better in your hands!

Obvious differences can be seen here between the Performance Center .22 Victory Target Model (top) and the .22 Victory Target. Note the fluted barrel and muzzle brake on the Performance Center version.

.22 VICTORY TARGET

If there's anything handier for setting up housekeeping than a good .22 I don't know what it is. The first gun I ever shot was a Harrington & Richardson .22 Top Break belonging to my uncle. When I was 8 years old, I learned to shoot on his farm and also drive a tractor. While he had to put wooden blocks on the tractor's pedals, the .22 sixgun was perfect for my small hands just as it came from the factory.

Every new shooter could do themselves a real favor and also speed up the learning curve by starting with a .22. This applies whether a first firearm is a rifle, sixgun or semi-automatic pistol. The positive attributes of a quality .22 are very little recoil, low noise level and relatively inexpensive ammunition — all of which promote practice. Everyone in my family — myself, Diamond Dot, all the kids and all the grandkids — started with .22's. Now we have our first four great grandkids and you can bet they'll begin with the same.

APPEALING OPTION

Several years ago S&W offered the Victory Model, a very reasonably priced .22 semi-automatic pistol with adjustable rear sight matched up with a fiber-optic front sight. Now we have the improved Victory Target which, for me, is greatly improved as it features target sights consisting of a fully adjustable black rear sight matched up with a black post front sight on a ramp. For me this is the best sight combination. It also features a target trigger with an adjustable trigger stop. The trigger pull measures an acceptable 4½ lbs., but I would prefer a pound less.

The pistol comes with two 10-round magazines that have a button on the side to depress the magazine spring for easy loading. An HKS loader for the S&W also helps here, especially when we get to loading the last two rounds. Unloaded weight is 36 oz. This weight combined with a barrel length of 5½" and excellent stocks give the Victory Target an exceptionally good balance in my hands.

The pistol is constructed of stainless steel and has textured polymer grip panels which, combined with the checkered back- and front-strap, provide a very secure feeling when shooting. S&W has done something quite unusual with their polymer grips. The Victory comes with a flat grip on the right side matched up with a thumbrest grip on the left side. If one happens to be left-handed this is taken care of by the fact S&W supplies two extra grip panels with one flat on the left side with a thumb rest grip on the right side. This allows two ways for setting up the Victory, or one can choose to use two thumbrest grips or two flat grips. The latter way is what I chose as it feels the best to me.

Part of the package optionally included with the Performance Center Victory Target is a Viper Red Dot optic.

THE NEXT LEVEL

Want a bit more from your Victory pistol? Luckily for you, S&W has its Performance Center, basically a custom shop taking standard production models and offering many special extras. They recently turned their attention to the Victory Target Model and made something very special.

In addition to internal smoothing and setting the trigger pull at just over 3 lbs., the Perfomance Center added a flat-face trigger and two set screws that allow the shooter to reduce both pre-travel and over-travel. Other obvious differences

The Performance Center Victory Target Model takes a great rimfire and makes it even better. It comes with a protective zippered bag.

TAFFIN TESTS

readily seen include a fluted barrel with an attractive muzzle brake/compensator installed. This is removable, and a thread-protecting bushing is provided. Fiber-optic fully adjustable sights, a larger push button magazine release and larger custom rubber grips with an aggressive pattern for a very secure grip feeling round out the package.

I fired over 600 rounds through the Performance Center pistol and the only malfunction was the typical failure to fire on the first hit you often get with some rimfire ammo. This happened with four rounds and all fired when the cartridges were rotated 180 degrees. This is most likely a fault of the priming compound not being complete around the rim of the cartridge.

In addition to great target sights, both the Victory Target Model and the Performance Center Target Model are supplied with a Picatinny-style scope base. To install the rail, the front screw on the rear sight assembly is removed, allowing the entire assembly to slide out from under the back clip that helps hold it in place. The rail replaces it, the front screw returned and it's ready to accept scope rings. What this means is the scope base is held in place by only one screw.

The same set up works fine with the rear sight assembly, but I wondered how it would perform with the scope in place. I tried both a standard Victory Target model and the Performance Center version with optics to test this out. I soon found after about 20 to 30 shots on the standard model the inertia of the scope, in this case a 4X EER Leupold, would cause the front screw to loosen on the scope base. On the Performance Center version I installed a Viper Red Dot, which is offered as an option with the pistol. I found I could get about 100 shots off before the base would loosen.

Hands On

More than 20 different brands/versions of .22's were put to the test in the Performance Center Victory Target Model. As long as the screw remained tight it performed exceptionally well with the red dot in place, with many loads giving me groups in the 1" or less range for nine shots at 25 yards. The most accurate load proved to be the Winchester T 22 Target with a 7/8" group with a muzzle velocity of 1,057 fps. Other loads in the 1" range included Winchester Power Point HPs, which is one of my favorite .22 LR hunting loads; CCI Mini-Mags and Mini-Mag HPs; Federal Lightnings; and American Eagle HPs.

In regards to the loosening screw concern, I didn't try Loc-Tite so I don't know if this would solve the problem.

My engineer friend says one of the problems is the fact the base is plastic and he felt an aluminum or steel one would serve much better. An aftermarket aluminum scope mount base is available and this may help to solve the problem.

Switching to the excellent fiber optic adjustable sights, I also received excellent performance for nine shots at 20 yards. Many of the loads gave me 1" or tighter groups. The same loads already mentioned work just fine with iron sights as well. The best performing loads in addition to these included CCI Standard Velocity, Remington Thunderbolt and Winchester High Velocity HP, all of which gave me 7/8" groups. The fiber-optic sights consist of a high-visibility green dot in the front sight and a green dot on both sides of the rear sight. For me and probably for most shooters green is easier to see than red.

The Performance Center Victory Target Model comes in a zippered padded case with two 10-round magazines for an MSRP of $672, and it's available with a Viper Red Dot optic for $868. It's a keeper for me, and neither the standard Victory Model nor the Performance Center version will be going back. It's impossible to have too many semi-automatic .22 pistols, and checks are easier and cheaper to mail!

MAKING BETTER-

MICHAEL O. HUMPHRIES

Mike's new M&P M2.0 Compact 9mm went to Apex Tactical for a new flat-faced set trigger, "Apex Grade" barrel and "failure-resistant" extractor. Note the zazzy blue color for the trigger.

EVEN BETTER

Until I wrote this, I didn't realize how much of a Smith & Wesson fan I am. I knew I had a lot of their guns and liked them, but it really struck home when I started digging through the gun safe. My first revolver? A .357 Smith Model 581. My first auto? A 9mm 5906. My first carry gun? A Model 642 J-Frame .38 Spl. My first .40? An M&P. In fact, my current carry gun is an S&W M&P9 full-size pistol, judiciously customized by Apex Tactical. See a trend here?

SIG SAUER V-Crown JHP, Federal Hydra-Shok Deep and Inceptor ARX +P ammo all performed fine.

A Milt Sparks Versa Max 2 IWB holster in horsehide and matching mag carrier worked great.

I'd been wanting something a tad smaller — without going the full "subcompact" route — and have been very curious about the new M&P M2.0 series of pistols. When Smith released the M&P M2.0 Compact, I jumped at the chance to see just what the difference is.

A Solid Foundation

What does the 2.0 bring to the party? Enhancements both inside and out. Internally, the 2.0 has a stiffened polymer frame through an extended stainless steel chassis as well as a redesigned trigger for a crisper and cleaner pull, with a tangible reset. Externally, the pistol's texturing was made more "aggressive" — and by this, I mean it's reaching the level of 220-grit sandpaper. Seriously, this gun is not going to move in your hand. In addition, the pistol comes with four interchangeable palmswell inserts to fit hands ranging from petite to bear paw sized.

The new M2.0 Compact also brought something notable to the M&P line — a completely new size. While the original M&P line had an M&PC compact variant — yep, I have one of these as well — it was more of a subcompact-sized pistol. As a result, you had pretty much the full-size and a much smaller compact from which to choose. To all of the Goldilocks out there, the new M2.0 Compact is a "just right" addition to the line. With its 4" barrel — although a shorter 3.6" barrel version is also available — and 15-round magazine in 9mm, the new Compact fits right in the middle of the older M&P offerings.

For someone like me who prefers guns closer to the full-size range for EDC, the new Compact was just about

Mike had the pistol topped off with a set of Trijicon's excellent HD XR Night Sights. Note the racking ledge on the forward face.

The pistol comes with two handy "grip extensions" for getting a full grip when using the longer mags.

While the Compact has a shorter grip frame than a full-size, you can still use the longer mags.

S&W M&P M2.0 COMPACT

perfect. Small enough to carry, but big enough to be a "real" gun. While it's also offered in .40 and .45, I selected the M&P M2.0 Compact in 9mm. I also like the variant with the ambi manual safety.

The Next Level

No sooner had I put in an order for the pistol when I got an email from Apex Tactical they had just released a "failure-resistant extractor" for the M2.0. Curiosity sent me to their site to see what else they were offering for the new pistols. What I found was a treasure chest of goodies. I put in an order for the extractor which had brought me there, as well as the new M&P M2.0C Apex "gunsmith fit" barrel and one of the company's iconic flat-faced forward set triggers.

During my discussions with Apex, the question of trigger color came up. As I already had a red Apex trigger in an M&P Shield — yep, I have one of these, too — I asked if blue would be a possibility. They explained they plan to offer red, but all custom color requests such as this one go to Legion Precision for Cerakoting. So, I packed up the pistol and sent it on to Apex for the install

work. I also included a set of Trijicon's excellent orange HD XR Night Sights for installation while they had it.

For me, the Trijicon sights offer the best of all worlds. They are three-dot tritium units, but the front sight has a large colored ring for picking it up easily. This way you get the three dots for low light, but pretty much just the high-visibility front sight in daylight. Add in a racking ledge on the rear sight and a slim front post, and you have just about everything I would ask for in a sighting set.

Hands On

I had spent the time waiting for the pistol to be finished by Apex gathering ammo and accessories. I went with my favorite holster rig, a Milt Sparks Versa Max 2 horsehide inside-the-waistband unit with a matching belt and single mag carrier, and I picked up a 17-rounder full-size M&P 9mm magazine to be my spare. I noted the Compact comes with two 15-rounders as

well as two handy polymer "grip extensions" for 17-round magazines, slipping over the magazine body giving you a full grip with the longer mags.

When I received the reworked pistol, I was wowed by the work. The new "Apex Grade" stainless steel barrel was attractive and seemed to be well fitted, and the flat-faced trigger was terrific. Apex had set it at 5 lbs. for me since I explained this would be a carry gun, and it exhibited a clean and crisp break right at this weight.

I headed out to the range with Inceptor 65-gr. ARX +P, Federal Hydra-Shok 135-gr. "Deep" and SIG SAUER 124-gr. JHP V-Crown ammo. I settled in at the bench at 15 yards with the Compact on a rest and began shooting groups. I had a few failures to fully feed malfunctions early, but this soon cleared up. I suspected the tightly fitted barrel was "wearing" in, typical of an auto. I shot the pistol with the original and the new barrel and noted the Apex unit did tighten up the groups. The pistol showed a preference for the ultra-light Inceptor ammo, with a smallest group of 3/4", but still shooting well with all three loads.

I really like the new Compact M2.0 from Smith & Wesson. The "bones" of it are exactly what I wanted in a new carry gun, and the Apex upgrades and Trijicon sights took it to the next level. The MSRP of the basic pistol is a very reasonable $569, although my customizing added up to more than the original cost of the pistol. However, in the big picture I think you get a lot for your money either way.

The M2.0 brings a lot of upgrades to the M&P platform. One of these is highly aggressive texturing and a total of four palmswell inserts to fit almost any hand size.

THE MAGICAL MODEL 12

(L-R) A former Hong Kong cop Model 12 Roy chopped and customized for carry years ago. The blued 2" Model 12 came next some years ago, and recently Roy talked Tiger out of the nickel one, a Model 12-3 third gen. The old Winchester flashlight is just for fun.

LIGHTWEIGHT, ACCURATE — AND A SIXSHOOTER!

Here a Model 12 is hiding a stock square butt 4" Model 10 behind it. But the light weight, round butt and shorter barrel of the 12 makes it much more carry friendly.

(L-R) The Colt Cobra (with shroud) is classy and holds six shots but doesn't handle as well as the Model 12 next in line. At top, the early Agent also has six rounds but is both more austere and exhibits that "stacking" Colt trigger, like the Cobra.

I've always been enamored — is it okay to be enamored? — with the Model 12. If you're not up to speed, it's a K-Frame S&W with an aluminum alloy frame weighing about 18 oz. in the 2" version. Early guns were made for the Airforce and even had aluminum cylinders, but it was soon found they just didn't hold up. Introduced to the commercial market around 1953, the same gun with aluminum cylinder suffered from the same ills — go figure — so the aluminum cylinder got tossed for a steel one. Problem solved. From then until about 1986 the Model 12 (in four "generations") remained in the Smith catalog in blue or nickel. I'm blessed with one of each flavor thanks to my talking Tiger McKee out of his nickel one lately. Don't hate me Tiger.

When I was a new cop, I stumbled onto a blued police trade-in Model 12 with a 4" barrel from, of all places, the Hong Kong police department. It even had a lanyard loop. It was just an old cop gun in those days and I think I paid something like $125 for it. It was actually minty inside with little sign of being fired, just carried a lot. While I loved J-Frames and D-Frame Colts — and still do — the K-Frame sized Model 12 simply handles better. Being a "full-sized" K-Frame, the bigger grip, better sights, longer/smoother action make it much easier to handle and shoot accurately.

I took to that Model 12 fast and carried it off and on for quite some time. I did have the sense not to beat it up with hot ammo — they just can't take +P stuff — and with a diet of primarily .38 Special Target Wadcutters, it's still alive and kicking. I did customize it in the late 1980s — check out the picture — and snubbing the hammer and shortening the barrel to about 3" really made it handy.

To put some perspective into things, a J-Frame Model 36 (steel) weighs about 19 oz. and carries five rounds. An "Airweight" J-Frame like the classic Model 37 weighs pretty close to 14 oz. depending on the grip style.

So with a 2" Model 12, you get all the advantage I talked about, in about the same weight range. Speaking of weight, for more reference, that elegant little .22 LR in the pic on p. 96, the Model 43, has an aluminum cylinder and is a feathery 14 oz. The Colt Cobra in another pic manages a comfy 16.5 oz. while the more austere early Agent (with Tyler T-Grip) is about 15 oz. give or take. Almost birds of a feather, if you will.

But we're back to what I learned earlier. Even with six shots, the Colt models are smaller than the Model 12, but the distinctive Colt action which sort of "stacks" as you pull the trigger, makes them not quite as friendly to shoot as the bigger Model 12. You'll feel it the instant you pick them up. For shooting, I'd take the Model 12, while for simply carrying around, with little shooting, the smaller guns win — barely. Slightly bigger means a bit tougher to conceal in a pocket, sure, but lord, the 2" Model 12's are delightful to shoot! And frankly, as accurate as any 4" at 15 or 25 yards. Decisions, eh?

Model 12 Secrets

Okay, not really secrets, but in all honesty it wasn't until just a few years ago I found out the frames of the first

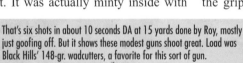

That's six shots in about 10 seconds DA at 15 yards done by Roy, mostly just goofing off. But it shows these modest guns shoot great. Load was Black Hills' 148-gr. wadcutters, a favorite for this sort of gun.

Leathersmith Thad Rybka makes this nifty strong side simple scabbard and Roy likes it for his Model 12. Ammo is the full-wadcutter defense load in .38 Special from Buffalo Bore (standard pressure) in the strip, and the classic 158-gr. soft lead SWCHP in the HKS speedloader. Both are Model 12 friendly.

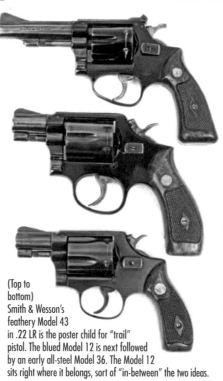

three generations of Model 12's are about 0.08" narrower than standard Model 10 frames. I put a set of stock Model 10 grips on a Model 12 once and there was a gap under the grip panel at the side plate. Huh? What? A bit of research yielded the reason and once I knew it, I could "see" it when I handled the guns. The Model 12 does feel "slimmer" — not by much, but it's there to a practiced eye and hand. The final Model 12-4 introduced in about 1984 went full-width. Oh, and any of them through the years could be had in square or round-butt, with round butt being my favorite. There's a joke somewhere nearby, but I won't go there.

Our friends at S&W introduced the "Night Guard" series some years ago as a new line of lightweight revolvers. One model, the 315 Night Guard, was essentially a Model 12 but modernized. They sold out and the line is discontinued, but you can find them on Gunbroker.com and the like. Worth a look if you ask me. The amazing thing is today, a nice, clean Model 12 (any generation) can go for a low of about $500 for a basic shooter to upwards of $1,200 for a minty one in a box and such. If you stay away from +P ammo and just enjoy the gun, you can't go

(Top to bottom) Smith & Wesson's feathery Model 43 in .22 LR is the poster child for "trail" pistol. The blued Model 12 is next followed by an early all-steel Model 36. The Model 12 sits right where it belongs, sort of "in-between" the two ideas.

wrong, and it will always be worth what you paid for it or more.

Carrying And Shooting

I enjoy carrying mine around my place here now and again just to exercise it, and have found my Thad Rybka belt holster to be about perfect for the job. Come winter time, it also finds its way into town with me under a coat. Out to about 25 yards, it's a laser beam, and even my 80-yard torso gong gets tired of being wanged by it and those 148-gr. wadcutters. I swear that target taunts me, "Sure, go ahead, you'll never hit me!" Followed by "Bang, Clang, Ouch! Hey, stop it, that hurts!" Gotcha.

Speaking of shooting, that target you see in the pic on p. 98 is a 15-yard, 2" group I shot double action in about 10 seconds using Black Hills target wadcutters. I was mostly just goofing off, but that's six shots and if I took my time, I'll wager that group would easily be 1.5" or better. Like I said, they shoot like laser beams if you do your stuff. One of these days I'll follow this up with a gala 100-yard shoot-fest with these cool old guns. That'd be fun. I especially like the fact both of mine shoot mostly right to point of aim.

Note the blued one has the flat cylinder latch putting it as a very early gun. The nickel is a Model 12-3. Between the two, I like the blued a tad better due to the smoother action and the fact it's a bit of a seasoned gentleman — sorta' like I am. Is that the same as just being called old?

Bye for now, but I promise more later.

APEX RUGER UPGRADE

The Apex Action Enhancement Kit for Ruger MK IV 22/45 .22 pistols basically changes everything! But seriously, my test gun, a new production MK IV 22/45, went from a kinda' gritty, creepy 5.5+ lb. trigger to a crisp, sweet 4.25 lb. trigger, with significantly reduced over-travel I could feel easily. The kit includes the Apex Enhancement Trigger (red or black), Apex Action Enhancement Hammer, Apex Safety Plate and Apex Magazine Safety Delete. The Magazine Delete allows the gun to fire without a mag inserted and is recommended for competition only. The install was easy and the videos Apex has posted on their website walk you right through it, step by step. Kits are $89.95. Don't be skeered to do it yourself. *For more info: www.apextactical.com, Ph: (623) 322-0200.*

BARRANTI CCW VEST

The Swift Cover Vest from Barranti Leather is simple, functional and rugged as all get-out. I really like the fact it simply covers your gun and doesn't try to be a 100-item pocket-tool of a vest. No hidden snaps, Velcro enclosures or padlocks — it just hides the gun while allowing you to get to it easily. And it looks like a "Western" vest rather than an urban-commando "shoot-me-first" flashing strobe. Doc designed it from the get-go for concealed carry and it's custom-made by a family member for him, not made out of swamp-reeds from China. You can have a lapel or not, and I especially like the sewn-in weights to both keep the vest in place, and to help toss the side out of the way during a draw. List is $125 and this is first-class stuff. *Find it at www.barrantileather.com, Ph: (412) 860-4804. Let Doc know you saw it here.*

ADD IT UP

214
Millions in the U.S. using Facebook.

26.5
Millions of users aged 45-65.

5
Percentage of social media users who trust it.

68
Percentage of users who don't trust what they see.

331
Justifiable homicides by private citizens in 2016.

A pair of S&W 657's in .41 Mag. The 6.5" model (L) wears a Trijicon RMR reflex sight. The 7.5" is fitted with a Leupold 4x scope. Both are ready for close encounters.

CLOSE ENCOUNTER WHEELGUNS

Hunting with a handgun can certainly spice up your outdoor experience. The variety of circumstances you may stumble onto in the field is always uncertain — but highly anticipated. Many handgunners hunting the wide, open spaces in western states prepare for long-range opportunities normally found while pursuing antelope and mule deer. Even on my farm here in south Missouri, hunting over food plots for whitetail will often yield shooting opportunities beyond 100 yards. But not all hunts involve long-range pokes on big game. If you really want to get the heart pumping, close-range encounters with whitetail, bear, or wild boar will definitely elevate the old heart rate!

I'm in the process of preparing for our upcoming whitetail season. It's fun but involves a lot of work too tidying things up. Many of our elevated deer blinds are situated where a 300-yard shot is possible. Normally I pack one of the single-shots for these stands. We also have several ground blinds where 75 yards is the maximum shot. This is a prime time opportunity for revolvers, and the fun is choosing the particular model for the season.

REVOLVERS WORK FINE

For years I've had an older S&W Model 686 resting under the bed serving as a home protection piece. I haven't shot it much lately so I decided to change things up a bit. A good friend sent me a Leupold base and rings so a scope could be fitted. I had a Leupold 4x scope on-hand and it made a nice fit on the 6" barrel. The original grips were swapped for a pair of attractive Altamont Bateleur grips. These grips are eye-pleasing, also providing a comfortable, secure grip. Our good friends at Mag-na-port gave this 686 a quality trigger job and suddenly — we have a really nice .357 Mag for hunting.

This S&W 686 is a real pleasure to shoot. It's very accurate with a variety of factory loads, including Hornady's 158-gr. XTP. One of our ground blinds allows for only a 60-yard poke and I plan on taking the 686 to this spot when conditions are right. While I consider the .357 Mag. a tad on the light side for whitetail, the cartridge will work fine with proper shot placement. I'll be careful and hold off on shooting until a broadside shot presents itself. With careful, well-executed shot placement, venison will be forthcoming.

For some unknown reason — a syndrome we all experience at times — I picked up a couple of S&W 657's in .41 Mag. A Classic Hunter with 6.5" barrel was first to seemingly magically appear in my safe. Then shortly after, a 7.5" model became available and I succumbed — not sleeping well until it was home. Both of these models feature full under-lugs, unfluted cylinders and really good triggers.

I mounted a Trijicon RMR reflex sight on the 6.5" and this 2.5 MOA dot is ideal for hunting in the woods. I fitted a Leupold 4x scope on the 7.5" version thanks to Jack Weigand's base and rings. So we have two .41 Mags with different optics capable of handling a variety of close-range encounters. Now here comes the dilemma — which one gets to hunt? Hey, this is all part of the fun.

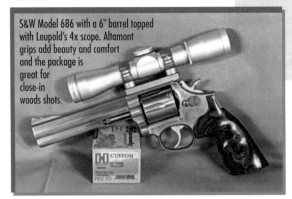

S&W Model 686 with a 6" barrel topped with Leupold's 4x scope. Altamont grips add beauty and comfort and the package is great for close-in woods shots.

TOO MANY CHOICES!

I figured a trip to the range to see just how they would perform would help me make a decision. The .357 Mag shot really well with Hornady's 158-gr. XTP. With the gun now sighted-in at 50 yards, I felt confident this revolver would get to see some action. It's often intriguing to see what changing grips, making slight modifications, and switching sighting options can do to enhance the performance of a handgun. I hadn't shot this 686 much over the last few years but suddenly it was like I got a new toy.

Both S&W 657's were too much fun to shoot. I couldn't decide which one I liked best. Both guns received a diet of Remington factory 210-gr. loads, Vor-TX 180-gr. XPB, Federal 180-gr. Barnes Expander, HSM 210-gr. JHC and Buffalo Bore's 180-gr. Barnes. Then I just had to shoot some of my friend Dick Thompson's powder-coated cast bullets. Lots of good choices and any of them will deck a whitetail or hog with a thump.

Optics play an important role on any hunting handgun. Certain situations lend itself to the 4x scope. The RMR red dot is also a great option. If I enjoyed young eyes there's no doubt iron sights would come into play. These aging peepers need some help so the reflex sight with the red dot is beneficial. Straight 2x or 4x scopes also work well for close-range chances. Now I just need to make a decision or two!

Are you ready for your next close encounter?

THE PERFORMANCE CENTER'S DINO-BLASTER!
2240 FPS!

The sheer size and weight of the 460
helped tame recoil. Mark said the hand-filling
rubber finger-grooved grips made a big difference too.

S&W MODEL
460XVR

MARK HAMPTON

Even sans-scope, the
S&W Model 460XVR
is a brawny beast
of a handgun at
almost 5 lbs.!

The 460 is versatile and can handle (L-R) the .45 Colt, .454 Casull and 460 S&W Magnum cartridges. Lots of options among them in factory ammo.

There's no doubt, most Americans like things big — really big. We like big trucks with big tires and big motors. Big boats, big homes, big farms, you name it — and we like it big. And we have big appetites, "Give me a number four and super-size it!" It's a good thing they don't offer mega-size or we'd order it. Well, if big is better then biggest is surely best. So, if you're in that category, you'll definitely like the Smith & Wesson Model 460 XVR.

That XVR stands for "X-Treme Velocity Revolver." This is a large revolver tipping the scales at 77.8 oz., and that's unloaded, and before mounting any optics. We're talking almost 5 lbs. of power here. Yes, this 5-shooter is a serious hunting handgun for big game pursuits. If you're looking for a conceal-and-carry rig, you'd best move along now.

S&W touts the 460 S&W Magnum cartridge as the highest velocity factory round at well over 2,240 fps with a 200-gr. bullet!

Beasty Boy

Our test gun arrived in a nice black carrying case embroidered in gold with the Smith & Wesson Performance Center logo. The revolver is based on S&W's massive X-Frame, originally intended for their .500 S&W Mag cartridge. The colossal unfluted cylinder holds five rounds. There's plenty of steel in the cylinder walls to accommodate magnum, teeth-rattling, dynamite loads, should you desire. The barrel/cylinder gap is so tiny you can barely see light past it, and lockup is tight.

This revolver features a greenish, HiViz fiber optic front sight, and the rear sight is an adjustable square notch with white outline, if you stay with "irons" — which I doubt you will. I'll admit, though, there's something about the bright green fiber optic sight making it easy for the eyes to acquire

and get on target. For those who can't get enough shooting with irons, this works well.

The unique looking barrel is 7.5" long and is equipped with an effective muzzle brake. The slab sided barrel has "Performance Center" etched on one side and "460 S&W Magnum" on the other. The ejector rod is housed in the underlug, so things are tidy there for a field gun. Underneath the barrel lies a small hole designed for a sling, supplied with the gun. After all, this would be a load to pack around in any type of holster and makes a Walker Colt look like a pocket pistol.

An integral scope base comes with enough space and slots to mount your optic with lots of flexibility. You can either mount a red dot or reflex

Mark found the Leupold 4X scope to be about perfect. Rugged and predictable it stood up fine to the hefty recoil. Note the stock muzzle brake on the barrel.

sight of some sort or go with a scope. Like all other current models, this revolver comes with a key-locking system.

The Performance Center hand-tuned action is silky smooth and didn't disappoint at all. This test gun had a real nice trigger and broke crisply at around 3 lbs. The double action was almost charming, although I'll probably never

Mark used factory ammo for tests. Keep in mind the 460 can also handle .45 Colt, .454 Casull as well as the 460 cartridge.

WHICH GUN

is right for you?

TURN
HERE
for help

S&W 460XVR

shoot the gun in that manner.

The overall fit and finish is superb and is what the Performance Center is all about. I really liked the black finger groove rubber grips that contrasted well with the all stainless steel revolver. They had a slight texture so your hands won't slide around. The grips were very comfortable and that's an asset when shooting 460 magnum rounds. The wide hammer spur is checkered providing a positive surface when cocking, which is likely the way you'll be shooting this brute.

Glassing It

Before going to the range I wanted to mount a scope on the mighty 460 Mag., and not just any scope. Under this amount of recoil, you really need a scope able to handle severe punishment. Fortunately, Leupold's FX-II 4x28mm handgun scope rides to the rescue. This fixed power scope has been abused in the past and continues to digest brutal recoil from the biggest monsters I've had it on. I had plenty of confidence the Leupold would hold up to the 460 Mag.

To make sure the scope wouldn't slide around under recoil, I installed Warne rings. Not only is the selection of scope important, the rings play a critical role in the equation too. In the past I've used Warne rings and bases on some heavy hitters and these quality items have never failed — ever. Warne rings are available in blue or silver so you can match your rings to scope and gun. When looking for scope bases and rings to withstand severe punishment, Warne will deliver. And, as a sort of added benefit, they look good too.

Ammo-Up

Checking the ammo bin I found plenty of factory stuff to keep me busy. Included in the testing process were two loads from Winchester, their 250-gr. JHP and their 260-gr. DJHP Bonded Hunting load. DoubleTap offers a 275-gr. Barnes XPB, Federal 275-gr. Barnes Expander, Hornady 200-gr. FTX, Buffalo Bore 300-gr. J.F.N. and two "old" loads from Cor-Bon, a 275-gr. DPX and in their previous Hunter line, a 325-gr. FPPN load.

I also found out it doesn't take long to find your real friends when you ask around for help to shoot something like this 460!

The 460 S&W Mag. is a stretched out .454 Casull and a step up in both length and power. The versatility of the 460 Mag. lies in the fact you can shoot .454 Casull and .45 Colt also. I have not handloaded for the 460 Mag. but there are many options and great bullets available. The 460 benefits from a flatter trajectory compared to the .500 Mag. The company states the Model 460 XVR has the highest muzzle velocity of any production revolver on earth. That's a pretty tall statement but I can't argue with them about it.

Numb Hands

Shooting the big 460 was exactly what I was expecting. The Performance Center revolver is well made, finely tuned, and performed flawlessly. Before you jump to any conclusion the gun is too heavy you need to shoot it first. You'll quickly appreciate the weight. Obviously recoil is robust with full-house factory loads, but Winchester's 250- and 260-gr. loads were pleasant, shooting well, with 50-yard groups running a tad over 2". Those finger-groove rubber grips and muzzle brake are assets.

It was early morning when I set-up the Oehler 35 P, with temperatures running in the mid-40s. Launching Hornady's 200-gr. FTX load out of the 7.5" barrel, let's just say I was impressed at the velocity. At first, I thought my eyes were deceiving me, but they weren't. From a revolver, 2,243 fps, pushing a 200-gr. bullet is mighty impressive!

All other loads tested shot respectable groups, including Hornady's FTX. Big bore handguns, especially revolvers, always seem to have guilt-edge accuracy with just about any load. I was also pleased to note, at the end of the day, Leupold's 4x scope held up fine, coming as no surprise. Don't mount a cheap scope on the 460 Mag. and expect it to survive very long.

For serious big game hunting, the 460 S&W Mag. provides plenty of horsepower for any critter. Hunters and shooters not wanting to digest a steady diet of magnum rounds can shoot .45 Colt all day long without fatigue. When elk, moose, bear, or other big game is on the menu, there are plenty of options with factory offerings. The gun and cartridge are capable of delivering long-range shots beyond what standard revolver cartridges can muster.

I couldn't be more pleased with the fit and function of this big Performance Center revolver. It shoots great and is capable of taking big game on any continent. If I were to carry the revolver in the field, the sling would be the way to go. Whether you're hunting whitetail on your back 40, chasing big mean hogs, or tracking eland on the Dark Continent, the S&W Model 460XVR will serve you well. It's a serious handgun — for serious hunting. MSRP is $1,770.

THE "I"s HAVE IT

The I-Frames can be real shooters! If you don't believe it, check out Clayton's group here.

A nice touch on the I-Frames is the pinned barrel — although perhaps not required for the lowly .32 Long.

CLAYTON K. WALKER

As we've been told so often, there's no "I" in team. But you do need it to spell words like interesting and iconic. Similarly, there's no Smith & Wesson without "I" as the wheelguns we know and love arguably all began with the company's "I-Frame." While the frame size has been out of production for several decades, these great guns are far more than just a historical footnote.

Prior to the I-Frame, Smith and Wesson's bread and butter lay in producing designs relying on a hinged frame. Think of classics like the Schofield and Model 3 as well as the Safety Hammerless designs affectionately — or perhaps

While no longer made, the Smith & Wesson I-Frame still holds a lot of appeal. A svelte little .32, this late model version shows the pinned barrel and is hiding the nifty "flat latch" cylinder release on the other side.

I-Frames varied much in terms of finish, stocks, sights and latches across the production run.

derisively — nicknamed "lemon squeezers." Ingenious as those auto-ejecting top breaks were, there was a limitation to the design: Since the frame wasn't solid it placed a ceiling on the power of the cartridges it could handle.

Trend-Setter

S&W introduced its first I-Frame, the .32 Hand Ejector, in 1896. It was so named because, quite literally, the user had to swing the cylinder out of the solid frame and eject the empties *by hand*. It's surprising to think this was a radical departure for the time, but there you have it. Three years later in 1899, S&W introduced a scaled-up version of the I-Frame capable of handling the higher pressures of the .38 Special cartridge. This gun, the venerable .38 Military & Police, was built on a sturdier "K" frame and eventually morphed into what we know today as the Model 10.

Admittedly, Smith's .32 Hand Ejector wasn't the first-ever solid frame design with a swing-out cylinder, but it was the model essentially defining the "before" and "after" periods of the company's revolvers. From the I-Frame forward, just about every revolver coming out of Springfield, Massachusetts, generally *looked* like we think a Smith is supposed to. The company did make a few adjustments to the lock work, including moving the cylinder stop from the bottom to the top of the frame, and by 1903 the cylinder release was relocated to where we're used to seeing it.

Really, the only thing antiquated about this I-Frame is the cartridge it shoots. The .32 was introduced chambered for the .32 S&W Long, a round intended to give the 32 S&W a little more oomph. By any modern standard, it's still anemic, pushing a 98-gr. bullet at about 718 fps for about 112 ft.-lbs. of energy. By comparison, your rack-grade .32 ACP will produce about 158 ft.-lbs. of energy and a .380 ACP will clock in at about 200 ft.-lbs.

Where It Counts

If you absolutely have to press your .32 Hand Ejector into the role of a self-defense gun, Buffalo Bore has some rounds they developed, in their words, "after countless customer requests for ammunition that will make this cartridge lethal...." While the round-nosed .32 Longs of yore are better than harsh words, let it be known this cartridge isn't a man-stopper in a conventional sense.

No matter. Aside from the fact this revolver is like a tiny little jewel in terms of its size and craftsmanship, it's also worth owning because it's scarily accurate. Shooting a quarter-sized group at 7 yards with any full-sized handgun is an accomplishment for me on an good day. I was gobsmacked when I was able to cloverleaf shots with my I-Frame after only a few cylinders worth of warm-up. Now, sure, I had to modify my grip with my pinky underneath the butt of the gun to be able to get a straight-line purchase on the trigger. That said, I'd stand on one leg and put my thumb in my ear if it allowed me to regularly print groups like the one pictured. It's worth the hassle!

A Common Treasure

The good news is if you want an I-Frame like mine, you'll likely be able to find one. Smith made hundreds of thousands of the little guns up until 1961, at which point it became hard to justify I-Frame production with the similar-but-stronger J-Frame in their product catalog.

Since purchasing my first I-Frame, I've since added another, and I'm sure more of these diminutive and eminently fun revolvers are in my future. Find one and shoot one, and I have no doubt you'll fall in love.

The .32 Long, while not a powerhouse, is still a handy little round. From left to right: .22 LR, .32 S&W, .32 Long and .357 Magnum.

> "THIS REVOLVER IS LIKE A TINY LITTLE JEWEL IN TERMS OF ITS SIZE AND CRAFTSMANSHIP, IT'S ALSO WORTH OWNING BECAUSE IT'S SCARILY ACCURATE."

MAG-NA-PORT'S S&W MOD. 69 .44 MAGNUM

HAKA!

ROY HUNTINGTON

INFUSED WITH A WARRIOR'S FIGHTING SPIRIT

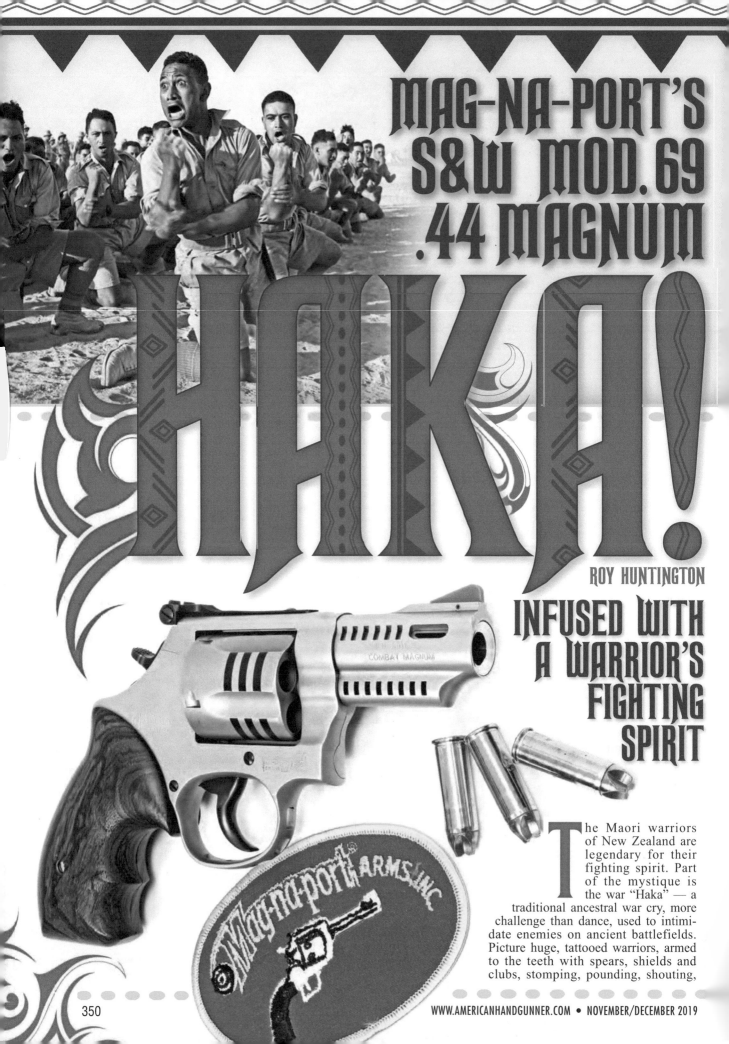

The Maori warriors of New Zealand are legendary for their fighting spirit. Part of the mystique is the war "Haka" — a traditional ancestral war cry, more challenge than dance, used to intimidate enemies on ancient battlefields. Picture huge, tattooed warriors, armed to the teeth with spears, shields and clubs, stomping, pounding, shouting,

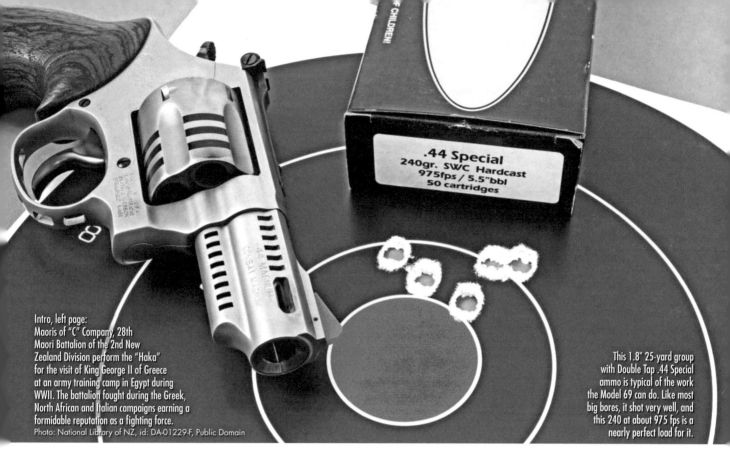

.44 Special
240gr. SW/C Hardcast
975fps / 5.5"bbl
50 cartridges

This 1.8" 25-yard group
with Double Tap .44 Special
ammo is typical of the work
the Model 69 can do. Like most
big bores, it shot very well, and
this 240 at about 975 fps is a
nearly perfect load for it.

glaring, poking out their tongues gro-tesquely, daring their enemies to fight — or run.

Today though, a Haka might be per-formed at a funeral to honor a cherished departed friend, a comrade in arms killed in battle, to welcome respected guests, or to acknowledge a great achievement. Look it up on *youtube.com* to get an idea of what we're talking about here. I promise it leaves a lasting impression.

During WWII the Maori Battalion's service against the German forces in the Mediterranean became legendary. After one successful bayonet charge in the North African campaign, Germans seri-ously began to fear them, calling them "scalp hunters." The Maori soldiers were without mercy — and to attack, attack, attack was their mantra.

The Maori Battalion gained such respect by the allies they were often used as the spearhead unit during assaults. Bernard Freyberg, the General Officer Commanding the 2NZEF (including the Maori Battalion) commented: "No infantry had a more distinguished record, or saw more fighting, or, alas, had such heavy casualties, as the Maori Battalion."

No less an enemy than General Erwin Rommel (who faced the Maori Battalion in North Africa) said this: "Give me the Maori Battalion — and I will conquer the world."

Such are the roots of the Haka.

Pedigrees

Mag-na-port's craftsmanship and the Maori's penchant for aggres-sive fighting against their enemies has resulted in this eye-catching S&W Model 69 .44 Magnum. While the 69 is a great field revolver — light enough to tote (34 oz.), but heavy

The 18-degree
muzzle crown
squares things up
and contributes to accuracy.
Black Hills HoneyBadger .44
Special loads are peeking out.

Many of the touches by Mag-na-port are just for the eye. The bold war-stripes, barrel cuts and trigger guard piercings set the tone. This barrel is 2.75" by the way, and take note of the smoothed and shaped trigger.

Just to show you what they can do, here's a custom Ruger Super Blackhawk Hunter Dwight Van Brunt sent to Mag-na-port to turn into a bear-defense gun. Dwight pronounces it perfect and 280-gr. A-Frame bullets tear the bullseye out of a 25-yard target. Leather is by Galco. Handsome is as handsome does.

A genuinely impeccable personal revolver, the Haka! begged for a rugged, practical holster. Roy worked with Karla Van Horne of Purdy Gear to come up with this flapped, paddle-backed field rig good for strong-side or cross-draw. Versatile — like the .44. Small Bowie is by Billy Helton. A satisfying trio.

enough to be steady — I think its forte is as a defensive/fighting handgun. Compact, but still able to handle full-power .44 Magnum loads, more modest .44 Specials and even CCI shot cartridges, this versatility gives the original design legs. But, even competency in a category can be improved upon.

When I first chatted with Ken Kelly of Mag-na-port about this gun, I basically told him I pictured it as an "all-the-time" gun, not a safe queen. If someone needs a serious trail pistol, back-up in Alaska, a "final-word" defensive gun, or "every-day-carry" to be relied upon, I think the L-Frame Model 69 is a nearly perfect starting platform. Mag-na-port's sage modifications give it panache — and hone usability.

I turned Mag-na-port loose on the base gun with those few general thoughts, and when I saw the final result — the stout, "tattooed" look — the Haka's powerful legacy leapt to my mind. And *Haka!* it became, heartily endorsed by Ken Kelly at Mag-na-port.

The Model 69's character covers more than just a basic palate of options. The adjustable sights assure zeroing to your favorite load, the round-butt means easier carry and the 2.75" barrel is long enough

for balance yet short enough for convenience. The base gun also incorporates many features S&W has introduced over the past 10 years or so.

The barrel looks "solid" but is actually sleeved or shrouded. There's a longer barreled version available (4.35") and since this is based on S&W's classic L-Frame, it's pretty much indestructible. From my own experience shooting it, you will wear out long before the gun does. Being compact and relatively light, the downside of this convenience is shooting full-house .44 Magnum loads tends to be attention-getting. I think the real way to go here is to use a stout .44 Special and something even milder for fun and trail use.

S&W has had to design in a "ball-detent" lock at the junction of the crane and the frame. It's a bit like the old "Triple Lock" third lock-up point, only this simply takes the place of the normal forward lock where the

ejector rod used to "snick" into a detent. This model drops the forward detent, substituting the ball-detent. It seems to work just fine and I think in all honesty does a better job than the old system.

In spite of all these features, I challenged Ken to dig deeper and come up with improvements.

And he did.

Haka! Is Born

Mag-na-port is famous for their excellent hand work and built their business by inventing the Mag-na-port process of barrel porting, lowering recoil and muzzle flip. The process works, and tens of thousands of guns have been modified over the years. The business grew under Ken's dad, Larry (who founded the company) and for many years since Larry's passing, Ken has continued to develop the company. Today's Mag-na-port is as modern as you could ask for, staffed by hard working, smiling people, all delivering amazing work in handguns and rifles. I think it's also good to know Mag-na-port basically "invented" modern big

Mag-na-port used their EDM process to "machine" a cut-out in the rear sight for the white outline. The bright orange front is hand cut and fitted and stands out if you're moving fast.

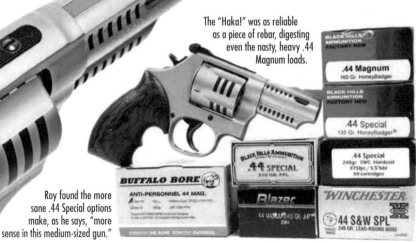

The "Haka!" was as reliable as a piece of rebar, digesting even the nasty, heavy .44 Magnum loads.

Roy found the more sane .44 Special options make, as he says, "more sense in this medium-sized gun."

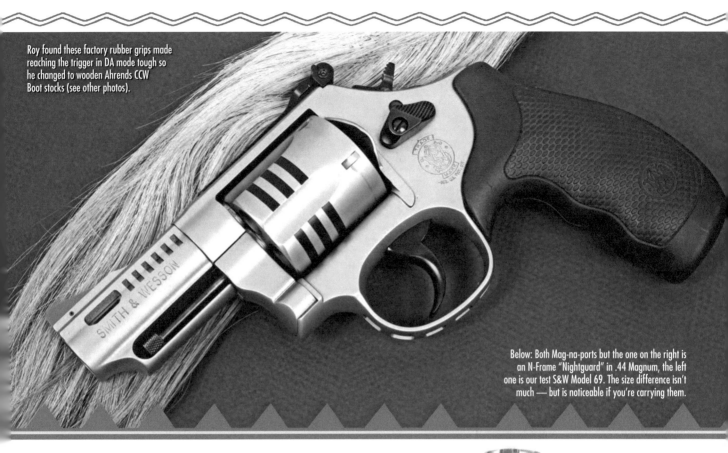

Roy found these factory rubber grips made reaching the trigger in DA mode tough so he changed to wooden Ahrends CCW Boot stocks (see other photos).

Below: Both Mag-na-ports but the one on the right is an N-Frame "Nightguard" in .44 Magnum, the left one is our test S&W Model 69. The size difference isn't much — but is noticeable if you're carrying them.

bore snubbie revolvers — well before there were any factory offerings. So there's that too.

The Haka! got the full porting treatment for sleeved barrels and a "Velvet Hone" soft bead blast finish. Ken's team did their "Mini-Bob" to the hammer spur, making it handier and less "grabby" when under clothing. The trigger got a full radius and the hammer, trigger, latch and screws were matte blued. They used their EDM process to cut and inlay a white outline on the rear sight blade, then custom fit and installed a bright orange front blade.

The base gun also experienced Mag-na-port's famous complete action job. Checking headspace, cylinder gap, smoothing internals, removing creep, lightening trigger pull, timing work, forcing cone tuning and numbering chambers are among the specific touches there. Can you say "night and day" from the original factory gun?

Adjusting the muzzle crown squares things off and often really contributes

Five rounds of .44 (magnum or special) fit neatly into the L-Frame cylinder. Note numbered chambers, a Mag-na-port trademark.

HAKA!

to better accuracy. Ken also used the magic of EDM machining to cut a series of vertical cut-outs in the barrel shroud (Maori ritual scarring?), pierced the trigger guard to help identify "Tribe Mag-na-port" — ending with a bold trio of robust black stripes around the cylinder. I upped the ante some by changing-out the factory rubber grips with a set of Concealed Carry Boot Stocks from Kim Ahrends.

The result is a revolver you can identify as yours at a glance — even from across a room. There's no doubting Mag-na-port did the work, or whether the Haka! is up to any task undertaken.

Because it is.

Doing Battle

In the spirit of being a fighting pistol, I loaded the Haka! with full power Winchester 240-gr. .44 Magnum loads right off the bat. I also admit I might not have entirely thought things through at that point. I have a 10" heavy steel plate hanging on chains about 20 yards downrange from my back porch. The first round not only smacked my hand hard enough to smart but at least sent the plate dancing too.

Since I still had feeling in my hand, I sent four more rounds in about as many seconds downrange, leaving the plate swinging — and me flicking my hand at my side while doing the "this hurts" dance. That's similar to the spider web dance, but keeping the muzzle safe at the same time and saying things like "Ouch" and "Oh goodness, that hurt" and "My, my, I'll think hard before doing this again" is part of the drill.

Or at least words to that effect.

Donning a shooting glove I shot a bit more of the heavy stuff — I know, I know, sometimes it takes me a long time to learn — but honestly did finally realize enough was enough. Can the Model 69 shoot full power .44 Magnum loads? Certainly, and in a pinch, a hard cast 240 at 1,100-1,200 fps is possible, and would likely save your skin. And I predict you wouldn't hear a thing or feel a single bit of recoil.

But in the real world, would I shoot the stuff in this gun for fun? Again?

Nope.

You ever hit a steel post with an aluminum baseball bat with no gloves on? It's sorta' like that. Don't ask me how I know. I can't imagine this without the Mag-na-porting too, by the way. Call me sissified, but also call me still able to use both of my hands without spilling my coffee from the shakes.

In a more sane world, I shot a "mild" but highly effective .44 Magnum load from Black Hills, their HoneyBadger. It's

a 160-gr. solid copper fluted bullet chronographing at an honest 1,425 from the 2.75" barrel. As fire and brimstone as this sounds, recoil is manageable since it's a lighter 160-gr. bullet. I think it'd stop just about anything walking on the planet.

Their sort of matching .44 Special HoneyBadger — a 125 with the same bullet design — flew at 1,135 fps from the short barrel. It was exceptionally fun to shoot, not to mention very accurate. I've seen the gel work on it and it penetrates deeply and reliably. For me, I think I found my main load for the Haka!

I ran some other .44 Special loads and found just about anything in the 240-gr. range at less than 850 fps to be okay, if not always entirely enjoyable to shoot. The classic 246-gr. lead round-nose .44 Special load chrono'd around the 625 fps range. I could actually see the bullet go and was tempted to race it to the target. But it was great fun to shoot, I'll admit.

Accuracy was typical S&W style, and characteristically big-bore excellent. Say, 1.75" (Black Hills HoneyBadger .44 Special and about the same for their cowboy load at not quite 700 fps) to about 3.5" for the uglier .44 Magnum loads — mostly due to me gritting my teeth and likely shutting my eyes just before the big noise.

My 100-yard steel torso target got tired of being wanged. Bang, clang, bang, clang more often than not was the drill. Easy-peasy comes to mind when using the .44 Special loads. A fun thing is you can often watch the big bullets sort of lope in before hitting the steel at this distance. I kept laughing out loud at that. Who needs a flat-shooting magnum anyhow?

So?

So, it's fun, that's what. As I always say, sell off some of your commodity guns and put the money to work on something really fun, likely to hold its value — and even grow — and will deliver a complete lack of buyer's remorse. These sorts of projects also tend to cause you to grin for no apparent reason, and at inappropriate moments. Pair it with a beautiful, practical holster — like the flapped field paddle rig by Purdy Gear, shown — and the grin will extend from ear to ear.

Thanks Ken, and thanks Mag-na-port. The Haka! helps to make the Huntington family sleep more soundly at night in these semi-scary times. I have to admit, the idea of a Maori warrior standing guard duty does have merit.

Made in United States
Troutdale, OR
12/06/2024

25996725R00197